Poland Alone:

Britain, SOE and the
Collapse of the Polish
Resistance, 1944

Poland Alone:

Britain, SOE and the Collapse of the Polish Resistance, 1944

Jonathan Walker

The
History
Press

For Hanna Zbirohowska-Kościa
and her mother
Halina Czarnocka

First published 2008

The History Press Ltd
The Mill, Brimscombe Port
Stroud, Gloucestershire, GL5 2QG
www.thehistorypress.co.uk

© Jonathan Walker, 2008
Maps Copyright © The History Press

The right of The Author to be identified as the Author
of this work has been asserted in accordance with the
Copyrights, Designs and Patents Act 1988.

British Library Cataloguing in Publication Data.
A catalogue record for this book is available from the British Library.

ISBN 978 1 86227 474 7

Typesetting and origination by The History Press Ltd.
Printed in Great Britain

Contents

List of Maps		7
List of Plates		14
Acknowledgements		17
Introduction		21
Chapter One	The Rape of Poland	25
Chapter Two	The Polish Home Army	56
Chapter Three	Operation 'Wildhorn'	86
Chapter Four	Auschwitz	114
Chapter Five	SOE – a Lifeline?	145
Chapter Six	Soviet Onslaught	172
Chapter Seven	Warsaw Erupts (August 1944)	204
Chapter Eight	Warsaw in Flames (September 1944)	235

Chapter Nine   Chaos and Collapse   262

Chapter Ten   Epilogue   283

Conclusion   295

Appendix   Equivalent Military Ranks   299

Glossary of Terms and Abbreviations   300

Bibliography   303

Index   315

List of Maps

1 The German Occupation of Poland   8

2 Relief Routes to Poland   9

3 The Auschwitz Camps   10

4 Soviet Offensives – Summer 1944   11

5 Warsaw Rising   12

6 Clash on the Vistula   13

Occupied Poland, 1939–1944

— Poland, 1939   --- Frontiers, 1939

Incorporated into the Reich

General Government

Soviet occupied until June 1941

○ Extermination camps

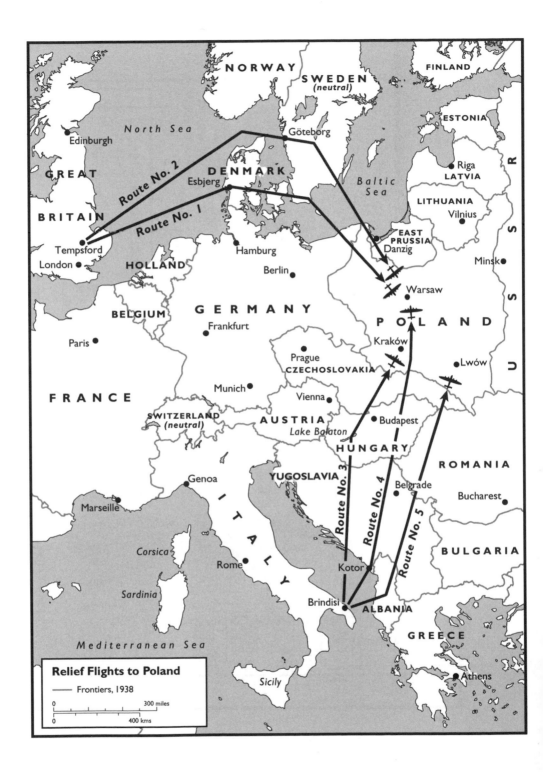

Relief Flights to Poland

— Frontiers, 1938

0 _____ 300 miles
0 _____ 400 kms

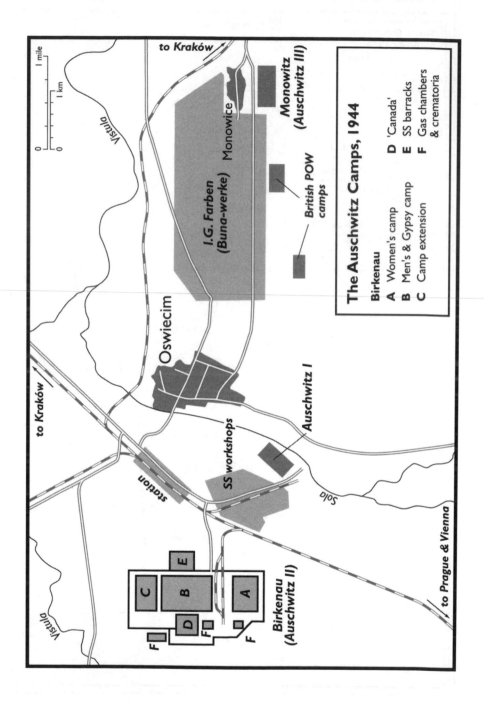

The Auschwitz Camps, 1944

Birkenau

A Women's camp
B Men's & Gypsy camp
C Camp extension

D 'Canada'
E SS barracks
F Gas chambers & crematoria

to Kraków

Vistula

I.G. Farben (Buna-werke)

Monowice

Monowitz (Auschwitz III)

British POW camps

Oswiecim

Auschwitz I

SS workshops

station

Soła

Vistula

Birkenau (Auschwitz II)

to Kraków

to Prague & Vienna

1 mile
1 km

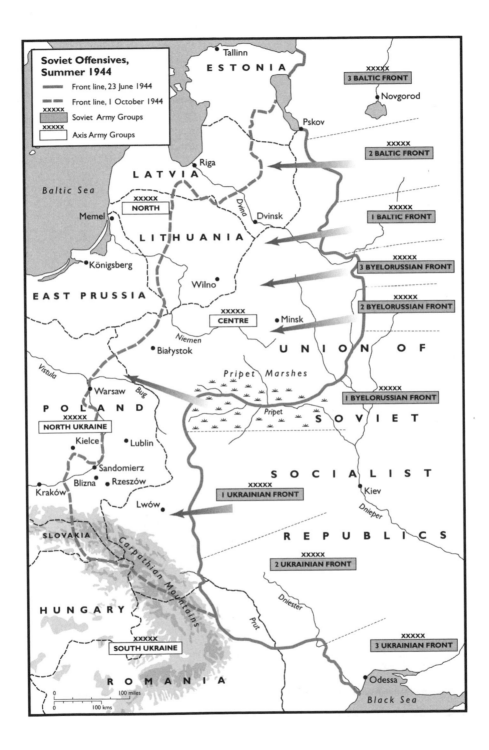

Soviet Offensives, Summer 1944

Front line, 23 June 1944
Front line, 1 October 1944
Soviet Army Groups
Axis Army Groups

Tallinn

ESTONIA

3 BALTIC FRONT

Novgorod

Pskov

2 BALTIC FRONT

Riga

LATVIA

Baltic Sea

Dvina

Dvinsk

1 BALTIC FRONT

NORTH

Memel

LITHUANIA

3 BYELORUSSIAN FRONT

Königsberg

Wilno

2 BYELORUSSIAN FRONT

EAST PRUSSIA

CENTRE

Minsk

Niemen

UNION   OF

Białystok

Vistula

Pripet Marshes

Warsaw

Bug

Pripet

1 BYELORUSSIAN FRONT

POLAND

SOVIET

NORTH UKRAINE

Kielce

Lublin

Sandomierz

Blizna   Rzeszów

SOCIALIST

Kraków

Lwów

Kiev

1 UKRAINIAN FRONT

Dnieper

SLOVAKIA

Carpathian Mountains

REPUBLICS

2 UKRAINIAN FRONT

HUNGARY

Dniester

Prut

SOUTH UKRAINE

3 UKRAINIAN FRONT

ROMANIA

Odessa

Black Sea

0   100 miles

0   100 kms

II

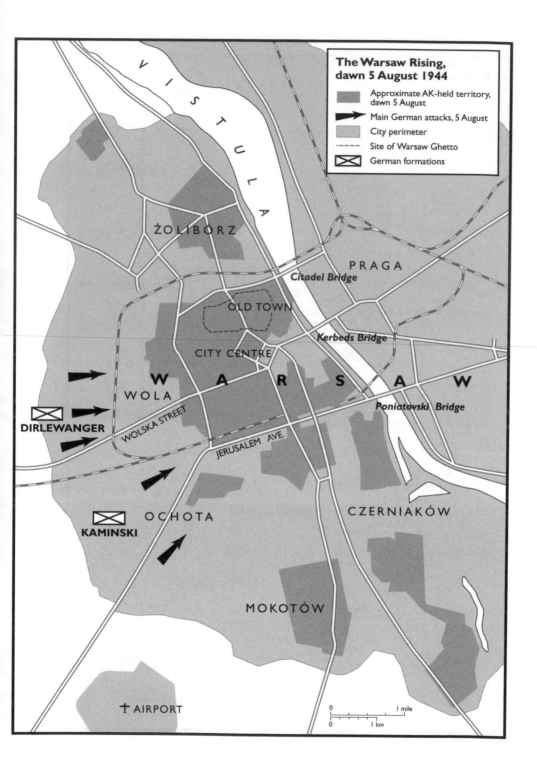

The Warsaw Rising,
dawn 5 August 1944

Approximate AK-held territory, dawn 5 August

Main German attacks, 5 August

City perimeter

Site of Warsaw Ghetto

German formations

V I S T U L A

ŻOLIBORZ

PRAGA

Citadel Bridge

OLD TOWN

Kerbeds Bridge

CITY CENTRE

W A R S A W

WOLA

DIRLEWANGER

WOLSKA STREET

Poniatovski Bridge

JERUSALEM AVE.

OCHOTA

CZERNIAKÓW

KAMINSKI

MOKOTÓW

✝ AIRPORT

0   1 mile

0   1 km

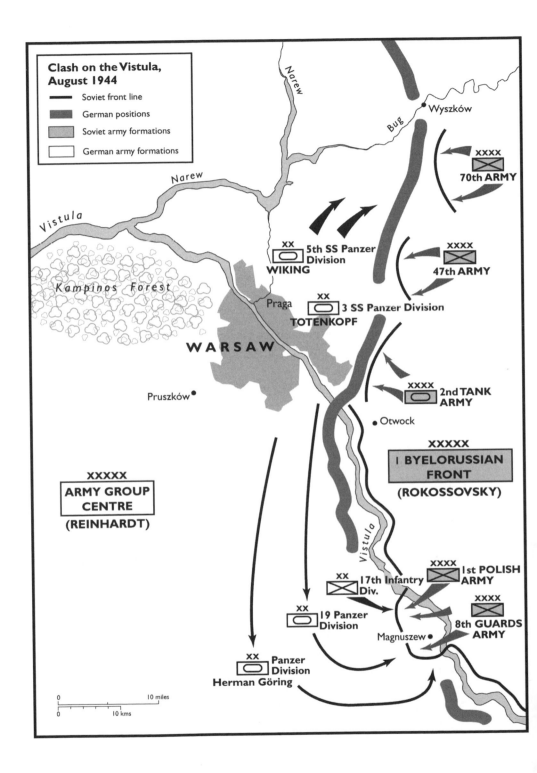

**Clash on the Vistula,
August 1944**

— Soviet front line

German positions

Soviet army formations

German army formations

Narew

Bug

Wyszków

XXXX
70th ARMY

Narew

5th SS Panzer
Division
WIKING

XXXX
47th ARMY

Vistula

Kampinos Forest

Praga

3 SS Panzer Division
TOTENKOPF

WARSAW

Pruszków

XXXX
2nd TANK
ARMY

Otwock

XXXXX
I BYELORUSSIAN
FRONT
(ROKOSSOVSKY)

XXXXX
ARMY GROUP
CENTRE
(REINHARDT)

Vistula

XXXX
1st POLISH
ARMY

17th Infantry
Div.

19 Panzer
Division

XXXX
8th GUARDS
ARMY

Magnuszew

Panzer
Division
Herman Göring

0   10 miles
0   10 kms

List of Plates

1 SS Reichsführer Heinrich Himmler and Governer-General Hans Frank – Dinner at Wawel Castle, Kraków. *United States Holocaust Memorial Museum # 15074.*

2 Lieutenant-Colonel Harold Perkins – one of SOE's 'toughies'. *Special Forces Club.*

3 'Against the odds' – a rare photograph of Special Duties Halifax II aircraft from No 148 Squadron, flying in formation. *RAF Museum # P009950.*

4 FANYs with Polish servicemen at Audley End House, Essex. *Polish Underground Movement Study Trust # 22-001.*

5 Flight-Sergeant John Ward – 'soldier of the Home Army'. *National Archives # HS4/256.*

6 V-2 Rocket. The quartered markings were to detect the amount of roll in flight. *Imperial War Museum # BU11149.*

7 Blizna testing ground. One of several blast shelters still remaining today. *Author's collection.*

8 'Motyl' landing ground today. Scene of Operation 'Wildhorn III' and the retrieval of rocket parts. The monument in the foreground shows the *Polska Walcząca* ('Fighting Poland') emblem. *Author's collection.*

9 Halina Czarnocka – 'important member of the resistance and survivor of Auschwitz'. *Hanna Zbirohowska-Kościa.*

10 Home Army (AK) wireless operators – possession of a set was punishable by death. *Muzeum Armii Krajowej.*

11 'Providing a lifeline' – Polish service personnel in Italy. *Polish Underground Movement Study Trust # 33-001.*

12 Auschwitz – US bombs intended for IG Farben, but accidently falling on Birkenau, 13 September 1944. The captions were added in 1978 by CIA analysts. *United States Holocaust Memorial Museum, # 03198.*

13 Auschwitz – After selection at the railhead, a Jewish mother and her children move towards the gas chambers (summer 1944). *United States Holocaust Memorial Museum # 77217.*

14 Auschwitz – SS officers from the camp singing at their retreat at nearby Solahuette. Front row: Höcker, Höss, Baer, Kramer, Hoessler, Mengele. *United States Holocaust Memorial Museum # 34739.*

15 Soviet troops achieve a river crossing. *Imperial War Museum # RUS 4272.*

16 Warsaw erupts – the beginning of the Rising. Looking due north, the River Vistula can be seen on the right together with its three vital bridges. The suburb of Praga lies beyond. Mokotov is in the foreground. *Polish Underground Movement Study Trust # 3513/6.*

17 German Tiger tank, Poland 1944. *Bundesarchiv # 1011-695-0406-15.*

18 Hanna Czarnocka with her brother, Bohdan – 'ready to serve the Home Army'. *Hanna Zbirohowska-Kościa.*

19 'Warsaw Erupts' – Home Army soldiers defend their trenches *Polish Underground Movement Study Trust.*

20 German soldiers surrendering in the early days of the Rising. *Polish Underground Movement Study Trust # 2195.*

21 German infantrymen prepare remote-controlled 'Goliaths' during the Rising. *Bundesarchiv # 1011-695-0411-06.*

22 'German snipers rarely missed' – Running the barricades during the Warsaw Rising. *Polish Underground Movement Study Trust # 1819.*

23 Warsaw airlift – the crew of Consolidated Liberator B Mark VI of No 178 Squadron, Italy 1944. Sergeant John Rush RAF (pilot); Sergeant Derek Coates RAF (wireless operator); Sergeant Peter Green (mid-upper gunner); Lieutenant Keith Murray SAAF (navigator); Flight-Sergeant Derek Stuart RAAF (2nd pilot); Flight-Sergeant Kenneth Pierce RAF (tail gunner). *Imperial War Museum # CL 3557.*

24 'Strong wind could carry them miles off target' – Containers falling on Warsaw. *Polish Underground Movement Study Trust # 1819.*

25 'A successful drop' – *Polish Underground Movement Study Trust # 1976.*

26 Polish post and courier girls during the Warsaw Rising – 'an uncertain fate'. *Muzeum Armii Krajowej.*

27 SS soldier with Flamethrower flushes out resistance fighters. *Bundesarchiv # 146-1996-057-10A.*

28 SS Gruppenführer Heinz Reinefarth together with Cossacks serving under his command – Wolska Street, Warsaw. *Public domain.*

29 SS troops brutally clear the Warsaw streets. *Bundesarchiv # 146-1973-113-23.*

30 The last days of the Rising – an AK soldier is pulled out of his sewer refuge. *Bundesarchiv # 146-1994-054-30.*

31 The end of the Rising – General Bór-Komorowski and SS General von dem Bach, 3 October 1944. *Imperial War Museum # MH 4489.*

32 'Help never came' – The AK surrender their arms. *Bundesarchiv # 146-1984-079-09.*

Illustrations credited to PUMST are copyrighted and cannot be reproduced in any format without the Trust's consent. They can be contacted at the following address:

11 Leopold Road, London W5 3PB.

Acknowledgements

I wish to thank those who provided personal testimonies and who were involved in this story of Poland's dark days. Particularly, Hanna Zbirohowska-Kościa (née Czarnocka), Colonel Mieczysław Wałega and his wife Adela, together with help from Dorota and Jurek Hostyńska. Also, my appreciation for the help given by Michael Saltern and Clare Thomas of Ilford Park Polish Home, Stover, Devon in securing interviews with veterans, Mieczysław Juny, Bolesław Majewski and Adam Wykrota. From the British side, I would especially like to thank ex-servicemen Bill Steed, Walter Davies and Brian Bishop for their testimonies and support.

I am most grateful to fellow author, Professor Donald Thomas for his help and advice on British attitudes to press censorship during the Second World War. As ever, Dr John Bourne of the University of Birmingham continues to inspire writers of military history and willingly provides help through his wide knowledge of sources and contacts. My thanks also for support from the prolific writers and historians, John and Celia Lee.

My thanks to Janek Lasocki for his deep knowledge and understanding of Poland and her relations with Eastern Europe. He has also helped me with an endless stream of Polish names and place-names, which I have endeavoured to spell correctly and consistently. Similarly Magda Mitra has been a great help in translating Polish documents and I appreciate the early assistance of Andrew Duchenski and his family.

I am fortunate to know a band of knowledgeable friends and associates who have helped with tracking down relevant sources; my sincere thanks to Rev Robin Laird, Michael Walker, Anthony Edwards, Keith Northover, Donald Richards, Peter Whicher, Richard Dennis, Ted Emerson and especially my good friends Mark and Geraldine Talbot for their generous hospitality and support. Local libraries are a splendid research tool and I thank Gill Spence and her team at Sidmouth Library; Meriel Santer, Victoria Luxton, Sylvia Werb and Joss Edwards, for tracking down endless and invariably weighty tomes.

For the testimonies of RAF Officers, I extend sincere thanks to Roger Walker and Chris and Caroline York for providing access to their family records. Simon Tidswell was again an excellent source for RAF material and Professor Peter Simkins, who has a vast knowledge of military history was, as always, most helpful and encouraging, particularly on US Army Air Force sources. I am also grateful to Nick and Paul Kingdom, who explained the techniques of take-off and landing on airstrips, an appreciation of which is so important in understanding the difficulties of 'bridging' operations to an occupied country.

My thanks to Dr Andrzej Suchcitz, Keeper of Archives, Polish Institute and Sikorski Museum, Kensington, London for making the Institute's resources available. Since 1988, the Polish Underground Movement Study Trust (PUMST) in Ealing, London has been amalgamated with the Institute, and continues to offer the researcher a particularly friendly and approachable environment. The Chairman, Dr Krysztof Stoliński, Hanna Zbirohowska-Kościa, Archivist, Krysztof Bożejewicz, and other volunteers have all given me the benefit of their extensive knowledge of the *Armia Krajowa*. The PUMST's written and photographic archives are supplemented by a very useful and authoritative English language website.

The world of Special Forces continues to intrigue. By their very nature, theirs is a small, closed world, but I am most grateful to Ernest van Maurik for his anecdotes and glimpses into the world of SOE. Likewise my gratitude and thanks to Jeremy Chidson, whose grandfather Lieutenant-Colonel Monty Chidson was one of the more experienced hands in D Section, SIS, and removed a large quantity of diamonds from under the noses of the Germans as they entered Amsterdam in May 1940. Duncan Stuart, SOE Advisor at the Foreign and Commonwealth Office 1996–2002, offered friendly advice on sources for SOE material in the public domain.

I am indebted to The Countess of Avon, for permission to quote from the papers of her late husband, the Earl of Avon. I am also grateful to the following for allowing me to examine or quote from archival material within their collections: The Trustees of the Liddell Hart Centre for Military Archives; The Trustees of the Imperial War Museum; The Trustees of the Polish Underground Movement Study Trust; The Special Collections Department, University of Birmingham. While Crown copyright still subsists in material held in the National Archives, Kew, London, since 1999 permission to publish extracts is not required in the case of documents unpublished at the time they were deposited.

An extraordinary and moving archive devoted to the Holocaust is to be found in Washington. My thanks to Caroline Waddell and the United States Holocaust Memorial Museum for their assistance; it should be noted that the views or opinions expressed in this book and the context in which the images are used, do not necessarily reflect the views or policy of, nor imply approval or endorsement by, the USHMM.

My thanks also to Joanna Jastrzębska and the splendid *Muzeum Powatania Warszawskiego* (Museum of the Warsaw Uprising), in Warsaw, for assistance and permissions. Likewise Remigiusz Kasprzycki and the Museum of the *Armia Krajowa* (Home Army) in Kraków; the *Bundesarchiv* (German Federal Archives) in Koblenz; the Special Forces Club, London; Andrew Renwick and the Trustees of the Royal Air Force Museum, London.

Every effort has been made to trace and obtain permission from copyright holders of material quoted or illustrations reproduced. I acknowledge permission to quote passages from the following: The Continuum International Publishing Group for *The Unseen and Silent* by George Iranek-Osmecki; Roman Antoszewski for *Red Runs the Vistula* by Ron Jeffery; Pollinger Limited and the Estate of T. Bór-Komorowski for *The Secret Army* by Tadeusz Bór-Komorowski; Orion Publishing Group for *The Pianist* by Wladylaw Szpilman (translated by Anthea Bell); Hippocrene Books for *Fighting Warsaw* by Stefan Korboński; Vallentine Mitchell Publishers for *A Warsaw Diary 1939-1945* by Michael Zylberberg; Tom Wood for *Karski* by Thomas Wood and Stanislaw Jankowski; Editions Robert Laffont and Orion Publishing for *The Forgotten Soldier* by Guy Sajer; AM Heath & Co. Limited for *Berlin Diary: The Journal of a Foreign Correspondent* by William Shirer; Penguin Group for *Speak You Also* by Paul Steinberg; The Random House Group for *A Writer At War* edited by Anthony Beevor and Luba Vinograda and

Those Who Trespass Against Us by Countess Karolina Lanckorońska and *The Second World War Diary of Hugh Dalton 1940–45* edited by Ben Pimlott; Casemate and Greenhill Books for *Blood Red Snow* by Günter Koschorrek and *War on the Eastern Front* by James Lucas; David Higham Associates for *The Memoirs of Lord Gladwyn* by Lord Gladwyn; Rolf Michaelis for *Die Grenadier-Divisionen der Waffen SS Part I*.

As always, I appreciate the help and advice of Jamie Wilson, Shaun Barrington, Clare Jackson and Miranda Jewess of The History Press. Finally my warm thanks to my wife Gill for all her support and her work in reading endless drafts, and my thanks to my family for their encouragement during this project.

Introduction

On a bitterly cold Christmas Eve in 1940 Hugh Dalton, Britain's Minister for Economic Warfare arrived in Perth, Scotland to address Polish troops. Flanked by the exiled Polish Commander-in-Chief, General Sikorski and the Polish President, Władysław Raczkiewicz, Dalton gave his audience a rousing oration: 'On the day of victory, Poland, as the first nation to stand up to Hitler, should ride in the van of the victory march'.[1] The 200 Polish soldiers greeted the speech with great enthusiasm. They were, after all, in a friendly host country – with an ally who had gone to war over their plight; they, the Poles would fight on behalf of Britain and in return they would receive Britain's support to free their land from both German and Soviet occupation.[2] It was a simple and trusting belief, but one that ignored the brutal maxims of international power, as well as simple logistics. The Poles made huge sacrifices on behalf of the Allies but never received their freedom with Allied help, let alone a place in the victory march in 1945. British attempts to help the Poles in their crisis period of 1944 were, at best, limited, but how much more could they have done?

In reality, Britain had very few strategic interests in Poland. When Hitler invaded Poland in September 1939, Britain declared war on Germany. She did so because of Prime Minister Chamberlain's guarantee of support to Poland, given six months before. Perhaps it was no more than a gesture against aggression in Europe as a whole, but the fact that Britain was in no shape to fulfil that guarantee and her failure to materially help Poland, weighed heavily on ministerial hearts during the war years.[3]

Poland was subsequently carved up between Germany and the Soviet Union, and Hitler singled Poland out for special treatment, murdering over five million of her citizens. British voices declared their determination to see, one day, a strong and independent Poland, but this took no account of the predator on her eastern border. The Poles were understandably hostile to Soviet intentions. The Soviet Union had, after all, effectively been an ally of Germany for nearly two years, before she was invaded in June 1941, and only then embarked on her huge sacrifices in the 'Great Patriotic War'. It was left to Poland's underground press, rather than Britain's largely pro-Soviet newspapers, to declare the true nature of Stalin's rule.

Polish military spirit was kept alive in the form of the Polish Home Army (*Armia Krajowa,* or AK), an organisation with strong connections to the Britain's Special Operations Executive (SOE). Its intelligence services, who wisely insisted on keeping their own secret cypher codes, nevertheless made a huge contribution to Allied intelligence. In return, Poland only ever received a paltry 600 tons of supplies via SOE. This compared to 5,796 tons for Greece and 10,000 tons for both France and Yugoslavia.[4] Even this limited support was hampered during 1944 by the periodic banning of flights to Poland. This was largely to prevent high casualties among the highly trained Polish Special Duties crews. Yet senior Polish Air Staff had to remind the British Air Ministry that over 2,000 Polish airmen had already been lost while fighting for Britain under RAF Command.[5]

In terms of sheer loss of human life on Polish soil, the events at Auschwitz and other Polish concentration camps dwarf all other events. We now know the huge scale of the Holocaust and modern scholars have the benefit of a large number of archives and oral testimonies, even including statements from those who perpetrated the crimes. Given this knowledge, the feeble British and American response to contemporary reports of the slaughter seems inexcusable. Furthermore, the Holocaust in Poland did not see the sudden eruptions of barbarity typical of other genocides. It was planned and methodically executed over a very long period, with its own warped, but entrenched economic thoroughness.[6] With such a long build-up – from the pre-war concentration camps (seen by many as just severe penal institutions) to the full-blown extermination camps of the war years – western officials should have had all the more time to detect it. Yet such a long period may have merely served to blunt the impact of the atrocities. Were the Nazi smokescreens convenient to those in the west who read the reports but closed their minds to the unthinkable? All Britain's national resources were diverted to the sole aim of winning the conflict and other humanitarian issues had to wait. Without the achievement of the former, could the latter ever be resolved?

Poland in 1944 was also the scene of important trials for the V-2 rocket. The story of the German development of flying bombs and rockets has received much attention in recent years. Emphasis has been placed on the role of certain personalities involved in their development, such as Wernher von Braun and Walter Dornberger, or those involved with their discovery, such as Constance Babington-Smith of the RAF Photographic Analysis unit. The considerable Polish role is usually minimised, yet it is doubtful whether Britain's Joint Intelligence Committee could have made such progress in analysing the threat, without Polish reports on the secret weapons.[7]

It is ironic that Britain went to war for Poland and yet the main victim after the Allied victory was Poland. Was the only choice facing Churchill and his government the simple one of accepting Soviet domination of Poland and Eastern Europe as the bill for defeating Hitler? Or could Britain and its instrument of irregular warfare, SOE, have done more to save the Polish people in their crisis year of 1944?

NOTES

[1] Ben Pimlott, (Ed.), *The Second World War Diary of Hugh Dalton 1940–45* (Jonathan Cape, London 1986), pp. 132–3.

[2] Notable contributions were made by Polish airmen in the Battle of Britain; the Polish Navy; General Maczek's 1st Armoured Division; General Kopanski's Carpathian Brigade; General Ander's II Corps; General Sosabowski's Parachute Brigade at Arnhem.

[3] On 24 May 1944 Major Vyvyan Adams MP, entreated the House of Commons not to be consumed with issues of Poland's borders, claiming Britain went to war for altogether wider concerns. See 'Discussions in Parliament' in *Polish Fortnightly Review*, No. 93, 1 June 1944, PRM.132a, Polish Institute and Sikorski Museum, London (hereafter PISM).

[4] Józef Garliński, *Poland, SOE and the Allies* (George Allen and Unwin, London 1969), p. 147.

5 Minutes of Meeting at Air Ministry, 31 August 1944, HS4/156, NA. This figure quoted at the meeting referred to the position in late 1944 and included 287 airmen lost as Prisoners of War. Total losses of Polish airmen during the war, while under RAF Command amounted to 2,258. This includes training and operational losses. See Jerzy B Cynk, *The Polish Air Force at War: The Official History, Vol. 2, 1943–1945* (Schiffer Military History, Atglen, US 1998), p. 654.

6 Richard Overy, *The Daily Telegraph*, 15 September 2007.

7 Professor Jan Ciechanowski has attributed this lack of Polish recognition regarding the 'V Weapons', to Western European researchers not pursuing Polish language sources; see Tessa Stirling, Daria Nałęcz and Tadeusz Dubicki (Eds.), *Intelligence Co-operation between Poland and Great Britain During World War II, Volume 1: The Report of the Anglo-Polish Historical Committee* (Valentine Mitchell, London 2005), pp. 34–5; see also 'Operation Underwriter', 18 July 1944, HS 4/180, National Archives, Kew, London (hereafter NA).

Chapter One

The Rape of Poland

It was a bizarre plan, even by the standards of Reinhardt Heydrich, head of the SS Security Service (SD). As a pretext for Germany's invasion of Poland in September 1939, some twenty bogus border incursions by Polish troops were arranged. Under the hardly discreet codename 'Operation Himmler', a number of condemned criminals were to be dressed in Polish Army uniforms, killed by lethal injection and their bodies shot and arranged as if they had fallen in attacks on German territory. In one particular action, Heydrich employed Alfred Naujocks, an SD henchman with some experience in 'incident creation' to organise a feigned assault on the Gleiwitz radio station, just inside the German border. Naujocks was in position at the station before dawn on 1 September 1939 and duly received his consignment – a half-dead Polish Silesian, Franciszek Honiok. An impervious Naujocks later testified:

> I received this man and had him laid down at the entrance to the station. He was alive, but he was completely unconscious. I tried to open his eyes. I could not recognize by his eyes that he was alive, only by his breathing. I did not see the shot wounds, but a lot of blood was smeared across his face. He was in civilian clothes. We seized the radio station as ordered, broadcast a speech of 3 to 4 minutes over an emergency transmitter, fired some pistol shots, and left.[1]

As German radio bellowed out accusations of 'outrageous' Polish incursions, the unfortunate Honiok was finished off and left as 'evidence' of a Polish assault – probably the first casualty of the Second World War. *Blitzkrieg* was swiftly unleashed against Poland. Nearly 1,600 first-line aircraft attacked bridges, installations and airfields in support of German armoured units. Air supremacy was achieved within twenty-four hours. Despite the courage of the Polish pilots, their outdated fighters were no match for the cannons of the Messerschmitt 109E, while the JU87 Stuka was used to terrifying effect. With its ability to dive at an angle between 65° and 90°, delivering one 500lb and four 100lb bombs within a 50–yard radius, it was a fearsome machine. Its screaming 'Jericho' sirens on its undercarriage legs further demoralised victims.

On the first morning of Hitler's invasion plan, *Fall Weiss* (Case White) the speed of the advance was extraordinary and even Warsaw was bombed. Unlike defences in Western Europe, Poland had a porous border with Germany and was bereft of integrated fortifications, allowing swift access for panzer units across level terrain. Under the control of Army Group North, General von Kluge's Fourth Army swept across the Polish Pomeranian corridor at the same time as General von Kückler's Third Army burst out of East Prussia, drove south and blocked off Warsaw from the east. Polish resistance was fierce but hopelessly out-manoeuvred. There were many stories of great bravery on the part of the Poles with units such as the Pomeranian Cavalry Brigade charging German infantry with sabres drawn. However, while German commanders conceded that the Polish Cavalry were 'superb', the appearance of German armoured cars caused devastating casualties amongst the Polish Lancer squadrons.[2]

An American documentary film-maker was caught up in the rush to escape the German attack:

> The Nazi planes covered the entire interior network of the Polish railways, completely destroyed train after train, killing and wounding 50 of 300 people on our train alone, including our engineer. As soon as the Nazis found there was no anti-aircraft protection on our train they gave up bombing, power-dived sometimes within 20 feet of the top of our train; what luck we had, jumping out of the windows, reaching the woods before they reached our car: for others were caught, and we filmed them between attacks, wounded, bleeding, dying or dead in their seats. The planes followed the survivors, strafing their hiding places in the woods, killing them in the open fields nearby. In one station, a crazy woman

standing calm in her straitjacket seemed the only intelligent human being in a flock of frantic, frightened human sheep.[3]

Meanwhile, Colonel-General von Rundstedt's Army Group South made similar rapid progress, though its Eighth Army met stiff resistance after reaching Łódź and faced a week-long counter-offensive from Polish troops advancing across the Bzura River. The German Tenth Army raced from Lower Silesia towards Sandomierz, while von List's Fourteenth Army moved out of Moravia and Slovakia to take Kraków and the south-east of Poland.[4] Senior Army commanders, unhindered by Hitler, had carried out much of this meticulous planning. As *Generaloberst* Franz Halder, Deputy Chief of the General Staff for Operations observed, 'Hitler did not interfere in Army preparations, except that he planned down to the smallest detail the attack against the Bridge at Dirschau'. It was ironic that this was one Polish operation where the Germans were thwarted, for the Poles pre-empted the German attack on this important bridge over the Vistula by blowing it up.[5] Nevertheless, those who worked closely with him conceded that Hitler did have a grasp of small unit tactics:

> With his personal experience of the last war in the ranks, he had gained a very good knowledge of the lower level of warfare – the properties of the different weapons; the effect of ground and weather; the mentality and morale of the troops – he was very good at gauging this.[6]

The German invasion of 1939 ended nearly twenty years of relative freedom and independence for Poland. Such freedom had been a novel experiment as Poland's recent history was largely one of foreign domination, sandwiched between the Teutonic powers of Saxony and Prussia in the west, and Russia in the east. During the Great War, much of modern Poland's territory was occupied by Germany, who from 1915 pushed the Eastern Front boundary beyond Warsaw. In the hope that the Poles would support the German war effort, the Kaiser imposed a surprisingly benign tenure, allowing some religious tolerance and even reinstating the Polish language in education and government administration. As the German monarchy collapsed, so Polish nationalists came to the fore, including Józef Piłsudski, while the Versailles Peace Conference re-established the country as an independent republic, albeit with ill-defined boundaries, especially to the east. Following a plebiscite, the important industrial and mining region of Upper Silesia in the west was granted to Poland in 1921, but her independence was far from guaranteed. To the east, Lenin still hoped to export the Bolshevik revolution to the centre of Europe and in 1920 war broke out. Polish and Ukrainian troops achieved early successes. However, an effective Red Army counter-offensive brought Poland to the international negotiating table, where a proposal for a settled eastern boundary known as the 'Curzon Line' was discussed.[7] This line, named after the British Foreign Secretary, was to be an armistice line but was soon ignored by the Bolsheviks who continued their march on Warsaw. The situation for the Poles appeared hopeless with only the River Vistula, on which the capital lay, remaining as a natural defence. But in an extraordinary reversal Józef Piłsudski's Polish army routed the Bolsheviks in the Battle of Warsaw, which became a legend known as 'The Miracle on the Vistula'.[8]

Piłsudski remained the strongman of Poland throughout the 1920s and early 1930s. A coup in 1926 consolidated his power and ushered in the *Sanacja* (sanitation) regime, which was to continue in office until 1939. This regime was certainly no democracy, but neither was it the fascist dictatorship described by some sources. However, it remained dedicated to a continuous search for security and this inter-war period saw a succession of treaties and pacts between Poland and her neighbours or allies. A Polish-French Alliance was signed on 19 February 1921, only to be tempered later by the terms of the 1925 Treaty of Locarno, which saw Britain and France guarantee that the German borders would remain static. Significantly, no international guarantees were given for Germany's border with Poland, and feeling vulnerable, the Polish Government signed a non-aggression pact with the Soviet Union on 25 July 1932, followed by a similar pact with Germany in January 1934.

With the death of Piłsudski in May 1935, the *Sanacja* regime lost its unifying force at the very time when the country was subject to increased nationalist agitation, for included in a population of 32 million were some important minorities including Ukrainians (4 million), Jews (2.2 million), Byelorussians (1.5 million) and Germans (1 million). The Depression of the late 1920s and poor harvests had badly affected the population of Poland, of whom 64% lived off the land, and some communities became susceptible to envy of the Jews, who, by their industry, achieved representation in higher education, and dominated professions such as law and medicine. Some elements in Polish society felt excluded from further advancement and looked for scapegoats amongst such minorities. As a result of economic inequalities, there were some anti-Semitic riots, but their nature was sporadic, largely un-orchestrated and lacked the state sponsorship clearly evident in Germany.[9]

On 29 September 1938, the Munich conference began. Perhaps 'conference' was a misnomer, for yet again, Hitler dictated the European agenda, pushing the feeble British and French delegations into accepting the German annexation of the Sudetenland. Almost all of the Czechoslovak defensive positions lay within this region and the country, now totally exposed, anxiously awaited dismemberment. The Polish Government and especially the sharp and resourceful Polish Foreign Minister, Józef Beck, closely monitored events in their neighbouring state. In a move to pick over the Czech carcass, Poland gave the Czech government an ultimatum to remove its troops from the northwest corner of the Duchy of Teschen. On 1 October 1938, Polish troops seized this portion of Czech territory, much to the delight of the Germans who were happy to spread the blame for the ceding of parts of Czechoslovakia. Although Germany was deprived of this three-hundred-square-mile parcel of land containing important rail junctions, its seizure by Poland was opportunist and short-lived; it was also an action which appalled traditional friends of Poland, such as Winston Churchill, who accused the Poles of jumping 'on the back of Czechoslovakia in that moment of agony which helped to rend her in pieces.'[10]

Although Beck knew he had guarantees from Britain and France, he was enough of a pragmatist to realise that these agreements needed underwriting. He therefore looked to a wider plan for an east European block of Poland, Hungary, Romania, and the remains of Czechoslovakia, that might just be a bulwark against Germany and the Soviet Union. However, these plans soon foundered and in the winter of 1938–9 Germany bought off Hungary by giving her a sizable chunk of southern Slovakia. The remainder of Slovakia was encouraged by Germany to declare independence on 14 March 1939 and the following day, the President of Czechoslovakia, Emil Hácha, was invited to meet Hitler. Standing before the dictator, Hácha was berated and humiliated and, once he had been revived from physical collapse, was 'encouraged' to sign away Moravia and Bohemia. These two regions had formed the residue of the Czech part of the country and their new status as a German 'protectorate' and base for German troops would prove important as a springboard for the forthcoming attack on Poland.

The 1939 Anglo-Polish Treaty did not contain any guarantee for the integrity of Poland's pre-war boundaries, though on 31 March the British Prime Minister Neville Chamberlain surprised the House of Commons with a verbal assurance that if Poland were attacked, Britain and France 'would lend the Polish Government all the support in their power'. Three days later, after a series of customary rages, Hitler instructed the German High Command (OKW) to issue plans for the invasion of Poland. The simultaneity of these acts has prompted some sources to blame Chamberlain's assurances for pushing Hitler to accel-erate his plans for an attack on Poland, but it would seem that Hitler needed little encouragement.[11] And it was hard to see how Britain could not have given Poland a guarantee, for as Gladwyn Jebb of the Foreign Office observed:

> There was no hope of averting a war by not guaranteeing Poland. The more or less instinctive reaction of the Government, approved by the Foreign Office, was not therefore unpremeditated panic as suggested by some: it was a calculated defiance, and it was probably right.[12]

The British Government's belated stand against Hitler was rewarded with more than just points for morality. Increased co-operation between Britain and Poland was to reap significant benefits for the former, in the shape of intelligence. The Polish Intelligence Service had for some time since the early 1930s been decoding German military signals traffic. They had even managed to construct a replica 'Enigma' machine, from which they deciphered pre-war German Wehrmacht messages. However, German modifications to the military machine in late 1938 could not be discovered in time to enable Polish GHQ to read enemy ciphers in the critical period during August and September 1939. Nevertheless, the Poles were prepared to share what Enigma knowledge they held with British and French Intelligence. On 26 July 1939, Intelligence officers from the three countries met in the village of Pyry, just south of Warsaw. AG Denniston, Head of the Government Code and Cipher School (GC&CS) who attended the meeting, recalled that the Poles displayed 'a mass of telegrams they had read, concerning naval traffic between Berlin and the [German] fleet in Spanish waters'.[13] This hard evidence of their progress was followed up in August by the delivery to London, of a replica machine. This did not mean that the western Allies could read German signals immediately, because the settings and keys were regularly altered, but with the invaluable assistance and knowledge of Polish cryptanalysts, the British were eventually able to break the Enigma code.[14]

Meanwhile, to the east of Poland, Britain was lukewarm about talks with the Soviet Premier Josef Stalin and since the spring of 1939 had largely pushed away offers of a Soviet pact. In Moscow, distrust of the west was allowed to fester, with both Britain and France being seen as unreliable allies since their weak showing at Munich the previous year. It was a widely held belief that 'the [British] Government made allies with eloquence and great diplomatic skill, without being in a position to back up their words with suitable deeds.'[15]

As Germany piled on the pressure during August, the atmosphere in Warsaw remained strangely calm. William L. Shirer, an American correspondent with CBS who was based in the Polish capital, noted in his diary:

Walking home to the hotel at dawn, the air was soft and fresh and the quiet, soothing. All in all, the Poles are calm and confident and Berlin's gibes and Goebbels' terrific campaign of lies and invented incidents leave them cold. But they are romantic – too confident. You ask them, as I've asked a score of officials in the Foreign Office and the army this past week, about Russia and they shrug their shoulders. Russia does not count for them. But it ought to.[16]

Shirer was right. Both the Soviets and Germans saw Poland as a buffer state between their ideologies and a convenient Nazi-Soviet non-aggression pact would neatly divide Eastern Europe into areas of influence and control. More importantly for Hitler, it would relieve the threat of a war on two fronts, whilst for Stalin, it would allay his fears that he might be attacked from the west at the same time as any Japanese assault on his eastern borders. After overtures from Hitler, on 24 August 1939 Vyacheslav Molotov, the new Commissar for Soviet Foreign Affairs, signed a pact with his German counterpart, Joachim von Ribbentrop. The pact would keep Stalin out of a major war for the moment, but at a stroke, it had determined Poland's fate.[17]

Hitler now pushed the issue of the 'Polish Corridor'. This was a strip of land, some twenty-five miles wide, which was given to Poland through the Treaty of Versailles in order to allow her access to the sea. The practical effect was that it split off East Prussia from the rest of Germany, including the German-speaking seaport of Danzig, which had been declared a 'Free City' under the protection of the League of Nations. Hitler then put forward terms for his acquisition of Danzig and the Corridor, but while these terms were clearly unacceptable to the Poles, they found some favour in Britain. Chamberlain still hoped for peace and he was not alone. Hastings Ismay, Secretary of the Committee of Imperial Defence was prepared to allow the dictator one last chance, declaring to his colleague Robin Hankey:

> Danzig is no longer a place but a principle and in my opinion, we should make no more concessions of any kind unless and until Hitler himself makes a real *geste de rapprochement*. If he did that, and I thought it could be trusted, I would go a very long way to meet him.[18]

As *Blitzkrieg* enveloped Poland, the German Luftwaffe ensured that all strategic railways were bombed, thereby stopping reservists reaching their units and effectively debilitating Polish mobilisation. With Polish communications in chaos, urgent appeals were made to Britain and France for action. Chamberlain's Government prevaricated, initially issuing a 'warning' to Germany on the first day of the invasion, and it was only after uproar in the House of Commons on 2 September, that an ultimatum was issued to Germany the following day. The ultimatum was ignored and Britain declared war at 1100 hours, followed by France later in the day. But this declaration did not precipitate action. The Poles may have expected British bombers to attack Germany, and these bombers did carry out sorties over German cities, but it was only to drop leaflets. This timid British response was also mirrored by the French, who made much of a military diversion against the German Siegfried Line in the west, but this merely prodded the enemy defences and made no difference to the war in Poland.[19] Although British and French staffs knew that they would be unable to render material military support, the Poles remained confident that aid would come. After all, part of their strategy was based on a promised early French entry into the war, easing pressure on the Polish front, and thus allowing time for Polish reserves to mount a counter-attack against German forces. It was a forlorn hope. The Poles were alone but still managed to hold the enemy back until the last of the major Polish armies was destroyed at the Battle of the Kutno Pocket. By 17 September, Warsaw lay open.

Generaloberst Franz Halder maintained that he had no wish to 'raze' Warsaw as the Polish Army had been defeated, but he alleged that Hitler had other ideas:

> Hitler said, 'No, Warsaw must be attacked.' The war against Poland would only be over when Warsaw had fallen. He then started to describe how the skies would be darkened, how millions of tons of shells would rain down on Warsaw, how people would drown in blood. Then his eyes nearly popped out of his head and he became a different person. He was suddenly seized by a lust for blood.[20]

On 17 September 1939 the Soviets announced that due to the German invasion, the Polish state had ceased to exist, rendering any current treaties null and void. The old standby was employed of 'rescuing Soviet friends' (Ukrainians and Emigré Russians) in Poland who were at the mercy of the Germans. At the very moment that Polish units were falling back on Warsaw, or heading for the Romanian border in the south-east corner of Poland, Soviet troops poured across the entire length of Poland's eastern borders. They were ordered to advance to the new German line and partition Poland in accordance with the Molotov-Ribbentrop Pact, and 'protect' the Polish territories of Ukraine and Byelorussia. This thin veneer of Soviet protection was soon breached when Molotov admitted that there were 'serious encounters between our troops and Polish troops and consequently there were casualties. The total casualties of the Red Army were 2,599.' No doubt this figure was understated, for although this eastern area was pacified within a week and only lightly defended by Polish troops, the Soviets claimed to have captured over 900 guns, 10,000 machine-guns, 300,000 rifles and 300 aircraft. It was a fair tally for capturing half of Poland's territory together with 13 million inhabitants.[21]

Some elements in eastern Poland believed that Soviet rule might even be benign. In reality it was every bit as brutal as German control in the west. The arrival of Soviet troops shocked fourteen-year-old Bolesław Majewski, who lived with his family on a farm just east of Brest-Litovsk:

> Shortly after we heard the Russians had invaded our country, my father was advised to leave his post in the Polish police, as it was every man for

himself. My elder brother and I continued to look after the animals on the farm. Early one morning I came back into the farmhouse after feeding them and was startled by a huge Russian soldier standing in the doorway with bayonet fixed. 'Who are you?' he barked. My father appeared and told him I was his son. He seemed to accept this and ordered us all to collect a few things and report to the village school. When we arrived there, we saw a lot of other villagers we knew. There were many Russian soldiers and an NKVD man standing in the centre with a list of all our names. They had done their homework in advance. We were shipped out in trucks and then in railway wagons up to Archangel in the north where it was bitterly cold. We were then put to work in the Russian railways and timber yards.[22]

While Stalin would never retreat from his captured Polish territory, Churchill was never going to force the issue, as the British Government considered that the eastern Polish frontier should be along the 'Curzon Line', which approximated to Stalin's new front-line. Ultimately, 'on the frontier position, the British views were therefore closer to the Russians than to the Poles.'[23]

As the Soviets swept in from the east, refugees streamed out of Poland, many crossing the border into Romania. This neighbour state kept her borders open, despite pressure from her military and certain sectors of her government, who had now rejected the old military alliance with Poland. Although Romania was inclined to Germany and she interned many leading members of the Polish Government, other senior military commanders were allowed to escape. As well as a steady stream of Polish refugees, the human column was enlivened by a Rolls-Royce bearing an upright British Ambassador, together with another car carrying Colonel Beck, the Polish Foreign Minister. Also among the refugees were the members of the British Military Mission from Warsaw. This Mission was headed by the legendary Major-General Adrian Carton de Wiart VC, and included Lieutenant-Colonel Colin Gubbins as GSO1, Peter Wilkinson, Captain Harold Perkins and Captain Mike Pickles. The aim of the twenty-strong party, which included representatives from Military Research, Intelligence (MIR), was to establish resistance contacts within Poland for the supply of weapons and transmitters. But they had spent barely two weeks in Poland before being evicted by the German invasion. Even the indestructible Carton de Wiart, who had lost an eye, a

hand and had been wounded three times in the Great War, realised that
this time the odds were too heavily stacked against his team. The party
eventually reached France and set up liaison with the fledgling Polish
Government-in-exile, based in Paris.[24]

Meanwhile, in eastern Poland, countless families were torn apart by
the sudden Soviet occupation. Those Poles who were seen as educated
or professional were immediately arrested and sent eastwards in railway
cattle trucks. In freezing, overcrowded conditions in the rail trucks, many
died and were thrown out onto the tracks, but in extraordinary acts of
bravery, some priests managed to squeeze into the trucks to administer
to the sick, knowing that they would share the same fate. It is estimated
that some 1.7 million Poles were deported to the Soviet Union, most
to be dumped in penal camps in the wastelands of Siberia and the
Arctic Circle.[25] Whole families were split and twelve-year-old Hanna
Czarnocka was shocked by the turmoil:

At the start of the war we lived in Krzemieniec, Volhynia, in eastern
Poland, and we had a comfortable lifestyle as my father was the *Kurator*
(Rector) of the *Liceum Krzemienieckie,* an important and historic school in
the region. My mother, Halina, was a social welfare worker, town council-
lor and supported the very large Jewish community in the region. When
the Germans invaded, refugees started pouring into our town and that
included Józef Beck and other government ministers, who sheltered in
the Hotel Bona. This soon became a target for German bombers, though
most of their bombs fell on the nearby market place killing many civilians.
Our school's German teacher, who quickly disappeared after the incident,
was strongly suspected of being the spy who caused the bombing. Many
local traders were frightened and left the town, heading south with the
government representatives. As goods were in short supply, my mother
started helping with local services as well as supporting refugees.

We were only 20 km from the Soviet border, so when the Soviets invaded
on 17 September, they arrived in our town three days later. I remember my
father dreading their arrival and he started burning papers; everywhere we
saw black wisps of charred paper floating in the air. Other groups in the
town welcomed the Russians, including some Jewish families, who knew
of the Nazi atrocities and hoped that the Russians would protect them. The
young Russian soldiers were so drab. They had no hems on their uniforms
and their rifles were slung over their shoulders with string. A platform

was built in the local school grounds and we were all forced to attend and listen to propaganda speeches. The men, in hats with red stars on, spoke in Russian, Ukrainian and Polish about 'how good Stalin was'. We were then sent home and soldiers came to our house to arrest our father, who looked sadly back at us as he was taken away under armed guard. A family friend made a parcel of food and clothes and managed to find him in a prison. She said that his captors claimed that 'as he had worked for the former Polish state, he had committed a criminal offence'. It was incredible; the Russians seemed to know who everybody was and where they were educated, there was no escaping this. Then one day, my mother received a note written on cigarette paper, from our father. It read, 'Tomorrow they will send me to deepest Russia and you will be sent as well. Take the children and escape to the German occupied zone'. It was February 1940, and the first transports were about to go to Siberia and while waiting to be deported, some children froze to death at the local railway station. My grandmother had already been taken ill and died in hospital in Lwów in terrible conditions. It was minus 20°C. My aunt, Wanda had already left for Warsaw, and my mother, my younger brother and myself, quickly packed and left for what was to be an extraordinary journey.[26]

Warsaw fell on 27 September, but elements of the disparate Polish Army fought on and indeed some of the toughest fighting occurred as Polish units battled their way south towards the Romanian border. General Kazimierz Sosnkowski managed to establish a bridgehead there, allowing valuable time for troops and much of Poland's government to escape. German and Soviet troops met near Brest on 28 September and by 5 October the fighting was effectively over. It is estimated that the Germans suffered nearly 50,000 casualties and lost some 500 aircraft whist inflicting 200,000 casualties on the Polish Army.

On 8 October, by Hitler's special decree, German–occupied Poland was divided almost in half, with the economically important western region including Danzig and the Polish Corridor, Poznan, Łódź and Upper Silesia being incorporated into the Reich. Those who could prove they were *Volksdeutsche* (of German origin) were allowed to stay, and in the important regions of Upper Silesia and Pomerania, over 40% were registered as such. The remaining population were classed as 'Poles' and either driven out to the east, or treated as a sub–human category, deprived of their homes and education and subjected to hard labour. In the eastern part of German occupied Poland, a new administration was formed. This administrative block included Warsaw, Lublin and Kraków, an area of some 100,000 sq km, and was to be controlled by a 'General Government'. In this sector, the population was to be subjected to particularly harsh treatment; semi-starvation, forced labour, mass executions and transportation were characteristics of the new order. Even before the total extermination policies were determined in 1942, Hitler's plan was simply the expansion of the German race into Poland to create *lebensraum* (living space), while the Poles were to be evicted and spread like a waste product over the vast tracts of the Soviet Union.[27] The German commander, von Rundstedt, temporarily filled the post of Governor-General until 26 October, when Hitler appointed Hans Frank as his successor. The forty-year-old lawyer had been Hitler's personal legal adviser and was a former Reich Commissar for Justice. Frank had served his apprenticeship with Hitler in the 'Beer Hall Putsch' in 1923 and had been an *Obergruppenführer* in the pre-war SA, but his recent military service was confined to the role of reserve officer. He later claimed that his promotion was a surprise:

> I was training my company and on 17 September I was making final preparations before going to the front when a telephone call came from the Führer's special train ordering me to go to the Führer at once. The following day I travelled to Upper Silesia where the Führer's special train was stationed at that time, and in a very short conversation, which lasted less than ten minutes, he gave me the mission, as he put it, to take over the functions of Civilian Governor for the occupied Polish territories.[28]

Despite his subsequent loyal service, Frank (and any member of the legal profession) was never really trusted by Hitler, who ensured that the SS (*Schutzstaffeln*) and Gestapo remained, officially at least, directly responsible to the SS-Reichführer, Heinrich Himmler. Nonetheless, this brutal security apparatus was available to Frank to implement his Führer's policies – policies Frank was to enthusiastically enforce, especially those concerning the suppression of the Poles and annihilation of the Jews. Referring to his new fiefdom, he noted in his diary, 'this territory in its entirety is the booty of the German Reich'. As well as Governor, Frank was also leader of the National Socialist Party in the state, and he was directly subordinate to Hitler and in time would even be allowed control over the Higher Chiefs of the SS and SD.[29] From his base in

Kraków, he surrounded himself with the trappings of power, as Countess Karolina Lanckorońska recalled:

> The existence of the Poles was becoming increasingly difficult. Ever more strongly, and at every step, it was emphasised that we Poles were *Untermenschen* (sub-humans)…we felt ourselves defenceless in the hands of the German General Governor Hans Frank, who resided at Wawel Castle, and whose deeds vied with those of all his predecessors who had borne that terrible title on the soil of Poland. I saw him once only. I was going through the Market near Bracka Street when five motor cars and a posse of motorcyclists, moving at top speed, emerged from Franciszkańska Street and drew to a halt in front of the Nazi Party HQ. SS men with hand-held machine carbines jumped from their cars and, at the speed of lightning, formed a double cordon from the pavement to the main door. At the same time, walking quickly came a man in uniform with very black hair and eyes. A pace to his rear a couple of aides were almost running to keep up. Had I not recognised his face – his photograph was everywhere – I would not have known who he was by the immense fear that he did nothing to hide, peering round to left and right at every step till he disappeared behind the door, which shut immediately.[30]

Meanwhile Stalin was busy consolidating the East European states to the north of Poland. In October 1939, the Baltic states of Latvia, Lithuania and Estonia were coerced into a pact with the Soviets, which gave Stalin access to ice-free ports. It was no surprise that within nine months a total Soviet occupation took place. Stalin had repeatedly voiced concern before 1939 as to the unreliability of treaties with Britain or France. On 30 November 1939 he disregarded his non-aggression pact with Finland and invaded her. It turned out to be a poor advertisement for Soviet military prowess, for the result was incomplete and the whole bitter adventure reinforced Hitler's belief that Stalin's forces were ill-disciplined, under-equipped and would not withstand a future German invasion.[31] Surprisingly, once hostilities ended, Stalin agreed to exchange prisoners with the Finns, something that was certainly not on his agenda for Poland in 1940, where large numbers of Polish troops, academics, clerics and civil servants had been rounded up for 'processing' by Stalin's secret police, or NKVD (*Narodny Komissaryat Vnutrennikh Del*). Adam Wykrota found himself caught in the net:

I was twenty-four when the war started in Poland and I was based with my battalion at Wilno. When the collapse happened, the regiment was disbanded and I fled to Lithuania thinking I would be safe. Then the Russians arrived there as well and I was arrested and sent to an internment camp near Smolensk and twenty-five miles from Katyn. We lived in cowsheds and were separated from our officers. Then one day, it was some time in 1940, the officers were taken away and we never heard of them again.[32]

The NKVD had, by the spring of 1940, sifted through their captives, allowing Lavrenti Beria, head of the security organisation to propose to Stalin that nearly 22,000 Poles, including half the Polish officer corps, should be eliminated. It is highly likely that Wykrota's officers were among those men massacred by Soviet forces in the spring of 1940 and buried in Katyn Forest. Katyn – and the other two NKVD execution sites at Mednoye and Kharkov – were to remain a secret for another three years and, even then, the Soviets would escape the blame.

Since their flight via Romania, many senior Polish political and military figures had established themselves in Paris. A discreet revolution had overthrown the old Polish *Sanacja* regime and a new Polish Government-in-exile was formed with Władysław Raczkiewicz as President. General Władysław Sikorski, a veteran of the 1920 war, was appointed both Prime Minister and Commander-in-Chief of the Polish Armed Forces. The new government of 'National Unity', which was speedily recognised by Britain and France, comprised leading figures of the main national parties, such as Stanisław Mikołajczyk and military commanders such as Kazimierz Sosnkowski. Sikorski, who was untainted by association with the *ancien régime*, started to rebuild the Polish Armed Forces and the intention was to create four divisions out of the 35,000 troops who had escaped, together with 45,000 Polish immigrants resident in France. A Highland Brigade was also formed as well as a revitalised 10th Mechanised Cavalry Brigade, equipped with French R–35 tanks.[33]

Meanwhile much of the Polish Merchant fleet had managed to escape to friendly waters and due to a pre-war plan by the British Admiralty, three naval destroyers sailed to the safety of British ports during the German invasion, followed shortly afterwards by several Polish submarines. While other Polish submarines were interned by neutral Sweden for the rest of the War, the Polish Navy continued a proud service record, operating under the Royal Navy and supplemented by ships leased from Britain.[34]

Hitler now turned his attention to the west. As dawn broke on 10 May 1940, along a front of over 175 miles running from the North Sea down to the Maginot Line, German forces swept into Holland, Belgium and Luxembourg. Within an hour of the alert, aircrews were scrambled from RAF 226 Squadron, part of the Advanced Air Strike Force, based at Rheims. The three-man crews took off in their Fairey Battle light bombers to attack strategic targets ahead of the German advance. The 'Battle' was one of the first British bombers to see action and great hopes were placed on the Merlin-engined aircraft, which had twice the bomb load and could cover twice the distance of its predecessors. One aircraft flown by Flying Officer Cameron, together with his navigator Sergeant Hart and Wireless Operator Sergeant John Ward made good progress towards the target, a bridge near Diekirch in Luxembourg. But as they closed on the bridge, enemy flak erupted around their aircraft and machine-gun fire ripped through the fuselage. Cameron wrestled with his controls, but an explosion in the cockpit blew off part of his arm. Nevertheless, he managed to crash-land the aircraft. As they lay in the smouldering wreck, Germans soon surrounded them, but the quick-thinking Ward called out that there were bombs on board. The Germans hastily retreated, enabling him to burn any secret papers, before the airmen were dragged out. The crew were then removed to a hospital, where Ward and Hart recovered but Cameron died on the operating table. The surviving RAF men were separated and interned in POW camps. During the next year, Ward was moved around various camps until he ended up in Upper Silesia, near the old German/Polish border. He escaped from this camp and crossed into the General Government sector of occupied Poland, where he joined the underground movement and became, on his own initiative, a British Intelligence source. He was to be one of the very few British witnesses to the terrible events in Warsaw in 1944.[35]

As Queen Wilhelmina and her Dutch government escaped to London, Holland surrendered just five days later. 10 May was a momentous day for other reasons. As Hitler was poised to conquer the Low Countries, the political situation changed abruptly in London. Despite the obvious failure of Chamberlain's policies in the light of Hitler's latest actions, it was the poor performance of British forces in the Norway campaign which brought him down. By the evening of 10 May, Winston Churchill was installed as Prime Minister and he quickly gathered an all-party cabinet around him. His famous offer of 'blood, toil, tears and sweat' brought great heart to the Poles, wearied by the recent diet of British indecision.

Following Hitler's swift occupation of Holland, Belgium capitulated soon after on 28 May, despite a brave showing by Belgian troops against hopeless odds. However, in the last days of that month, over 125,000 Allied troops had been evacuated from Dunkirk, though Polish units were not among them. Their fate was determined by French Army operations, which floundered in front of Hitler's sweep into France. The Polish Highland Brigade, which had recently seen service in the lacklustre land campaign in Norway had been pulled back to France to assist her defence, only to be overwhelmed a week later together with the partly formed Polish 3rd Division, in heavy fighting on the Bretagne peninsula.

A similar fate befell Colonel Maczek's 10th Mechanised Brigade, which was severely mauled in actions in the Champagne region. Meanwhile, of the two Polish divisions that were fully formed, the 1st Grenadier Division under the command of General Duch fought a brave rearguard action covering the retreat of the French 20th Army Corps and lost nearly 50% of its men. However, the other completed unit, the 2nd Rifle Division, was compelled to move across the border into Switzerland, where it was interned for the rest of the war. In the light of the disastrous French campaign, it was miraculous that any Polish troops managed to escape. Although 55,000 Polish troops were lost or captured in France, some 19,000 men, including 5,000 aircrew, did manage to escape to England to re-form and re-fit. They remained part of the Polish Republic's armed forces, but now came under Allied Command.[36]

The Fall of France was a shock to the Poles. 'There was terrible disappointment at the French collapse,' wrote Countess Karolina Lanckorońska, 'to whom we had all looked up to for so long. This frustrated love of France was redirected all the more intensely towards England – powerful, wise, immeasurably upright and yet, so far, hardly known to us.'[37] This warmth of feeling between the Poles and Britain grew during the summer of 1940, strengthened by the courageous roll of Polish pilots in the Battle of Britain, when twenty-nine out of ninety-eight Polish pilots were lost. And more importantly, that bond was cemented during the months leading up to the German invasion of the Soviet Union in June 1941, when 'Poland-in-exile' was Britain's only significant ally.[38]

Poland's Government-in-exile had to move to London, and set itself up in the unlikely surroundings of the Hotel Rubens, near Buckingham Palace. In London, the Polish leaders, unlike the Czechs, were unfamiliar figures. They were known in the US, where there was a large Polish immigrant population and they had left behind a large number of contacts in France, but new relationships had to be forged in Britain. The capitulation of France and the move to Britain was also a further disruption for Polish troops who had been on the move since their own country fell, and were desperate to stay in the war. Second Lieutenant Mieczysław Juny's adventures were typical:

> Having been a young officer in the Polish Reserve Army, I was recalled before the war started and was commanding a unit of reserve men [Territorials] in the Carpathian Mountains along the southern border with Hungary. After the Germans invaded, I was ordered with my men to cross the border into Hungary, where we were held temporarily. The Germans must have put much pressure on the Hungarians and Romanians to intern us, but they were our friends and it was a fairly easy stay. To my amazement, my fiancée also managed to cross the border and find me, and we married there and then. I left her in a safe place and we made our way down to Yugoslavia, then Bratislava and Greece and finally we embarked on 'The Constanza' and crossed the Mediterranean to Beirut, which was French controlled. While we were there, awaiting the formation of a Carpathian Brigade, France fell. We were now under the control of a French officer who was taking his orders from the Germans. He commanded us to surrender our arms, but luckily we were with some tough French Foreign Legionnaires who sided with us and he had to back down. We were all determined to get away to fight again, and we were soon moved to Palestine and then down to Egypt, in order to move up to Tobruk to face the Italians.[39]

From 1939, right up until its invasion by German forces in June 1941, the Soviet Union was still a German ally, and as such, helped her with trade and economic support, as well as offering naval facilities at Murmansk. Stalin continued this support right up until 'Operation Barbarossa' in the belief that Hitler could not do without his help. There were of course German strategic 'side-shows' such as Yugoslavia and Greece which further wrong-footed Stalin, but despite repeated intelligence that the

Germans were about to invade, Stalin resolutely refused to accept the notion.[40] Yet German plans for the invasion had been in preparation for some time. On 5 December 1940, the German OKH (*Oberkommando des Heeres*) Commander-in-Chief, *Generaloberst* Walter von Brauchitsch, presented the final plan to Hitler for the invasion of the Soviet Union. Von Brauchitsch and his Chief-of-Staff, *Generaloberst* Franz Halder stood before their Führer, who immediately amended their overworked plans and directed that Moscow was no longer the main objective. Instead, German Army Group North and Army Group Centre would advance through the Baltic States and the Ukraine, while Army Group South would occupy the oil-rich Caucasus. This new *lebensraum* (living space) would indeed incorporate Moscow, but perhaps mindful of Napoleon's disastrous Russian campaign, Hitler did not make the city the focus of his plans. After all, France had capitulated without a major strike at Paris. But his overriding consideration was that the Soviet Army had to be destroyed west of the River Dnieper, avoiding the Wehrmacht being drawn too deep into Soviet territory to fight a war on stretched resources.

Despite the disquiet of his fellow commanders, von Brauchitsch put up little resistance to Hitler's fateful plans. In fact, von Brauchitsch had long since given up the unequal struggle with his supreme commander:

> General Brauchitsch said privately to a small circle of German generals, 'Why should I tell Hitler the truth when everyone else lies to him?' At the same meeting the German plan for the Caucasus was discussed. Almost all present were against it and begged Brauchitsch to explain to Hitler the difficulties of executing it. Brauchitsch made the above excuse. Hitler is not accurately informed about the material, technical and physical possibilities of continuing the war, nor is he told the truth about German losses, because he would then put the blame on the generals. At war councils he indicates with his finger on the map the objectives he wishes to attain. The generals do not carry out his instructions strictly, because he forgets very easily, but they give him the report after the event. Anyone who tries to tell him unpleasant things is treated to an explosion of temper.[41]

Operation 'Barbarossa' started in the early hours of 22 June 1941. It was heralded by German newspaper headlines, screaming '*Abrechnung mit dem rotten Pack*' (Settlement with the red rabble). The scale and success of the initial Wehrmacht thrust was staggering. Originally deploying along a front of over 1,700 miles, an Axis army of 3 million men would crash through 750 miles of Soviet-held territory within the next six months, which was equivalent to travelling the distance from London to Rome.[42] Stalin was at first thrown off balance and it took him some hours to issue his first military directive. His first thought was that the German attacks were some sort of large-scale provocation until he received the official declaration of war at 0530 hours. By then, the assault was well under way and Soviet communications were seriously damaged with many frontline units cut off from central HQs. The tortured report and confirmation system inherent in the Soviet system meant that com-manders like Konstantin Rokossovsky, commander of 9th Mechanized Corps, could not go into action until he had opened a top secret opera-tional envelope. This contained orders from his Fifth Army Command, which had to be opened in the presence of the People's Commissar for Defence. Rokossovsky then had to confirm its contents with District HQ, Army HQ and the People's Commissariat for Defence and then, even as a Corps commander, consult with his Chief of Staff, Political Deputy and Special Section Chief. In the meantime the Germans had bombed Kiev and cut him off from his District Command.[43]

As the Wehrmacht swept through the old eastern part of Poland, the special operational units of the *SS Einsatzgruppen* were never far behind. Hitler's declared aim for 'Barbarossa' was the defeat of the 'Bolshevik/ Jewish conspiracy', a wide brief that included the extinction of much of the Polish intelligentsia. Lists drawn up by the pre-war German Embassy and Consulates assisted the brutal exercise, but terror became indiscriminate. In a typical exercise, *Brigadeführer* E. Schöngarth's SS police unit arrested and summarily shot twenty-five Polish professors from the Lwów Polytechnic School, together with their relatives and house-guests.[44] Considering all four *Einsatzgruppen* mustered no more than 4,000 troops altogether, their capacity for creating mayhem was extraordinary. But these 'mission squads' did not have a monopoly on brutality. Poles, in areas formally under Soviet control and now under German occupation, were also capable of atrocities. At Jedwabne, the Jewish community were slaughtered by their former Polish neighbours in an act that may, or may not have been inspired by local German *Einsatzgruppen*.[45] However, it was also evident that because they were so small in number, the *Einsatzgruppen* could not have functioned with such appalling efficiency, without the help and connivance of Wehrmacht units. Nonetheless, such diversions did not slow the rapid Wehrmacht advance, and by November 1941 German forces were within sight of Moscow. Within a month their fortunes were dramatically reversed due to stubborn Soviet resistance, exhausted lines of communication and appalling weather.[46] With a short breathing space to gather reserves, the Soviet Army unleashed a series of counter-strokes east of Leningrad and at Rostov. These successes then enabled Stalin to launch a general offensive early in 1942 across the whole front running from Leningrad in the north, to the Black Sea in the south.[47]

While 'Barbarossa' was a critical challenge to the Soviet Union, it also marked a turning point for Poland. Because Stalin was under pressure, he was compelled to enter into a Polish-Soviet agreement, whereby the Poles interned in the Soviet Union since 1940, including large numbers of Polish POWs, would be released under an amnesty. However, many Poles had perished in the camps through execution, disease and sub-zero temperatures, and a tally had revealed that virtually all Polish Army officers captured in the early months of the war had disappeared, later to be accounted for in the Katyn massacres. However, about 114,000 soldiers and civilians were allowed to leave Soviet territory with General Władysław Anders, a former cavalry officer, who was intending to create a new Polish Corps. This large body of Poles entered neighbouring Iran, where under British jurisdiction, General Anders set about creating a II Polish Corps, thus relieving six Soviet Divisions of occupation duties.[48] The release period was tense and collusion between senior Polish officers and the Soviets was rare. Large numbers of Poles had been slaughtered and those who had endured spells in the grim gulags of Siberia were not inclined to any further contact with the Soviets. There were some who, through pro-communist sympathies or opportunism, decided to remain in the Soviet Union, but there were more who were simply unable to travel the long distances or obtain the necessary documents to join Anders. From among these ranks Stalin ordered the creation of a Soviet-sponsored 1st Polish Army. Zygmunt Berling, a former Polish Army officer had spent many months languishing in Soviet jails and camps before he was 're-educated' and began a meteoric rise to the head of this army, which would become one of Stalin's tools for the control of Poland.

Until 'Barbarossa', Britain and its one ally, Poland had stood alone against Hitler. It was therefore a huge relief to Britain when the

Soviet Union was brought into the war. The attitude of the press and public to the Soviets was therefore one of gratefulness, but the BBC hardly needed to be reminded of that. Its output, particularly from its European News Directives was unashamedly pro-Soviet, while the Home Service's 'Russian Commentary', was written by Alexander Werth, a known admirer of communism and the 'Soviet experiment'. Stalin's birthday was even celebrated by special performances by the BBC Symphony Orchestra, and radio programmes featured articles on Soviet life as well as her activities on the battlefield.[49] Although Stalin's collusion with Hitler in 1939 was now conveniently ignored, all this build-up of admiration for 'Uncle Joe' and the Soviet system made it very difficult for the British Government to backtrack on its relationship with Stalin. Once news of Soviet atrocities started to leak out, could it ever admit to a sceptical public that it had been in league with a mass-murderer and were unaware of his antics?

Meanwhile, the Poles, who were certainly more versed in the ways of their Soviet neighbour, continued their vital cooperation with the Allies, especially in the area of intelligence. When the Polish General Staff were set up in London, the II Bureau (Intelligence) became an important component and was directly responsible to the Chief of Polish General Staff (PGS). Colonel Leon Mitkiewicz was the first Head of II Bureau, to be followed in December 1941 by the more experienced Lieutenant-Colonel Stanisław Gano. Although the lines of communication to their home country were even further stretched by the move to London, they continued to provide reliable intelligence to the British SIS (Secret Intelligence Service), an organisation distinctly lacking in foreign contacts since the fall of France.[50]

Polish intelligence made a huge contribution to Allied planning. The value of the breaking of the German Enigma ciphering machine cannot be underestimated and tremendous work was undertaken by men such as Mieczysław Słowikowski ('Rygor') in facilitating the escape of Polish troops left behind after the fall of France, as well as in the setting up of the Intelligence network 'Agency Africa'. Słowikowski's work in French North Africa, and in particular the efforts of the Polish Military Intelligence unit in Algiers, paved the way for the November 1942 Allied landings. Known as 'Operation Torch', this venture in turn made possible the later invasion of Italy, and until a new western front could be opened, 'Torch' quelled Stalin's anger over the lack of a fresh Allied front.

And as German forces took over control of the Vichy sector of France in November 1942, the work of Polish agents in France became crucial.[51]

The brief alignment of Poland with the Soviet Union came to an end in April 1943, when the Germans finally discovered the graves of over 4,000 Poles in Katyn Forest. Those murdered included not only army officers but also NCOs, pilots, officials, professors, writers, teachers – in fact anyone who might have played a part in a revived, independent Poland. It was later revealed that the scale of the atrocity was much greater and that the Soviet Security chief, Lavrentiy Beria, had engineered the simultaneous murder of not only 4,421 Poles at Katyn, but also 3,820 Poles near Kharkov, 6,311 in the Ostashkovo district and a further 7,305 in POW camps.[52] When the Soviets denied the slaughter, the Polish Government-in-exile demanded a Red Cross-sponsored investigation. Hoping to capitalise on an allied split, Germany made similar requests and this brought dividends for Reich Propaganda Minister, Josef Göbbels. On 26 April, the Soviet Union broke off diplomatic relations with Sikorski's government, claiming 'disgust' at Polish collusion with Germany. As Polish/Soviet relations reached a new low, a terrible tragedy befell the Polish leadership. On 4 July, a Liberator carrying General Sikorski crashed into the sea as it was taking off from Gibralter runway, killing him together his daughter Zofia, members of his staff and a British Liaison officer, Lieutenant-Colonel Victor Cazalet MP. Although evidence pointed to an accident, conspiracy theories abounded and accusations were even made against Churchill and SIS, as well as several Polish antagonists – accusations that were fuelled by German propaganda.[53] Various suspects were produced, including one man, Wing Commander Kleczynski, who claimed the previous year to have found a bomb on Sikorski's aircraft. However, such claimants were eventually ruled out by British intelligence after investigation by Britain's Special Operations Executive (SOE):

> SOE have informed this office informally that W/C Kleczynski is believed to be a dope fiend, suffers from hallucinations and, in the words of a prominent and reliable SOE official, is a 'pathological exhibitionist'.[54]

Tragically, Kleczynski was a gallant and decorated airman, who had been on many bombing raids over Germany and had also been wounded in action. He subsequently threatened to take his own life.

Sikorski's death was a serious blow to Polish hopes. As both head of the Government-in-exile and Commander-in-Chief, he had welded together the many disparate voices in the Polish establishment and as far as Britain was concerned, he was a trusted and valued ally. Churchill had respected him and, as the diplomat, Frank (later Sir Frank) Roberts observed, 'Sikorski provided a welcome contrast to that other much more difficult Allied military leader in London, General de Gaulle'.[55] The Polish President, Władysław Raczkiewicz remained in office, but it was decided to split the late General Sikorski's role between Stanisław Mikołajczyk, leader of the Polish Peasant Party who was appointed Prime Minister, and General Kazimierz Sosnkowski who was promoted to Commander-in-Chief. Mikołajczyk, who shared Sikorski's pragmatism on foreign affairs but lacked the international contacts, was well aware that Britain was not prepared to fight for Poland's eastern borders and consequently pursued a foreign policy similar to that of Sikorski. While he did not rule out a deal with the Soviet Union on borders, General Sosnkowski took a more intransigent view and rejected anything that might lead to the 'gradual Sovietisation of Poland'. This put him at odds with Churchill, who reportedly told a Polish colleague, 'you have a general called Sozzle-Something. We don't want him. He would upset the Russians'. Nonetheless, Sosnkowski was appointed to his new post by his ally, President Raczkiewicz, but it was without reference to the rest of the Polish cabinet and precipitated a political crisis. The storm died down but deep divisions remained over Polish policy towards the Soviet Union.[56]

While internal divisions pre-occupied the Polish Government-in-exile, their interests were hardly championed at the highest level. When Churchill, Roosevelt and Stalin met at the Tehran Conference on 23 November 1943, the question of Poland's eastern borders was raised. On the eve of the conference, Mikołajczyk requested meetings with both Churchill and Roosevelt, but was turned down on the basis that any prior meetings between the western leaders and the Polish Premier, 'might prompt Stalin to back out'.[57] The British Foreign Secretary, Anthony Eden had already stated that any deal on Poland's borders would only be sanctioned by the 'Big Three' with Polish agreement. But 'Polish agreement' was never a likely outcome, even if Churchill had insisted. The 'Big Three' were rapidly becoming the 'Big Two' as Roosevelt tried to ingratiate himself with Stalin at the expense of the British Prime Minister. In fact, when the contentious issue of the Polish borders was discussed, the American President made a conscious effort to side-step the awkward question. Hugh Dalton, Britain's former Minister for Economic Warfare observed:

> As to the Poles, Stalin wants the Curzon Line, but is quite prepared for Poland to go as far west as the Oder, with transfer of German population westward. Eden said they had some discussion on the eastern frontier and Stalin said, 'we regard that as all settled. Here is our line on the map.' Eden said, 'Do you mean the Ribbentrop-Molotov Line?' Molotov looked rather disconcerted at this, but Stalin said, 'we generally call it the Curzon Line. It is the same thing, isn't it?' Then there was some discussion about Bialystock, where Eden said the people were mainly Poles and Stalin agreed and redrew the line on the map to exclude them. We tried very hard to get Lwów for the Poles, but Stalin insisted that although there were a lot of Poles in the city, the countryside was entirely Ukrainian. Stalin also thought that the Russians ought to have Königsberg, as a 'warm water port', but Eden thought this was going a bit far. Stalin did not speak very ill of the present Polish Government in London, but complained that the Poles were killing Partisans on their territory, and that a situation was developing very much like that in Yugoslavia. The President [Roosevelt] with his mind full of the elections, did not want to get involved in a discussion on Poland and this, therefore, was entirely an Anglo-Russian affair, the President sitting in a corner and feigning sleep.[58]

To the British Government, the Allies' capitulation to Stalin at Tehran was the inevitable cost of keeping the Soviet Union on board. To the Poles, it was a betrayal, and sceptical observers, such as the British writer, George Orwell saw the *rapprochement* as naïve and without a future. In fact, he based the last scene in his book, *Animal Farm*, on the events at Tehran. In the climax to his parody of communism, Orwell had 'Farmer Pilkington' (representing Churchill and the leaders of Britain) sitting down with 'Napoleon' (Stalin) and exchanging toasts, amid feelings of mutual admiration. The next minute they fell out over a card game and were furiously attacking each other. The Polish borders were indeed, 'a busted flush.'[59]

NOTES

[1] Alfred Naujocks Affidavit, 2751-PS, *Trial of the Major War Criminals before the International Military Tribunal, Nuremberg 14 November 1945-1 October 1946,* Vol. IV (International Military Tribune, 1947). The private war journal of Generaloberst Franz Halder, Chief of the General Staff (OKH) provides interesting background on 'Operation Himmler', see 17 August 1939 entry, MF 321-322, Liddell Hart Centre for Military Archives, King's College, London (hereafter LHCMA).

[2] It is often erroneously stated that the 18th Uhlans (Lancers) mounted and charged German tanks. For an assessment of Polish strengths and weaknesses, see 'General Hasso von Manteuffel Interrogation', November 1945, LH 15/15/149/8, LHCMA.

[3] Unamed US journalist to Basil Liddell Hart, 29 October 1939, LH 9/24/222, LHCMA.

[4] For the German view of the September campaign in Poland, see Dr. Otto AW John, 'Synopsis of the German Campaign Against Poland in September 1939', *The Army Quarterly,* July 1950. The synopsis was prepared in connection with the later trial of Field-Marshal von Manstein, together with his annotations.

[5] Chester Wilmot, 'Interrogation notes on Generaloberst Franz Halder', October 1945, LH 15/15/150/2, LHCMA.

[6] 'Interrogation notes on General of Armoured Troops, Hasso von Manteuffel', November 1945, LH 15/15/149/1, LHCMA.

[7] The two countries did not take up the Curzon line at the time. Lord Curzon merely signed the document marking the line and had no hand in its construction. It was actually drawn by the Oxford philosopher, HJ Paton.

[8] For authoritative English language histories of Poland, see Norman Davies, *Heart of Europe: a short history of Poland* (London, 2002); Jerzy Lukowski and Hubert Zawadzki, *A Concise History of Poland* (Cambridge University Press, Cambridge 2006); Richard M Watt, *Bitter Glory. Poland and its Fate 1918–1939* (Hippocrene Books, New York 1998).

[9] 70% of the Jewish population in Poland was concentrated in the cities of Warsaw, Lwów, Łódz and Kraków. See also, Adam Zamoyski, *The Polish Way,* (Hippocrene Books, New York 2006), pp. 344–50. Also, Lukowski, op. cit., pp. 233–5.

[10] Richard M Watt, *Bitter Glory. Poland and its Fate 1918-1939* (Hippocrene Books, New York 1998), p. 386. 'Teschen' is the anglicised version of the Polish *Cieszyn.* For Churchill, see WSC to Foreign Secretary, 15 February 1944, AP20/12/53, Lord Avon Papers, Special Collections, University of Birmingham (hereafter UB).

11   Basil Liddell Hart, LH 11/1960/3, LHCMA.

12   Lord Gladwyn, *The Memoirs of Lord Gladwyn*, (Weidenfeld and Nicolson, London 1972), p. 92.

13   Robin Denniston, *Thirty Secret Years: AG Denniston's Work in Signals Intelligence 1914–1944* (Polperro Press, Clifton-upon-Teme 2007), pp. 64–5, 118–20. Also FH Hinsley, *British Intelligence in the Second World War: Its Influence on Strategy & Operations* (HMSO, London 1979), pp. 487–95.

14   Although this remains a controversial area of research, the capture of an original machine during the Norway Campaign in 1940 was not enough for British code-breakers to make the breakthrough. The contribution of the Poles remains inestimable. See Tessa Stirling, Daria Nałęcz and Tadeusz Dubicki (eds.), *Intelligence Co-operation between Poland and Great Britain during World War II. Vol. I: The Report of the Anglo-Polish Historical Committee* (Valentine Mitchell, London 2005), pp. 443–62. Also, John Gallehawk, 'Some Polish contributions in the Second World War', in *The Bletchley Park Reports No. 15, July 1999* (Bletchley Park Trust 1999). See also, Józef Garliński, *Intercept: The Enigma War* (Magnum Books, London 1981) and Ronald Lewin, *Ultra Goes to War* (Arrow Books, London 1980). The National Archives HW series of papers from the Government Code and Cipher School of Bletchley Park contain interesting documents on the work of Polish cryptographers.

15   Lothar Kettenacker, 'The Anglo-Soviet Alliance and the Problem of Germany 1941–1945', p. 437, in *Journal of Contemporary History*, Vol. 17 Number 3, July 1982. Stalin's real name was Josef Dzugashvili. He used the alias 'Stalin' because it meant 'Man of Steel'.

16   William L Shirer, *Berlin Diary: The Journal of a Foreign Correspondent 1934–1941* (Hamish Hamilton, London 1941), p. 144.

17   Richard Overy, *Russia's War* (Allen Lane Penguin Press, London 1998), pp. 44–50. See also David Glantz and Jonathan House, *When Titans Clashed* (Birlinn, Edinburgh 2000), pp. 1–11.

18   Ismay to Hankey, 16 June 1939, Ismay Papers, 4/16/20, LHCMA.

19   EDR Harrison, 'The British Special Operations Executive in Poland' in *The Historical Journal*, 43, 4, (2000), pp. 1072–5; also Richard Watt, op. cit., pp. 420–30.

20   Chester Wilmot, 'Notes on interrogation of General Franz Halder', LH 15/15/150/2, Liddell Hart Papers, LHCMA.

21   Edward Rozek, *Allied Wartime Diplomacy. A Pattern in Poland* (John Wiley, New York 1958), pp. 35–7. The capture of this eastern territory also gave the Soviet Union 90% of Poland's natural gas production.

22   Bolesław Majewski to Author, 15 March 2006.

23   Sir Frank Roberts, quoted in *Sikorski: Soldier and Statesman* (Orbis Books, London 1990), pp. 11–12.

[24] For an account of the No. 4 Military Mission to Poland, see Peter Wilkinson, *Foreign Fields: The Story of an SOE Operative* (IB Taurus, London 1997). For Carton de Wiart, 4/5/42a, Ismay Papers, LHCMA. For a witness on the border, see Clare Hollingworth, *Front Line* (Jonathan Cape, London 1990), pp. 41-3.

[25] This figure is generally accepted by Poles, but recent research based on Soviet archives conducted by separate Russian (Zemskov) and Polish (Ciesielski, Hryciuk, Srebrakowski) historians put the maximum number of deportees at 400,000. However, anecdotal evidence of deportees' descriptions, combined with poor Soviet documentation indicates a much higher figure. Janek Lasocki to Author 28 September 2007. The story of the deportees is told in *A Forgotten Odyssey*, an independent film production, written and directed by Jagna Wright.

[26] Hanna Kościa to Author, 22 September 2006. There were also poor members of the Byelorussian and Ukrainian peasantry who believed that they might benefit from the Soviet system; see Norman Davies, *Rising '44. The Battle for Warsaw* (Macmillan, London 2003), p. 173.

[27] Jerzy Lukowski and Hubert Zawadzki, *A Concise History of Poland* (Cambridge University Press, Cambridge 2001), pp. 260–1. *Generalplan Ost* codified this brutal policy in April 1942.

[28] Frank is often described as a former Reich Minister of Justice, a post, he claimed was held by Dr Franz Guertner. Frank later denied he was ever a member of the SS, but had been an *Obergruppenführer* in the SA (*Sturmabteilungen*), the assault section of Hitler's early political fighting force. His main power base before the General Governorship was the legal department of the National Socialist Party. For Frank's account of his career, see his personal affidavit, 18 April 1946, *The Trial of German Major War Criminals by International Military Tribunal*, Part 12, HMSO, 1947.

[29] Ibid. For 'booty' quote, see GM Gilbert, *Nuremberg Diary* (Eyre & Spottiswoode, London 1948), p. 70.

[30] Karolina Lanckorońska, *Those Who Trespass Against Us: One Woman's War Against the Nazis* (Pimlico, London 2005), p. 62.

[31] Glantz op. cit., pp. 15–20.

[32] Adam Wykrota to Author, 5 May 2006.

[33] For the formation of the Polish Government-in-exile and its early policies, see Anita Prazmowska, *Britain and Poland 1939-1943: The Betrayed Ally* (Cambridge University Press, Cambridge 1995), pp. 10–27. Also S. Mikołajczyk, *The Rape of Poland: Pattern of Soviet Aggression* (Greenwood Press, Westport US, 1948), pp. 7–16.

[34] M. Peszke, 'An Introduction to English Language Literature on the Polish Armed Forces in World War II', in *Journal of Military History* 70, October

2006, p. 1038. For a study of Polish naval operations, see M. Peszke, *Poland's Navy, 1918-1945* (Hippocrene Books, New York 1999). The Polish Navy lost 404 killed and 191 wounded in their 1,162 operational missions during the war.

[35] Twenty-three Fairey Battles were shot down on 10 May 1940. The aircraft proved to be outdated and was soon withdrawn from service and employed as a trainer. For Ward's extraordinary testimony see, 'MI9 Report on Sergeant John George Ward, 226 Squadron RAF', 13 April 1945, HS4/256, NA.

[36] S. Zaloga, *The Polish Army 1939–45* (Osprey, Oxford 1982), pp. 14–15.

[37] Karolina Lanckorońska, op. cit., p. 45.

[38] EDR Harrison, 'The British Special Operations Executive and Poland' in *The Historical Journal*, 43, 4 (2000), p. 1074. Also Memo to CAS, 8 September 1944, AIR 20/7984, NA.

[39] Mieczysław Juny to Author, 5 May 2006. Juny was lucky to be alive. While transported in a destroyer, he and his men were dive-bombed by Stukkas off the North African coast. He was then seriously wounded in the attack on Gazala, Tobruk in 1942. He was evacuated by *HMS Devonshire* and transferred to *The Empress of Canada*, which was then torpedoed. He eventually made it back to the UK where he trained and served in the RAF.

[40] Richard Overy, op. cit., pp. 53, 70–1.

[41] Report by Dr. Todt to British Intelligence, 21 December 1941, C13950, FO371/26515, NA.

[42] The operation was named after Emperor Frederick Barbarossa of the Holy Roman Empire. For statistics of Barbarossa and the Eastern Front, see David Glantz, Introduction, in Keith Bonn (Ed.) *Slaughterhouse: The Handbook of the Eastern Front* (Aberjona Press, Bedford US 2005).

[43] K. Rokossovsky, *A Soldier's Duty* (Progress Publishers, Moscow 1985), pp. 12–13. For the effects of Germany's surprise attack on Soviet communications, see Amnon Sella, 'Barbarossa' in *Journal of Contemporary History*, Vol. 13, No. 3, July 1978.

[44] This crime is examined in Karolina Lanckorońska, op. cit.

[45] Jan T. Gross, *Neighbors: The Destruction of the Jewish Community in Jedwabne, Poland* (Princeton University Press, Princeton 2001). Gross does not delve into the reasons for the crime, but the implication of Poles is beyond doubt. Historians still debate the extent of the pogrom, but in 2001, the Polish President, Aleksander Kwasniewski publicly apologised to the Jewish people on behalf of his Government.

[46] Wehrmacht troops were released from judicial responsibility for atrocities against civilians under the 'Criminal Order' of 13 May 1941. For the role of the Wehrmacht in atrocities, see Norman Naimark, 'War and Genocide on the Eastern Front 1941–1945', in *Contemporary European History*, Vol. 16:2,

May 2007. An example of the connivance of senior Wehrmacht command-ers in SS and Police atrocities can be seen in Truman Anderson, 'Incident at Baranivka: German Reprisals and the Soviet Partisan Movement in Ukraine, October–December 1941' in *The Journal of Modern History* Vol. 71, No. 3 (Sept. 1999). For involvement of a typical infantry division, see Christopher Rass, *Menschenmaterial Deutsche Soldaten an der Ostfront* (Verlag Schöningh, Paderborn 2003).

[47] For an annotated chronology of Soviet operations during 1941–1945, see David Glantz in *Slaughterhouse* op. cit., pp. 15–66. Following the lessons from battles on the Eastern Front in 1941–2, Soviet forces were transformed as professionals started to regain control from NKVD commissars. Officers' insignia and saluting returned and the tortuous reporting system was eased.

[48] General Anders, who had been tortured by the NKVD and released, also set up recruiting camps in Palestine and Iraq. A Polish 1st Corps had already been established in Scotland.

[49] PMH Bell, *John Bull and the Bear: British Public Opinion, Foreign Policy and the Soviet Union 1941–1945* (Edward Arnold, London 1990), pp. 68–71.

[50] Tessa Stirling (Ed.), *Intelligence Co-operation*, op. cit., p. 82.

[51] For a study of Slowikowski's work see, John Herman (Ed.), *In the Secret Service. The Lighting of the Torch* (Windrush Press, London 1988).

[52] Benjamin Fischer, 'The Katyn Controversy: Stalin's Killing Field', www.cia.gov/csi/studies/winter99-00. For a detailed analysis of those murdered at Katyn, see Nataliya Lebedeva, 'The Tragedy of Katyn', *International Affairs (Moscow)*, June 1990.

[53] Conspiracy theories continue to be popular in Poland today, usually involving Russia. Janek Lasocki to Author, 28 September 2007.

[54] 'Attempted Sabotage, BOAC Liberator AM 262', 5 April 1942, KV3/275, NA. For an investigation into the death of Sikorski, see 'The Death of General Sikorski' in *After the Battle* No. 20, 1978.

[55] Sir Frank Roberts (et al), in *Sikorski: Soldier and Statesman* (Orbis Books, London 1990), p. 10.

[56] For an unreferenced British assessment of Sosnkowski, see 'General Sosnkowski', 28 September 1944, HS 4/146, NA; also Stirling et al, *Intelligence Co-operation* op. cit., p. 71.

[57] Mikołajczyk, op. cit., p. 47.

[58] Ben Pimlot (Ed.), *The Second World War Diary of Hugh Dalton 1940–45* (Jonathan Cape, London 1986), p. 687.

[59] Bernard Crick, *George Orwell. A Life* (Secker & Warburg, London 1980), p. 309. Orwell himself was the subject of MI5 investigation for communist leanings. A report for the Security Service in 1942 bizarrely warned that 'he dresses in a bohemian fashion both at his office and in his leisure hours',

see KV 2/2699, NA. The British publishers, Victor Gollancz, Jonathan Cape and Faber & Faber were all frightened of publishing *Animal Farm* during the war, as it might be perceived as 'against the national interest'. It was finally published in August 1945. For the implications of Tehran, see Anita Praźmowska, *Britain and Poland,* op. cit., pp. 191–2; also George Kacewicz, *Great Britain, the Soviet Union and the Polish Government in Exile 1939–1945* (Martinus Nijhoff, The Hague 1979), pp. 164–82. For a copy of the Tehran Agreement, see ref AP6/2/159, Lord Avon Papers, UB.

Chapter Two

The Polish Home Army

Despite the surrender of the Polish Armed Forces in early October 1939, Poland itself had never surrendered. Even as Hans Frank was installing himself in Wawel Castle, Kraków, the Underground State (*Państwo Podziemne*) was starting to function. Because much of Poland's history had been one of occupation or oppression, guerrilla warfare and clandestine operations were familiar to the Poles and early resistance organisations, such as *Polska Organizacia Wojskowa* were revered. However, these ideas of resistance were not the preserve of a minority as in most other occupied European countries, but were ingrained in all Poles. Nevertheless it was always expected that guerrilla tactics would be employed initially against the Soviet Union rather than Germany, and there remained the difficult question of how to weld together the disparate political and military resistance movements.

The Polish Government-in-exile, under the firm leadership of General Sikorski, pulled together the main political parties including the Peasant, National Democratic and the Polish Socialist Party to form the nucleus of a civil underground state. Only the extreme right-wing Nationalist Party and the communist Polish Workers Party, who were eventually to set up a competing government and army, refused to join the coalition. However, those political leaders who chose to remain in Poland and go underground were constantly in fear of their lives. Early losses included the leading members, Mieczysław Niedziałkowski and Maciej Rataj, who after arrest and interrogation at Gestapo HQ in Warsaw, were taken to a killing ground in the Kampinos Forest, just west of Warsaw and executed in June 1940.[1]

For reasons of security and to improve liaison with the Allies, as well as to co-ordinate Polish military units worldwide, the Polish Government-in-exile remained in London. From there, it directed the administration and policies of both an underground civilian administration and military resistance movement in occupied Poland. This clandestine civilian Underground State, or 'Home Government' (*Delegatura Rządu*) comprised numerous departments to look after the needs of a suppressed population. The preservation of a Polish press, culture, education and welfare system were of paramount importance and even 'shadow' departments of Trade, Industry, Communications and Agriculture were established in the hope that they would, one day, form part of an independent Polish government.

During the years of occupation, the Germans stripped Poland of its industry and financial means of support. They also destroyed the Polish educational system by closing all schools except technical colleges, capable of producing tradesmen for the Reich. Professors, teachers and lecturers were expelled from their *gymnasia* (lower secondary schools) and higher education, or even eliminated. Yet the Underground State still managed to organise the secret education of Polish children in safe houses, by teachers who had survived the round-ups. And the shutdown also provided an unexpected boost for the resistance; for at a stroke, large numbers of science and research academics were sent home and could turn their minds wholeheartedly to devising plans to undermine German control.[2]

The main practical way to oppose the enemy was by military resistance. The main military underground organisation within Poland was initially the Service for the Victory of Poland (SZP), which operated from September to December 1939. Then on the orders of General Sikorski, the SZP was integrated into a new formation known as the Union for Armed Struggle or ZWZ (*Zwiazek Walki Zbrojnej*). The first military commander of ZWZ was briefly Major-General Michał Tokarzewski-Karaszewicz ('Torwid'), who left to command the military resistance in the Soviet controlled Polish sector and was replaced by General Stefan Rowecki ('Grot').[3] The ZWZ operated as an important intelligence gathering, sabotage and propaganda organisation until its re-birth on 14 February 1942 as the *Armia Krajowa* (Home Army or 'AK'). Again, the extreme nationalist militia (NSZ) and communist

Polish People's Army (*Armia Ludowa*) were excluded, but the strength of the new organisation was that all levels of the resistance were now subordinate to the Commander-in-Chief, General Grot-Rowecki and the Home Army High Command; ultimate control was still exercised by the Government-in-exile in London. The AK had become the largest and most powerful resistance organisation in occupied Europe, with a formidable structure and a High Command split into seven separate areas of responsibility, known as bureaux (or in Polish, *Oddziały Sztabu Generalnego WP*). These bureaux covered operations, personnel, welfare, supply, command and communications and most famously, 'Intelligence and Counter-intelligence' (Bureau II) and 'Information and Propaganda' (Bureau VI).[4]

The organisation of AK resistance had to be based in the central General Government sector, where it enjoyed widespread support, for the western part of Poland, incorporated into the Reich, was largely untouchable. There, Germans had been introduced into the local population and together with *Volksdeutsche*, they provided the German security forces with a formidable eavesdropping source, making clandestine operations extremely difficult. Although the AK was an underground army, it was organised and officered in very much the same way as a conventional army. In place of regiments based on county affiliations, units were assembled according to 'provinces', which were further broken down into districts, regions and areas, each with their own commander. These chiefs had the traditional military accompaniment of adjutants, staffs, quartermasters and liaison officers, together with attached specialist intelligence and signals units. However, although there were higher commands, such as divisions, these lacked transport and normal divisional arms such as artillery, and numbered far fewer men than a conventional British Army division; in the case of the 27th Vohlynian Infantry Division, the unit listed 7,300 soldiers, including 500 women and a divisional staff of 126. The basic and widespread operational unit remained the platoon and it was estimated there were over 6,500 platoons in the General Government sector, each consisting of approximately fifty men. But for all the courage and dash that these units possessed, by 1944 the estimated 350,000-strong army was still handicapped by a chronic lack of arms, with perhaps only 12% of the soldiers possessing a weapon.[5]

Home Army detachments were made up of all social classes, ranging from the poor peasant and forest dweller through to professionals, such as doctors and lawyers. There were AK men who spent their entire war years in the service of the Home Army, while there were others who worked in civilian jobs by day and took part in clandestine operations at night. Then there were those who were on the run from the Gestapo or escapees from prisons and penal camps, who joined armed bands in the forests across Poland. Consequently, some never donned a uniform and if they did, it could range from pre-war Polish kit to British Army 'battle-dress', which had been dropped in containers by parachute. Use was even made of German army uniforms, though captured Wehrmacht smocks would always bear the red and white armband. Similarly, German helmets would be adorned with a white eagle or the red and white band, together with the underground unit's insignia.

RAF supply drops containing charges and explosives were eagerly awaited by AK units but most had to make do with local materials. The explosive compound, Cheddite, was a favourite but procuring its main element, potassium chlorate, took ingenuity – stocks had to be stolen from factories or rolling stock. Other stolen chemicals were put to good use when the resistance broke into rail yards, and added the chemicals to the grease on the wheels of railway engines, making the brakes sieze. They would also apply time-fused bombs to petrol wagons awaiting dispatch. But more often than not, trains would have to be attacked in open country with varying degrees of success. If a single explosive was placed on the track, which blew up as the train passed over it, only limited delays of perhaps four hours, would result. However, on occasions the AK were able to lay charges at intervals along the track so that when recovery trains came to retrieve a damaged engine, further explosions occurred which wrecked these trains further down the line; chaos ensued and lines could be out of action for several weeks.

In April 1944, The Polish Government-in-exile in London ordered the AK to carry out numerous rail sabotage missions as part of 'Operation Jula'. Such concerted action was designed to show the Soviets that the AK were capable of mounting operations that could materially assist the Red Army advance. One member, 'Szyb' was only too keen to take part:

> We set out at dusk, taking ladders with us to fix the charges properly under the low railway bridge. We went with a numerous escort. We from Warsaw had four bren-guns as our personal weapons...we squatted under the bridge, though not without having to scramble away when a five-man

patrol walked over the bridge. The charges had been placed during an interval between trains. At a given moment, we saw a bright flash in the direction of the River Wisła; some seconds later we heard a powerful explosion, followed by the staccato of rifle and automatic fire. Tadzunio and Felix had done their bit.

And then our turn came. Two trains were coming, one in each direction. They were going to pass each other on the bridge. One locomotive thundered over the bridge and already a long stream of trucks was following. I waited as long as I could; then as the second locomotive was coming over the bridge, we detonated the charges...The bridge collapsed along its entire length and fell with one train into the river.[6]

The Germans immediately retaliated from two nearby pill-boxes and shot one of 'Szyb's' colleagues as well as the AK photographer, who had been called in to report on the action. The wounded were taken to the nearby house of a forester, who, as 'Szyb' recalled, 'before the action had long told tales of his unswerving loyalty and past services to the Underground; but after the rather energetic German display of shooting, he went completely yellow and refused to hide the wounded'.

Sabotage by AK teams against the German transportation system proved to be very successful and in one six-month period, SOE reported that the AK had wrecked 1,268 railway engines, damaged 3,318 trucks, derailed 25 trains and cut 148 signals – and at the same time as carrying out a number of successful assassinations of Gestapo officers.[7] These actions were carried out nationwide, and on a regular basis by men such as twenty-four-year-old Mieczysław Wałęga, a Second Lieutenant who had originally served with the Polish 17th Regiment:

It was a hard, but not very long fight. When the Germans overran us in 1939, those of us who survived in the Rzeszów region hid our weapons and shed our uniforms, knowing that the battle was only just beginning. All ex-officers were required to report to the Germans, but obviously we went into hiding. For the next few years, we carried on a war of sabotage against the enemy and I became an area commander. By the winter of 1943–4, I was receiving orders to blow up two or three trains a week, using explosives stolen locally or supplied in containers by the Allies. To help us, we had drops of specially trained Polish saboteurs, who had received their instruction in the US and Canada, as well as in England.

The object was to prevent German troop reinforcements from travelling by rail towards the eastern front, in order to stem the Red Army advance. As the Russians drew near to our border, communist partisans attacked the Rzeszów electricity plant and the Germans just rounded up sixty civilians and executed them on the spot. That hit our morale, but what always helped our spirits were the stories we heard over the wireless about Polish troops abroad – especially tales of the Polish II Corps in Italy and the eventual raising of the Polish flag over Monte Cassino in May 1944.[8]

When the Germans invaded in 1939, many Polish soldiers had indeed hastily buried their weapons, knowing the fight would resume. While possession of a weapon was punishable by death, most underground members were more concerned by the lack of serviceable ammunition. By 1944, many of these small arms were unusable or had been lost to the Germans, though a number of heavier weapons such as mortars, heavy machine-guns and anti-tank weapons (PIATs) had been saved. They were extremely valuable, but were still unable to lift AK actions beyond light attacks on small enemy installations. Greater reliance had to be placed on newer home-made weapons. Basic hand-grenades could be home-produced and through the connivance of Polish factory workers, iron sheeting was dispatched (with forged invoices) to AK manufacturing units to produce flame-throwers. Steel plate and wire were utilised for pistol parts and copies of the British Sten or Polish-made *Błyskawica* submachine-gun. However, the most useful source of weapons in Poland was the Wehrmacht itself, or units of their less committed allies, the Hungarians. Automatic pistols, rifles and occasionally machine-guns could be stolen or bought with bribes and ammunition was plentiful and reliable. As the Germans were pushed out of Poland during 1944, their morale dropped and this trade became easier, though Gestapo 'stings' were always a risk.[9]

Home Army units were sometimes named after old Polish cavalry or infantry regiments who had been garrisoned in the region, or after the pseudonym of the commander. There were hundreds of these organised bands in cities, towns and villages throughout the country, as well as many units in the forests and mountain areas, which also contained cavalry units for reconnaissance. Operations were frequent but because of their secret nature, many remain unrecorded. But what was remarkable was the large involvement of women and children in the resistance. The youth of the country were heavily involved through the 'Grey Ranks' Scouts organisation. They were split into age groups such as *Zawisza* (twelve to fourteen-year-olds, for runners and postmen), 'Fighting Schools' (fifteen to seventeen-year-olds, for minor sabotage and reconnaissance) and 'Storm Groups' (over seventeen-year-olds for partisan operations). They managed to combine clandestine academic studies with para-military training, for it was hoped that one day the Grey Ranks would make a contribution to running a free and independent Poland.[10] Young women also had a part to play. Eighteen-year-old Adela Wałęga lived with her parents in the southern town of Rzeszów, ninety miles east of Kraków, and was immersed in the underground movement:

My father was a German from Sudetenland in Czechoslovakia, but he had married my mother who was Polish. I was born in Tarnów but we lived in nearby Rzeszów, in the centre of the town in the quarter reserved for *Volksdeutsche*. Because we were in this district, the Germans requisitioned part of our house and we had Wehrmacht and a Gestapo man (who insisted on the best bedroom) living with us downstairs. My parents were required to act as their janitors and see that they had everything they needed.

Meanwhile, my teenage friends and myself began to be involved in underground activities. Because we were young, we were keen, but many of the youngsters made silly mistakes and were easily captured by the Gestapo. It was tragic. A group of about twenty, who I knew well, were caught and all executed in a nearby forest.

I had married my husband, Mieczysław in 1941 and he was heavily involved in the AK, being adjutant to Captain Japlinski, the district commander. It was extraordinary, because my husband came and went from the house under an alias and I started working for the 'organisation' as a secretary and courier and we set up a base in our house upstairs. All the while, the Germans were below us. Because they would never believe we would do this sensitive work so close to them, we got away with it. Though we had several close encounters. My husband would bring in reports on operations for me to type up for transmission to London. One evening he arrived home and came upstairs. Our Wehrmacht lodgers were out, so we thought it safe to get the typewriter out and begin the report. Suddenly we heard German voices downstairs that did not belong to our 'usuals' and they were starting to come up the stairs. We were really worried as we had all our secret papers spread out on the bed, as well as

a number of machine-pistols and ammunition hidden behind the bedroom dresser. We had to think really quickly. We leapt up, opened the door
slightly and stood just inside and started kissing. As the voices neared the
landing we realised they were German police. We got more amorous and
luckily they were too embarrassed to come in, just shouting at us that we
had left our light on during the blackout.[11]

Women and girls also played an important part in the propaganda war,
distributing underground newspapers and leaflets to maintain Polish
morale. Part of this brief was also to undermine enemy confidence. To
this end, 'N' section of the Information and Propaganda produced vast
amounts of leaflets, usually in German, and aimed at Wehrmacht soldiers.
Titles such as *Der Soldat* or *Der Frontkämfer* ridiculed the German High
Command and warned ordinary German troops of the retribution that
would come if they committed atrocities. Women also ran courier services inside towns and cities as well as those linking rural communities.
In combat situations, they distinguished themselves as nurses, running
first aid centres and assisting in field hospitals as well as acting as runners
during fire-fights and bombardments. In some cases, such as the unit
commanded by Wanda Gertz, they ran their own sabotage units.

While AK units had no shortage of volunteers or potential enemy
targets, they were in desperate need of outside support and supplies. For
the British, providing help was not straightforward; until parts of Europe
could be liberated, any flights of supplies or men would have to come
from airfields in eastern England. The sheer distance involved – a 2,100
mile round trip to the Warsaw region – meant that only the western and
central areas of Poland were in reach and even then, aircraft had to be
reduced in weight to accommodate extra fuel. 'Special Duties' squadrons, notably 138 Squadron RAF, based at Newmarket, Suffolk, had been
available since the creation of SOE in 1940, to drop agents or supplies
into occupied Europe. However, they only had access to the short-range
Lysander or the longer-range but slow, Whitley bomber.

On 15 February 1941, the first Poles were dropped into Polish territory by a lumbering Whitley bomber, at the very extent of its range. It
dropped the first two officers and one courier into Bielsko, part of the
country annexed to the Reich.[12] From then on irregular drops were
made of Polish agents and trained saboteurs, as well as containers of supplies. For continued missions to Poland, the heavy Whitley bomber was

really out of the question, so the more suitable Halifax B II bomber was used, once weight adjustments could be made. These alterations invariably brought their own problems; the heaviest and most obvious candidates for removal were the 0.303 gun turrets, one mid-fuselage and one in the nose, leaving just the rear gun as the sole means of defence. But this in turn resulted in the aircraft becoming more vulnerable to night-fighter attack. So, to avoid concentrated anti-aircraft fire over France and Germany, the missions had to fly either through Sweden or via Denmark. And as the journey was at the very limit of the standard tanks, extra fuel tanks had to be fitted to the Halifax, which further reduced its carrying capacity from 2,100kg to 1,200kg.[13] In addition to these logistical problems, operations could only take place in autumn, winter and spring, when dark nights were long enough to cover both the outward and return trips, and taking into account the moon's phases, only about forty missions to Poland could be planned each year.[14] Given the priorities of British Bomber Command and its commitments elsewhere, it was all that could be offered. Yet to the Poles it was nowhere near enough support for their desired aim of a national revolt.

Between 1941 and October 1943, when SOE organised sorties from Britain via the Sweden/Denmark routes, 316 Poles were flown out and dropped by parachute into their occupied home territory. As well as politicians, and couriers such as the legendary Elzbieta Zawacka, a particularly brave group of agents known as the 'silent and unseen' (*cichociemni*) were dropped into Poland to assist in sabotage operations, and more importantly to fill specialist posts within the AK; these ranged from district commanders and staff officers to intelligence and weapons specialists. Apart from clothing, each agent carried two automatic pistols with fifty rounds, a small shovel, torch, compass, knife and first aid kit, as well as a small phial of poison concealed in a button. This suicide pill, sometimes called an 'L' tablet, was small, round and rubber-coated to prevent it dissolving in the mouth. When crunched and sucked, death followed in a matter of seconds.[15]

Thus prepared for any eventuality, the parachutist duly boarded the aircraft for the five-hour flight to Poland. When the aircraft finally approached the drop zone, the pilot lowered his altitude down to 2,000 feet, falling to 600 feet over the actual drop zone. Meanwhile, back in the bomb bay, the bombardier prepared his parachutist, or 'Joe', according to strict instructions:

1) Running in should be given over interphone at the start of the final run (approximately two minutes before dropping). At the command 'running in', the 'Joe' scoots up next to the hole and is in readiness to swing his legs into the hole.

2) Action Station is given two to five seconds before Go. Give Action Station clearly over the interphone and by Red Dispatcher's light. At this signal the 'Joe' swings his legs into the hole and is poised for the jump.

   Go is signalled by green light and interphone. On a 'Joe Mission' Go is given immediately after toggling containers.

No member of the crew will give any operational information to the 'Joes'. This includes flight plan, route, altitudes of the present flight.[16]

On landing, the parachutist was supposed to be greeted by an AK reception committee but despite his training and the best efforts to organise a drop zone on the ground, plans often went awry. One operative, 'Gora' found himself alone as soon as he landed:

I picked myself up from the ground. While pulling my parachute off a pine tree, I was thinking of the English chucker-out, who had been unable to tell us whether we were over the reception station or the emergency area. He just shouted 'Go! One! Two! Three!' There were no lights and no reception committee. I crossed a small wood, carrying all the equipment and came to a standstill before a river, which barred further progress. I noticed on the other side something very much like a spread-out parachute. I peered at it for a long time and came to the conclusion that it was a patch of light-coloured sand. I had no idea where I was and I could see nothing around to enable me to get my position fixed.[17]

'Gora' managed to swim across the ice-cold river and eventually linked up with the local AK unit. It was only then that he discovered the fate of his colleague:

We learned the depressing news that 'Alec' had been killed during his jump. Now I understand why I saw no one in front of me after leaving the plane. He went down like a lump of lead, and while I was looking for him in the air he was already dead. The lighter patch on the opposite bank of the river really had been his parachute.

In March 1942, 138 Squadron was moved to RAF Tempsford in Bedfordshire, a recently constructed airfield that was earmarked for SOE operations.[18] The special duties squadron was joined a month later by 161 (Special Duties) Squadron, both of which were to be employed not only on Polish missions, but also on the more numerous SOE flights to France and the Low Countries. Squadron Leader Tony Walker DFC, one of the youngest pilots of his rank in the RAF, piloted a Halifax on these special missions, and when flying with 161 Squadron, was later tragically lost with his crew on a mission to France. In his diary, he described what it was like to run the night-time gauntlet of enemy defences:

> Hit the Danish coast at 0100 hours and everything seemed exceptionally quiet when suddenly the searchlights opened up and in 5 minutes we were caught in a cone of about 12. That in itself wasn't much fun, but the thing was, the attack from the fighters which was bound to follow. It must have been the perfect set-up for the enemy, and sure enough he came in behind when we were still doing a steep diving turn at 12,000 ft. Tracer zipped past and into our kite and three bullets shot through the front Perspex, about 12" from my head. By this time we were in a terrific dive and doing well over 300 mph and still the searchlights held us. I've only just recovered from the effect of that dive on my ears! We pulled out at 500 ft just over the coast and at last the lights lost us and in a few minutes we shook the 'Me109' off. They fired a lot of flares up at us as well. We climbed up over the sea but found that oil was leaking from the port engine, also TR9 had been shot up, aerial shot away and that George was a fatal casualty, so we decided to S/C for base.[19]

While RAF special duties flights were now enhanced by the use of the faster and larger capacity Halifax II, General Sikorski continued to press the case for an independent Polish flight. On 1 April 1943, 'C' (Polish Flight) was created as one of three flights of a reorganised 138 Squadron and operations involving Polish crews began the following month. They were used not only for flights from Tempsford to Poland but also for other SOE operations in Europe and North Africa. Then, in September 1943, three Liberator B-24 bombers were added to the complement of Halifaxes. The Liberator, with its four Pratt & Whitney engines, quicker take off and landing, and with an operational cruising speed of 180 mph, was the best of the Allied heavy bombers available; though for night missions, the bright flames from the turbo-supercharger exhausts could illuminate the aircraft for enemy night-fighters, so special baffles were added to hide the flames. And as night-fighters invariably attacked from behind, all the 0.50-calibre machine-guns were removed from the nose, belly turrets, and beam (side) to save weight, leaving the two upper and four rear guns to provide defence.[20] Now at last the numbers of air-craft on Polish sorties were steadily increasing and on the night of 14/15 September 1943, eleven Halifaxes containing both British and Polish crews, took off to drop agents and supplies into Poland. But the cost was high. Two British crews were shot down over Denmark on the way out, and one was shot down crossing the German coast on the return, while one Polish Halifax hit a house near its drop zone and crashed.[21] Such losses bolstered the case of those in the British Air Ministry who argued against risking valuable aircraft on Polish operations.

While this erratic support system got underway, the rest of the British relief package was similarly piecemeal. The British Foreign Office appeared to have scant knowledge about the AK. In spite of the contacts between the Polish Government-in-exile and the British Government, as late as May 1943 Denis Allen of the Central Department of the Foreign Office admitted that his information on Poland was five months out of date. The department even needed a report by Colonel Gubbins of SOE to remind them of the AK's existence:

> There exists in Poland a very widespread and well disciplined organisation [AK] obeying the orders of General Sikorski, who in turn follows closely the Directives issued from time to time by the Chiefs of Staff...instruc-tions are despatched to Poland that attacks should be directed against German transportation to the Eastern Front. The Polish organisation faithfully carries out these Directives.[22]

For the hundreds of thousands of displaced Poles, there was no hope of outside help – families had to fend for themselves. After their flight from Ukraine, Hanna Czarnocka, her younger bother, Bohdan and her mother, Halina made for Warsaw, a city where they had contacts and some chance of anonymity. They had a desperate journey, travelling via Białystock in deep snow in an attempt to leave the Soviet-controlled area and cross over the River Bug into the designated German-controlled General Government zone. Before they could make the crossing they were arrested and interrogated. Hanna recalled that she and her family escaped into No Man's Land between the German and Soviet borders and had to move quickly:

> Nearby we could hear a train and every so often the Germans fired flares to light up the night sky. The German barbed wire was very taut and it tore our clothes as we squeezed through the narrow gaps in the fence. We could hear gunshots; they were hunting those illegally crossing the border. We crawled towards a small light. Once we got close we saw it was a cottage and a dog started barking. We rushed to the door. The light went out and a woman let us in. 'Lie down on the floor. The Germans are out on patrol and shooting. I'll give you some straw and feed you tomorrow'. The following day we left and were taken by cart to a railway station. It was fortunate that we had money to pay these good, brave people. At the station I was shocked to see an overweight *Bahnschutz* (railway police officer) hitting and kicking a small boy, who was probably Jewish.[23]

Eventually, Hanna and her family reached Warsaw, where her mother, Halina, immediately joined the ZWZ, and with her experience was given her first job of training Girl Guides as couriers for the underground. She instructed the girls in the use of 'dead-letter boxes', which were used to avoid other couriers knowing their colleagues' identities, and each courier was ordered to take routes long enough for them to check if they were being followed. Halina became secretary and adjutant (with codename 'Maryla Bonińska') to Colonel Tadeusz Pełczyński, when he was Chief-of-Staff, ZWZ and continued her work with the successive *Armia Krajowa*. She still carried out dangerous courier work herself and this sometimes involved passing messages direct to other operatives. As her daughter Hanna knew, it was one of the most risky jobs in the underground:

> Arrests took place all the time in Warsaw. Sometimes it was just random, and sometimes they knew who you were. One day – it was Good Friday, 1943 – my mother had just met another courier in the street and passed her a message from General Rowecki which stated that any Polish policeman who maltreated Jews would be dealt with by an AK court and severely punished. She and the other courier had parted and as my mother walked away, she heard a car pull up at the kerb behind her. The

next thing she knew, two men had got hold of her by the arms. She played innocent but they shouted, 'this is the police, now get in the car.' The Gestapo took her to their HQ in Szucha Avenue. They began interrogating her and hitting her across the face. She didn't admit anything, but she knew that she had an incriminating message in a secret lining in her coat. The assault continued until she pleaded to go to the lavatory. Surprisingly, they let her go under guard and she managed to flush the message away. The interrogation began again, but as the Gestapo made no progress, she was sent to Pawiak Prison. In her cell, in solitary confinement, she was able to scribble a beautiful poem to me and my brother, urging us to be brave and good and to continue our studies and with hope, we would all meet again. A Polish nurse smuggled it out for us. I still have this poem.

After two weeks of being dragged backwards and forwards between Pawiak and Gestapo HQ, they finally gave up and sent her to Auschwitz. She was put on the same transportation as Józef Garliński.[24]

As Halina Czarnocka found, despite the brutal activities within Pawiak jail, it was still possible to pass forbidden information to the outside world. The Gestapo were short of reliable prison warders and retained a number of former Polish warders in the jail. Similarly, a number of former doctors and nurses continued to make daily visits from their homes in Warsaw. So, with regular contacts inside Pawiak and in numerous other penal and concentration camps, the AK were able to build up reliable data about prisoner movements.[25]

Although AK members were also required to carry out retaliation against those *Volksdeutsche* who were informers for the Gestapo, retribution was not always a clean operation, as 'Mira' discovered when he was ordered to assassinate an informer known as 'Herr Koch' in his favourite bar:

My carefully laid plans came to nothing because of my, and my men's inexperience. As I was walking up to the counter to ask for cigarettes, my number one, seeing an ordinary military patrol approaching along Czerniakowska Street, lost his head, dashed into the room, and, without waiting for the order, fired twice at Koch, after which he dashed out through the kitchen door. He had the jitters, fired in a hurry and missed. I, too, lost my head, and seeing Koch pull a gun out of his pocket, fired the contents of my magazine at him. As I learned later, only three bullets found their mark in his chest, and one unnecessarily wounded the waitress.

At first I thought I had killed him, but there were shots fired back in my direction. There is no denying, he was a tough nut.[26]

While the resistance was able to penetrate German organisations, the Gestapo in turn were sometimes able to penetrate the AK. However, the underground's cell structure, whereby only one member of a unit had touch with a higher authority, and then only through an intermediary, helped to mitigate the problem. Occasionally, when a high-ranking member of the AK was arrested, his colleagues could bribe the local Gestapo into releasing him. In 1944 Szymon Jan Zaremba (also known as Alun Morgan), a reception officer for supplies and agents dropped by Britain, was arrested by the Gestapo at Tomaszow and swiftly taken to Radom. Zaremba was then tortured by his captors and although he refused to give any information, was released in return for a 200,000 zloty bribe paid to the local police chief.[27] Even when the Gestapo did not succeed in extracting information, their methods could produce results elsewhere. For several years, informers and collaborators had delivered top underground commanders to the Germans and in the Kraków region alone, four successive AK leaders were arrested and murdered during the War. Even the Commander-in-Chief of the AK, General Stefan Grot-Rowecki was arrested in Warsaw on 30 June 1943, and later perished in Sachsenhausen concentration camp.[28] His successor, General Tadeusz Bór-Komorowski was well aware of the thorough Gestapo tactics:

> In order to secure descriptions and photographs of members of the underground, the Germans frequently used agents disguised as beggars. One pair was notorious in Warsaw. A supposedly blind man used to play an accordion at street corners. His inseparable companion was a woman who sang to his accompaniment. Whenever they appeared, arrests would follow shortly after in the vicinity. Both were sentenced to death as Gestapo agents and executed by us.[29]

Although the number of collaborators in Poland was very small compared to other occupied countries such as Czechoslovakia, nevertheless a problem did exist, as one SOE officer recalled:

> Certain Poles did collaborate with the Hun. During the war it was the policy of the Polish Government to present a united front and declare that

within Poland there was no collaboration whatsoever. They minimised the fact that there existed the right-wing NSZ, who were bordering on collaboration, especially after the Russians entered Polish territory.[30]

Underground Courts of Justice were set up by the AK, to try collaborators or dispense justice for lesser crimes. Stefan Korboński, a leading figure in the 'Directorate of Underground Resistance' and responsible for the clandestine justice system, recalled that in the case of informers or enthusiastic supporters of the German administration, the death penalty was often exacted in public, with several shots from a revolver when the miscreant was alighting from a tram or simply going into his office. Any medium seen to be assisting German morale, such as theatre productions, was penalised, with Polish actors warned not to appear on stage. Those actors who persisted faced unusual retribution from the AK:

On the selected day, just when the rehearsal was about to begin, a dozen or so armed men invaded the little theatre. They secured all exits and windows and several of them made for the stage. From among the terrified actors they called forth the culprits; and after reading them a complete list of their offences, they administered, in the full glare of the footlights, the prescribed number of strokes to one of them and shaved off the other's hair. The executors of the sentence, with a lawyer at the head, conducted themselves with great dignity. News of this punishment spread throughout the theatre world.[31]

The main tools of the AK were always sabotage and intelligence, whilst militarily conserving the organisation for a large uprising. Initially it was hoped that the Allies, with General Anders II Polish Corps, would thrust up through Italy in 1943–1944 and into Austria, Slovakia and thereby enter Poland from the south. This would coincide with an AK uprising as the Germans retreated through Poland. But with dogged German resistance in Italy the Allied advance was overtaken by events on the Eastern Front where Soviet forces made rapid headway.

On 3 January 1944, Soviet forces crossed the old eastern Polish border, putting further pressure on the AK. The Polish underground were now faced with a hostile invader from the east, who did not recognise the validity of their Government-in-exile or its military arm. Bizarrely, the AK were now approached by the Germans with offers of arms to defend themselves against the Soviets, but they resolutely refused and so remained the only occupied country in Europe not to supply a national detachment to fight for the Reich on the eastern front. With options evaporating, the AK planned to implement 'Operation Tempest' (*Burza*) and rise up behind German lines and assist the Red Army to defeat the Germans. The 'Tempest' plan envisaged AK units engaging the enemy only in areas where he had started retreating, rather than attempting one simultaneous rising throughout the country. However, the AK presumed that it was of equal power to the Soviet Union and that it could act as the host of a liberated country, whose Government-in-exile would return from London. This of course depended on Stalin's respect for Poland's pre-war boundaries, which was manifestly absent. But the AK did not know that at Tehran the previous year, Stalin and Churchill had already agreed that the Curzon Line should be the marker.[32] It was no accident that Soviet troops had first crossed the Polish border into the Volhynia (Wołyń) region. This area of Western Ukraine lay between the rivers Pripet and Bug and was the gateway to the important city of Lublin, a bastion of the emerging communist 'Union of Polish Patriots'. It was here that Stalin planned to set up a rival government to the Polish Government-in-exile, and enforce its rule through the Red Army and Berling's communist 1st Polish Army. But before destroying the AK, Stalin first needed their assistance in clearing German forces out of eastern Poland. However, a German counter-attack stalled the Soviet advance around Żytomierz, and it would take months for Soviet troops to break out of Volhynia. In February and March, AK divisions, including the 6,000-strong 27th Volhynian Division, launched co-ordinated attacks with the Red Army against German formations, notably capturing Turzysk. It was, in all but name, the beginning of 'Operation Tempest', and during the spring of 1944 numerous AK units attacked German forces in the rear, engaging in heavy fighting especially around Kowel, which helped the Soviet advance towards Chełm and Lublin.[33]

Initially, there were cordial relations between AK commanders and their Soviet counterparts, but once the Germans had lost a sector, the Soviet NKVD swiftly moved into the captured territory and began to implement their terror methods. In fact they proved a more formidable foe to the AK than the Gestapo, through their use of pre-prepared lists of 'enemies'. When they arrived in a locality, the NKVD knew exactly who the local AK officers were, and with an estimated 10,000 commissioned officers and 70,000 NCOs in the underground, this was a considerable intelligence feat. The NKVD also ensured that large parts of the forests of eastern Poland came under their control, denying rural AK units cover and sustenance.[34]

The NKVD ensured that AK officers were summarily shot or transported and their men pressed into Berling's Army. Yet despite this brutal policy, the AK command continued to urge its units to co-operate with the Soviets, at the same time pleading for Allied air drops. Throughout the spring and early summer of 1944, AK units assisted the Red Army in behind-the-lines operations, and, reversing the previous policy of keeping out of urban areas, Bór-Komorowski ordered his troops to assist in the capture of Wilno on 13 July, Lublin on 23 July and Lwów on 27 July.[35] But although the AK suffered in Soviet hands, not all its units, or at least bands associated with the AK, were blameless. In the region of Poland's border with Lithuania, there was long standing resentment of the way some Lithuanians collaborated with the Germans and in the disputed Vilnius district, a number of Lithuanian police atrocities were countered by AK assassinations of alleged Lithuanian collaborators. The antagonism came to a head in June 1944 with the slaughter of civilians in the Lithuanian village of Dubingiai, by a unit under AK command, who appeared to have acted in retaliation for Polish deaths, though the circumstances remain controversial.[36]

As the Soviet advance into eastern Poland rolled inexorably onwards, Stalin also had the instrument of Berling's 1st Polish Army. This had grown steadily, assisted by Soviet air drops and pressed reinforcements, so that by March 1944, it had outgrown its Corps status and become an Army, numbering over 100,000 men. Berling's ranks had been swelled by ex-POWs and further deportees from the gulags, but the Army was still chronically short of Polish officers and most positions were filled by Byelorussians or Ukrainians and staffed by NKVD officers.

When AK operations against German targets were successful, retaliation was inevitable. An order from the Higher SS and Police Leader *Ost* on 28 June 1944, made perfectly clear what retaliation could be expected:

> The Reichsführer SS [Himmler], with the approval of the Governor General [Frank], orders that in all cases where assassinations or attempts at assassinations of Germans have taken place, or where vital installations are destroyed by saboteurs, not only should the culprits be shot, but, beyond

that all the men in the family should be executed and the women over sixteen sent to concentration camps.[37]

In practice, Frank managed to exceed Himmler's demands, boasting in his diary, 'I have not been hesitant in declaring that when a German is shot, up to 100 Poles shall be shot too.'[38] He was as good as his word. Small local acts of sabotage usually resulted in twenty people being rounded up, but if an assassination or murder of a guard was carried out, 100 names would be posted in a public place and the executions carried out in full view of everyone. The retaliation was random and included both men and women and this penalty weighed heavily on those AK operatives about to carry out attacks. Yet, such brutality largely failed to deter the resistance and merely reinforced Polish hatred of the occupying forces.[39]

Despite retribution, assassinations of carefully targeted German security officers and their Polish collaborators continued. 1943 had seen the killing of Otto Schultz, a particularly sadistic Gestapo officer, together with Emil Braun, who organised round-ups of civilians and numerous small functionaries. Then, on 1 February 1944, the commander of the AK's Special Operations Directorate, Colonel August Emil Fieldorf ordered his Warsaw unit, named 'Pegaz', to strike a blow against the SS by assassinating General Franz Kutschera, *Gauleiter* and Chief of the Warsaw Police District. In a plan as daring as the killing in Prague of the Deputy *Reichsprotector* for Bohemia and Moravia, Reinhard Heydrich, the assassins awaited the arrival of Kutschera's convoy in Warsaw's central boulevard, the *Aleje Ujazdowskie*. With perfect timing, a conspirator's car came out of a turning and smashed into the convoy. The startled Police Chief was then confronted by two men who emptied their sten-guns into him. The SS escort returned fire and wounded the gunmen, who still managed to escape. Corporal Bronisław Pietraszewicz ('Flight'), and his brave accomplice died later that night, but the audacious attack, which did much to raise Polish morale, was followed by brutal retribution. Three hundred Warsaw civilians were arbitrarily taken away by the SS and executed.[40]

Security was much tighter in Kraków, the seat of the General Government, evidenced by the failed assassination attempt on Kutschera's counterpart, General Koppe in July 1944. Consequently most AK operations were concentrated away from the city and included the release of prisoners from jails, raiding money transports for much needed cash and the disruption of railway transports. It was this latter activity that often brought spectacular results. AK 'Operation Jula' in early July 1944, managed to simultaneously destroy a railway bridge, two rail viaducts, and several trains, all of which set back German transports in the region. And one commander, Jan Piwnik, known as 'Ponury' because of his gloomy expression, who was dropped into Poland on 8 November 1941, became a legend after organising one audacious jailbreak operation.

On 18 January 1943, 'Ponury' targeted the jail in Pińsk, a town some 200 miles from Warsaw and fortified with a German garrison of over 3,000 mcn. His brief was to release a number of important AK prisoners and he duly set up his support and escape teams near the prison compound. It was late in the afternoon when 'Ponury' arrived at the main gate in the back seat of a captured SS Opel car. With the engine running, a colleague, who was dressed in SS uniform jumped out of the front passenger seat and immediately berated the sentry. The startled soldier opened up the prison gates and 'Ponury's' car swept into the main yard. Once inside, the successful routine was repeated and the car drove right into the inner square. Then armed AK men sprang from the car and sprayed the prison guards with bursts from their semi-automatics. The prison gates were opened, allowing more AK men to join the assault and soon the prison warders were overpowered and relieved of their cell keys. Some forty men were released, including seven Soviet partisans and all were bundled into the back of waiting lorries, which sped off from the scene. As they drove away, they released goads onto the road, which punctured the tyres of any pursuing vehicles.

The Pińsk jailbreak was a textbook operation, carried out without casualties and news of the audacious raid soon spread. The adventure was published in the underground press and spread throughout Poland, though the story of Soviet partisans being rescued by the AK was vigorously suppressed by the Soviet propaganda agency. 'Ponury' went on to command successful guerrilla actions in the Radom-Kielce region, keeping to his mission of sabotage and enemy assassinations. Despite German retaliation, such as the razing of the village of Michniów and the slaughter of its inhabitants, he continued to operate from bases deep inside forests, where he successfully evaded capture. However, the Gestapo were determined to catch him and as a lure, they arrested the mother of 'Motor', one of 'Ponury's' most trusted lieutenants from the Pińsk operation. 'Motor' eventually caved in to blackmail by the Gestapo, turned informer and as a result many of the 'Ponury' band were arrested or shot. 'Motor' was eventually exposed as a spy and was executed by the AK in January 1944, while 'Ponury' managed to evade the Germans for another six months, finally falling in battle while commanding the AK 77th Battalion in the Nowogródek region.[41]

News of AK operations soon started to come back to British intelligence via an unofficial source. There were always a number of British POWs in hiding in Poland at any one time, including Gris Davies-Scourfield, who was concealed in a house in Warsaw, and recalled that the women looking after him had five other British POWs hidden at various addresses in the city. However, unless a POW could offer the underground a particular skill, and especially if he couldn't speak Polish, he could prove a liability. So, often the best course was for him to escape via the Soviets. The AK would make sure he had a letter in Polish, English and Russian explaining who he was and that he was a POW escapee, while his precise details would be transmitted to England.[42] Exceptionally, a POW might gain the confidence of the AK and eventually join them in operations. Sergeant John Ward achieved this distinction, but only after a protracted journey. He had been shot down in 1940 and was interned in a number of hospitals and POW camps near the Polish border. He escaped, was caught, interned in a local prison and while awaiting re-internment, escaped again:

> During the night I broke the strands of barbed wire across the window of the room at the police station at Gostyn by bending them several times. When I had made a hole large enough, I climbed through the window and walked across the yard. I discovered that the yard was surrounded by a wall about ten feet high with broken glass on top, so I decided to attempt to get through the gate, where there was a sentry. I looked around for a weapon and found a brick. It was very dark so I walked up to the guard quite openly. When I reached him I hit him on the head with the brick using all my strength. He was wearing a forage cap and fell to the ground without making very much noise. I then ran off.[43]

Ward trekked to the town of Sieradz, where he went to the nearest Roman Catholic church, made a confession to the priest and asked to be put in touch with the local underground movement. The priest spirited him away and after much interrogation, Ward was put into the hands of the AK in Łódź, verified and given false papers. He did not disappoint his new adopted army:

> I was then taken to Warsaw. It was the intention of the underground move-ment to send me to Russia, but the outbreak of war between Germany and Russia had made this impossible. I met Otto Gordziałowski, a lawyer, who was editor of *Dzień,* an underground newspaper in Warsaw. This man offered me the job of taking down the BBC news broadcasts in English, which were to be translated into Polish and published in the newspaper. I accepted the job and moved to his flat, where I stayed until 4 October 1944…I began to construct wireless receivers and transmitters, which were supplied to various underground political organisations in Warsaw. I bought a Gestetner duplicator, paper, ink etc. using funds supplied to me, and with these materials I began to publish an underground newspaper called *Echo.* After nine months, the daily distribution of this paper was two thousand copies. Mrs Gordzialowska, who was an accomplished linguist, worked with me as my secretary but I used my own discretion about what should, or should not, be published. Eventually, I handed this newspaper over to the underground and I continued to supply the news through my information bureau.[44]

Ward, whose ingenuity knew no bounds, was carrying out a dangerous job and risked his life on a daily basis:

> In January 1943, I was walking along a street in Warsaw carrying a pistol and various incriminating papers on my person. A German gendarme stopped me and pointed a pistol at me. He wanted to search me and examine my identity papers. I knocked his pistol arm down and hit him on the jaw with my fist. He fired his pistol as I hit him and the bullet entered my right thigh. As he fell I ran off and mingled with the people in the street. I then hired a cab and left the vicinity. I was confined to bed for three months until my wound healed.[45]

While Ward provided one of the very few direct links between the AK and Britain, other options for contact were opening up in Italy since the Allied invasion in 1943. The British Eighth Army had landed on the 'toe' of Italy on 3 September and progress had been swift in moving up the 'heel' of the country. The ports of Taranto and Brindisi fell quickly, followed by Bari to the north and the airfields around Foggia were soon in Allied hands. The airfields were vital if the Allies were to press home their strategic bombing of Germany and the key Romanian oilfields of Ploesti, as well as opening up air routes to the Balkans.[46] The importance of these airfields was not lost on the Soviets, who pressed for access for their aircraft, ostensibly to support the partisans in Yugoslavia. But an SOE-sponsored Balkans Air Force was in the process of being established at Bari in 1944 and fortunately Eden soon squashed the idea of Soviet 'help', realising that it would allow the Red Air Force to build up a substantial presence in Italy.[47] Moreover, these airfields also had to be given over to special duties flights, especially valuable for the Polish effort now that flight times could be substantially reduced. In October 1943 Brindisi was selected as the main operational airfield for support to Poland, with the Polish HQ (known as Base 11) at Latiano and the SOE HQ (known as Force 139) based at nearby Monopoli. This town was sandwiched between Bari, about twenty miles north along the Adriatic coast, and Brindisi, which lay thirty miles to the south.

The SOE HQ occupied two floors of an undistinguished building in a muddy back road to Monopoli, whose only claim to notoriety was that it was the birthplace of Al Capone.[48] Meanwhile, the town of Brindisi had become well known for other reasons, for following the Allied invasion and Mussolini's expulsion from power, King Victor Emmanuel III, together with Italy's provisional government had set up their base in the city. In addition, Brindisi boasted an important port, but it was the airfield that the Allies were most keen to utilise. A complicated command structure for airfield operations soon evolved, but essentially they were directed locally by an SOE officer, Lieutenant-Colonel Henry (later Sir Henry) McLeod Threlfall, who had to defer to SOE in London for policy issues, and to Major-General Stawell, Chief of Special Operations Mediterranean (SOM) for administration. In addition, all flights were under the ultimate control of Deputy C-in-C Mediterranean Allied Air Forces (MAAF), Air Marshal Sir Jack Slessor.[49]

With the Italian air bases now secure, operations to Poland out of Tempsford, England, could now cease. But the No. 1 and No. 2 tortuous routes across Denmark and southern Sweden, had not been in vain. During 1943, 1586 Polish Special Duties Flight, which had been formed out of the old 'C' Polish Flight, had achieved sixty-four sorties to Poland. This had resulted in forty-eight successful drops, putting 105

agents and forty-two tons of supplies into the country. It was a tally that
the Flight now looked to increase during 1944, and new training stations,
including parachuting and radio transmitting, sprung up around Brindisi.[50]
1586 Polish Flight, which had now split off from an unhappy relationship
with 138 Squadron, left their temporary base in Tunis, North Africa and
arrived at Brindisi on 23 December 1943 with an initial establishment of
three Halifaxes and three Liberators. But in the context of total SOE
strength in the Mediterranean, this was a very moderate allocation.
By the end of January 1944 SOE had at its disposal thirty-two other
aircraft for flights to the Balkans, so it was no surprise that for the next
two months, 730 sorties were planned for the Balkans and North Italy,
while only 150 sorties could be allocated to Poland.[51] Three new routes
were now marked out to reach into southern Poland. Route 3 crossed
Lake Balaton in Hungary, and flying west of Budapest then crossed the
Tatra Mountains and went on to approach Kraków, a round trip of over
1,300 miles. Route 4 flew over Kotar, in Yugoslavia, then passed to the
east of Budapest and approached Warsaw (1,800 miles return). Further
to the east, Route 5 crossed Albania and headed for Lwów (1,400 miles
return).[52]

Although the distance was now reduced, one of the biggest problems facing the airmen was the weather. In the winter of 1943–4, Italy
suffered the worst weather for twenty years and the new Brindisi base
struggled to dispatch successful flights to Poland. It boasted only one
runway, and that was exposed and near the sea, which was subject to
violent cross-winds, and some of the early missions ended in disaster.
On the night of 5/6 January 1944, Polish airmen in three Liberators and
one Halifax took off to drop supplies into Poland. The Halifax and one
Liberator soon had to return to base, having been battered by gale-force
winds, while the other two Liberators went on. Unable to find the drop
zone in the appalling conditions, they had to return to Italy, but as the
aircraft approached Brindisi, they found that the local electricity grid
had broken down and there were no landing lights. They circled for
two hours in the hope that emergency lights would come on. With fuel
expended, one Liberator attempted to land at Brindisi but the pilot, finding he was about to over-shoot the runway, climbed steeply and stalled,
sending the aircraft crashing into the docks. Meanwhile, the second aircraft attempted to reach the nearest airfield at Taranto, but lack of fuel
prevented it climbing above the adjacent mountains and it crashed into

Poland Alone: Britain, SOE and the Collapse of the Polish Resistance, 1944

a hillside. Both crews, with the exception of one member, were killed. With two of the remaining Halifaxes out of commission due to engine failure, the Polish Flight was left with just two serviceable aircraft.[53]

To alleviate this desperate situation, 148 Special Duties Squadron, under the command of Wing Commander W.D. Pitt, joined 1586 Polish Flight at the end of January. This was a welcome addition, as their establishment comprised thirteen Halifax B IIs. These aircraft were distinguished by their metal 'Tempsford' nose in place of a glazed nose, together with the addition of a paratroop door in the floor, aft of the bomb bay.[54] Despite the cold winter, aircrews and ground crews from 148 Squadron relished their new posting to Italy, as Flight Mechanic Bill Steed, recalled:

It was a great relief to come to southern Italy after the intense heat, dust and flies in North Africa. Our new facilities were so much better, our food improved and we had attractive Italian women to look at – what more could a young man want – so our morale was high. We soon set about our task of preparing the Halifaxes for dropping supply containers to Poland, North Italy and Yugoslavia. To service each Halifax, we had four flight mechanics (one per engine), two airframe riggers, one armourer for guns and one for bombs, who would also do the electrical work. So in all, the ground crew would be eight men with a sergeant in charge. I remember our aircraft were fitted with a 'rest position', which was a bunk bed in mid–fuselage for casualties, as well as extra fuel tanks for the Polish trips.

We would load fifteen containers for a supply drop. Nine would go in the bomb bay and three under each wing next to the inner engines. Then anything that was non-breakable, such as clothing and boot supplies would be put into kit bags and so they could be dropped through the fuselage. On board, it was the bomb aimer who organised the dropping. If containers were dropped with a parachute they tended to drift, but if accuracy was important, the aircraft would go in at about 100ft and almost down to stalling speed. The partisans would often mark out the drop zone with our old white parachutes.

Depending on the weather at Brindisi, the aircraft normally took-off out to sea. When a mission returned, a morse lamp would flash the letters 'FS', which was our squadron sign, followed by 'A' or 'B'. If the aircraft landed safely, it would taxi round, the aircrew would get out and the first thing the ground crew would do was survey all the engines for any damage. Underneath the cowling was a tank which contained coolant and that was always very vulnerable to SAA fire. But the cross-winds at Brindisi made landing difficult. An aircraft could make it back on three engines if it wasn't returning with a full load, but if it crash-landed and was wrecked, which was quite frequent, the medics would be straight on the scene to see to any casualties. Then any serviceable parts would be salvaged, particularly tyres, which were always in short supply.[55]

During February and March 1944, aircrews were mainly allocated to missions over the Balkans but when Poland was back on the agenda, bad weather and mechanical faults often conspired to abort the missions. While the Poles continued to be buoyed by hopes of massed sorties, Lord Selborne, the Minister in charge of SOE, privately admitted that his organisation had overstated intended British support and 'made errors in suggesting 300 sorties to the Poles'.[56] Even if the flights were to be limited, the newly-arrived aircrew from 148 Squadron, including twenty-three year old Flight Sergeant Walter Davis, remained committed to the task:

Our seven aircrew had all served together for some time, though we had tragically lost our bomb-aimer on a previous mission, when he had fallen out of the bomb-bay in mid-flight and simply disappeared. We were a close team and had complete confidence in our skipper, Warrant Officer Tom Storey, though he was a tough disciplinarian and there was never any chat allowed over the intercom during missions.

At this stage of the war we were still flying the Halifax B II, whose only armament was a rear four-gun turret (other armament was shed to save weight). For the ten hour round trip to Poland, we had extra fuel tanks in the bomb-bays. I was the wireless operator and sat underneath the pilot with the navigator directly in front of me, and we also had on board a bomb-aimer/supplies dispatcher and a flight engineer as well as rear gunner. We usually operated alone, even flying without fighter escort and it was frequently a rocky ride – crossing the Alps at 15,000ft resulted in the aircraft lifting violently and it was equally tricky crossing the Carpathian mountains into Poland. Navigational aids were few and the weather predictions usually wrong. I remember the conditions were atrocious that spring.[57]

While Allied support was yet to render significant dividends for the AK, the resistance movement continued to help British Intelligence. One of the lesser-known Polish contributions was to keep the Air Ministry supplied with information on the repair work carried out on Heinkel bombers in Polish air bases and factories. This was of great value in assessing the Luftwaffe Order of Battle. And AK intelligence provided regular updates on aircraft parts production in numerous Polish factories, including Focke-Wulf in Poznań and Daimler Benz in Rzeszów. Reports and plans were also sent to London on over 300 German airfields in Polish territory, and Polish agents managed to obtain useful technical detail on the German Panther tank, as well as information on mini-submarines and anti-tank manufacture.[58]

Time was slipping away for the Poles. Although Operation 'Overlord' heralded the opening of a long awaited western front in June 1944, it was also a reminder to the AK that the value of their stock was falling. Britain and the Allies had once looked to the AK for help in tying down and disrupting German troop movements to the west, but now the Soviet Union had taken on that role. Despite the undoubted value of their intelligence work, cynics suggested that the AK were no longer worth supporting. Those in Britain who believed they were, faced an uphill struggle.

NOTES

[1] It is estimated that over 2,000 politicians, academics, writers and opponents of Frank's regime were murdered at Palmiry in the Kampinos Forest, just west of Warsaw. See Stefan Korboński, *Fighting Warsaw, The Story of the Polish Underground State 1939–1945* (Hippocrene Books, New York 2004), pp. 26, 46.

[2] Norman Davies, *Rising '44: The Battle for Warsaw* (Macmillan, London 2003), p. 184.

[3] General Tokarzewski was arrested by the Soviet authorities in March 1940. After Barbarossa, the Soviets released him, and he assumed a command within the Polish Corps in the Middle East.

[4] Bureau I (Personnel, Welfare and Legal); Bureau II (Intelligence); Bureau III (Operations); Bureau IV (Quartermaster); Bureau V (Command & Communications); Bureau VI (Information); Bureau VII (Finance). For details see, Marek Ney-Krwawicz, *The Polish Home Army 1939-1945* (Polish Underground Movement Study Trust, London 2001), pp. 11–21.

[5] For details of AK organisation, see T. Bór-Komorowski, op. cit., pp. 146–51. John Erickson, ob. cit., p. 263. For weapons see SOE memorandum, 'Conversation with Captain Podoski', 7 December 1942, HS4/160, NA.

Although estimates of AK strength differ wildly, the figure of 350,000 is taken from an SOE report in 1944, see 'The Polish Secret Army' in HS4/160, NA.

6 George Iranak-Osmecki, *The Unseen and Silent* (Sheed and Ward, London 1954), pp. 89–90.

7 Colonel Gubbins, 'Notes on Polish Activities June 1942–Jan 1943', HS4/142, NA.

8 Colonel Mieczysław Wałęga to Author, 2 September 2006.

9 'The Polish Secret Army', an assessment in HS4/160, NA. Also Colonel Mieczysław Wałęga to Author, 2 September 2006.

10 Dr Andrzej Suchcitz, 'The Grey Ranks (1939–1945)' in www.polishresistance-ak.org.

11 Adela Wałęga to Author, 2 September 2006. Captain Japlinski was arrested by the Red Army as soon as they arrived in Rzeszów.

12 The drop comprised two soldiers (Major Stanisław Krzymowski and Captain Józef Zabielski) and one political courier (Czesław Raczkowski).

13 Polish Air Force Association, *Destiny Can Wait: The Polish Air Force in the Second World War* (William Heinemann, London 1949), p. 214. For capacities, see Air Ministry to HQ, MAAF, 10 February 1944, HS4/157, NA.

14 The first 'special duties' Halifax flew to Poland on the night of 7 November 1941. See Brian J Rapier, *Halifax at War* (Ian Allen, London 1987), p. 88.

15 'Hints for Bombardiers on SO Aircraft', Reel 5, Vol. 6, #0735, OSS Microfilm, MF 204–211, GB99, LHCMA.

16 Ibid.

17 Iranek-Osmecki, op. cit., pp. 43–5.

18 Tempsford airfield was returned to agriculture after the war and remains private property.

19 Diary entry, Squadron Leader Tony Walker, 10 May 1941. I am indebted to Roger Walker for making his brother's papers available.

20 Martin Bowman, *Combat Legend: B-24 Liberator* (Airlife, Shrewsbury 2003), p. 58.

21 Full details of all operations and losses are contained in the comprehensive study by Jerzy B Cynk, *The Polish Air Force at War. The Official History Vol. 2, 1943–1945* (Schiffer Military History, Atglen USA 1998), pp. 453–68. See also 'Polish Operations, 6 March 1944', HS4/146, NA.

22 Gubbins report attached to WD Allen letter, 11 May 1943, HS4/142, NA.

23 Hanna Kościa to Author, 23 July 2007.

24 Ibid.

25 Józef Garliński, *Fighting Auschwitz* (Fontana, London 1976), p. 156.

26 Iranek-Osmecki, op. cit., p. 97.

27 This officer, later known as Captain Alun Morgan, assisted with the SOE Operation 'Freston' in 1944-5. See Brigadier GA Hill to Colonel Graur, 7 April 1945, HS 4/142, NA.

[28] During the years 1942–1944, Colonel Spychalski, Colonel Godlewski and General Rostworowski were captured and murdered, while Colonel Miłkowski was arrested and remained missing. See, T. Bór-Komorowski, *The Secret Army*, (Victor Gollancz, London 1950), pp. 64–5.

[29] T. Bór-Komorowski, op. cit., p. 117.

[30] Letter to Sir Colin Gubbins, unsigned, dated 7 May 1946, HS4/293, NA.

[31] Stefan Korboński, op. cit. pp. 141–2. Korboński details the whole underground judicial system, see pp. 115–141.

[32] For arms offer see Anthony Eden to Prime Minister, 25 January 1944, AP20/1/23, Lord Avon Papers, UB. For 'Burza' see Professor Jan Ciechanowski, 'Operation Tempest', Article # 9, www.polishresistance-ak.org

[33] Ney-Krwawicz, op. cit., p. 59.

[34] Norman Davies, *Rising '44,* op. cit. p. 173.

[35] Tadeusz Pelczynski, *The Polish Home Army and the Warsaw Uprising* (Museum Armii Krajowej, Kraków). Also, Tessa Stirling, *Intelligence Co-operation*, op. cit., pp. 73–4.

[36] Estimates of those slaughtered vary between Lithuanian historians (100-200) and Polish historians (27).

[37] Document L-37, Exhibit USA-506 in affidavit from Hans Frank, *The Trial of German Major War Criminals Part 12*, ob. cit.

[38] Quoted in GM Gilbert, op. cit., p. 70.

[39] Colonel Mieczysław Wałęga to Author, 2 September 2006.

[40] Norman Davies, *Rising '44,* op. cit. pp. 197–8. Heydrich had a token superior in his fiefdom – *Reichsprotector* Constantin von Neurath.

[41] Józef Garliński, *Poland, SOE and the Allies* (George Allen and Unwin, London 1969), pp. 106–34. See also, Marek Ney-Krwawicz, op. cit. pp. 52–3.

[42] For Warsaw see Gris Davies-Scourfield, *In Presense of My Foes: Travels and Travails of a POW from Calais to Colditz via the Polish Underground* (Pen & Sword, Barnsley, 2004). For Soviets, see Lanckorońska, op. cit., p. 68. There was no direct liaison between MI9 (the British intelligence section responsible for the escape and evasion of POWs) and their Soviet counterparts. Any negotiations took place between service attachés in London and Moscow; see MRD Foot and JM Langley, *MI9: Escape and Evasion 1939-1945* (Bodley Head, London 1979).

[43] Ward MI9 Report, op. cit., HS4/256, NA.

[44] Ibid.

[45] Ibid.

[46] For 'The Winter Campaign in Italy 1943–44', see *The Army Quarterly*, April 1945. In April 1944, the US 15th Army Air Force, using Italian airfields, resumed attacks on Ploesti.

[47] Anthony Eden to Sir Winston Churchill, 17 March 1944, AP20/11/168, Lord Avon Papers, UB.

48 Peter Kemp, *No Colours or Crest* (Cassell, London 1958), p. 252.

49 Józef Garliński, *Poland, SOE*, op. cit., p. 141. Threlfall was assisted by Majors Klauber, Morgan and Truszkowski. For the complicated layers of SOE responsibilities in the Mediterranean, see William Mackenzie, *The Secret History of SOE: Special Operations Executive 1940-1945* (St Ermin's Press, London 2000), pp. 405–8. Threlfall was a businessman before the war and joined Siemens after 1945. He became chairman of Siemens (London) Ltd on 5 July 1973.

50 The last parachute drop mission left Tempsford, UK in October 1943. Three supply drops were made out of Tunis in December 1943, before missions started from Brindisi.

51 CAS to Air Marshal Slessor, 22 January 1944, HS4/157, NA. Also 'MAAF Plan for SOE Operations to Balkans, Italy, Poland and France', HS4/157, NA.

52 Polish Air Force Association, op. cit., p. 217. Route 3 via Lake Balaton had to be abandoned in April 1944 due to the volume of enemy ack-ack batteries and night-fighters in the Budapest-Balaton region.

53 For a full list of crews and casualties, see Jerzy B Cynk, op. cit., p. 463. For the disastrous January mission, see CAS to Sir Jack Slessor, 10 February 1943, AIR 19/816, and Lord Selborne to Sir Archibald Sinclair, 24 January 1944, HS4/157, both NA.

54 The improved Halifax B V did not arrive with the Special Duties units until June 1944. For the dire shortage of aircraft, see D Colyer to General Sosnkowski, 24 January 1944, HS4/157, NA. For aircraft strengths, see 'Aircraft and Crew State of SD Squadrons for SOE/SIS Purposes', 25 January 1944, HS4/157, NA.

55 Bill Steed to Author, 8 December 2006.

56 Air Ministry estimates were 100 sorties. J.A. Easton to CAS, 3 February 1944, HS4/157, NA. Also Lord Selborne to Sir Archibald Sinclair, 21 February 1944, AIR 19/816, NA.

57 Walter Davis to Author, 19 January 2007.

58 H Perkins to Sir Colin Gubbins, 7 May 1946, HS4/293, NA. See also, Tadeusz Dubicki, 'Air Force Intelligence' in Tessa Stirling, *Intelligence Co-operation*, op. cit. pp. 501–11. Also 'Summary' p. 552.

Chapter Three

Operation 'Wildhorn'

British Intelligence had few assets in occupied Poland. At the time of the German invasion in 1939, even the British Military Mission beat a hasty retreat, and from then on, great reliance was placed on Polish intelligence. As a measure of this dependence it has been estimated that Polish agents passed on over 80,000 reports to British agencies during the course of the war.[1]

The overriding problem in moving Polish agents, couriers, politicians and soldiers between Britain and Poland, was always distance. While SOE could utilise the single-engine Lysander aircraft for drops into France and the Low Countries, it was out of the question for the 1,800 mile round trip from Bedfordshire, England to sites in western Poland. Apart from its small fuel capacity, the Lysander could only carry two passengers at a squeeze, although its short take-off and landing ability (within 300 metres), as well as its ability to land in rougher terrain, compared well against the heavier Halifax bomber. The Halifax did score however, on its sheer capacity; extra fuel tanks could be fitted at the expense of shedding armament and it could carry six parachutists in addition to the crew. It was an uncomfortable, cold and long flight of over nine hours, but it was just possible without touching down. However, if a clandestine landing in a forest clearing in Poland was required, it did pose real problems for a larger aircraft. Winter operations were desirable because of the long hours of darkness, but it invariably meant sodden ground and a Halifax needed 1,300 metres for take off, even on a concrete runway.

There was also the added hazard of flying over occupied Europe, which meant running the gauntlet of ground fire as well as enemy night-fighters. Landing in inland waters was considered, but the Catalina, the only flying boat with sufficient range to reach a landing on a Polish lake, only flew at 100 mph and therefore could not make the round-trip in darkness. For these reasons, Major Harold Perkins, head of SOE's Central European Section, covering Poland, Czechoslovakia and Hungary had, as late as July 1942, quashed ideas of a two-way bridge between the countries.[2]

Couriers did make the long and dangerous journey between Britain and Poland by land. It always took several weeks, if not a month, by which time the information they carried was often out of date. So it was vital to form some type of 'air bridge' (*Most*) between the countries, both to support the AK and to bring back to Britain important intelligence on the eastern front. While SOE and the British Air Ministry debated the issue of suitable aircraft, the AK set about finding accessible landing sites (described by the Poles, as 'ponds'). These had to be square or rectangular, so that a plane could come in or take-off from one of several angles, taking particular account of headwind, which gave important lift to an aircraft attempting to take off on a short landing strip. This landing ground, which also had to allow 1,000 metres in each direction, had to be firm and free of rocks or tree stumps and clear of deep snow. Such requirements were not easily found in Poland, a land of forests and harsh winters, and those areas that were available were usually taken by the Germans. If a site could be found, it would have to be photographed for the Air Ministry's satisfaction and, as Perkins stressed, 'It is highly improbable whether photographs of landing areas in Poland can be procured. The Mosquito flight to Danzig when the German battle cruisers were photographed was near maximum effort.'[3]

While aircraft bound for Poland continued to fly out of Tempsford airfield, in Bedfordshire until October 1943, they were always on drop missions and never landed. Following the losses of aircraft on the Tempsford-Poland missions, there was continuing disquiet in the British Air Ministry over the allocation of the valuable Halifax for SOE operations, when they were needed elsewhere. For since 1941, the Soviet Union had been engaged in her monumental struggle on the eastern front and in lieu of the opening of a second Allied front in the west, Churchill had offered Stalin an Allied bomber offensive on German cities; in the three months to September 1942, RAF Bomber Command had dropped 11,500 tons of bombs and incendiaries on enemy targets. In addition, the landings in North Africa in November 1942 had eased the tension between the two leaders, with Churchill confirming to Stalin that 'Torch is flaming well and General Eisenhower and our own commanders have every hope of obtaining complete control of French North Africa and building up a superior air power at the tip of Tunisia.'[4] Nonetheless, in the winter of 1942–3, the Red Army continued to be engaged in a desperate and bitter contest, particularly at Stalingrad, and there remained huge pressure to make every RAF bomber aircraft available for attacks on Germany.

In addition to the problems of aircraft allocation, SOE, in its early years, had few friends in RAF Command. Commander-in-Chief of Bomber Command, Air Chief Marshal Sir Arthur Harris was no ally, calling them 'amateurish, ignorant, irresponsible and mendacious', while the Chief of Air Staff, Air Chief Marshal Sir Charles Portal could barely allow himself to be associated with 'assassins'.[5] Such poor relations hardly helped negotiations between the British Air Ministry, the SOE Polish Section, the Polish VI Bureau in London and the AK organisation in Poland. However, despite these drawbacks, on 21 May 1943 agreement was finally reached on allowing the 'Bridge' operations to go ahead, but without using precious Halifaxes. Instead, the Lockheed Hudson III was proposed, but even then, the Air Ministry were reluctant to allow the former maritime reconnaissance aircraft to be used for missions to Poland:

> This is cutting the safety margin on flights to the bone. Even with all the overload and reinforcing tanks, the Hudson is barely within its range. We are not prepared to make any further concessions; this is the absolute limit.[6]

The codename 'Wildhorn' was allocated to these bridging operations, which were scheduled to begin in October 1943 from Tempsford, and without notice to the Soviet Union. However, in the meantime, the Allies had successfully landed on the tip of southern Italy, and Italian airbases such as Brindisi, in the 'heel' of the country became available. However, by the time SOE had set up its base in southern Italy it was already late autumn, verging on winter. This was a thoroughly undesirable season to be landing on 'home-made' sites in Poland and Lieutenant-Colonel

Perkins was adamant that only safe landing sites could be contemplated. Writing to Major Jan Jaźwiński, head of Air Support ('Office S') in the Polish VI Bureau, he cited Air Ministry concerns:

> The Air Ministry state that in view of communication difficulties and the great handicap of being unable to obtain photographic reconnaissance, it is necessary that detailed arrangements should be made well in advance, to include:
>
> 1) The selection of a suitable ground would have to be undertaken during January or at the latest February, which might well prove impossible if the ground is covered by more than two or three inches of snow, since ditches, holes and obstructions would be obscured. No one could carry out a survey adequately with snow on the ground.
> 2) If a thaw sets in at the time of the operation, it is improbable that many surfaces would carry the weight of the aircraft.
> 3) The surface must be firm and hard, e.g. pasture land or stubble over which a loaded dray can be drawn without the dray wheels making an impression more than ¼" deep.
>
> I do not think they [Air Ministry] will allow a Polish crew, their reason being that considerable experience is required to land this aircraft on an emergency field at night; this experience would of course be more necessary in Poland than in other countries, in view of the fact that the aircraft will be landing with considerably greater weight of petrol, owing to the long return flight.[7]

The other delay on SOE flights during the winter of 1943–44 was caused by a sudden cessation order issued on 1 December by the Deputy Chief of Air Staff, Air Marshal Norman Bottomley. The reason was the discovery by the Air Ministry that the entire Dutch SOE network had been penetrated by the Germans and that they had effectively controlled it since 1942. SOE flights over Europe were banned until the extent of the disaster could be determined. In the event, the rot had not extended beyond Holland but relations were further soured between SIS and SOE, as the Secret Intelligence Service claimed its warnings had been ignored by the latter. After all the quibbling, on the evening of 15 April 1944, a Douglas Dakota FD919 took off from Brindisi bound for a site near Lublin. The Dakota C-47 was now chosen for Operation 'Wildhorn I' as it had a greater range and capacity than the Hudson. With a normal crew of three, the transport could carry up to twenty-eight passengers but for the Polish trip, it had to be fitted with eight extra fuel tanks, limiting its capacity to about six men.

The aircraft was piloted by Flight Lieutenant E. Harrod (RAF 267 Squadron) and Flight Lieutenant B. Koprowski (1586 Special Duties Flight) and the object was to land, drop off two couriers, Captain Narcyz Łopianowski ('Sarna') and Lieutenant Tomasz Kostuch ('Bryła'), each carrying a parcel of documents, and then collect five important AK commanders and Polish politicians for return to London. As the Dakota neared the landing site 'Bak', some fifteen miles from Lublin in the General Government sector, an AK reception unit, equipped with shovels and ropes were waiting for them. They were commanded by a 'dispatch officer' who controlled the landing lights and there were wireless-operators in the immediate vicinity of the drop. The officer also directed armed units, who had recently been engaged in bitter fighting to secure the area, to defend the landing ground and all the approach roads to the site. Stable lamps were placed at eighty metre intervals to mark out the landing zone, with green flares to light the approach and large oil flares to mark wind direction. As the twelve-ton aircraft came in to land on the second pass, the wind direction changed and the pilots had to negotiate a difficult landing, hardly helped by the landing gear sinking into the soft ground.[8]

However, it only took ten minutes to execute the change-over of personnel and the operation was not detected by the Germans. Of the five men whom clambered on board the Dakota, the most important was the forthright General Stanisław Tatar ('Tabor', 'Turski', 'Erazm', 'Sokół') who was travelling to London to take up the post of Deputy Chief of the Polish General Staff.[9] The others were Lieutenant-Colonel Marian Dorotycz-Malewicz ('Hancza' or 'Roch'), who would go on to command the Polish 'Base 11' at Brindisi in July, Captain Andrzej Pomian ('Dowmunt'), a propaganda specialist from VI Bureau and two politicians, Zygmunt Berezowski, and Stanisław Ołtarzewski. On arrival at Brindisi, General Tatar and his colleagues transferred to an aircraft for the onward trip to Britain, landing at Hendon airport, on the outskirts of London.[10] It was vital to SOE that the party should not come into contact with any other 'outside organisation', so on arrival they were closely guarded and immediately debriefed by SOE officers, who found their information very revealing:

> The bringing back of the first Wildhorn party provided an opportunity for proper consultation and the results were illuminating. Instead of Intelligence reports on EATON [German] defence preparations and accounts of railway sabotage, the party produced Order of Battle Maps of the Underground Army showing the plans for military action at various stages of the EATON retreat. These plans were submitted to the Combined Chiefs of Staff, who dismissed them with a polite homily. The divergence between the intentions of the FIELD [AK] and the plans of the Allies was thus finally made clear.[11]

So, even at this stage the Allied Chiefs of Staff seemed resigned to Soviet domination on Germany's eastern borders, as the price to pay for defeating Germany. Consequently, AK resistance could become increasingly irrelevant to them, and Polish determination to resist – an irritation. Yet the Chiefs had some unlikely allies; Sir Alexander Cadogan, Permanent Under-Secretary of State for Foreign Affairs, reported that some influential Poles, and in particular, General Tatar, seemed flexible in their attitude to the Soviets:

> While the party confirmed that the people of Poland fully acknowledge the Polish Government [in exile] as their official legal representative... General Tatar stated that the forces under his command would in no way be used in a fruitless attempt to secure control of Polish territory, in the event of a Russian occupation.[12]

But General Tatar's acceptance of overwhelming Soviet might did not deter him from his real mission in London, which was to gauge and rally support for an uprising in Poland. He was well qualified for the job and although many Poles arrived in London optimistically requesting meetings with Churchill, it was Tatar who gained quick access to the Premier, meeting him on 25 April. At forty-eight, Tatar was still a professional soldier, having been an artillery officer, graduate of the General Staff Academy in Warsaw and lately Chief of the 3rd Operational Bureau of the AK. Yet for all his establishment credentials, he was something of a radical, and was a severe critic of the pre-war

Polish government. He espoused a form of national communism for Poland, free of the Soviet Union and such left-wing views may have allowed him to view Stalin with a less cynical eye than his colleagues. Indeed, this was apparent in his talks with western leaders during the months before the uprising and merely reinforced their view that Stalin was a man who you could do business with; or in the words of the US President Theodore Roosevelt, the Soviet Marshal was 'not an imperialist, just a realist'.[13]

Although 'Wildhorn I' had delivered some influential Polish leaders to the west, the operation was not without some fall-out, as the Germans discovered the landing site soon afterwards and carried out the customary local reprisals. Nonetheless, there was further pressure to repeat the success of the mission. SOE had already earmarked the most important man to bring out of Poland on the next bridge, or as they coded it, the next 'trunk' operation. He was Józef Retinger ('Salamander'), an extraordinary intriguer, adviser, adventurer and 'contact man', who moved among the world's most influential elites. Born in Kraków in 1888, he had been an early close friend of the Polish novelist, Joseph Conrad and, after establishing contacts with the leaders of some diverse countries, became an intimate of the Sikorski circle, which included SOE's Colonel Colin Gubbins. Surprisingly among this circle, Retinger held fervent socialist views but this did not hinder his contacts with either the Vatican or the British Government; in fact he became something of a go-between for both the Soviet Union and Western Europe. With close contacts in both SOE and, it should be assumed SIS, the fifty-six-year-old was parachuted into Poland together with Lieutenant Tadeusz Chciuk, in early April 1944. His mission has always been shrouded in mystery, but it was most probably to report back to Premier Mikołajczyk on the real effectiveness of the AK. According to another Polish emissary, Jan Karski, Retinger later claimed that the British Government had told him:

> We want to send an emissary to Poland who would be totally independent. His role would be limited. He would get access to all British secret documents referring to the position of the Polish Government on the international scene. His mission would be to convey this information to the highest authorities of the underground in Poland, so that they would realise what kind of position the Polish Government is now faced with, particularly in view of the territorial demands of Russia.[14]

After all, the Polish Government-in-exile had been separated from its homeland for over four years and although regular messages came through to them, it was rare to receive reports first-hand by a man of Retinger's calibre. He covered much ground in Poland during the spring of 1944, with clandestine meetings with General Bór-Komorowski and Government Delegates. Considering that the Gestapo knew he was in the country, it was a surprise to many that he was never arrested.[15]

Meanwhile Force 139, SOE's base at Monopoli near Brindisi, had an agenda of its own. The base, commanded by Lieutenant-Colonel Threlfall allowed the next bridging operation, 'Wildhorn II' to go ahead without the knowledge of the SOE Polish Section in London. Even a new landing site, which allowed for a better take-off, had been secretly located. The site known as Butterfly (*Motyl*) was twelve miles north-west of Tarnów in southern Poland and was a large flat landing ground, bordered on one side by a forest, and previously used by Luftwaffe reconnaissance aircraft. At 1950 hours on the night of 29 May, an unarmed Dakota KG477 took off from Brindisi, escorted until darkness by two Liberators. On board were two passengers, General Tadeusz Kossakowski ('Krystynek'), an armoured warfare specialist, and Lieutenant-Colonel Romuald Bielski ('Bej'), a sabotage expert. It was a good landing, the passengers disembarked and a new party climbed on board for the return flight. The new group comprised Group Captain Roman Rudkowski ('Rudy'), Chief of Air Intelligence AK, Major Zbigniew Leliwa ('Kuna'), Active Operations AK, and Jan Domański ('Barnicki'), a politician; but there was no sign of Józef Retinger.[16]

When Perkins heard reports that the 'Wildhorn II' operation had gone ahead without his knowledge, he berated Threlfall for a lack of communication. He was not even impressed by the calibre of the Poles who were lifted out. On 4 June, when the dust had settled, Perkins pointed out to his subordinate that a great opportunity had been missed:

CD [Gubbins] when summoned to see QUEEN [Mikołajczyk] on a most important matter, assured him that although such a TRUNK [bridging operation] might be feasible at some distant date, we knew of no immediate possibility. The reason for QUEEN'S interest was of a very high political nature which could not be disclosed under any circumstances to the DAYS [Polish Government-in-exile], the purpose being to bring from KENSAL [Poland] someone who would replace SHINE [General Sosnkowski] in his role as President elect, and to place at the head of that side of their affairs, a figure not only acceptable to KENSAL but also to the world in general including DULWICH [Soviet Union].[17]

It appeared that SOE were facilitating the removal of the ardent anti-Soviet, C-in-C of the Polish Armed Forces, General Sosnkowski, in favour of someone who was approved by Moscow, and Retinger had a part to play in such scheming. Sosnkowski, as C-in-C, was also nominally 'President Designate' of the Polish Government-in-exile, but those who opposed his strident position on the Soviets did not wish to see him ever appointed to the post. Tomasz Arciszewski, a veteran socialist politician with strong, recent links to the underground state, was being lined up for the job of President elect, but he also needed lifting out of Poland.[18] SOE were doing the British Government's bidding, for Perkins stressed, 'DULWICH [Soviet Union] loathes and suspects the whole of the DAYS' [Polish Government-in-exile] activities under SHINE [Sosnkowski], and it is only through QUEEN [Mikołajczyk] and his work that we can allay this suspicion'. The chance of lifting Retinger and Arciszewski had been missed until a further 'Wildhorn' operation and Perkins reported that his superiors were not pleased:

> Bowler hats were again hovering in close proximity. 'How was it possible for such a TRUNK [bridging operation] to take place and be prepared without our knowledge?' My lords and masters suspected that the whole thing was out of hand. There were stormy meetings at the DAYS [Polish Government-in-exile] office. In fact a good old PORTMAN [British] flap... We now fear for PAISLEY's [Retinger] life. Who knows how much better a position we would be in today, and KENSAL [Poland] in general, had we received news of the WILDHORN TRUNK 14 days before it happened.[19]

Perkins had every right to fear for Retinger's life, for while in Poland, the emissary was poisoned, possibly by elements of the AK who dreaded a poor report on their organisation. However, the attempt failed although the poison partially paralysed Retinger; so before another attempt was made to finish him off for good, SOE desperately wanted him lifted out by a 'Wildhorn' operation.[20]

The next bridge operation was 'Wildhorn III' (known to the Poles as *Trzeci Most*, 'Third Bridge', and by SOE sometimes as 'Underwriter'). This was to be an extraordinary adventure, which involved Hitler's secret weapons programme and amounted to one of the greatest Polish contributions to Allied Intelligence during the Second World War. The centre for the testing and research of these secret weapons had been carried out since 1937 at Peenemünde, a small fishing community on Germany's Baltic coast. Historically it was the Wehrmacht that had nursed the more sophisticated A-4 (later known as V-2) ballistic rocket project, while it was the Luftwaffe who went on to develop the cruder and cheaper flying-bomb (V-1) from the end of 1942, in response to their failure to sustain a bombing campaign against Britain. However, it was the A-4 rocket project that was to captivate Hitler. The missile, which had a range of 230 miles, was designed to climb fifty-eight miles into the thermosphere, at which point the engine would cut out and it would plunge to earth at a speed of 2,100 miles per hour. On impact, its warhead would explode, creating a large crater. Overall, liquid fuel engines, as used in the A-4, were far more efficient and provided more thrust for their weight than their solid-fuel counterparts, but the disadvantage of liquid oxygen was its availability, which would severely limit launch rates. And while it could take only five and a half minutes for an A-4 rocket to reach its target, it was inaccurate and unpredictable. Nonetheless, as small details started to emerge about the German secret weapons, fear arose in British scientific and intelligence circles as to the capacity of such weapons.[21]

By early 1943, there were over 15,000 forced labourers at Peenemünde and it was inevitable that information would start to leak out. Jan Szreder, a Pole, and Roman Träger, a Pole of Austrian descent, who were both working at Peenemünde, had reported on the secret weapons site to the AK in the early spring of 1943. Wasting no time, an AK agent, Antoni Kocjan sent a short report to London and followed it up with a map of Usedom, the island on which Peenemünde was situated. Further reports came in from Polish agents concerning the 'rocket airplanes' and their associated research buildings. This tallied with other information about the activities on the island coming into London via agents in France, Luxembourg and Belgium, but even though more convincing aerial photographs were taken on 14 May 1943, the details of the actual rockets remained sketchy and conflicting.[22]

Duncan Sandys, Parliamentary Secretary, Ministry of Supply and Churchill's son-in-law was appointed to co-ordinate the rocket analysis, which was already under way in the Scientific Section of SIS. But there was much disagreement about the capacity of the A-4 rocket.

While Sandys was convinced that 'a single rocket could cause up to 4,000 casualties', Churchill's scientific adviser, Lord Cherwell, believed the rocket project to be a German hoax. R.V. Jones, Head of the SIS Scientific Section and one man who, more than any other, had briefed himself on the German rocket threat, recommended an attack on Peenemünde. He argued that at the very least, it was a major experimental establishment worthy of destruction, an argument that won favour with Churchill at a late night meeting on 29 June 1943.[23] The Defence Committee of the War Cabinet acted swiftly and approved 'Operation Hydra', a raid designed to kill leading V weapon engineers and paralyse production at the site. During the night of 17/18 August 1943, 65 RAF Pathfinders and 433 bombers dropped 1,875 tons of explosives and incendiaries. Due to the nature of most bombing missions, many bombs fell outside the target area and those that fell within, killed 213 forced workers but only two engineers; forty-one bombers were shot down and production was only partly disrupted.[24] However, the raid exposed the vulnerability of Peenemünde and following further RAF attacks on electronics facilities at Friedrichshafen, the Germans moved their ballistic testing beyond the range of Allied bombers. There was still some limited A-4 production at the Peenemünde site, but most large-scale assembly now took place at the underground Mittelwerk plant near Nordhausen. It was here that the SS controlled a slave labour camp, 'Dora', which was itself a sub-camp of Buchenwald concentration camp. In appalling conditions, the labour force created an underground world with full production facilities, though at a terrible cost. It has been estimated that over 20,000 inmates were worked to death or died of disease and malnutrition in these tunnels and caves.

The bombing of Peenemünde was also a catalyst for change in the Nazi Party leadership. Though Himmler had always coveted the role, the secret weapons programme was always the preserve of the Reich Minister of Armaments, Albert Speer. Himmler, with his twisted logic, wanted to be closely associated with any 'miracle' weapon in the hope that some of the magic would rub off on him; he also realised that control over the project would boost the economic power of his SS empire and at the same time diminish that of his adversary, Speer. Even as the smoke was clearing from the bombed rocket establishment at Peenemünde, Himmler was on site, suggesting how his legions of forced labour could rebuild the damage – an offer that was eagerly accepted by Hitler.[25]

With a safe production centre deep underground in the centre of Germany, the Wehrmacht required further firing sites for the A-4 rocket in Western Europe, as well as a testing ground far enough to the east to escape Allied bombers. Despite damage inflicted by RAF bomber raids in 1943 on the bunker and firing platform complex near Watten, in the Pas de Calais in northern France, a replacement bunker was soon completed,[26] and to the east the Germans established a new secret and isolated testing site in Poland. Access to a local labour force was necessary, as well as a good rail network to transport rockets and fuel. An ideal site was found within an existing SS training complex in southern Poland. This vast training base, with its numerous sub-camps was spread over 200 square miles of heathland between Tarnów and Rzeszów. Construction of the original camp, *SS Truppenubungsplatz Ost-Polen* had commenced in 1939, using slave labour from a penal camp set up within its confines in Pustków.[27] By 1942, the SS had renamed the vast base, 'Dębica', as many of the local town's pre-war munitions buildings had been incorporated into the plan. Then in 1943 the base became known in documents as 'Heidelager' (literally 'heath camp'). By then it had developed into probably the largest SS training ground in the east, commanded by *SS Brigadeführer und Generalmajor der Waffen SS* Bernhard Voss, with a strength of 12,000 men. The whole area consisted of numerous infantry firing ranges, tank exercise grounds, as well as accommodation and workshops at Pustków, serviced by four 'horseshoe-shaped' concrete roads. At Kochanowka there was a large transit camp and de-lousing unit to deal with troops returning from the eastern front. However, it was in the centre of Heidelager, where there was an artillery testing ground established around the village of Blizna, that a two square-mile area was selected for the new secret weapons testing site. As with many of the other villages within Heidelager, Blizna was razed and the Polish inhabitants expelled. In the autumn of 1943, slave labourers from Pustków concentration camp were marched the five miles to Blizna each day, where they created a network of concrete service roads as well as barracks, shelters and stores to serve a rocket testing unit of 400 officers and men.[28] A new rail link was built, connecting Blizna to the Kraków-Lwów line and this enabled the heavily disguised rockets and liquid fuel to be regularly delivered from manufacturing sites, rather than risking storage at Blizna.[29]

The first A-4 rocket was fired from Blizna on 5 November 1943, but it was not a successful launch. In the winter of 1943–4, British SIS received continuous reports of activity at Blizna via Polish Intelligence in Warsaw, including a photograph of a missile in flight.[30] From early 1944, when reliable production commenced at Mittelwerk, rockets were continually transported east to Blizna, where local Polish AK units monitored the trials, though they could never get close enough to examine the methods of launching. However, they did record the times, dates and direction of launches from information supplied by nearby forestry workers and from a network within the Dora penal camp at Nordhausen, which continued to supply shipment details to British intelligence. Between January and June 1944, by which time the A-4 rocket was supposed to be operational, there were 118 test launches from Blizna, but many of these rockets failed to reach the target zone, having either failed to take off or exploded in mid-air. Subsequent insulation of the fuel tanks partly solved the problem, but in the time allowed, Blizna would never demonstrate consistent, reliable rockets.[31] In response to persistent Polish reports of these missile launches and of rail trucks arriving at Blizna with 'liquid air', on 15 April 1944, 60 Squadron RAF took advantage of a break in the weather and made a successful reconnaissance sortie over the area. Polish maps had provided clear intelligence and a lack of cloud cover enabled good photographs to be taken. However, because they were taken at high altitude to avoid enemy flak, the RAF interpretation team at Medmenham could identify V-1 'ski' ramps but had difficulty in picking out details of any A-4 rockets on the ground:

> The Blizna area has clearly been used for some sort of experimental work and is active. There is a ramp 155 feet long of apparent steel rail construction at 724983 which points N. 40° E and has an inclination approximately 10°…A number of small objects on open ground either side of the ramp are not seen clearly enough to be interpreted; two of them look like small guns in open rectangular emplacements.[32]

Photographs were taken over the whole Heidelager area, including the horseshoe-shaped camps at Pustków, whose purpose clearly confused the RAF interpreters, and more aerial reconnaissance was called for. Further photographs were taken over Blizna on 5 May and this time, British Intelligence had more success. Medmenham reported cranes, gantries and 'three flat wagons carrying a cylindrical object, similar to those reported at Peenemünde and Friedrichshafen'. The discovery of a twenty-five metre diameter crater, three miles from Blizna, also caused great interest, but 'Ultra' traffic was leading the way to a greater discovery. Wireless intercepts of German analysts at Blizna had indicated that there was a crater near Sidlice, 160 miles from Blizna. R.V. Jones now knew that missiles fired from Blizna included long-range rockets, as well as flying-bombs.[33]

In the early hours of 13 June 1944, barely a week after the D-Day Normandy landings, the first V-1 flying bombs landed in London, Kent and Sussex. The opening salvo of ten, fired from Pas de Calais launch sites was not the promised 'onslaught'. Five crashed immediately, one fell in the Channel, while the remainder droned on to explode in southeast England. But more deadly salvoes were released over the next few weeks, including one on 18 June, when a flying-bomb crashed into the Guard's Chapel at Wellington Barracks, killing 121 people. On 30 June, a similar bomb fell into The Aldwych in London, killing forty-eight.[34] At this point, the only defensive measures the British could muster were AA guns, barrage balloons and fighter aircraft. Flying Officer Jim York of 85 Squadron was one airman trusted with this mission:

> To give extra speed, because the flying bomb flew at over 400 mph, our Mosquitos were fitted with special high compression Merlin engines with stub exhaust shrouds and using 150-octane fuel. We did a dozen flying bomb patrols in July. Our total score was four destroyed. The flying bombs usually came over in batches of six, flying at about 1500 feet. We patrolled at 6,000 to 8,000 feet and were directed by radar ground control on the same course, ahead of the batch. You could see them below you as a bunch of bright lights. When you were over the top of them, you stuck your nose down and opened the throttles wide and you closed in until you could see the bomb's jet engine casing glowing red-hot. You then knew you were too close and dropped back before firing. You only had one chance because a Mosquito, even with special engines, had not got the speed to catch up the flying-bomb again. If you hit it, you had to fly right through the explosion as you couldn't avoid it. It was a bit of a bump.[35]

The threat to London was immediate, though had the flying bombs been directed in greater numbers and towards the embarkation ports on the south coast, the 6 June D-Day landings, 'Operation Overlord' could have been seriously hampered. After the initial firings, euphoria rose within the Nazi hierarchy at the prospect of new war-winning weapons and Göbbels claimed that, at his suggestion, the secret weapons should now be called 'V Weapons' (*Vergeltung* or revenge), with the flying-bomb gaining the title V-1, while the A-4 rocket was re-branded as the V-2.[36]

Polish reports on activities at Blizna in early 1944 had continued to talk of some sort of 'aerial torpedo'. There was also information from AK sources in Warsaw that two casualties from a car crash in the city were from Mielec near Blizna, and were secret weapons specialists. The mystery 'torpedoes', often painted in a black and white chequered pattern to determine the roll in flight, were launched from Blizna in a northerly direction. Generalleutnant Walter Dornberger later admitted that one V-2 was fired into a concentration camp but 'consoled himself with the thought that it would be chalked-up to the SS rather than the Wehrmacht'.[37] However, most rockets landed in the districts outside Warsaw, Lublin and Radom, leaving large craters, and because the warhead was usually loaded with sand, there was no explosion to scatter the parts. German motorised units were always quickly on the scene to recover everything and only small fragments were ever left for AK units to find. However, local AK maps of the Sarnoski region, east of Warsaw showed that nearly thirty rockets had fallen within a five-mile radius between Siemiatycze and Sarnaki, along the River Bug and all had exploded or were retrieved by the German reception units. But on 20 May 1944 the AK 22nd Infantry Regiment finally managed to retrieve a fallen 'torpedo', before the German recovery unit arrived. The V-2 rocket had fallen into swampy ground on the banks of the River Bug, near the hamlet of Klimczyce close to Sarnaki, some seventy-five miles east of Warsaw, and luckily failed to disintegrate. The local AK unit managed to hide the rocket until the Germans gave up their search, then with the aid of two pairs of horses, they dragged the missile onto waiting carts. This was no mean feat, for the weapon was fourteen metres long and weighed nearly four tons after the fuel was expended. Handling it was extremely awkward as the base diameter with fins was 3.6 metres and the fuselage diameter was 1.6 metres.[38] The rocket was hauled off to a barn in the nearby village of Hołowczyce-Kolonia, while the scientists Professors Janusz Groszkowski and Marek Struszynski were called in by the AK to dismantle and examine the fuel and radio components.

Meanwhile, Antoni Kocjan, a glider pilot, engineer and member of the AK Research Committee, was charged with organising a succession of these experts to take photographs and make drawings of the rocket. It was a dangerous mission for Kocjan, who had been arrested once before, thrown into Auschwitz, and freed after nine months when a large bribe had unusually secured his release. But after making repeated trips back and forth to Warsaw, he was arrested again by the Gestapo on 31 May 1944. This was a crisis for the rocket retrieval operation, for should Kocjan be broken by interrogation, then Wildhorn III would collapse. In the event, he was severely beaten at Gestapo Headquarters and then carried to Pawiak Prison on a stretcher. In a cell, he had his fingers systematically broken and was burned with hot irons. He repeatedly passed out, was drenched in cold water and given electric shocks, yet he still remained silent, allowing the AK vital time to carry on their rocket examinations.[39]

Contact was made with the British SIS for a way to be found to transport details of the rocket back to London. The AK Research Committee soon drew up a report on the V-2 rocket, 'Special Report No. 242', which included detailed drawings of the rocket components and analysis of the fuel and activator system, containing what appeared to be liquid oxygen and alcohol, together with numerous photographs. There were also records of rocket launches and the size of resulting craters, as well as details of the Blizna testing ground itself, showing launch pad dimensions. The vital importance of this report about the workings of an intact rocket should not be overlooked in favour of the more dramatic retrieval of V-2 parts, especially as the number of these parts had to be restricted – there were severe weight restraints on any aircraft flying to Poland, not to mention the unacceptable risk of moving the larger parts of a rocket across Poland. Consequently, only eight rocket components weighing a total of approximately 50kg could be despatched to Britain and these were carefully packed into cylinders to await transportation to Britain on the next 'Wildhorn' operation.[40]

Although most V-2 testing had been moved to Blizna, there were still sporadic firings from a newly rebuilt station at Peenemünde. On 13 June 1944, the same day that the first V-1 fell on England, a V-2 test rocket was fired from the new pads on the Baltic coast and instead of landing in the sea, it careered on and crashed near Malmö in neutral Sweden. Despite her neutrality, Sweden gave British agents access to the rocket and, taking advantage of the much shorter flight, large rocket parts were collected and brought back to Farnborough on 16 July. Once re-assembled, the scientists found that this rocket was an experimental hybrid fitted with a sophisticated form of remote control, together with 'gas vanes'. However, it was vital to know whether this remote control system was just a 'one off' or whether it was the standard control system for all V-2 rockets. Hopefully the rocket parts collected by the 'Wildhorn III' operation would provide the evidence.

The bridging operation planned to use the *Motyl* (butterfly) landing ground again. The Air Force section of the AK had overall responsibility for the organisation of *Motyl*, and they directed the Kraków Area AK to put together a reception committee, armed guards and signals unit to cover the landing. The local commander was the Area Inspector, Lieutenant-Colonel Stefan Musiałek–Łowicki ('Mirosław'), who had 9,000 AK men within his inspectorate, though by his own admission, only 15% at most were ever armed. Because of the cell structure of the AK, briefings were limited to very small numbers on a 'need to know' basis and within 'Mirosław's' staff, only the Chiefs of Intelligence and Communication knew the identities of any passengers and the true nature of any cargo.[41] It was imperative to find a secret store for the rocket parts as well as a marshalling area for the outgoing passengers, prior to the aircraft's arrival; so 'Mirosław' utilised a large fuel depot, 'Drewno' in Krakowska Street, Tarnów. Picquets were posted and secure hideouts were located at the depot to house the secret V-2 parts.

On 3 July, the outgoing party started to arrive in Tarnów. Firstly, Jerzy Chmielewski ('Raphael'), who arrived with the leader of the group, Czesław Miciński. The following day saw Tomasz Arciszewski ('Stanislaw'), together with the incapacitated Józef Retinger ('Salamander') who was carried by his bodyguard, Second Lieutenant Tadeusz Chciuk ('Celt'). The pair had travelled down from Warsaw to Kraków and on to Tarnów with false papers, on trains packed with Germans, who amazingly failed to question them. They were then ferried through the back roads in a horse and cart, driven by a fellow conspirator who, according to Retinger, resembled the famous Dickensian coachman, Sam Weller. Securing Retinger was a great relief to the SOE Polish Section in London, whose operations controller, Major Mike Pickles knew that the Polish Government-in-exile were also extremely anxious to bring 'Salamander' out.[42] Once in Tarnów, the party were found a variety of safe houses in the city, pending their embarkation, while Mirosław organised the movement of the rocket parts:

On 4th July, we received a van at our secret depot, which had come down from AK headquarters in Warsaw. Included in the load were two oxygen cylinders, which contained the most important parts of the dismantled V2 rocket. After opening the cylinders, the parts were removed and put into sacks, which we hid in the Drewno offices. On 6th July, we collected all the V2 parts from the depot, together with any underground mail which had been delivered and decided to move it all towards the landing ground, about eight miles away. We used a peasant's horse and cart loaded with a quantity of wood to disguise the valuable packages. I ordered Major Stanisław Marek ('Jagoda') to organise the transport, together with a bicycle escort, secretly armed with pistols, who would keep at some distance from the cart. On 8th July, 'Jagoda' was given false documentation to show that the wood was destined for the community of Radłów and that he was authorised to take the consignment. He moved off with it and safely reached the landing area.[43]

Meanwhile, in London, R.V. Jones and his team had deduced some surprising features about the V-2 warhead. The remote control found in the Swedish rocket was so sophisticated that the scientists thought that only a large warhead could warrant it, and craters near Blizna, shown on RAF photographs taken on 5 May, enforced this view. From measurements of the craters, Jones initially estimated that the warhead weighed approximately five tons. But it was important to obtain more hard information from the test site at Blizna, before any V-2s were launched at Britain. By mid-July, the site was in the line of the Soviet advance and there was a danger that its secrets would be lost to Stalin. Churchill urgently code messaged the Soviet leader on 13 July:

> There is firm evidence that the Germans have been conducting the trials of flying rockets from an experimental station at Dębica in Poland for a considerable time. According to our information this missile has an explosive charge of about 12,000 lbs [over 5 tons] and the effectiveness of our counter-measures largely depends on how much we can find out about this weapon before it is launched against our country. Dębica is in the path of your victorious advancing armies and it may well be that you will overrun this place in the next few weeks…I should be grateful, therefore, Marshal Stalin, if you could give appropriate instructions for the preservation of such apparatus and installations at Dębica as your armies are able

to ensure, and that thereafter you would afford us facilities for the examination of this experimental station by our experts.[44]

Several days later, Stalin consented to Churchill's request, though ominously he undertook to 'take personal care of the matter'.[45] While a British investigative team was being assembled to leave for Moscow, R.V. Jones persevered with his own photographic analysis and on 17 July he finally detected the outlines of rockets on the Blizna photographs, together with square concrete pads. Though their method of launching and propulsion was still unconfirmed and the size of the warhead would have to be re-assessed, he calculated that the rockets could be launched from a small pad with the aid of mobile cranes. This was enough for Jones to see off his detractors in the 'Crossbow Committee' as well as rocket doubters, such as Lord Cherwell. It was the height of the V-1 flying-bomb attacks on London and Jones himself feared for his life, leaving details of where his latest research notes were to be found, in the event of his death by a flying-bomb. He was also instrumental in devising a deception whereby double agents, including the legendary adventurer, Eddie Chapman, would notify Berlin of the actual site of any flying-bomb overshoots and claim them as undershoots. Subsequent re-adjustments by the Germans on their firing sites in north-west Europe, resulted in many flying-bombs wildly missing their target.[46]

Because of the short hours of darkness over Poland in the summer, SOE also looked at the feasibility of an aircraft flying to Poland, collecting men and materials and then refuelling in the Soviet Union before returning to Brindisi. Lieutenant-Colonel Threlfall, of SOE's Force 139 contemplated the use of heavy signals apparatus, which would need to be hauled onto a Soviet airfield before such a landing could be attempted. But Threlfall made light of the political dimension, which had became all-important as Stalin was distinctly cool about allies landing on his territory. Refuelling and refitting on Soviet soil was really out of the question, so a long two-way trip was devised, based on the previous Wildhorn operations. At 1930 hours on the evening of 25 July, during a non-moon period, a Douglas Dakota C-47 (KG477) took off from Brindisi.[47] It was piloted by New Zealander, Flight Lieutenant Stanley Culliford together with co-pilot and translator, Flying Officer Kazimierz Szrajer, who was a veteran of ninety-seven operations. Flying Officer J. Pemberton-Williams (navigator) and Flight Sergeant John Appleby (wireless operator) completed the crew.[48]

The Dakota had one Liberator as escort until it crossed over Yugoslavia and then it was on its own – unarmed and extremely vulnerable. There were also a number of 'anonymous' Poles on board, unknown to the crew but highly important to the AK for their forthcoming uprising, including Lieutenant Jan Nowak, a military courier coming to Poland with messages from General Sosnkowski for General Bór-Komorowski. The party also carried nineteen suitcases of equipment, together with mail and large quantities of cash.[49]

The 1km long '*Motyl*' landing site was marked out inside a much larger clearing, bordered by a forest and road on one side and drainage ditches on the other and was clearly identifiable from the air for some distance. The AK established observation posts all around the site, together with first-aid points and a radio station across the field at Zdrochec. Yet it was hardly a remote site. The Soviet front was only 100 miles away to the east, and in the nearby village of Wał Ruda, about one mile away, there was a detachment of the Wehrmacht. The approach roads to the landing site were full of retreating motorised or horse-drawn German columns, and even two Feisler Storch reconnaissance aircraft had landed in the field that very afternoon, but luckily took off again before nightfall.[50] Knowing the aircraft was on its way, 'Mirosław' and the reception party looked anxiously to the sky:

At last, about 2400 hours, someone in the awaiting crowd hears the drone of the approaching airplane. Lieutenant 'Włodek' recognizes the typical sound of a heavy transport plane – a Dakota. It flies over the airstrip, but does not give identification signals. 'Włodek' is the first one to give a signal. The Dakota replies. The aircraft lights come on and so do tens of stable lamps, marking the edges of the airstrip. The lamps have their sides covered with paper so the light is visible only from the air. The crew servicing and maintaining the airstrip have done their job exceptionally well and quickly. The aircraft circles the airstrip, lowering its altitude in order to land but it does not land – it circles the airstrip once again. Then just as its nose is lowered, the pilot raises the plane up, and circles a third time. Finally, it decides to land.

The Dakota taxis along the landing strip with its propeller still in motion. Everyone is now running towards the aircraft, and I lead, arm in arm with Tomasz Arciszewski. Our horses and carts come out of the darkness and approach the plane. When we reach it, the wind from the revolving propeller blows off Arciszewski's hat and it tumbles into the middle of the airstrip. The man stops, turns round, and wants to catch it. I shout, 'There is no time.

You can buy yourself a new hat in London', and I pull him towards the fuselage of the plane. The doors open, the passengers come out quickly, one after another, with hand luggage. Second-Lieutenant 'Skory' catches them and leads them in the direction of horses and carts standing nearby. Then with the help of the reception crew, big suitcases and parcels (about 20 in all) are quickly unloaded and piled up on the carts. After the last packet has been unloaded, one of the aircrew members leans out of the plane (Second Pilot, Lieutenant Szrajer) and issues commands in Polish for the order in which items and passengers can be loaded: first of all, parts of the V2 rocket and the post, then 'Rafal' (Chmielewski); next, Dr Retinger, together his special courier 'Celt' (Chciuk), and finally, the leader of the departing party – I think, it was Miciński. The name of Tomasz Arciszewski is not mentioned at all. However, I push him into the plane anyway. Lieutenant 'Włodek' is discussing something with Lieutenant Szrajer. Finally, words and gestures of farewell and the doors are closed. I look in the direction of the horses and carts, but not a trace! The passengers, as well as the luggage, have all disappeared. The whole operation has only taken 12 minutes.

Meanwhile, what is happening in the nearby village of Wał Ruda? What are the Germans doing? Nothing – they are asleep, though there are very powerful reflector lights switched on there and it looks like a sunny day in the village. On the edge of the landing field, 300–400 metres from us, soldiers' heads from Lieutenant 'Deska's platoon are starting to appear above ground, after lying in position as security guards. There are our machine-gun crews huddled together, with their backs to the plane, attentively watching Wał Ruda for any movement. All around are our guard posts, looking out across the meadows, which are lit up by the lights of the Dakota. I can see the fences of gardens on the edge of the village and in the distance, the outline of a German guard with his weapon slung over his shoulder, leaning with his back against a fence. He is observing our activity, yet miraculously he doesn't do anything about it – perhaps he thinks we're Germans. The German soldiers are billeted in a school behind the houses of this village, and our men are out there covering the building, but we don't know why this guard is out in a village garden overlooking the meadows.[51]

'Mirosław's mission was not yet over. While the Germans remained ignorant of the operation, the Dakota still had to take off with the valuable and heavy consignment of V2 parts, together with the detailed rocket plans and the passengers. As the aircraft doors slammed shut, the engines started:

The plane begins to shudder and its tail suddenly rises up (to a man's height). It isn't going anywhere. After several minutes the engines are switched off. Lieutenant Szrajer leaps out of the plane together with the main pilot, Lieutenant Culliford and announces that the plane isn't moving because the brakes are stuck. With Lieutenant 'Włodek', he bends down and examines the wheels then climbs back into the plane and starts the engines again. The Dakota shakes as if it has a fever and the tail is raised up, but it fails to move. After 5 minutes, the engines are switched off and Lieutenant Szrajer disembarks from the plane and announces that the plane won't start now because its wheels have sunk into the soft ground. The plane's Captain, Culliford suddenly demands that the plane must be emptied of its cargo, in order to destroy it and prevent it falling into the German hands.

At Lieutenant Culliford's orders, the passengers begin to leave the plane. Lieutenants Culliford and Szrajer disembark along with them and approach us. I make it clear to the two pilots that I do not agree with having the plane destroyed, but Culliford is very upset and agitated. So I point out the German guard standing by the fence and tell him that the Germans must assume that the Dakota is a German plane and they are not at all interested in it.[52]

'Mirosław' had won his argument for the moment, and having bought more time, dashed off with some of his men to strip a nearby barn of useful lengths of timber. These were broken up and pushed under the aircraft wheels to give some traction. After twenty minutes, the job was done and the crew climbed back into the aircraft, followed by the passengers. Lieutenant 'Włodek and forty men from the signals unit crowded around the Dakota and as the engines turned for the third time, everyone pushed. Again, the engines roared but the aircraft failed to move. It was 0045 hours on 26 July and it was just several hours until dawn. Lieutenant Culliford climbed down from the aircraft and demanded that the passengers and packages be removed again and the Dakota destroyed. But this time the Polish ground crew protested that the passengers and goods (they were unaware of the V-2 parts) must be sent to London and there followed fevered attempts to put some grip under the wheels. Culliford was prepared to try one last time. Miraculously, on the fourth attempt, the aircraft ploughed along and 'finally waffled into the air at 65mph'. The relieved AK units stood in silence as the aircraft disappeared over the trees, and they quickly dispersed. Even the take-off din from the twin Pratt & Whitney engines failed to alert the slumbering Wehrmacht.[53]

On their return to Italy, Retinger rested briefly at Brindisi, while Arciszewski and Chciuk left for Rabat to meet Premier Mikołajczyk, who was on his way to Moscow. The next day Retinger was flown to Benghazi and then on to Cairo to meet Mikołajczyk again, catching the Premier on 31 July, on the final leg of his journey.[54] From there, an exhausted Retinger was flown to London to update Anthony Eden on events in Poland. Retinger flattered Eden by presenting him with a cigarette box, which contained secret partitions and which had been used by a commander of the AK in Warsaw. The box contained a message, which the Foreign Secretary found 'embarrassing and which is past my power to do anything to deserve'.[55] Meanwhile, Chmielewski and Miciński flew on to London, via Gibralter, arriving with their important haul of V-2 parts at Hendon aerodrome on 28 July.[56] SIS took control of the party for debriefing purposes, but Jerzy Chmielewski remained with his sack containing the rocket parts. Speaking no English, he pulled out a knife and fiercely protected his prize from anyone who came close. He had orders to only hand it over to the Polish VI Bureau, so their representative was called in to receive the contents and decipher the report. The Poles then passed on the rocket parts and translated report to the British scientists, who were able to compare them to the parts recovered from the Swedish rocket. The important find from Poland was the radio device, which confirmed that the V-2 could only send and receive regular signals but could not be operated by remote control.

As SIS were talking to Chmielewski in London, the Germans were hastily evacuating the testing ground at Blizna as Soviet forces closed in. The site was now very vulnerable. On 20 July, an AK unit launched an attack on the camp, which was repulsed and on 24 July the last V-2 test rocket was fired from Blizna. The Germans then hastily dismantled their equipment and moved the test site northwards into the safer territory of the Tuchola Woods, about 160 miles northwest of Warsaw.[57] Although the rest of the vast Heidelager camp would not be cleared of Germans until 23 August, Blizna itself was a priority for the Soviets, who occupied it on 6 August and started immediate investigations. Although the summer months were to see concerted and successful RAF raids against V-1 and potential V-2 launch sites and storage bunkers, London still awaited its first attack by V-2 rockets. In the meantime, the British investigative team had set off, bound for Blizna, but floundered around in Europe, waiting for Soviet consent to enter their frontline zone.[58]

NOTES

[1] According to the report of the Anglo-Polish Historical Committee, it must be concluded that the files of the Polish II Bureau (Intelligence), handed to Britain's SIS in 1945, have been destroyed. This was probably to protect the identity of Polish agents in a post-war communist Poland. See Tessa Stirling (et al), *Intelligence Co-operation*, ob. Cit., pp. 11–12, 166, 549.

[2] Polish VI Bureau Memorandum, 26 November 1942, ref. 3.10.3.1/1, Polish Underground Movement Study Trust, London (hereafter PUMST), refers to Perkins' position during the summer of 1942. See also H.B. Perkins to VI Bureau, 7 December 1942, ref. 3.10.3.1/2, PUMST.

[3] Józef Garliński, *Poland, SOE and the Allies* (George Allen, London 1969), pp. 156–9. If a large enough site could not be found, SOE contemplated two adjacent fields, one with a north-south run, the other with east-west, H.B. Perkins to J. Jazwinski, 30 October 1943, ref. 3.10.3.1/9, PUMST. For photography, see H.B. Perkins to Polish VI Bureau, 7 December 1942, ref. 3.10.3.1/2, PUMST.

[4] Winston Churchill to Premier Stalin No. 85, 13 November 1942, *Stalin's Correspondence with Churchill and Atlee 1941–1945* (Capricorn Books, New York 1965), p. 76.

[5] Norman Dixon, *On the Psychology of Military Incompetence* (Pimlico, London 1994), pp. 293–4.

[6] Wing Commander W. Lockhart to VI Bureau, 2 July 1943, ref. 3.10.3.1/7, PUMST.

[7] Lieutenant-Colonel H.B. Perkins to Major J Jazwinski, 30 October 1943, ref. 3.10.3.1/9. PUMST.

[8] H.B. Perkins to Polish VI Bureau, ref. 3.10.3.1/5, 30 June 1943, PUMST. Also, J. Podoski to HB Perkins, 15 May 1944, ref. 3.10.3.1/41, PUMST, and Garliński, *Poland* op. cit., p. 158.

[9] Part of Tatar's brief was also to set up a separate independent archive of Polish Intelligence material, independent of official channels. The fate of this archive is unknown; see Stirling et al, *Intelligence Cooperation*, op. cit., p. 20.

[10] For passengers and landing zone for Wildhorn I, see ref 3.10.3.1/17 and 98, 99, PUMST. Also 'MP3' to H. Perkins ('MP'), HS4/183, NA. Berezowski was the latest leader of the Popular Democratic Party, his five predesessors having been killed. Ołtarzewski was a contender for the post of Vice-President in the Government-in-exile.

[11] 'MP21' to 'MP1' (Major Boughey), 'General Policy for Kensal', 4 September 1944, HS4/146, NA. See also Major Mike Pickles to 'D/AIR', 23 November 1944, HS4/180, NA.

[12] A. Cadogan to Churchill, 22 April 1944, AP20/11/273, Lord Avon Papers, UB.

13 Ney-Krwawicz, op. cit., p. 24; also Davies, *Rising*, op. cit., pp. 52-3, 66–8. Tatar returned to a communist Poland in 1949, but was imprisoned, released and rehabilitated in 1956. He died in 1980.

14 E. Thomas Wood and Stanisław Jankowski, *Karski: How One Man Tried to Stop the Holocaust* (John Wiley & Sons, New York 1994), pp. 221–2.

15 Norman Davies, *Rising* op. cit., pp. 213–9. Also Lieutenant-Colonel Stefan Musiałek–Łowicki ('Mirosław'), '*Lądowanie Alianckich samolotów w Polsce*', p. 1, ref. 3.10.3.2, PUMST. The story of Retinger's parachute jump into Poland is told in John Pomian (Ed.), *Joseph Retinger: Memoirs of an Eminence Grise* (Sussex University Press, London 1972), pp. 147–77.

16 Lieutenant-Colonel H Threlfall to Lieutenant-Colonel H.B. Perkins, 30 May 1944, HS4/183, NA.

17 H.B. Perkins (MP) to H Threlfall (MP1), 4 June 1944, HS4/183, NA.

18 For Arciszewski, see 'The Polish Situation', 30 December 1944, HS4/145, NA. He later became Premier after Mikołajczyk resigned on 24 November 1944.

19 Ibid.

20 For poison story, see Norman Davies, *Rising*, op. cit., p. 216. Stefan Korboński maintains that Retinger's injuries resulted from being accidently tipped out of a stretcher cart on his way to be collected by 'Wilhorn II'. However, after meeting Retinger several times, Korboński does confirm that the emissary feared for his life, see Korboński, op. cit., pp. 296–301; also Pomian, op. cit., 177–9.

21 Steven J. Zaloga, *V-2 Ballistic Missile 1942–52* (Osprey, Oxford 2003), p. 20. For the German assessment see also 'The V. Weapon Offensive' in Horst Boog, Gerhard Krebs, Detlef Vogel, *Germany and the Second World War. Vol. VII, The Strategic Air War in Europe and the War in the West & East Asia 1943–1944/5* (Clarendon Press, Oxford 2006), pp. 420–58.

22 The US sister organisation to SOE, OSS, claimed that it was their agent in Switzerland who furnished British intelligence with two vital reports. For transcripts of these reports, see 'OSS Reports, Vol. 8 to 1 January 1945', pp. 67–8 on mf # 204–211, Reel 8, GB99, LHCMA.

23 The arguments are detailed in R.V. Jones, *Most Secret War. British Scientific Intelligence 1939-1945* (Hamish Hamilton, London 1978), pp. 430–41.

24 Józef Garliński, *Hitler's Last Weapons* (Julian Friedmann, Magnum 1979), pp. 54–7, 78–97.

25 Joachim Fest, *Speer: The Final Verdict* (Weidenfeld & Nicolson, London 2001), pp. 176–85. Nearly 6,000 V-2 rockets were to be manufactured at the new underground plant, Mittelwerk. Of these, almost 3,600 rockets were fired at Britain; almost a quarter failed because of airburst.

26 Alan Cooper, *Beyond the Dams to the Tirpitz: The Later Operations of 617 Squadron* (William Kimber, London 1983), pp. 81–92.

27 'Political Memorandum from Stockholm', 25 September 1944, HS 4/157, NA. Pustków was initially inhabited by Jewish prisoners, most of whom had been worked to death by 1941. After Operation Barbarossa, large numbers of Soviet prisoners were brought to Pustków and with hopelessly inadequate housing, most died of exposure or starvation. Having virtually eliminated all the camp inmates, the SS re-constructed a new penal camp in June 1941, in 'Ring 4', one of four concrete roads built in the shape of a horseshoe. Two years later, the Pustków penal camp was officially designated a concentration camp, moved several miles away and began to receive Jewish and Polish prisoners to work on the construction sites across Heidelager. In the face of the Soviet advance, Pustków concentration camp was evacuated in early August 1944, when the SS destroyed all the buildings. 'Hill 218', where countless bodies were cremated, still stands as a reminder of the 15,000 prisoners who perished there. See also Ben A Soifer, *Between Life & Death: History of Jewish Life in Wartime Poland 1939–1944* (Janus, London 1995), pp. 170–5. Also 'Sanders' Commission: report on visit to South and East Poland', HS4/146, NA.

28 The Blizna testing ground can be reached today by exiting the E40 between Tarnów and Rzeszów at Dębica, taking the 985 Road towards Mielec and turning right towards Blizna. It is rarely visited but bomb-proof shelters and concrete platforms still remain near the recently rebuilt hamlet and foundations of installations can be found in the woods. For a contemporary map, see AIR 42/2157, NA. Also 'Report of Sanders' Commission – Visit to South and East Poland' HS4/146, NA.

29 For the role of Polish intelligence in the detection of Blizna, see Michał Wojewódzki, *Akcja V-1, V-2* (Instytut Wydawniczy, Warsaw 1970) and enlarged pbk. edition 1984; in secondary sources, 'Heidelager' is the name often given just to the SS artillery ground, but was in fact the name for the whole 200 square-mile SS area; see 'Report of Sanders Mission' (including map), AIR 40/2517, NA; HS4 /146, NA; Ben Soifer, op. cit., pp. 170–1; T. Dungan op. cit., pp. 83–6.

30 *Intelligence Co-operation* op. cit., p. 441.

31 Following German evacuation of the site at the end of July 1944, testing was moved to the Tuchola forest in northern Poland, where it carried on until overrun by the Soviets in January 1945. For launch statistics and crash sites, see Michał Wojewódzki op. cit., pp. 451–2.

32 'RAF Medmenham Report', 26 April 1944, AIR 40/2517, NA.

33 For photo recce, see 'RAF Medmenham Report', 3 June 1944, AIR 40/2517, NA. For Ultra, see R. V. Jones, op. cit., p. 544. 'Enigma' was the German name for their coding machine, while 'Ultra' was the British name for the high-grade intelligence received from code-breaking.

[34] V-2 casualties in mainland Britain amounted to 2,541 killed and 5,925 injured. For V-1 and V-2 statistics, see Frederick Ordway III & Mitchell Sharpe, *The Rocket Team* (Heinemann, London 1979), pp. 78–9; also Bob Ogley, *Doodlebugs and Rockets* (Froglets Publications, Westerham 1992) and Peter Cooksley, *Flying Bomb* (Robert Hale, London 1979).

[35] Flying Officer L.J.York DFC, Memoir July 2002. I am grateful to Christopher York for making this available.

[36] Elke Fröhlich (Ed.), *Die Tagebücher von Joseph Goebbels*, 14 June 1944 (KG Saur, München 1995).

[37] CSDIC report re Dornberger in conversation with Generalmajor Bassenge, 2–7 August 1945, WO 208/4178, NA.

[38] For full technical data, see Steven J Zaloga, op. cit.; T.D. Dungan, *V-2. A Combat History of the First Ballistic Missile* (Westholme, Yardley, USA 2005), pp. 27–56.

[39] Jósef Galiński, *Hitler's Last Weapons* (Magnum, London 1979), pp. 154–7.

[40] 'Operation Underwriter', 14 July 1944, HS 4/180, NA. A number of published sources have wrongly indicated that the whole, or greater part of the V-2 rocket was dispatched to Britain.

[41] In his testimony, Musiałek-Łowicki was unimpressed with the memoirs of his colleagues concerning 'Wildhorn III', stating that too many myths had grown up around the operation. For composition of his AK district, see 'Ląowanie Alianckich', op. cit., pp. 4–5.

[42] M.J.T. Pickles to Lieutenant-Colonel Protasewicz, 5 July 1944, ref. 3.10.3.1, PUMST; also AK Memo 98, ref. 3.10.3.1, PUMST.

[43] 'Laowanie Alianckich', op. cit., pp. 55–9.

[44] Churchill to Stalin, 13 July 1944, No. 295, *Stalin's Correspondence with Churchill and Atlee 1941–1945* (Capricorn Books, New York 1965). Messages between Churchill and Stalin were normally sent in code to the British Embassy in Moscow, de-coded and the resulting text in English was delivered by diplomatic post.

[45] Ibid., No. 297, Stalin to Churchill, 15 July 1944.

[46] Ronald Lewin, *Ultra Goes to War* (Arrow Books, London 1980), pp. 321–2; also R.V. Jones, op. cit., p. 551. Chapman's exploits were later the subject of a feature film, 'Triple Cross' (1967).

[47] The Dakota C-47 was the designation given to the military version of the civilian DC-3 aircraft; see also Major Pickles to Lieutenant-Colonel Protazewicz, 5 July 1944, HS 4/180, NA. For Threlfall's report, see 'Operation Wildhorn X', 13 July 1944, Hs 4/180, NA.

[48] Warrant Officer Appleby, from Cwmbran, South Wales, was a veteran of thirty-four relief flights to partisans in the Balkans. He was awarded the Polish Cross of Valour for the 'Wildhorn III' operation. In 2001 his medals,

including his DFM, came up for auction; see Spink (London) Orders & Decorations Catalogue, 25 September 2001. The Author appreciates the assistance of Keith Northover for bringing this to his attention.

49 The other passengers were AK specialists Major Bogusław Wołniak, Captain Kazimierz Bilski and Second Lieutenant Leszek Starzynski. See also 'Polish Operation', 25 July 1944, HS 4/180, NA.

50 The landing ground 'Motyl' has now been marked by a commemorative stone and Polish emblem together with a large-scale map of the operation and viewing platform. For a contemporary description of the ground, see 'Operation Underwriter: Description of landing ground', 14 July 1944, HS 4/180, NA; also map of 'Motyl', ref. 3.10.3.1, and 'Platoon Plan', ref. 3.10.3.2, PUMST.

51 This account of the arrival and take-off at 'Motyl' has been translated from the Polish document '*Lądowanie Alianckich samolotów w Polsce*', (Landing of Allied Planes in Poland as related by the Participants), ref. 3.10.3.2, PUMST, testified by Stefan Musiałek on 18 December 1972. The document runs to 107 pages, and pages 1–89 deal in particular with 'Motyl' and 'Wildhorn III'.

52 Ibid.

53 Ibid. For other accounts, this time in English, see Pomian, op. cit., pp. 182–90; also Kenneth Merrick, *Flights of the Forgotten: Special Duties Operations in World War Two* (Weidenfeld Military, London 1989); also Bernard Newman, *They Saved London* (Werner Laurie, London 1952).

54 Mikólajczyk was accompanied on his Moscow mission by Professor Grabski and his Foreign Minister, Tadeusz Romer. In his memoirs, Mikólajczyk makes no mention of meeting any of the Wildhorn party, though he does refer to stops in North Africa and Cairo. See Mikólajczyk op. cit.

55 Frank Roberts to Anthony Eden, 17 August 1944, together with Eden's hand-written note in margin, AP 20/41/92, Lord Avon Papers, UB. For Retinger, see Norman Davies, *Rising* op. cit., pp. 216–9.

56 Cypher to New York, 28 July 1944, HS 4/183, NA.

57 T.D. Dungan, op. cit., p. 109.

58 Report of Sanders Mission, AIR 40/2517, NA.

Chapter Four

Auschwitz

1944 was to see momentous events in Poland, but in terms of premeditated murder, nothing could approach the scale of the frenzy which occurred at Auschwitz in the early summer of that year. Yet by this time, Britain and the US were in possession of more evidence of German atrocities than ever before. Was their feeble response the result of geographical distance or even German deception, or was this inertia caused by overworked officials with a lack of imagination? The inability to believe in the scale of this horror was not just restricted to the Allies; some Jewish councils were just as doubtful in the face of the evidence, as nothing in their experience had ever prepared them for it. And anyone looking into the Nazi camp system from outside had to contend with a bewildering array of prisoner categories and camp descriptions, which were all too easy for the SS to camouflage.

By 1944, the Germans had constructed a vast network of camps throughout Poland. These ranged from detention, POW, or penal camps through to concentration and extermination camps. Some of the larger concentration camps, where the majority of prisoners were worked to death, had their own sub-camp systems. But regardless of the size of the complexes, most were expanded beyond their original capacities, causing starvation, disease and appallingly unsanitary conditions. Amidst this tide of human misery, the Poles as a nationality were singled out for particularly brutal treatment, and over 2,700,000 Polish Jews were destined for extermination.[1]

The early years of the war had seen Polish Jews herded into nearly 400 sealed ghettos across the country, each with an imposed 'self-government' called the *Judenrat*. Following 'Barbarossa' and the German occupation of eastern Poland in the summer of 1941, larger numbers of Jews came within the grasp of the SS. But by the winter, the German offensive had faltered within sight of Moscow and it was becoming clear that the Wehrmacht was unlikely to defeat the Soviet Union, at least in the short term. Without vast areas of land under his control, Hitler's vision of a huge 'dumping ground', or *lebensraum* for non-Soviet Jewry was not materialising. His order to deport the Reich Jews to the east had created further pressure and there was a grim determination, confirmed by the Wannsee Conference in January 1942, for the 'Jewish Problem' to be dealt with by 'a final solution'. It was the green light for the expansion of many existing penal concentration camps into extermination or death camps, mainly sited in occupied Poland.[2]

In their occupied territory, the Germans immediately shot any Soviet commissars who were identified among the POWs, while Soviet Jews were singled out for 'special treatment'. To the Nazis, being both a Slav and Jewish, and perhaps a communist, rendered the individual sub-human, whose only destiny was to be butchered. Initially, the killings were carried out by mobile units, employing small arms, and in the summer of 1941 Himmler visited an occupied region of the Soviet Union to witness anti-partisan operations and to see for himself how large numbers of unfortunates were dealt with. His host for several days was the Higher SS and Police Chief for the district, Erich von dem Bach.[3] This East Prussian professional SS officer, himself of Polish/German origin, was becoming an expert in resettlement, expropriation of property and mass murder, operating in the Rear Zone of Army Group Centre in the former Byelorussian SSR. However, it appeared that over long periods, dispatching victims at close quarters with small arms fire was having a detrimental effect on SS executioners. In short, it was affecting their fighting ability, and was considered 'inefficient'. *Gruppenführer* von dem Bach's complaints seemed to galvanise Himmler's thinking about more industrial methods of extermination.

One part of the 'Final Solution' in Poland was enacted under Operation *Aktion Reinhard,* named after the co-ordinater of the slaughter, Reinhard Heydrich, which came into effect between July 1942 and October 1943. Its aim was the extermination of Jews in the General Government and

Białystok regions. To facilitate this terrible programme, the two exist-ing penal and extermination camps at Auschwitz and Majdanek were expanded, while four small camps were established, purely for extermi-nation, in the isolated areas of Treblinka, Bełżec, Chełmno and Sobibór, near the eastern borders with the Soviet Union. These latter camps were tiny by comparison, because Jewish arrivals were gassed almost imme-diately and only a small number of prisoners were kept alive to run the plant. At Treblinka, a surprisingly small detachment of twenty-five SS, and 100 Ukrainian guards oversaw the slaughter and incineration of an estimated 800,000 Jews. Reporting directly to Himmler, this small and secret band of Reinhard SS operatives were forbidden to transfer to other units in order to maintain secrecy, but information on the atrocities did start to leak out to Allied news agencies during 1942. Newspapers, such as *The Times*, *Daily Telegraph* and *Manchester Guardian* ran reports, and there were broadcasts by the BBC, via the Polish Government-in-exile and the Jewish Labour Bund.[4] The British Foreign Office, while believing that killings were taking place, imagined that there was some sort of 'weeding out' going on, rather than the wholesale slaughter of a race. The SS tactic of creating penal camps alongside extermination centres may well have created a slave labour force, but it also conven-iently camouflaged the true intent of the operation. To this end, in the south-west of Poland, in that part of the country annexed directly to the Reich, a vast industrial, penal and extermination complex was taking shape around the town of Oświęcim.

Oświęcim, or as the Germans named it, Auschwitz, was an unre-markable town. At the turn of the century, it was just inside the Austro-Hungarian border and had warranted a brief mention in *Baedeker's Guide* for its respectable railway restaurant and important railway junction. After incorporation into Poland, the town hosted a cavalry barracks which soon fell into disuse, but the buildings sur-rounding a large horse-breaking yard were still standing by the time the Germans arrived. In March 1940, Himmler picked SS *Sturmbannführer* Rudolph Höss to be the first Commandant of the new camp. It was a role that the SS Major accepted without hesitation, later commenting, 'I had nothing to say; I could only say *Jawohl!*'[5] The following month, he arrived with a small team and, after demolishing local Polish houses to pilfer building materials, he set about constructing a penal camp around the old barracks to house mainly Polish political prisoners.[6] He adopted the mocking phrase from the Dachau camp '*Arbeit Macht Frei*' (work makes you free) and erected the words over the main gate. It was not long before Himmler saw the possibilities of expanding Höss's small camp, because it had one great advantage – its geographical position near the Silesian coalfields. Coal was the raw material for fuelling the manufacture of synthetic oil, essential to the German war machine, and if there could also be a guaranteed slave labour force, it would be a suitable place to site a factory run by the German chemical giant, IG Farben. In one of his many grandiose schemes, Himmler also planned a new model Nazi town at Auschwitz, which would be financed by IG Farben.[7] This town would have excellent rail communications and it would also be isolated from the threat of enemy bombing raids. But Hitler had bigger plans for the town – plans that would transform Auschwitz from a number of severe penal colonies into an extermination centre. The invasion of the Soviet Union in 1941 meant that vast numbers of Soviet civilians and POWs would come under the control of the SS, and according to warped Nazi logic, these millions would either have to be eliminated on site or transported away. Auschwitz, sitting on an axis of the European railway system, could prove to be the ideal repository for this population.

During the winter of 1941–2, the camps around the Polish town were expanded, though in Allied documents relating to reports about the camp, they were still not referred to as 'Auschwitz'.[8] New barracks were added to the old camp, Auschwitz I, and a vast new extermination camp was constructed at the nearby village of Brzezinka. This settlement, which had a pre-war population of about 4,000 Poles, lay about a mile to the west of the old main camp. The village was soon demolished and the new camp erected with the new German name 'Birkenau' (from the German *Birke*: birch), which also became known as Auschwitz II. About three miles to the east, the IG Farben plant was constructed, known as Buna-Werke, and was serviced by two nearby British POW camps together with the Monowitz penal camp (Auschwitz III). The three Auschwitz concentration camps were therefore to become the centre of a regional group of over 40 sub-camps in Poland and four in Czechoslovakia. During 1942, as the systematic killing got underway, the camps took in Jews from outside Poland for the first time. These included Jews deported from Slovakia, whose government, like others who were subservient to Germany, had paid for the Nazis' transport costs as part of the appalling price for domination. Considering the now international scale of the operation, it is staggering that so much was kept secret for so long. This was partly due to the climate of fear inspired by the Nazi security apparatus, which permeated every facet of life in occupied countries.[9]

This German security and intelligence network was indeed complicated, with agencies overlapping each other at every level. The Nazi Party itself had its own security system, the *Sicherheitsdienst* (SD), which operated quite independently of the Wehrmacht's intelligence service, *Abwehr*. Then there was a separate security empire presided over by the Minister of the Interior, Heinrich Himmler, which was divided between the Ordinary Civil Police (*Ordnungspolizei*, only for German territory) and the Security Police (*Sicherheitspolizei,* who could operate in occupied territory). It was this latter organisation that generated most fear, with its brutal methods and paranoid operatives. This unit was again split between the *Kriminalpolitzei*, who pursued ordinary criminals, and the Secret State Police, or 'Gestapo' (*Geheimistaatspolizei*).

The Polish General Government was split into districts and Himmler's writ was imposed in each district by a 'Chief of Police and SS' known as the *Höhere SS und Polizei-Führer*. Most concentration camp guard duties were given over to members of the *SS-Totenkopfverbände* (Death's Head Organisation) and latterly, to men from the Waffen-SS. But they were not a huge compliment and it is estimated that no more than 25,000 SS guards together with their auxiliaries, controlled the whole concentration camp system throughout occupied Europe. Nonetheless, the operation could not have proceeded without the compliance of thousands of railwaymen and Customs officials, as well as numerous petty officials in occupied countries.[10]

Himmler's decree of July 1942 that all Polish Jews in the General Government sector should be 'resettled', gave new impetus to other death camps in Poland. Treblinka, which would become second only to Birkenau in the number of prisoners murdered, remained a very small camp; so small that 95% of Jews who arrived there were dead within several hours.[11] Very few were kept alive, unlike Auschwitz, which became a mixture of slave labour, torture and extermination, all sited in a large complex. The old penal camp, Auschwitz I, became the scene of appalling brutality. Within its confines lay twenty-eight prison barracks including Block 11, or the 'Death Block', with its adjacent execution wall. It was well known that this was a centre for interrogation and torture of Polish political prisoners, intellectuals, priests, AK members and anyone considered part of Poland's elite. However, after Barbarossa, Auschwitz I had taken in increasing numbers of Soviet POWs and after 1942, increasing numbers of Jews.

There were a mixture of nationalities in Auschwitz I, but the Poles always comprised the largest contingent. In the penal camp at the beginning of 1944, there were 18,418 prisoners, including 8,649 Poles, 3,830 Jews of all nationalities, 2,989 Soviets, 742 Germans and 155 French. Most of the German prisoners, although convicted criminals, still enjoyed special privileges and often worked as overseers, known as *Capos,* some Polish political prisoners, mainly from Silesia, also worked as camp functionaries or block seniors. However, because the Jewish prisoners received the harshest treatment, they were rarely given good camp jobs or work in the penal parties and consequently had less chance of organising escapes.[12] In Birkenau, the system of 'Capos' and overseers was copied, but only a minority of new arrivals would live long enough to experience their brutality. Although there were nearly 250 prison blocks, most trains bringing prisoners into Birkenau passed through the main gatehouse, into the camp and emptied their human cargo onto a railhead near the crematoria. Subdued and bewildered, every man, woman and child was then sorted into groups – one for immediate gassing and one for those deemed fit to work. A young Jew, Paul Steinberg, together with his friend Philippe arrived in one such consignment and was herded towards the SS guards:

> Philippe was sent to the line on the left. The oldest officer, the one in the middle – I later found out he was Mengele – asked me, '*Was ist mit dem Fuss, gebrochen?*' (What's wrong with your foot? Is it broken?)
>
> '*Nein, Herr Offizier, ein Abszess an der Fussohle*'. (No sir, an abscess on the sole).
>
> He looked at me, surprised by my accent, consulted one of his henchmen with a glance, and sent me off to rejoin Philippe in the line of the living. The line on the right, with the exception of a few young women, never saw another sunrise.[13]

Since July 1942, such selections had become routine. Those deemed unfit for work, including children, mothers with children, pregnant women and the elderly were gassed immediately. Most of the arrivals remained calm. There were instances of defiance at the railhead, but as it was situated deep within the one-square-mile camp, with a network of searchlights, savage dogs and machine-gun positions surrounding it, any rebellion was obviously hopeless. There was one instance in October 1943 when women attacked their SS guards in a gas chamber undressing room, wresting a pistol from one *Unterscharführer,* shooting him, and attacking other guards. However, they were swiftly overpowered and then gassed.[14]

As soon as prisoners arrived at the Birkenau railhead, any belongings were taken from them. Prior to their journey, there were German propagated stories of a new life in the east; of plots of land; that cash would be required. Consequently, the Jews arrived with their suitcases, duly labelled and full of possessions, only to be relieved of them straightaway.[15] Kitty Hart-Moxon, a young Jewess from Lublin, was one prisoner working in this area of the camp:

In May 1944 I was working in the 'Canada' warehouses, near where people were unloaded from the rail trucks. There was a pile the size of a three-storey building and every imaginable possession was put on top of the pile. It was nick-named 'Canada' because Canada was the country of plenty and so was this area. I didn't know I was to be brought so close to the crematoria and my hut faced one of them. There were 200 girls working day, and 200 working night – so it was working twenty-four hours around the clock. There was an abundance of possessions but you couldn't touch it for yourself. We had to sort through all the jackets, take out any valuables and drop them into a bucket. We formed our little families there, so we knew what was going on, and passing on food or shoes to another person could mean the difference between life or death. You never made such friendships after the war as there was never again such sacrifice. You couldn't trust anyone outside your family.

We saw the people walking past our hut. They were put into the woods beyond and the children started playing. The people sitting there seemed to have no idea what awaited them. Section by section, they were led away. You could hear muffled sounds coming from the gas chambers and the whole area was full of soot coming down from the chimneys. I saw this from May 1944 through to November, as they were bringing in the Hungarian Jews.

There were always SS men around us. There was one SS officer in particular. A man called Wünsch. He fell in love with one of our girls, who was a Czech. He saved her sister who had typhus but he was guilty of other murders and he was tried after the war. Then there was another SS man who had a glass eye. He used to walk with a walking-stick, and would beat people with it. His speciality was that he used to shoot tins off the top of people's heads – he was known as the William Tell of Auschwitz – and he would continue until he had shot the prisoner. I also saw this man kill many children. When they were playing in the woods while waiting to be gassed, they would pick flowers. He used to get irritated by this and would pick them up and kill them on the spot.

Someone in my group once threw a bottle of water at a passing group who were begging for water. A child, of eight or nine, caught the bottle. The same SS man saw this and picked up the child, threw him into the air and bayoneted him. He then came over to our group and asked who had thrown the water. No-one owned up. He picked out every fourth girl and shot her. Just like that.[16]

There were occasional glimpses of humanity amongst the camp establishment. Maria Stromberger, an Austrian Sister-in-Charge of the SS hospital, organised food for prisoners as well as introducing arms and explosives into the camp via AK contacts. But such 'angels' were rare. Most SS guards and their female *Helferinen* assistants were content to carry out their duties and those who had done 'good work' were rewarded by trips to the SS recreation resort of Solahütte, 30km south of Auschwitz.[17]

With such massive shipments of people, it would seem surprising if Britain remained unaware of such movements. Reports about atrocities in Auschwitz and other concentration camps had certainly reached the British Government by 1942, but remained unconfirmed. Its Code and Cipher School at Bletchley Park had already decoded messages from Waffen-SS and German Order Police units, who had been slaughtering partisans, Bolsheviks and Jews on the Eastern Front since Barbarossa in 1941. But due to the euphemisms employed in German Police cyphers, British analysts were far from clear that any holocaust was under way, or indeed, if Jews were being specifically singled out for 'special treatment'. Churchill was informed through his daily intelligence briefings of the slaughters in the east and there was no doubt that he identified with the Jewish struggle and was keen to state that 'the Jewish people know well enough that I am their friend.' Yet, reflecting Allied ignorance of Nazi intentions, his public speeches denouncing the atrocities in 1941 excluded specific mention of the Jews.[18] While reports on atrocities were reaching various departments of the Foreign Office including SIS, as well as the Air Ministry and SOE, there appeared to be no system of conferring or pooling evidence. Consequently, the idea of a vast and dedicated Nazi extermination policy did not build in the minds of Whitehall officials. Furthermore, by 1942–3, the Germans had become more wary of the vulnerability of their signals, and police decodes made far fewer references to mass killings or the persecution of Jews.[19]

If German Police messages were drying up, the British could now depend on the Polish AK for intelligence about Auschwitz. According to the AK C-in-C, General Tadeusz Bór-Komorowski, such reports were regularly passed on to the British:

> Our intelligence reports were regularly dispatched by radio to London and in the years 1942–4, numbered 300 per month. They contained details concerning every aspect of the war. Apart from radio transmission, the essential facts of our intelligence material were micro-filmed and sent every month to London by courier. We received from our Allies several official commendations of our work.[20]

Both the British Government and Polish Government-in-exile, had received emissaries from the AK and *Delegatura,* bringing news of the genocide of the Polish Jews. One such messenger was Jan Karski, who had reached London on 25 November 1942 and proceeded to see General Sikorski as well as the British Foreign Secretary, Anthony Eden.[21] Duly fired up, on 17 December Eden addressed the House of Commons with an emotional speech about Nazi barbarities and the whole House rose to its feet in respect for the lost souls. But such gestures, however sincere, had absolutely no effect on the relentless progress of the genocide in Poland. At one meeting with Karski, Eden was joined by the Minister for Economic Warfare, Lord Selborne, who promised moral support but drew the line at Karski's requests for money to bribe certain Nazis into releasing Jews. His predecessor, Hugh Dalton, who was pro-Jewish and a keen advocate of a Zionist state in Palestine, might have been more compliant.

In July 1943, Karski had met the US President, but it was the Polish/ Soviet border issues that dominated Roosevelt's mind. Despite the Polish emissary persevering with horrific stories concerning the 'Final Solution' and the scale of the death camps at Auschwitz, Majdanek, Treblinka and Belżec, the President diluted the matter amongst wider international issues. He did, however, arrange for Karski to meet with other US statesmen, Jewish leaders, Union chiefs and the leadership of the Office of Strategic Services (OSS). This latter group, the broad equivalent of the British SOE, were particularly interested in the strength of the Polish underground.[22]

On 18 April 1943 the first report was received in London from an eye-witness at Auschwitz, who had entered the camp on behalf of the AK, to confirm the camp's activities. There were inaccuracies, but the report was clear – mass extermination by gassing was being carried out at Auschwitz. Yet the report caused little reaction in the British Foreign Office, and neither did the momentous events of the following day.[23] In Warsaw, in the early hours of 19 April, Wehrmacht and SS troops surrounded the Jewish ghetto, in order to expel the remaining 70,000 Jews. But the SS encountered resistance from 500 fighters equipped with small arms, hiding inside the tenement buildings. There were a number of ferocious battles as SS and Lithuanian storm-troopers assaulted the Jewish positions, fighting street by street, using tanks and flame-throwers. The resisters held out for nearly a month before the last was caught and executed, by which time the Germans had systematically destroyed the ghetto.[24] Meanwhile, the remaining ghettos in the General Government sector were eradicated, though in some areas such as Lwów and Białystok, the Jewish underground again resisted and exacted a heavy price on their attackers.

With its large Jewish and Polish communities, the US Government at last responded to pressure and on 28 August 1943, issued a 'Declaration on German Crimes in Poland':

> Trustworthy information has reached the United States Government regarding the crimes committed by the German invaders against the population of Poland. Since the autumn of 1942, a belt of territory extending from the province of Białystock southwards along the line of the River Bug, has been systematically emptied of its inhabitants. In July 1943 these measures were extended to practically the whole of the province of Lublin, where hundreds of thousands of persons have been deported from their homes or exterminated.

> These measures are being carried out with the utmost brutality. Many
> of the victims are killed on the spot. The rest are segregated. Men from
> fourteen to fifty are taken away to work for Germany. Some children are
> killed on the spot…
>
> The US Government reaffirms its resolve to punish the instigators and
> actual perpetrators of these crimes.[25]

Again the declaration referred to the issue of deportations rather than
the ultimate destination of Auschwitz. Consequently, the declaration
carried no weight at all among the SS units and their auxiliaries, who,
in the following days at Birkenau, gassed half the transport of 1,004 Jews
from Holland. A transport of 1,000 French Jews, including many children, then arrived from Paris and within a few hours 662 were murdered.
Selections for extermination from the old and sick within the camp
proceeded as usual. Meanwhile, the British Foreign Office was reluctant
to issue a declaration and persisted in requiring further confirmation of
the slaughter. A Foreign Office official, writing in a memo to William
Cavendish-Bentinck, Chief of the Joint Intelligence Committee of the
Chiefs of Staff (JIC), urged his superior to exercise caution. He felt 'a
little unhappy' about the statement to be issued on the authority of His
Majesty's Government, that 'Poles are now being systematically put to
death in gas chambers'. The official went on to question German extermination methods:

> Personally, I have never really understood the advantage of the gas cham-
> ber over the simpler machine-gun, or the simpler starvation method.
> These stories may or may not be true, but in any event I submit we are
> putting out a statement on evidence which is far from conclusive, and
> which we have no means of assessing.[26]

And a hand-written note was added, 'However, you may not consider
this of sufficient importance to warrant any action.' Caution in these
matters sat well with Cavendish-Bentinck, who was critical of the US
statement and was already minded to temper the British response to the
extermination stories:

> In my opinion it is incorrect to describe Polish information regarding
> German atrocities as 'trustworthy'. The Poles, and to a far greater extent

the Jews, tend to exaggerate German atrocities in order to stoke us up. They seem to have succeeded.

Mr Allen and myself have both followed German atrocities quite closely. I do not believe that there is any evidence which would be accepted in a Law Court that Polish children have been killed on the spot by Germans when their parents were being deported to work in Germany, nor that Polish children have been sold to German settlers. As regards putting Poles to death in gas chambers, I do not believe that there is any evidence that this has been done.

I think that we weaken our case against the Germans by publicly giving credence to atrocity stories for which we have no evidence. These mass executions in gas chambers remind me of the story of the employment of human corpses during the last war for the manufacture of fat, which was a grotesque lie and led to the true stories of German enormities being brushed aside as being mere propaganda.[27]

While Victor Frederick William Cavendish-Bentinck was right in his assessment of the spoof story from the Great War, his continued scepticism about the current atrocity reports was surprising. He was, after all, a man of some experience in intelligence affairs. As an ex-Grenadier Guard, he entered the Diplomatic Service and served in Warsaw at the end of the Great War. Throughout the 1920s and 1930s, he held a succession of diplomatic posts and was appointed Chairman of the JIC in 1939, and his name was even discussed for the vacancy of head of SIS in 1941.[28]

If the Allies were showing such feeble resolve, the only salvation for the inmates of Auschwitz lay in escape. Yet with so many obstacles in their way, the chances for escape were remote. Throughout 1943 and 1944, the complement of guards for the whole Auschwitz complex was estimated at between 3250 and 6650 soldiers. This included Waffen-SS as well as 400 women from the *Helferinnen* SS auxiliary, and 850 Polish and Ukrainian fascists. Furthermore, the guards could count on 250 ferocious dogs and call on further support from nearby SS bases.[29] So the only real opportunities lay in escape from the penal squads who would be marched out each day to outside factories such as the German Armament Works (DAW), or the nearby Siemens or Krupp sites.

Despite the hopelessness of their situation, death camp prisoners could and did rebel. There had been large-scale breakouts at other camps, such as Treblinka on 2 August 1943, when the prisoners stole kerosene, set the camp buildings alight and attacked their guards. They were soon over-powered and some 1,500 inmates perished in the rebellion, with only 50 escaping. Then at Sobibór on 14 October 1943, 300 prisoners killed a dozen of their SS guards and fled through the wire. But most of those who survived the surrounding minefields were then hunted down by capture squads with dogs, and summarily executed. Some even survived for weeks in nearby forests, only to be murdered by roaming bands of partisans. Although such desperate action ended in heavy casualties, both revolts resulted in the camps being razed to the ground by the SS.

After every escape attempt, all inmates had to be accounted for. This Nazi obsession with recording and monitoring prisoners who were destined to be killed anyway, was indeed bizarre; for while Birkenau was the only concentration camp to tattoo its inmates on arrival, metic-ulous records of all transports were always kept, as well as daily roll calls. Missing persons meant reprisals and investigations and when one of the Polish leaders of the underground resistance within Auschwitz, Witold Pilecki, escaped on 27 April 1943, block leaders and clerks were all interrogated and any of Pilecki's associates were beaten or shot. Later that year, two more Poles, Jerzy Tabeau and Roman Cieliczko, having managed to short the electric fence and cut out the lights, made a suc-cessful bid for freedom, but their escape preoccupied camp authorities for weeks afterwards.[30]

The human accounting was even more rigorous for the sick. When *Konzentrationslager* (KL) Lublin (also known as Majdanek) was aban-doned in April 1944, those Jews who were not shot were transported to Auschwitz. It took eight days to transport one group of 2,000 sick men, of whom 276 died through lack of water. On arrival, most of the survivors were left on the ground for four days while tattooing and regis-tration took place, but when the 300 girls arrived at Auschwitz who had been responsible for sorting the effects of those murdered at Majdanek, they were registered and gassed within hours. Several days later, it was found that two of the girls had been left off the list and had sought sanc-tuary in one of the women's barracks. They were immediately dragged out of their new barracks, shot and burned, while retaliation was meted out to the arrival clerks.[31]

Rudolf Höss, as Camp Commandant continued to oversee this geno-cide, which had, until he was recalled to Berlin on 11 November 1943, involved the murder of 1,265,000 victims. Asked later how he nourished his anti-Semitic views, Höss confirmed a diet of Göbbels' weekly rants in *Das Reich* and Rosenberg's *The Myth of the 20th Century*. Bizarrely, Höss had been groomed by his father for the priesthood, but had turned against him, sought refuge in the Nazi Party and climbed the SS ladder.[32] His replacement, *SS-Obersturmbannführer* Arthur Liebehenschel continued this foul mission and managed to account for a further 500,000 prisoners, before he was 'retired' on 8 May 1944.[33] Meanwhile, attempts by couriers, such as Jan Karski, to broadcast the Nazi crimes in the west, continued throughout the early months of 1944. Karski returned to the US at this time, and he was joined in the US by other couriers, such as Zdzisław Jeziorański ('Jan Nowak') and Tadeusz Chciuk-Celt, who brought further news of the Holocaust to the Allies. The leading American newspapers, the *Los Angeles Times, Washington Post* and *New York Herald Tribune*, all ran stories on 22 March 1944 about the slaughter inside Auschwitz.

Another source of information for the British about the Auschwitz region came from German POWs of Polish origin, who were held in Britain. When Hitler incorporated the western area of Poland into the Reich, a large number of Polish youths from the Katowice and Gleiwitz regions were put to work in German factories. When the Wehrmacht suffered critical manpower shortages in 1942, these young men were drafted into the German Army and saw active service, particularly in North Africa. Those who were captured by the Allies gave interesting, if rather dated information on IG Farben, as one British intelligence officer reported:

The bulk of the information concerns Poland and is partly out of date. It relates largely to the period during which the various works in question were still being built, and details of production are, therefore, rather meagre. On the other hand, there is a good amount of description of lay-outs, locations, working conditions, sources of supply of raw materials...they do fill in some gaps and provide certain confirmations we were waiting for.[34]

Ironically, it was the Allied interest in bombing the IG Farben complex that led to the first accidental aerial photographs of the Auschwitz camps in the spring of 1944. The Allied priority during this period of the war was the elimination of oil storage and synthetic oil plants, such as the IG Farben installations at Auschwitz, and on 4 April a break in cloud cover allowed Allied aircraft to photograph the area. Because of its extreme distance, and because the Farben plant had only recently reached full production, this area had not attracted much Allied interest before. It must also be remembered that the cameras on reconnaissance aircraft only carried film for approximately 150 shots, which only allowed for images in, and directly around, the target area. When these photographs were taken back for analysis, the Auschwitz camps could be seen in the clips leading up to the main series of Farben photographs, but agonisingly, were interpreted just as penal camps. At the time, these images were not analysed, and were ignored in the interests of the prime objective – the bombing of IG Farben, several miles away.[35]

One other potential source of information about Auschwitz, which appeared to be discounted by British intelligence, was the nearby British POW camp. Split into two separate sites, the nearest of which was barely half a mile from the Monowitz (Auschwitz III) penal camp, Camp E715 was home to about 600 prisoners. Included in the complement was Corporal Brian Bishop of the Royal Corps of Signals, who had been captured south of Tobruk in May 1942:

> After I was captured, I was handed over to the Italians and shipped to Italy. I was moved around various Italian POW camps, ending up in the north. When the Italians capitulated in September 1942, the Germans rounded us up and sent us off to Germany. I was then transferred from a transit camp to a working duties camp in Poland. Until I got there, I had no idea where Auschwitz was.
>
> I arrived at the British POW camp no. E715 in the winter of 1942/3. It was split into two camps with the POWs working in the nearby IG Farben (Buna-Werke) factory. We heard fairly soon that our camp was very close to one of the Auschwitz penal camps, known as Auschwitz III (Monowitz) and we were also across the town from Auschwitz I, and the extermination camp at Birkenau. In our section of the POW camp there must have been about 300 men who all worked at the factory welding flanges onto large pipes. In the mornings we were assembled, counted, searched and marched to the Farben factory under Wehrmacht guard. It must have been the SS or police guards who made periodic searches of our barracks.

We had one particularly nasty guard called 'Ritler' who controlled the daily parade. If anyone failed to appear, he would draw his pistol and fire at the barracks. One morning he shot a man who was still lying in bed. Ritler, however, seemed to respect bravery. We used to pin our regimental badges on our breast pockets as we weren't allowed caps. One man was with the King's Royal Rifle Corps and his badge was like a Maltese Cross. Much to our amusement, Ritler was strutting about one morning, saw the man and immediately thought it was the Victoria Cross and began saluting and congratulating the puzzled soldier. We heard later that Ritler ended his days on the Russian front.

At IG Farben, we worked in our army uniforms and did most of our work outside (in the winter it was −11°c). We worked in small gangs, often alongside the Jews from Auschwitz in their striped clothes. If they spoke English we managed to get into conversation with them. I persuaded one Jew who was a carpenter to carve me a wooden pistol in exchange for some barter. This he did, though I was never able to use it in an escape as all the exits were heavily patrolled. I also knew two Jews who were lawyers from Toulouse. One of them wore a ragged jersey over his stripes with the whole front missing. I managed to get him some material to repair it and he hid it in his trousers when he left the factory that day. The following day he did not appear for work. We heard that on his return to Auschwitz, he had been searched and even the possession of spare material was a crime. We heard he was put into solitary confinement in a tiny cellar.

There were lighter moments. On the return from the factory one day, I noticed the man in front of me was always out of step, sort of waddling along and I nearly tripped over him. When we were searched, the German guards found that he had a dead duck down his trousers, swinging between his legs. He was told to explain himself and we thought he was 'for it'. There was a pond in the grounds of the factory and it appears that he crept up on a duck and managed to kill it. Anyway, he told the guards with a straight face that he was minding his own business and working away when the duck had attacked him and he had to kill it in self-defence. Unbelievably, the guards started laughing and said he could keep it.

Each morning you could hear the Monowitz orchestra strike up and you knew that the prisoners were being played out of the camp for work. The columns of Jews would arrive with 'Capos' controlling and sometimes beating them. One Capo, who was better than most, was a German criminal who had been jailed for murder in 1923 and when he was let out in 1942, he thought he had served his sentence. But no, he was not let out, but sent to Auschwitz to work as a 'Capo'. This must have been typical of many of them.[36]

Although officially it was forbidden for Jews to speak to the British POWs in the Buna-Werke factory, there were snatched opportunities when Capos were absent. Paul Steinberg, a Jewish prisoner who spoke fluent English, translated German war bulletins to keep British prisoners updated:

> I did it once too often. The Capo caught me and took me aside.
> 'You know, don't you, that this is strictly prohibited?'
> 'Yes', I admitted, looking contrite.
> 'What did you tell them?'
> 'I translated the bulletin for them'.
> 'And they, what did they say?'
> 'They thanked me'.
> 'What else did you say to them'.
> 'Nothing really. I only spent five minutes with them'.
> 'What did you write down?'
> 'Just the bulletin, in English. Nothing but the bulletin'.
> 'Who gave you a pencil?'
> 'They did'.
> He told me to follow him. I was starting to get worried. We both left the building where we worked and tramped for a long time through the factory. I told myself it wasn't possible – a Jewish Capo wouldn't hand me over to the SS. I was wrong. That's exactly what he did.[37]

There were chances for British POWs to help the 15,000 Jewish slave labourers who worked alongside them in the IG Farben factory. Sergeant-Major Charles Coward became known as 'The Count of Auschwitz' for his work in 1944 in saving Jews bound for the gas chambers. Coward, as an inmate of the E715 POW camp, knew that when Jewish prisoners from nearby Auschwitz III became sick or disabled, they were marched off to Birkenau to be gassed. In an ingenious plan, he bribed the guards and obtained a daily allocation of three Jewish corpses in stripes. Then, using outside help, he would rescue three men from the staggering column and lay the corpses beside the route, as if they had died on the march. With the meticulous record keeping of the SS, the total of those leaving and arriving tallied exactly and no suspicion arose, allowing Coward to organise the eventual rescue of over 400 Jews.[38] However, contacts between Jewish prisoners and British POWs were not always so fruitful, as Leon Grossman, a British Jew imprisoned in Monowitz in 1944, found to his cost:

> One day I saw a lot of British POWs in Farben. They said, 'you come and march out with us.' But how could I, with my face, my shaved head, my clothes. Whenever I could, I would speak to the POWs when my fore-man wasn't looking and say, 'keep on walking alongside me. I'm from London. Can you remember my name and where I live, to tell my family?' Suddenly, an SS man in civilian clothes, barked at me from behind. 'Why are you not with your Kommando?' I made an excuse. But the SS man went over to my foreman and said, 'that man has been talking to a British POW. Are you going to deal with it or am I?' So my foreman, called Abraham, says, 'I'll see to it.' He then hit me and I fell to the ground and then he kicked me. He said afterwards, 'I'm sorry I had to do that.'
>
> Another day, I saw a British POW going into the lavatories and I thought I would get a message to him. I followed him in and told him I was from London and had he any cigarettes. He simply said, 'Here, you and I are both prisoners, but in England it's the Jews who run the black markets.' And then he walked away.[39]

Despite the near total control that the SS exerted over camp inmates, a resistance movement survived within the complex. Witold Pilecki was one legendary figure in a movement that survived numerous SS attempts to crush it. The brief of the resistance movement within the camps included the recording of Nazi atrocities for later recriminations, as well as the organisation of food supplies and the care of the sick. There was also the business of eliminating informers. But any ideas of upris-ings or break-outs could only be contemplated with outside help from the AK, and to this end, a secret transmitter, which had been built by inmates and hidden in a cellar beneath a typhus infested block, sent out messages to the AK's Silesian District. The SS never found the trans-mitter, despite ripping up all the floorboards and tapping the walls, and its messages continued to reach the outside world and the AK's special Section for Jewish Affairs. This section, headed by Henryk Woliński, coordinated financial assistance to the Jews, as well as establishing contacts between the AK and Jewish military groups, both inside and outside the Auschwitz camps.[40]

But what outside military support would be forthcoming even if the prisoners could rebel? It was encouraging to learn that there were several AK formations within a fifteen-mile radius of Auschwitz, but most were small and by the winter of 1943–44, only the *Sosienki* group could claim to field over 100 men. Further away, the AK command in Kraków could muster a larger group but the overriding problem was lack of weapons and explosives. The *Sosienski* only boasted a dozen rifles and pistols, together with 20 grenades and the same number of Sten-guns, which had been dropped by the British. Escapees from Auschwitz would find support among these bands in the Beskid Hills, just south of the town, but the underground did not have the power to launch an assault against the machine-gun emplacements, watch-towers and mine-fields that surrounded the concentration camps. Furthermore, the AK knew from bitter experience that any attacks on SS units attached to the camp garrison would result in brutal reprisals against camp inmates.[41]

In order to preserve the Polish coal mines for German industry, local Poles were not expelled from Silesia, so any escapee from Auschwitz could certainly still find local Poles prepared to help. But he would have to reach them in the first place and in Birkenau many prisoners were riddled with disease and could hardly walk, let alone run and escape guard dogs.

By the summer of 1944, with the prospect of the arrival of Soviet forces, concern arose that the Germans might well attempt to destroy all physical evidence of Auschwitz, together with the reported 45,000 remaining prisoners.[42] The AK despatched Second Lieutenant Stefan Jasieński ('Urban'), one of the *cichociemni*, to investigate German intentions. He arrived in the Bielsko region and established contacts with AK units who were making plans to storm Auschwitz in the event of a countrywide uprising. He was gaining intelligence on German intentions for Auschwitz, when he was arrested at Kęty, and interned in Auschwitz I. Word came out of the camp that, despite brutal interrogation, Jasieński refused to give away any intelligence and perished in the camp some time after December 1944.[43] Nevertheless, the AK were able to put together a last-ditch rescue plan for Birkenau, which envisaged the AK attackers rescuing only some 300 prisoners while the remainder would have to make their own escape. Even if the attack was successful in breaching the camp's defences, expected casualties among the inmates would be huge. In the meantime, Jasieński's reports prior to his arrest had at last stirred action in the Allied camp, though the Polish Government-in-exile's response was hardly dynamic:

> The Polish Government are of the opinion that a joint declaration by His Britannic Majesty's Government and the Government of the United States of America warning the Germans against carrying out such murders on the prisoners at Oswięcim, under threat of the gravest consequences, might restrain the German authorities from proceeding with their monstrous plan.[44]

Draft statements for the British Government were then bounced around various Foreign Office departments, with some advisers cautioning, 'There is no use in reciting the past barbarities of the Germans in these matters: it only stiffens their attitude.' And the reaction in the United States was barely urgent, with the British Ambassador, Lord Halifax reporting that the US Government would reply with a declaration 'but doubt it will have much effect, though it would be a way of demonstrating Unites States solidarity with the Polish Government in London'.[45]

While escapees from Auschwitz could expect help from local Poles, Jewish escapees from camps in eastern Poland faced an uncertain reception from local civilians. Sometimes the ex-prisoners would be sheltered, while at other times they might be turned into the German authorities by civilians exercising 'simple greed and a desire to demonstrate loyalty to the occupation regime'. But there was always the threat of retribution, which hung over any effort to shelter Jews. Given that it usually took about ten people to organise the sheltering of one Jew, in the event of exposure there could be wide-scale executions. And the fact that large numbers of Polish Jews had never assimilated into Polish society before the war, with many speaking only Yiddish, meant that they found it difficult to merge inconspicuously into Gentile households.[46]

Michael Zylberberg, a Jew in hiding in Warsaw had an extraordinary encounter with a Gestapo officer who told him how to survive detection. The officer advised:

> How was it possible to pick out one suspect in a teeming, crowded street? The reply was simple. 'First of all, shave off your Polish-type moustache! All Jews in hiding try to pass as Poles and think that a moustache is the answer. That is ridiculous. Secondly, you should clean your shoes every day. You can always recognise Jews by their filthy shoes. Particularly, in streets like Marszalkowska and Kredytowa.[47]

Sue Ryder, who had numerous contacts with Poles through SOE, and spent many years in their country after the war, knew that many Poles went to great lengths to protect Jews:

> The Poles and their relations with Jews – I think many comments are unfair. There was certainly some anti-Semitism in Poland before the war. The Jews were very successful and perhaps, because they were a minority, irritated the Poles. I think it was disgraceful though that some Israelis should not give credit to those Poles who risked their lives for Jews. For example there were convents near the Jewish ghettos that hid Jewish children. Those convents which were discovered, were annihilated by the Germans. I can think of countless Poles who hid Jews. It is a pity that these many acts of heroism shown by ordinary Poles have been overshadowed by the acts of a minority.[48]

For some Poles, sheltering Jews had horrific consequences:

> A Polish woman, mother of two children, took a Jewish baby and kept it with her own children. The baby's parents, who had been living in the same house, had implored her to do so. The Polish mother felt she could not refuse, and took the child, keeping its origin a close secret. But it did leak out, and one day, two Gestapo men appeared at the flat and asked to see the children. The mother said there was only the little one at home, the two others were at school. The Germans answered quietly that they would wait for the children to return. In the meantime, they talked with the mother while the baby played on the floor. After about half an hour, the older children, a boy of six and a girl of five burst into the room.

The Gestapo men took out their revolvers and shot both children on the spot. At the door they turned back and said to the mother, 'Now you can bring up your Jewish brat alone' and walked out.[49]

The Commandant of Auschwitz, Rudolf Höss, came back to take over the liquidation of Hungarian Jews in the summer of 1944 – a frenzy that resulted in a further 300,000 deaths.[50] Following the German occupation of Hungary in March 1944, the first of the Hungarian Jewish transports arrived at Birkenau on 15 May and each day, some 15,000 Jews were offloaded, of whom 90% were immediately gassed and burned, while the remaining 10% were admitted, without tattoos, to the camp. Höss travelled backwards and forwards to Budapest to ensure the transports continued, while his former adjutant, *SS-Hauptsturmführer* Josef Kramer supervised the slaughter at Birkenau. Among those deported in the round-up of Hungarian Jews was a 47-year-old Glaswegian woman, Jane Haining. She was a Scottish missionary working in Budapest in a Church of Scotland Mission, which had included Jewish children. When she refused to leave her wards during the round-ups, she was deported with them to Auschwitz in May 1944. Separated from them on arrival, she was reportedly gassed with a group of Hungarian women on 16 August 1944.[51]

On 4 July 1944, as the furnaces raged, a detailed report on activities at Auschwitz reached the Foreign Office. It was written by two escapees, Rudolph Vrba and Alfred Wetzler, and clearly stated the enormity of the Nazi crimes, together with details of the starvation, gassing and burning of prisoners, as well as naming certain SS guards.[52] Above all, the report confirmed that Birkenau was not just an extension of the penal camp Auschwitz I, but a full-blown extermination camp.

As the Hungarian transports continued relentlessly throughout May, the Allies received the news that over 400,000 Hungarian Jews had already been deported to Auschwitz. Then on 6 July 1944 Anthony Eden received a deputation from the Jewish Agency for Palestine, an organisation that liaised with the British in the mandated territory. The Agency had always enjoyed a stormy relationship with the British Government, especially over restrictions on Jewish immigration to Palestine. Caving in to Arab pressure, the pre-war British Government had passed legislation capping the Jewish population in the territory at 75,000, and even with the Holocaust under way, such restrictions were still rigorously enforced.

However, the purpose of the latest Jewish deputation, headed by Chaim Weizmann, was to convince the British Government that they needed to buy time on the deportations; and the only way to do this was to play with a Nazi proposal to exchange trucks or gold for Jews.

The Agency also wanted pressure put on the Swiss and other neutral governments to accept Jewish refugees, while attempts should be made by the Allies to bomb extermination plants in the Auschwitz camps, as well as the railway lines between Budapest and Auschwitz. Weizmann wanted pressure applied simultaneously by Stalin. While Eden had no time for 'dealing' with the Nazis over the Jews, he immediately issued a memo to Churchill requesting action. The British Prime Minister, who had always stridently opposed anti-Semitism, instructed Eden to act in all haste.[53] Churchill had a long record of supporting the Jews, going back to his criticism of the French anti-Semitic campaign in the 1898 Dreyfus case, as well as his opposition to the Conservative Government's Aliens Bill in 1904. In 1921, he had spoken in the House of Commons in favour of Jewish land purchase in Palestine and more recently in 1940 had opposed the Chamberlain Government's restrictions on such purchases. He was intolerant of anti-Semitic views in the Armed Forces and proposed the removal of those officers in the Middle East who espoused such views.[54]

But for all Churchill's enthusiasm, it was the Foreign Office that determined the speed of the British response. In a draft letter of 13 July suggesting bi-lateral action, which was intended for Stalin, an FO official appended, 'I don't think this will do much good, but no doubt we must go through the motions.'[55] And Eden was fast losing patience with Sir Archibald Sinclair and the British Air Ministry, who replied to his requests for Allied bombing of the rail lines and gas chambers with the suggestion that 'it might be ineffective and even if the plant was destroyed, we are not clear that it would really help the victims.' Eden wrote beside this comment, 'He wasn't asked his opinion of this; he was asked to act.'[56] Throughout August, a welter of correspondence between the Air Ministry and the Foreign Office concerning correct procedures and 'clarification', submerged Eden's fresh impetus. As a memo indicated, it was British bureaucracy at its worst:

If in fact further information about the German's intentions in that particular camp has caused the Secretary of State for Foreign Affairs to revise his opinion, it will be necessary for him to inform the Secretary of

State for Air who will, no doubt, then modify or rescind the instructions which he has issued to Air Staff.[57]

Eden instructed the Air Ministry to carry out air reconnaissance as a prelude to bombing, but the Ministry delayed, stating that reconnaissance could not proceed without 'topographical information' on Birkenau from the Foreign Office – information, which officials conceded, was never ever received.[58] The Air Ministry's reluctance to act was not without foundation. They argued that to be effective, the raids would have to be constantly repeated as the Germans could normally repair railway lines within days. Furthermore, while flying as far as Poland, now feasible in 1944 due to the acquisition of Italian air bases, bombers usually had to forego fighter escorts for part of the dangerous mission. But the Air Ministry seemed ignorant of the fact that US aircraft had already flown as far as Auschwitz in April, taking reconnaissance photographs for anticipated bombing raids on IG Farben. A further batch of photographs were taken of the area on 26 June, clearly showing the three Auschwitz camps, but again their true purpose was not identified (the aerial photographs in the US archives were only annotated by the CIA in the 1970s). Even if the means were allocated to bomb the camps, hitting small targets within the camp, such as gas chambers or crematoria from a bombing height of perhaps 20,000 ft, without destroying the camp population, was expecting a lot (a large proportion of WWII bombs did not even fall within ½ a mile of their target).

On the same day that the Jewish Agency had met with Eden, the Hungarian Government, who had become fearful of Allied reprisals, finally stopped the deportation of Jews. This news reached the British Foreign Office, where officials seemed satisfied that this meant an end to all European deportations to Auschwitz:

> According to our reports, there has been a slackening in Jewish persecution and apparently a slackening and probably a cessation of deportations. It was therefore considered inadvisable (if the news regarding deportations could be verified) to pursue the proposal to bomb the camps, with the Air Ministry.[59]

Dr Weizman was the next to receive the disappointing news, though all mention of 'materials of vital importance at this critical stage of the war' not being diverted to help the Jews, was deleted from the final Foreign Office letter.[60] In the end, the news about the cessation of Hungarian deportations was pounced on by both the Air Ministry and Foreign Office as the excuse for inaction. However, British relief at the cessation of Hungarian deportations was premature. Unbeknown to them, during August, transports continued to arrive at Auschwitz from France, Rhodes and the Łódź ghetto, and the majority of arrivals were gassed immediately. Furthermore, there was at least one case where Adolf Eichmann, the SS Transport Administrator, arranged covert transportations of Jews, against the orders of the Hungarian Government. The early days of September saw the overthrow of the Horthy Government in Hungary and, with the return of the Gestapo, the deportations recommenced.

However, it was the advance into Poland by the Red Army that would finally ensure the release of concentration camp prisoners. On 23 July 1944, the Eighth Guards Army of the Soviet Union came across the first of the *Aktion-Reinhard* camp sites at Majdanek. The writer, Vasily Grossman, witnessed the scenes and spoke to the few survivors:

> A carpenter from Warsaw, Max Levit, survived. He was wounded and lay under the corpses of his comrades until it was dark, and then he crawled into the forest. He told us how, when he was already lying in the trench, he heard the team of thirty boys from the camp sing the song 'My Motherland is Vast' just before their execution. He heard how one of the boys shouted 'Stalin will avenge us.' He heard how the leader of the boys, the camp favourite, red-haired Leib, who fell down into the trench after the salvo, lifted himself a little and asked: 'Papa guard, you've missed. Please could you do it once again, one more time?'[61]

The camp at Majdanek, on the outskirts of Lublin was about 600 acres in size, with 144 barracks, accommodating approximately 30,000 prisoners. Like Auschwitz, it comprised both penal camp and extermination camp and according to survivors, was every bit as brutal:

> At the evening parade a list of the internees who had worked 'badly' was read to the SS men on duty, and they were beaten with straps, sticks and birches on a special bench. 25 or more blows were given and people were frequently beaten to death. Women were subjected to the same indignities and tortures. The chief supervisor Erich and the supervisors Braunstein, Anni, Devid, Weber, Knoblik, Ellert and Redli, all SS women, were distinguished by their cruelty. One witness stated that he saw the head of the cremato-

rium burn one Polish woman alive. Other witnesses stated that they had seen children taken from their mothers and killed in front of them.[62]

In addition to the Soviet journalists who soon rushed to Majdanek, there were two journalists from the west, H. W. Lawrence of *The New York Times* and Alexander Werth, a naturalised British war correspondent who had been based in the Soviet Union throughout the war. Within a month, Lawrence's report appeared in *Time* magazine but Werth's was buried in the September issue of *Christian Science Monitor*, probably untouched by leading London newspapers because of his notorious pro-Soviet sympathies.[63] A day later, Soviet forces arrived at Treblinka to find some parts of the small penal camp (Treblinka I) still intact, but little trace of the remains of the death camp at nearby Treblinka II. Evidence had already been obliterated the previous year, together with the other death camps at Bełżec and Sobibór, so that when Red Army troops arrived, they had little comprehension of the scale of the crimes. At Bełżec, the SS had destroyed everything and having buried the evidence, built a new manor house over the top of it. When Soviet troops arrived, they found a former SS auxiliary posing as a 'farmer' tilling his fields.

The British public's response to the discovery of these death camps was muted. Little news reached the west and even the discovery of the partially intact Majdanek camp hardly registered with the British public, consumed with news of events in Normandy. Even to the Jewish people at the time, the scale of the Holocaust was unimaginable. There were lessons of genocide from history such as the Armenian massacres during the Great War, but the Jews had nothing in their history with which to compare the 'Final Solution'. For many Jews in the west, it was beyond their comprehension. Even those within yards of the gas chambers could not imagine their fate. And if they could not understand the scale of the crime, it would have taken a huge leap in imagination for the mandarins of Whitehall to contemplate such genocide.

NOTES

[1] Zamoyski, op. cit., p. 359.
[2] Lukowski, op. cit., p. 260. Hitler's instigation of the Holocaust is discussed in Ian Kershaw, *Fateful Choices: Ten Decisions That Changed the World* (Allen Lane, London 2007).

[3] In 1940, von dem Bach officially dropped Zelewski from his surname. On 9 November 1941, he was promoted to *SS Obergruppenführer* and General of the SS. For von dem Bach's career, see his testimony, 7 January 1946, *The Trial of German Major War Criminals by the International Military Tribunal, Part 4*, HMSO 1947.

[4] For reports on Jewish deportations and massacres, see The *Jewish Chronicle*, 16 January 1942; The *Daily Telegraph*, 25 June 1942; *The Times*, 10 July 1942; The *Manchester Guardian*, 27 October 1942. On 25 November 1942, The *New York Times* specifically mentioned Treblinka, Bełżec and Sobibór. For BBC, see 'General Directive', 25 June 1942, BBC Written Archives Centre, Reading.

[5] G.M. Gilbert, op. cit., p. 150.

[6] Auschwitz I initially contained Polish political prisoners (some of whom happened to be Jews), together with some German criminals. From mid-1941, prisoners from occupied countries were brought into the camp, and by mid-1942, Jewish prisoners were moved to Birkenau. For details of movements, see Henryk Świebocki (Ed.), *London Has Been Informed: Reports by Auschwitz Escapees* (The Auschwitz-Birkenau State Museum, Oświęcim 2002), pp. 136–7.

[7] IG Farben was an extremely large and profitable concern. One of its subsidiary companies, Degesch manufactured 'Zyklon B' the infamous cyanide-based insecticide used in the gas chambers.

[8] Martin Gilbert, *Auschwitz and the Allies* (Michael Joseph, London 1981), pp. 51, 54.

[9] Janek Lasocki to Author, 17 October 2007.

[10] For further details of German Police units, see Gordon Williamson, *World War II German Police Units*, (Osprey, Oxford 2006). Also, Sue Rhyder, op. cit., p. 627; also Gerald Reitlinger, *The SS. Alibi of a Nation 1922-1945* (Lionel Leventhal, London 1981), pp. 262–88.

[11] It is estimated that at least 750,000 people perished at the death camp Treblinka II, including the four-months-pregnant Bula Liebling, mother of Roman Polanski. Polanski later became a famous film director and immortalised the wartime sufferings in Warsaw in his film *The Pianist*.

[12] Józef Garliński, *Fighting Auschwitz: The Resistance Movement in the Concentration Camp* (Fontana, London 1976), pp. 170–1. For Polish overseers, see Świebocki op. cit., pp. 140–1.

[13] Paul Steinberg, *Speak You Also* (Allen Lane, London 2001), p. 42. Josef Mengele was known as the 'Angel of Death'. As one of the camp's physicians, he carried out numerous human experiments on gypsy children and dwarfs. He also experimented with sterilisation, killing many patients with shock. After the war, he escaped to Argentina, and later died in Brazil in 1979, having escaped trial.

[14] Świebocki, op. cit., pp. 146–7.

[15] The slaughter of inmates also generated financial benefits for the SS. Currency, diamonds and other valuables were all extracted for SS coffers. Clothes and materials were sent to Germany. Hair shaved from the arrivals and those subsequently gassed was collected and processed by German companies for bedding and upholstery. Examples of this human misery, together with piles of labelled suitcases can be seen at the Auschwitz-Birkenau State Museum.

[16] Kitty Hart-Moxon, ref. 16632, IWM Sound Archive. The SS man, later identified as Gottfried Weise, was only finally brought to trial in 1988, when Hart-Moxon, with others, testified against him. Weise was released from prison in 1997 and died in 2000.

[17] Stanisław Kłodziński, 'Maria Stromberger' in *The Medical Review*, 1962. An extraordinary photograph album belonging to the camp commandant's adjutant, showing SS guards relaxing at Solahütte, has recently been acquired by the USHMM, see www.ushmm.org.

[18] In particular, Churchill's speech of 24 August 1941. For British reports on verbatim German Police messages, see series HW 16/6, 16/16 and 16/32, NA. These decodes were not released into the public domain until 1997. For Churchill see, Martin Gilbert, *Churchill and the Jews* (Simon & Schuster, London 2007), p. 309.

[19] Richard Breitman, *Official Secrets: What the Nazis Planned. What the British and Americans Knew* (Allen Lane, London 1998), pp. 110–11. Although the German cypher codes for the Order Police were decoded at Bletchley Park, they were not part of the Enigma system.

[20] Bór-Komorowski, op. cit., pp. 150–1.

[21] This was not the first report of the Nazi atrocities. Stories concerning the activities of the *Einsatzgruppen* and the gassing of Jews at Chełmno had already reached London via the left-wing Jewish Bund in May 1942.

[22] E. Thomas Wood, op. cit., pp. 170–2, 196–215.

[23] A copy of this report lies in the Yad Vashem Archive, ref 0-67, Jerusalem. See M. Gilbert, op. cit., pp. 130–1.

[24] For a detailed analysis of the Warsaw Ghetto Rising, see Israel Gutman, *Resistance: Warsaw Ghetto Uprising* (Houghton Mifflin, Boston 1998). One picture, more than any other, symbolises the cruelty of the Warsaw Ghetto. It is the photograph of a terrified little boy, with his hands up in front of German soldiers. The boy has been possibly identified as Tsvi Nussbaum, who was arrested with his aunt in July 1943. Miraculously, he survived the war and emigrated to the US.

[25] US Department of State press release, 28 August 1943, No. 362, FO 371/34551, NA.

[26] R Allen to W Cavendish-Bentinck, 27 August 1943, FO 371/34551, NA.

[27] Memo, V. Cavendish-Bentinck, 27 August 1943, FO 371/34551, NA. The 1917 scare story concerning 'body boiling' was run by *The Times* and the *Evening News* on 19 April 1917 and stated that the Germans were rendering the bodies of war casualties to produce fat. It arose from the mistranslation of the German word *Kadaver* as 'human corpses', which should have been translated as animal carcasses.

[28] Patrick Howarth, *Intelligence Chief Extraordinary: The Life of the Ninth Duke of Portland* (The Bodley Head, London 1986), p. 149. Cavendish-Bentinck succeeded as 9th Duke of Portland on the death of his brother in 1980. He died in 1990.

[29] Michael Elkins, *Forged in Fury* (Piatkus, Loughton 1981), p. 115 and Garliński, *Auschwitz* op. cit., p. 86.

[30] Świebocki, op. cit., pp. 16–24. Both men later joined elements of the AK. Tabeau was later wounded, while Cieliczko was killed in action in 1944. Witold Pilecki's extraordinary story is told in Garliński, *Fighting Auschwitz* op. cit., and MRD Foot, *Six Faces of Courage* (Leo Cooper, Barnsley 2003).

[31] Świebocki, op. cit., p. 278.

[32] G.M. Gilbert, op. cit., p. 160.

[33] Because the majority of Nazi records for the camp were destroyed, estimates for deaths varied widely. See Świebocki, op. cit., pp. 272–3 for sources of statistics.

[34] 'Notes on Interrogation of 173 Prisoners of War of Polish Origin', MEW Report January 1944, FO 371/39449, NA.

[35] For an analysis of the reconnaissance photos of 4 April and 26 June 1944, see Dino Brugioni and Robert Poirer, 'The Holocaust Revisited: A Retrospective Analysis of the Auschwitz-Birkenau Extermination Complex' in www.globalsecurity.org.

[36] Brian Bishop to author, 10 April 2007.

[37] Steinberg, op. cit., p. 113.

[38] Bernard Williamson, op. cit. Coward was the first Englishman to be accorded the honour of a tree planted in his name in the Avenue of Righteous Gentiles, Yad Vashem Memorial, Jerusalem, in 1960.

[39] Leon Grossman, ref. 9274, IWM Sound Archive.

[40] There were fewer than 1000 Jews within the actual ranks of the AK.

[41] Garliński, *Fighting Auschwitz*, op. cit., p. 152, 232.

[42] Telegram from 'McMillan' to Foreign Office, 29 September 1944, FO 371/39453, NA.

[43] Jasieński left some distinctive carvings on the back of his wooden cell door, in Block 11, which can still be seen today.

44 Tadeusz Romer to Sir Owen O'Malley, 18 September 1944, FO 371/39453, NA.

45 Halifax to Foreign Office, 8 October 1944, FO 371/39454, NA.

46 For collaboration see Leonid Rein, 'Local Collaboration in the Execution of the 'Final Solution' in Nazi-occupied Byelorussia', in *Holocaust and Genocide Studies*, Vol. 20, Number 3, Winter 2006. For problems in hiding see Richard C. Lukas, *Forgotten Holocaust: The Poles under German Occupation 1939–1944* (Hippocrene Books, New York 2005), pp. 143–4.

47 Michael Zylberberg, *A Warsaw Diary 1939-1945* (Vallentine Mitchell, London 1969), pp. 152–3.

48 Sue Ryder, 1987, ref 10057, Sound Archive, IWM.

49 T. Bór-Komorowski, op. cit., pp. 103–4.

50 Having set this massacre in motion, Höss was relieved on 29 July by 33-year-old *SS Sturmbannführer* Richard Baer. Under Baer's rule, a further 500,000 were to perish between May 1944 and the camp's liberation. The Germans attempted to extract a large consignment of trucks from the Allies, in return for the lives of the Hungarian Jews. The trucks were purportedly for use on the Eastern Front but it was a hollow gesture as Höss was already in place at Auschwitz to receive his Hungarian human consignment.

51 It has been estimated that a further six Scotsmen and women died in Auschwitz.

52 The full contents of this report can be seen as 4951/duv/44, 4 July 1944, in FO 371/42809, NA.

53 For the proposals to the Swiss Government, see Berne draft, 11 July 1944, FO 371/42809, NA. For Eden's memo to Churchill, see Eden to Prime Minister, 6 July 1944, AP/20/11/499, Lord Avon Papers, UB. For Churchill's response see Winston Churchill to British Ambassador in Washington (Halifax), 9 July 1944, AP20/11/528A, Avon Papers, UB.

54 Sir Martin Gilbert in *The Spectator*, 30 March 2007; see also Sir Martin Gilbert, *Churchill and the Jews* (Simon & Schuster, London 2007).

55 A.W.G. Randall to 'Private Secretary', 13 July 1944, FO 371/42809, NA.

56 Air Ministry to Eden, 15 July 1944, FO 371/42809, NA.

57 Air Commodore G.W.P. Grant to V. Cavendish-Bentinck, 13 August 1944, FO 371/42814, NA. See also voluminous FO correspondence during August 1944 in same file, including letters between FO Refugee Dept and Jewish Agency.

58 R. Allen to V. Cavendish-Bentinck, 22 September 1944, FO 371/42806, NA.

59 Foreign Office 'Note for the Secretary of State, 25 August 1944, FO 371/42814, NA.

60 Draft FO letter to Dr Weizman, 25 August 1944, FO 371/42814, NA.

61 Quoted in Anthony Beevor and Luba Vinogradova (Eds.), *A Writer at War. Vasily Grossman with the Red Army 1941–1945* (The Harvill Press, London 2005),

pp. 282–3. See also Corine Ducey, 'The Representation of the Holocaust in the Soviet Press, Literature and Film 1941–1968', in *East European Jewish Affairs*, Vol 36, Issue 2, December 2006.

[62] 'Statement by the Polish-Soviet Extraordinary Commission for the Investigation of German Atrocities at Majdanek', 16 September 1944, FO 371/39454, NA.

[63] *Time*, 21 August 1944; *Christian Science Monitor*, 18 September 1944. See Jon Bridgeman, *The End of the Holocaust: The Liberation of the Camps* (BT Batsford, London 1990), p. 20.

Chapter Five

SOE – A Lifeline?

In late May 1940, as France collapsed, the British Government sanctioned the creation of a Special Operations Executive (SOE). This was in response to the increasing reliance that Britain would have to place on 'home-grown' subversion in occupied Europe. In fact, at a time when resources for defeating the Wehrmacht in open battle were extremely limited, subversion ranked with bombing and blockade as one of the three major weapons at Britain's disposal. However, Britain's Chiefs of Staff realised that the success of nationalist uprisings would still hinge on Britain's ability to reinforce and re-supply such revolts by air, and if necessary, by sea. Co-ordination with nationalist forces would be a further problem, but in this period before the successful Soviet land battles in the winter of 1941–2, and before the entry of the United States into the war, assisting subversion became 'official British strategic doctrine'.

SOE did not have an easy birth and in its first year there was conflict with government ministries, notably the Ministry of Information, as well as the Foreign Office, to whom SIS was also responsible. SOE had, after all, been created out of three existing organisations; 'Section D' from SIS, 'Electra House', a propaganda unit from the Foreign Office, and MI(R), a sabotage research section from the War Office. SOE came under the control of the Minister for Economic Warfare (initially Sir Hugh Dalton), who maintained an uneasy relationship with the patrician Foreign Secretary, Anthony Eden. Rivalry and mistrust existed at all levels, particularly between senior, professional SIS officers and their 'amateur' counterparts in SOE.[1] After the SIS station evacuated Paris in 1940, it set up a separate P5 (Production) section under Wilfred Dunderdale to handle Polish affairs. The Foreign Secretary was determined that there should be no merging of SIS (for whom he was ultimately responsible) and SOE. He was adamant that the former should remain a separate, professional service whereas he felt SOE was always a temporary, amateur unit brought together for wartime expediency.[2] The armed services were also suspicious of SOE, who they felt were the creation of a civil authority in London and who were controlled directly by a government minister. Yet, although there was widespread friction, SOE could never have expanded to the force it became without the impetus of the War Office or SIS.[3]

SOE had a lot of ground to make up in Poland. Blitzkrieg in the summer of 1940 had destroyed most networks and British intelligence contacts in Western Europe, and those agents who remained in the Balkans, Hungary and Greece were soon compromised by German occupation. It was often down to individuals, such as Krystyna Skarbek ('Christine Granville', who would only later join SOE) to run the gauntlet of border guards in the Tatra Mountains to bring out Polish fighters, as well as Allied airmen on the run.[4] Dropping agents into Poland by parachute had, on the whole, produced better results. The first Polish drop took place in February 1941, and during the last quarter of 1941 SOE dispatched seventy-nine agents from airfields in Cambridgeshire into occupied Europe, including fifteen into Poland. This escalated over the next few years to a total of 316 agents and couriers dropped into Poland, as well as a further seventeen Poles parachuted into Yugoslavia, Greece and Albania. But of these, a total of 109 were killed or tortured to death by the Gestapo.[5] The BBC played their part in such clandestine operations, often inserting code-words into news bulletins to be picked up in occupied countries, though the familiar tones of Big Ben were no longer 'live'; recordings were played every hour, so that German Air Intelligence could not detect the weather in London at a particular time by the resonance of the bells.

The early concept of SOE inspiring and supporting large-scale insurrections was abandoned during 1940–1, as the organisation's role as 'a great strategic player' diminished. Furthermore, the entry into the war of the Soviet Union and the United States, with their vast conventional firepower, meant that SOE would now be restricted to supporting sabotage operations, albeit on a wide scale.

The US had their own clandestine organisation called the Office of Strategic Services (OSS), which was formed in July 1942. In many ways it was a sister organisation to SOE, but its brief was wider and included not only the use of guerrilla operations in support of the regular armed forces, but also the collection of all intelligence relating to 'national security'. While SOE and OSS operated in tandem in some European countries via their own Special Forces HQ (SFHQ), notably in France during and after the Normandy landings, most worldwide responsibilities were split geographically.[6]

While their US counterparts were allowed a certain amount of slack, SOE found themselves pinched not only by their subordination to the Chiefs of Staff, but also by the sheer lack of available resources. By early 1943, its finances and manpower had marginally improved, but the vision of its senior commanders such as Brigadier (later Major-General) Colin Gubbins that it should assist home-grown revolts in occupied countries by vast airborne drops, was not encouraged by either the Chiefs of Staff or the Air Ministry. Poland as well as Norway and Czechoslovakia were all identified as the most likely countries for wide-scale revolt, but to support such risings would have required virtually all the resources of Bomber Command. This was clearly an unacceptable gamble, for Britain's strategic bombing offensive was continuing to show the British people that the offensive was being carried into Germany. Any detraction from that goal was deemed undesirable.[7]

Since December 1940, SOE had always contained a Polish Section, which dealt with operations inside Poland's historic borders. This section was in turn part of a regional group comprising 'Poland, Czechoslovakia and Hungary'. The Poles were also represented by an SOE section that looked after Polish minorities in occupied Europe. Initially run by the dapper Major Ronald Hazell and known as the European Polish Minorities Section, or 'EU/P', it aimed to help and organise Polish resistance fighters outside their mother country, particularly in areas such as north-east France. The area around Lille, an important mining area of France, had seen particularly large Polish immigration between the wars, and after the Fall of France it was estimated that some 250,000 Poles still remained in the region. Major Hazell and his EU/P Section spent a long time trying to harness this manpower for subversion purposes under Operations 'MONIKA' and 'BARDSEA', but political meddling, Gestapo penetration and conflict with Poland's home-grown

'Secret Army in France' (POWN) neutered its potential. In addition to these SOE assisted operations, a large number of Poles fought with the French resistance.[8]

There had always been a close affinity between SOE personnel and the Poles. The first Minister for Economic Warfare, Hugh Dalton was resolute in his defence of Poland, writing to Basil Liddell Hart in 1939, 'I like the Poles and I would rather, if there must be war with Germany, have Poland active and armed and on the same side.'[9] Dalton, never a modest man, noted in his diary, 'They say that I am regarded by the Poles as their best friend in England, and that my name is known and loved throughout the Underground.' Churchill never liked Dalton, who hoped SOE would be a tool for social revolution in Europe and had been levered into the job by his fellow Labour Cabinet Ministers, so the Prime Minister was greatly pleased by his removal in April 1942.[10] Dalton's replacement was Roundell Palmer, 3rd Earl of Selborne, a good friend of Churchill's and politically on the right wing who, it was hoped, would push the SOE cause to the highest level. Dalton predictably thought him 'not to be very clever' but Selborne's appointment would certainly improve relations between SOE and the Foreign Office, soured in the past by a personal animosity between Dalton and Eden.[11]

Other senior figures in SOE also had good relations with the Poles. The Director of Operations for Western and Central Europe, Brigadier Colin Gubbins was a close confidant of General Sikorski, and knew Sikorski's inner circle, which included Major Victor Cazalet MP, and the adventurer Dr Józef Retinger. When Gubbins was appointed Chief of SOE in September 1943, he continued the good rapport with Sikorski's successor, Stanisław Mikołajczyk.

But good personal relations could only go so far in securing SOE help for the Poles. 1942 and 1943 saw SOE's flamboyant programme move towards a more realistic plan for resistance groups to be co-ordinated with Allied strategy. And Allied strategy, which was compelled to leave the Eastern Front to Stalin's designs, seemed to be offering Poland little more than symbolic support. This was due in part to the extreme logistical difficulties in dropping supplies, but more importantly, the War had moved on. The success and importance of the alliance with the Soviet Union was critical and British policy became shackled to the idea that Stalin's wrath should not be incurred by British assistance to a movement that he considered hostile. Yet, as planning for the Normandy landings in June 1944 began to take shape, there was hope amongst the Polish Government-in-exile that a Polish uprising could be linked to the opening of this second front. They believed that with this uprising they would obtain sustained Allied drops of supplies and Polish paratroops as well as the relocation, to a part-liberated Poland, of the Polish Air Force.[12]

Before the Soviet advance into Polish territory in early 1944, the strongest argument for assistance the Polish Government-in-exile could make to the Allies, was to point to the ability of the AK to hold down large numbers of German troops in the east. Writing to Lord Selborne on 23 October 1943, the Polish C-in-C, General Sosnkowski pressed his case:

> Even with the very limited support granted this Army [AK] up till now, its activities have forced the Germans to maintain a large number of armed forces in Poland. According to intelligence reports up to the 15th September, there were 710 Army, SS and SA battalions in Polish territory. In addition to this there are many base troops, aerodrome defence units, AA defence units etc., making a total of approximately half a million soldiers which the Germans have to maintain in Poland, most of them in the central provinces.[13]

General Sosnkowski lobbied Sir Archibald Sinclair as well as the Chief of the Imperial General Staff, General Alan Brooke to increase the number of special duties flights to Poland. He also concentrated on the new SOE Chief, Major-General Gubbins and other SOE officers, who encouraged Polish hopes of material support via their organisation. Sosnkowski was quick to remind Lord Selborne that Gubbins had confirmed the Poles could expect twelve flights on any night when weather conditions are favourable, 'and you should base your calculations on this'. On the basis of these forecasts Sosnkowski requested 250 supply flights for the quarter ended 31 December 1943 and a further 350 flights the following quarter. But this was only barely feasible if airfields in southern Italy could quickly come into operation, as regular missions from Britain using the old northern routes were unrealistic. However, less than 10% of these requested flights were ever carried out. Sosnkowski became desperate, pleading with Selborne:

> I wish to mention how difficult is my own position. It is not easy for me to tell my soldiers who have fought so long with great self-sacrifice and

courage against our common enemy that Great Britain, in the fifth year of
the war, is not in a position to allot a small number of aircraft for the support
of this Army [AK] in order to supply the means of continuing its fight.[14]

At a meeting of the War Cabinet's Defence Committee on 14 January
1944, Lord Selborne admitted that while the Allied Commander-in-Chief
effectively controlled SOE operations in most occupied European countries, Poland and Czechoslovakia were excluded. As the AK organised all
operations within Poland, SOE were excluded from planning missions
for Polish fieldwork and were only responsible for training agents, who
were then dropped into the country as reinforcements for the AK. In
short, SOE's brief was largely restricted to encouraging local acts of sabotage by the supply of equipment, arms and explosives. This equipment,
which was dropped in containers into Poland, came from both British
and Polish sources and was sorted at the RAF Packing Station at Henlow,
Bedfordshire.[15] This ensured that only stable materials were dispatched by
RAF aircraft and at the same time, SOE knew exactly what equipment
the Poles were sending to their homeland; otherwise, the British knew
little of what passed between the Polish Government-in-exile and their
resistance movement, and Allied Command continued to cast a covetous
eye over the Poles' own radio stations and secret cypher codes.

The occupied countries of Holland, Czechoslovakia and Norway all
had their own sections and like the Poles, carried out their operations in
their own countries, reporting back to their respective governments-in-
exile. But the Poles had one very important concession. They were the
only country allowed to keep their own cypher codes for radio communication – ciphers that were unknown to British code-breakers. This
policy, according to Sue Ryder, who worked for SOE, was supported by
Major-General Gubbins:

> General Gubbins was a remarkable man. He had a tremendously high
> regard for the Poles. He fought for every aircraft he could get and I'm sure
> that people in the Cabinet and Foreign Office couldn't stick his guts. He
> endorsed the Poles in keeping their own intelligence and signals and this
> further irritated them.[16]

Coded messages would come in from Poland to the Polish Radio station
at Stanmore, in north London and would then be transmitted to the

Polish Cypher Office in central London. There they were de-cyphered, translated and despatched to either the Polish II Bureau for onward transmission to SIS, or the Polish VI (Special) Bureau, who would pass on items they considered of interest to SOE. Consequently, SOE, whose normal communications remit only extended to training wireless operators or providing equipment, formed a close relationship with the VI Bureau.[17] The Poles were wise to retain this independence. For quite apart from the uncertainty of where the British-Soviet relationship was heading, SOE had hardly exhibited tight control over their existing fiefdom. It was only in the latter part of 1943 that they discovered that the organisation they had set up in Holland had been thoroughly penetrated by the Germans, at a terrible cost.[18]

By 1944, Major-General Colin Gubbins (acronym 'CD') and his Vice-Chief, Henry Sporborg ('V/CD'), a partner in the London City firm of solicitors Slaughter & May, headed the council of SOE. The organisation now consisted of a number of Directorates employing an estimated 13,200 men and women. The backbone of its activities comprised a number of regional and individual country sections. The regional department for Poland, Czechoslovakia and Hungary was headed by Lieutenant-Colonel Harold Perkins ('MP'), who was appointed as overall director. He was a tough, self-reliant man who had made his way in central Europe before the war. Running away to sea at sixteen, he had become a Master Mariner at twenty-three, but then changed direction and went to Czechoslovakia in the 1920s to work for a British engineering company. While he was there, he also studied engineering at Prague University, and then moved to Poland to set up a subsidiary company, becoming manager of the Benn-Bielsko steel mill in Silesia. Just before the war, 'Perks' as he was universally known, became a territorial army officer, and during 1939, a member of MI(R), the small sabotage research branch of the War Office, which helped spawn SOE.[19] Since working for SOE, his contact with Polish soldiers had earned him widespread respect. In the early days of dispatching parachutists from Tempsford, Perkins was often the last soldier they saw on British soil. Jerzy Lerski ('Jur') remembered his controller with affection:

Perkins, our British guardian angel, was in excellent humour. He drove us to the airfield in a luxurious limousine. He used his famous stick, with which he never parted, as a conductor uses his baton. 'Tell the Polish people', he said, 'that here in England live their true friends, who will never desert Poland.'[20]

The rabbit warren of SOE offices at 64 Baker Street soon spread out over the streets of Marylebone, London, as the organisation grew to incorporate more country sections.[21] Perkin's 'Poland, Czechoslovakia and Hungary' regional group was further broken down into individual country sections with operatives from the Polish country section working under code-names with the prefix 'MP'. This dedicated Polish Section was headed by a regular, Major Mike J.T. Pickles ('MPP'). Under him, there were a number of SOE officers with different responsibilities, such as Operations (Captain R.G. Colt-Williams – 'MPC'), Training (Captain C.T. Gregor – 'MPG') and Intelligence (Captain L.M. Massey – MPX1). Massey, like some of the other SOE officers, had received his higher education in Poland and in his case, being a reader in English at Poznań University had greatly assisted his work in document recognition.[22]

Despite the growing sophistication of the organisation, SOE rarely found favour with the senior officers of the RAF. Sir Charles Portal, Chief of Air Staff derided SOE tactics, including the dropping of agents dressed in civilian clothes as 'not an operation with which the Royal Air Force should be associated'.[23] Oliver Harvey, who was Principal Private Secretary to Anthony Eden, had no doubt as to the calibre of the early SOE recruits, reminding his master, 'the truth is SOE were a gang of toughs and quite ruthless.'[24]

Harvey didn't comment on SOE's senior officers, but some were every bit as tough. Harold Perkins was a big man, in physique as well as personality, and his stamina and strength were legendary. He could bend a poker in his hands or win any drinking game, including suspending himself full stretch on two beer bottles.[25] But he also had mental stamina and from the very start of the Polish presence in London he invested much time in establishing links with the Polish General Staff, based at the Hotel Rubens. By 15 February 1941, he had built good enough contacts with their VI Bureau and the RAF to organise a twin-engined Whitley aircraft to drop the first three personnel into Poland. The agents fell wide of the mark, but it was still a huge morale boost for the Polish Government-in-exile and their underground. Even though logistics prevented further drops until the following November, Polish hopes remained undimmed. Peter Wilkinson, one of the SOE's founder members conceded that his organisation had helped maintain these false hopes, recalling that 'we were so deeply committed to the Polish cause that we funked facing them with the realities of their situation.' Wilkinson was even instructed by his superior, Gubbins, to spend fruit-less time in planning joint operations with the Polish General Staff for an airborne invasion of occupied Poland – an invasion he knew would never happen.[26] Nevertheless, news of these plans was picked up by the Polish radio station, 'Radio Świt', which proceeded to broadcast details from England – a move which stirred up Stalin. The Foreign Office, who had taken a pro-Soviet stance for some time, stepped in and pressed the Polish broadcasters to concentrate just on anti-German rhetoric.[27]

One important constituent of SOE was the role of the First Aid Nursing Yeomanry (FANY). This was a Corps of women volunteers who had played an important civilian role assisting troops on the Western Front during the Great War and had, since 1927, been officially recog-nised by the War Office. Some were selected to work in SOE as cypher or wireless operators or packers of arms and explosives, while others became active agents in occupied Europe – a role that ended for some in concentration camps or death at the hands of the Gestapo. Sue Ryder, a FANY attached to SOE from its early days, was always mindful of the organisation's secrecy:

> My part of FANY was attached to the Baker Street HQ. We didn't really refer to the organisation as SOE but tended to call it all Baker Street. We also knew about the Polish Intelligence and of Bureau VI, though we never discussed them and certainly not with any outsiders.[28]

Other FANYs worked as driver/chauffeurs or on vehicle mainte-nance, both duties being popular around SOE bases in either England or southern Italy. For those working in the latter, home was the FANY HQ at Latiano, about twelve miles inland from Brindisi and from where they were called on to transport SOE officers, between Monopoli and the various air bases in the area. Other FANYs such as Sue Ryder, who would later become famous for her work in Poland and her charity foundation, contributed to SOE by escorting Polish agents right through their training to the final hours before their mis-sion. She recalled that 332 Polish agents, known to the FANYs as 'Bods', went through SOE training stations, and what really mattered to all of them was 'faith, loyalty and courage'.[29] At Brindisi and Bari, as well as for earlier operations at Tempsford, Ryder's Polish Section had its own holding station for Polish agents, together with segregated changing huts and facilities. This not only ensured secrecy but also generated a platonic bonding between agents and their chaperones. She recalled that it was a small, intimate world:

> One had a tremendous admiration for the agents. They were young and energetic but we were only allowed to have platonic friendships and this rule was never broken. We were asked to keep an eye on agents who were under special strain, who might give way after capture. It was quite a lot to ask of people our age. Some agents were very frightened of what they were going back to, especially if they'd already been arrested by the Gestapo or the Soviets. We had one boy, 'Robert' who had been captured before by the Gestapo. He would pace up and down, dreading that he would be tortured again. I think he went back and was killed. Those Poles who had already had a spell in some gulag in Siberia would talk of cannibalism and that the Soviet system was on a par with the Nazi system. They had been released in 1941 as a result of the Sikorski-Maisky Pact. Many had suffered typhus and huge numbers had died.
>
> You knew you would never be called on to do this sort of work again. And you were with people who were under a sentence of death. Therefore, we FANYs did get to know people very well. They would talk about things you'd never discuss in normal life. It was rather like talking to people with a terminal illness. You would be told things you'd never normally hear. It was emotionally intimate and extremely memorable. It consumed one. It became a way of life.[30]

Ryder had great admiration for these Polish agents who would be dropped into their mother country, and began to understand their tremendous spirit:

> Radio operators always seemed to have the worst time, because they had to carry these wretched receivers around with them and if they were caught, there was no way they could conceal them. Quite a lot of wireless operators were girls. Couriers also had a very difficult time as they had to break through the various frontiers in occupied Europe. We always had to check them before they left to make sure they had nothing incriminating

on them. We had to make sure that all clothing labels were made in Poland and that there was nothing traceable to England. The Poles were, after all, almost reckless in their courage, unlike the Czechs who were more solid and cautious. The Poles always said, 'it was right to do it,' whether they were going to lose or not – it just had to be done. They were like corks. The worse the situation for them became, they would pop up again.

In the first three months of 1944 appalling weather had frustrated SOE attempts to help the Poles. An SOE operations summary for the Prime Minister reflected their disappointment:

> Bad weather frustrated every effort to increase supplies to Poland. Only two dropping operations have been successfully concluded during the quarter and only 3½ tons were actually delivered to the field as against 6½ tons for the previous quarter and nearly 21 tons during the corresponding quarter in 1943. The AK managed to destroy 3 coaches of Governor Frank's train, but the fourth, carrying Frank himself, unfortunately remained undamaged. Lubbert, Chief of the Labour Bureau, has been executed after condemnation by the underground movement.[31]

The local SOE commander for Brindisi, Lieutenant-Colonel Henry Threlfall worked in concert with the Polish element, known as 'Base 11', who were commanded from January 1944 by the capable Major Jan Jaźwiński. This Polish officer was an experienced VI Bureau man and had been involved with many of the early parachute drops into Poland, and consequently was well aware of the limitations of air support to his country. This inevitably brought him into conflict with his C-in-C, General Sosnkowski, who believed that the Polish Air Force would be the saviour of the country in the event of a rising. Such false hopes did not sit well with Jaźwiński, who tried to warn elements in the Polish Government-in-exile in London that any rising could not depend on material air support.[32] Nonetheless, with the onset of brighter weather from early April 1944, attempts were made to ratchet up air relief. On the night of 3/4 April, sixteen aircraft took off from Brindisi, eight from No. 1586 Flight and eight from No. 148 Squadron. While some of the aircraft failed to find their AK drop zones, one of the Polish crews flying a Halifax V successfully dropped two couriers near Warsaw, one of whom was the important emissary, Józef Retinger.[33]

While Major Jaźwiński played the caution card with his British superiors, on the night of 8/9 April 1944 he was reported to have secretly authorized drops to the AK 27th Volhynian Division, fighting in the south-east corner of Poland. Despite orders forbidding drops in this sensitive area so close to the Soviet front, Jaźwiński could not ignore the plight of this AK unit, who were desperately short of arms and equipment. Collusion with SOE officers may well have taken place as Polish aircrews flew further unauthorized missions on this brief over the next few nights, dropping supplies into restricted SOE drop zones.[34] These 'irregular' drops into Poland may also have included large numbers of Polish pilots, put into the country to await the eventual rising; it was now no secret that General Sosnkowski was in favour of any move that would re-establish the Polish Air Force on Polish soil.

The good luck with the weather continued and night after night in mid-April 1944, combined sorties of Polish and British crews, often numbering ten or more aircraft, made flights to Poland. But the darkness did not always provide a cloak for the heavy, drumming aircraft, especially when an enemy squadron of *Nachtjäger* ('night hunter') fighters were scrambled from Hungarian or Romanian airfields. Many of these night-fighters serving in central and Eastern Europe lacked onboard radar equipment, such as the 'Naxos' radar receiver, so were vectored to attack incoming Allied aircraft by ground-based radar, often mounted on railway wagons. By 1944 the Luftwaffe had not only refined their original *Wilde Sau* ('wild boar') night tactics, but were also adapting a wider range of aircraft to attack Allied bombers or supply missions. The well-known single-engined Messerschmitt Bf 109G and Focke-Wulf Fw190A night-fighters were now supplemented by the twin-engined Messerschmitt Bf 110G and Junkers Ju88G. Apart from refinements such as long-range tanks, flame dampers and machine-gun flash suppressors, one German innovation was the painting of the under-surface of one wing of the aircraft in black; for when a night-fighter flew in amongst an Allied formation, any German searchlights playing on the aircraft would recognise the single illuminated wing and the night-fighter would not be targeted by anti-aircraft batteries.[35] It usually took more than 300 enemy machine-gun rounds to bring down a heavy bomber and therefore two or more night-fighters would have to take on each Allied aircraft. Despite the success of the *Nachtjagddivision* (night-fighter wing), SOE decided to increase the size of sorties flying to Poland and on the night of 23/24 April, nineteen aircraft, the largest number yet assembled, took off from Brindisi. Seven aircraft were detailed for drops on the AK 9th Infantry Regiment near Zamość, and among them was Halifax II JP224, whose aircrew included Flight Sergeant Walter Davis. The British airman recalled a very black night:

> It was like any other sortie. We all knew we were flying to Poland, but only the skipper and navigator were told the details. We never knew the contents of the containers, though they could have been anything from clothing, wireless kits or gelignite to gold for bribes. We took off into a very dark sky and once we'd crossed the Carpathians we dropped to 2000ft as we approached the drop zone. On the ground, we would normally expect the Poles to mark the DZ by five torches to indicate the wind direction. The bomb-aimer would attach static parachute lines to the canisters and I would assist him to bundle them out of the plane. Except it didn't work out like that on this mission. Four hours into the trip, after we'd crossed the Polish border, something happened and we were flying on three engines. I'd just been listening to a wireless broadcast and I heard the skipper say 'where's the Russian front?' Next thing we're down to one engine and losing altitude rapidly. I went back to the bomb bay to start throwing things out to slow our descent but I was ordered to bale out. I grabbed my chute and tumbled out at only 500ft and the others must have followed. The skipper baled out last at 300ft and I heard the aircraft crash shortly after. I landed uninjured and quickly buried my chute and 'Mae West'. I was alone in a forest.[36]

As the Halifax fuselage was larger than the Lancaster bomber, baling out was a slightly easier operation, but landing unexpectedly in any occupied country meant an uncertain reception. With luck, a parachutist might evade German search parties but the local partisan unit might not be friendly. There were cases where airmen were shot or beaten up before they had a chance to identify themselves, though MI9, the British Security Service branch charged with helping escapees, did later issue 'blood chits'. These were printed cards with a prominent Union Jack, informing anyone that a reward was available if the bearer was treated well. To the credit of most AK units, downed airmen were well-treated, hidden at great risk to the families concerned, and invited to share any meagre resources available.[37]

Even though British support for the Poles was proving extremely erratic, there was no let up by the Poles in sending large volumes of intelligence material back to Britain. The main conduit for Polish intelligence reaching the British SIS was the Polish II Bureau, based in the Hotel Rubens. The chief of this bureau for most of the war was Lieutenant-Colonel Stanisław Gano, a formidable and competent operator, with a wide experience of intelligence and diplomatic matters. Under his direction in 1944, Bureau II passed a vast amount of intelligence to SIS.[38] It has been calculated that in this year alone, the Poles passed on over 7,351 intelligence reports, 966 reports on foreign agents and 29,510 reports on deciphered signals. Furthermore, during the war, of the 45,770 intelligence reports provided to Churchill by Commander Wilfred Dunderdale (Head of Special Liaison Control, SIS) 44% were derived from Polish sources.[39] But gathering such intelligence on the streets of Poland's towns and cities was still fraught with danger. German security forces seemed to be everywhere, assisted in many cases by Polish police, who were usually recruited from among the *Volksdeutsche*. Part of the diet of terror were the regular police round-ups, which would be conducted by Wehrmacht and Gestapo units, assisted by local police, who would suddenly arrive by lorry in an area and cordon off the streets. Everyone within the cordon would be rounded up and their papers examined. If their documents stated that they worked for the General Government or the Reich, they would be sent away, if not, they would be arrested or beaten and thrown into the back of a lorry. Such arbitrary actions netted AK men and women for further interrogation or execution, as well as providing fresh sources of hard labour for the Reich.[40] Michał Zylberberg, a Jew hiding in Warsaw, experienced the aftermath of a round-up:

> Suddenly, an open van drove past. There were men sitting in a double row at the back, their hands above their heads. Standing between the two rows were SS men, machine-guns pointing and at the ready. I was terrified and rooted to the spot. I had no idea what had happened. The SS smiled at me and I smiled back but I sensed danger. The van passed and I heard a voice calling out from behind a gate, 'Lunatic! How can you just stand there when people are being rounded up to be shot.' I had been lucky. The number of people arrested had been large enough to satisfy the Germans. Possibly the Germans thought I was a member of

the secret police, otherwise I would surely not have been standing there so confidently returning their smiles.[41]

Probably the most dangerous undercover work was carried out by radio-telegraphists – the most unseen of all the underground soldiers. Their job was dangerous and difficult and the important results of this unspectacular job were never seen. Yet these volunteers carried out one of the most important tasks of an AK detachment – that of receiving orders from London or regional HQs and reporting results of operations. Captain Aleksander Jedliński ('Franek') ran the 'Orbis' communications base deep within the Kampinos Forest, which handled sensitive data transmitted between Poland and London.[42] In London (codenamed 'Martha') SOE-trained Polish receivers found it difficult to pick up signals from Poland. One London receiver, 'Malewa' found it was only a job for the experienced:

> Ordinary stations tried to drown down the pips of press agencies' radiograms, magnetic disturbances competed with technical faults, and everything together made a frightful din, at the bottom of which was hidden a thin wisp of sound...then he was on the air at once. First slowly, the heading; there mustn't be a mistake there. Then faster and faster. The Morse signals sped through the ether – numbers made up from dashes and dots, and groups from the numbers. Suddenly everything snapped. The earphones were drowned by the roar of a powerful station, which was succeeded by buzzing, whistling and crackling. The thin wisp of the clandestine station was torn to shreds. Then after a while everything was normal again, and in the ensuing quiet the dots and dashes lined the paper, like soldiers falling in. 'Ten groups lost, five uncertain. A request for a repeat of the message would be necessary. Here in London it only meant a few extra minutes: the worst that could happen was being late for supper. But for the fellow on the other end...[43]

The risk of being caught transmitting to London from inside Poland was high. Apart from Gestapo raids after tip-offs, there was always the threat that a traitor within the organisation might expose an AK network. In April 1944, one operative who had been turned by the Gestapo gave away the names of twenty-two Warsaw personnel, together with couriers and smugglers. Consequently, SOE and SIS had to abandon its few post-boxes and contacts inside Warsaw and start again.[44]

Other British-sponsored intelligence operations were well advanced in the summer of 1944 and could co-ordinate with the opening of the new front in north-Western Europe. The success of the deception plans and co-ordination with the French resistance during Operation Overlord at the beginning of June was a feather in the cap of SOE as well as SIS. Poles continued to work with British intelligence, notably as double agents. Men such as Roman Garby-Czerniawski ('Brutus') were invaluable for 'Operation Fortitude', which successfully deceived the Germans into believing that the D-Day landings would take place in the Pas de Calais region rather than in Normandy.[45] And SOE's EU/ P Section endeavoured to organise Polish resistance fighters to cause disruption behind German lines in northern France in the immediate aftermath of the landings. Under 'Operation BARDSEA', SOE would drop specially trained three-man Polish cells, together with arms and ammunition, into areas that would be overrun by the Allied advance within seventy-two hours. This rarely went according to plan and it is estimated that casualties were high, though the exact details of these operations have never been made available. It was also proposed to use Polish Special Forces for clandestine operations inside the Reich, an area where SOE were woefully underrepresented.[46]

Another area where Britain could help the Poles was with economic aid, for Britain helped fund both the Polish Government-in-exile as well as its resistance army. The original 1940 Anglo-Polish Finance Agreement, whereby a £5 million lump sum was provided to help finance Polish 'armies abroad', was soon exceeded by payments to support the political and military underground in Poland. By 1943, SOE, as well as the British Treasury and SIS, were sanctioning money transfers to Poland via the Polish VI Bureau. However, after Sikorski's death in 1943, and with the Soviet Army advancing ever closer, these donations and credits started to dry up. However, despite restraints placed on it by the Foreign Office, SOE still continued to send a reported £35m in gold and currency to the AK by secret couriers. Such was the volume of its transactions that even SOE themselves conceded that by 1944, 'SOE has the honour of being HM's principal procurer of foreign currency in the black markets of Europe and Asia.'[47]

Aerial support began to improve. The quarter April to June 1944 showed much better results for SOE, with 240 tons of equipment dropped into Poland.[48] Although the weather had improved, there was

1 SS Reichsführer Heinrich Himmler and Governer-General Hans Frank – Dinner at Wawel Castle, Kraków. *United States Holocaust Memorial Museum #15074*

2 Lieutenant-Colonel Harold Perkins – one of SOE's 'toughies'. *Special Forces Club*

3 'Against the odds' – a rare photograph of Special Duties Halifax II aircraft from No 148 Squadron, flying in formation *RAF Musuem #P009950*

4 FANYs with Polish servicemen at Audley End House, Essex. *Polish Underground Movement Study Trust #22-001*

5 Flight-Sergeant John Ward – 'soldier of the Home Army' *National Archives #HS4/256*

6 V-2 Rocket. The quartered markings were to detect the amount of roll in flight. *Imperial War Museum #BU11149*

7 Blizna testing ground. One of several blast shelters still remaining today. *Author's Collection*

8 'Motyl' landing ground today. Scene of Operation 'Wildhorn III' and the retrieval of rocket parts. The monuments in the foreground shows the Polska Walcząca ('Fighting Poland') emblem. *Author's Collection*

9 Hanna Czarnocka – 'imortant member of the resistance and survivor of Auschwitz'. *Hanna Zbirohowska-Kościa*

10 Home Army (AK) wireless operators – possession of a set was punishable by death. *Muzeum Armii Krajowej*

11 'Providing a lifeline' – Polish service personnel in Italy. *Polish Underground Movement Study Trust #33-001*

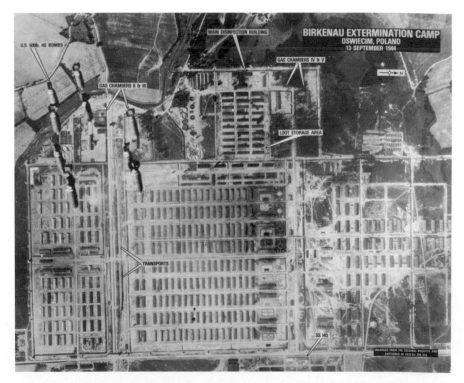

12 Auschwitz – US bombs intended for IG Farben, but accidentally falling on Birkenau, 13 September 1944. The captions were added in 1978 by CIA analysts. *United States Holocaust Memorial Museum #03198*

13 Auschwitz – After selection at the railhead, a Jewish mother and her children move towards the gas chambers (summer 1944). *United States Holocaust Memorial Museum #77217*

14 Auschwitz – SS officers from the camp singing at their retreat at nearby Solahuette. Front row: Höcker, Höss (leaning back), Baer (arms folded), Kramer (behind Baer's left shoulder), Hoessler, Mengele (immediately left of accordionist). *United States Holocaust Memorial Museum #34739*

15 Soviet troops achieve a river crossing. *Imperial War Museum #RUS 4272*

16 Warsaw erupts – the beginning of the Rising. Looking due north, the River Vistula can be seen on the right together with its three vital bridges. The suburb of Praga lies beyond. Mokotov is in the foreground. *Polish Underground Movement Study Trust #3513/6*

17 German Tiger tank, Poland 1944. *Bundesarchiv #1011-695-0406-15*

18 Hanna Czarnocka
with her brother, Bohdan
– 'ready to serve the
Home Army'. *Hanna
Zbirohowska-Kościa*

19 'Warsaw Erupts' – Home Army soldiers defend their trenches. *Polish Undergound Movement Study Trust*

20 German soldiers surrendering in the early days of the Rising. *Polish Underground Movement Study Trust #2195*

21 German infantrymen prepare remote-controlled 'Goliaths' during the Rising. *Bundesarchiv #1011-695-0411-06*

22 'German snipers rarely missed' – Running the barricades during the Warsaw Rising. *Polish Underground Movement Study Trust #1819*

23 Warsaw airlift – the crew of Consolidated Liberator B Mark VI of No. 178 Squadron, Italy 1944. (Left to right) Sergeant John Rush RAF (pilot); Sergeant Derek Coates RAF (wireless operator); Sergeant Peter Green (mid-upper gunner); Lieutenant Keith Murray SAAF (navigator); Flight-Sergeant Derek Stuart RAAF (2nd pilot); Flight-Sergeant Kenneth Pierce RAF (tail gunner). *Imperial War Museum #CL 3557*

24 'Strong wind could carry them miles off target' – Containers falling on Warsaw. *Polish Underground Movement Study Trust #1819*

25 'A successful drop' – Polish Underground Movement Study Trust #1976

26 Polish post and courier girls during the Warsaw Rising – 'an uncertain fate'. *Muzeum Armii Krajowej*

27 SS soldier with flamethrower flushes out resistance fighters. *Bundesarchiv #146-1996-057-10A*

28 SS Gruppenführer Heinz Reinefarth (extreme left) together with Cossacks serving under his command – Wolska Street, Warsaw. *Public domain*

29 SS troops brutally clear the Warsaw streets. *Bundesarchiv #146-1973-113-23*

30 The last days of the Rising – an AK soldier is pulled out of his sewer refuge. *Bundesarchiv #146-1994-054-30*

31 The end of the Rising – General Bór-Komorowski and SS General von dem Bach, 3 October 1944. *Imperial War Museum #MH 4489*

32 'Help never came' – The AK surrender their arms. *Bundesarchiv #146-1984-079-09*

also another significant reason why support for the AK was ratcheted up in this period. In the run-up to the Normandy landings on 6 June 1944, it was vital that there were no transfers of German troops from Poland to the west. To this end, it was important that the AK maintained its level of sabotage operations inside Poland to tie down as many German troops as possible. But as the Allies successfully established their bridgehead in the west and the Soviets penetrated further into occupied Poland, Allied Command saw the role of the AK as increasingly marginal. Quite simply, the Soviets had taken over the role of occupying German attention in the east.[49] A secret SOE memorandum confirmed this opportunistic policy:

The priority accorded to Kensal [Poland] during April and May was based on the Chief of Staffs' directive for cutting communications. It was, in effect, a bribe to the Field [AK] to achieve their necessary sabotage effort just before D-day. The effort proved not to be necessary as Dulwich [Soviet] pressure made transfer of reserves impossible. The results of the April and May operations were an increase in guerrilla activity and very considerable aid to the Dulwich [Soviet] advance over Kensal territory.[50]

An SOE officer communicating with Harold Perkins on 28 June 1944 realised that SOE and the AK were minnows swimming around a very large shark:

The Kensals [Poles] see things in the following way:

(a) Dulwich [Soviet Union] intends to annexe half their country.
(b) The remaining half, enlarged to the West, either to be nominally inde-
    pendent under a puppet government or to be attached as a federal
    republic.
(c) No action made by them is to be allowed to influence this decision;
    this is to be settled among the Big Three, and is irrevocable.[51]

The Poles were indeed trapped. Time was running out and a decision on an uprising in Warsaw had to be made. By mid-July SOE knew a rising was inevitable but had little idea of how widespread it would be:

The nature of the action is clear − there is to be an armed rising. This is both a psychological and political necessity, and the Poles are determined not to allow their five years of work, planning and suffering, to be dissipated by the liberation of the country before the Underground Army can undertake action. Even if it might appear to be the most sensible solution to allow the Russians to defeat the Germans, and then to come to terms with the Russians, the Poles have waited too long and will not abandon their project of an open rebellion against the Germans. So far as is possible they would like to have the Russians enter a territory already in the possession of the Poles and administered by them, so that the Russians would enter as allies but not as liberators.[52]

Unfortunately for the Poles, as the prospect of a rising came closer there was no parallel increase in SOE supply drops, which frustrated most SOE operatives. They wanted to help, but realised that either Allied Command were ignorant of Polish intentions or, more likely, wanted no part in the rising for fear of Soviet anger. There was even talk of a simultaneous rising in Slovakia, co-ordinated with the AK, who had strong forces in the sub-Carpathian, south-east region of Poland. But, whatever the nature of the rising, there was also the question of an almost total lack of British representation in 'the field' in occupied Poland. SOE operatives lobbied for a British Military Mission at the very least, so that their 'knowledge of Polish intentions would then, for the first time since 1939, be based on something more reliable than hearsay'.[53] However, having British agents on the ground in Poland was not so easy. Those British servicemen who as ex-POWs were in hiding in Poland realised how difficult it was to live and travel around in a German-occupied country. Lance-Corporal Ron Jeffery, who had been on the run for several years in Poland and was adopted by the AK, regularly ran the risk of exposure, especially if he had to move by train. On one occasion, travelling with his new Polish wife, Marysia, he kept a low profile while in a railway compartment shared with three German soldiers:

A couple of uniformed Hun railway policemen entered the compartment. Looking for Polish civilians unauthorised to use the *'Nur fur Deutsche'* railway wagons, the policemen's attention lingered for only a moment on the three soldiers, before one of them directed himself to me.
'Sind Sie Deutsche?'
'Jawohl, meine Papiere bitte'. With that, out came my various documents and with all their swastika plastered glory, rated only a brief glance.

'*Danke*'.

The policemen handed my papers back and addressed himself to Marysia.

'*Sind Sie Deutsche?*'

I certainly got a shock. My dear, new, sweet wife had been very busy since meeting me, learning English at every spare opportunity. Of German, she spoke only a few words.

'*Sind Sie Deutsche?*' repeated the policeman.

In perfect English, Marysia answered 'Y…Yes.' I jumped into action. Just as well that I had a few vodkas under the belt and I piped up immediately.

'*Verzeihen Sie, dass ist ja meine Frau.*' Excuse me but this lady is my wife.[54]

Luckily, the policeman was happy with this explanation, thinking that Jeffery was a *Volksdeutsche* with an English wife, and moved on. But one lapse of concentration had nearly cost them their lives. Nevertheless, Jeffery managed to evade capture and with the help of AK and SOE liaison, he returned to Britain, where SOE officers, Lieutenant-Colonel Perkins and Major Pickles were desperate to de-brief him. He was then passed on in turn to a bewildering selection of contacts including the Polish VI Bureau, Sir Owen O'Malley, Frank Roberts of the Foreign Office and the Duchess of Atholl, before returning to the normality of his old regiment – The Queen's Own Royal West Kent.[55]

Both British servicemen on the run in Poland, and agents dropped into the country could usually rely on local Polish help. When an agent landed in Poland, they had a contact address where an 'aunt' would be waiting for them, and when Allied airmen were shot down, a similar support system would often be available. The 'aunts' were young women, trained by the AK to instruct their wards in the way of life under occupation. They would feed and clothe their new arrival as well as making him familiar with the local geography and activities. Flight Sergeant Walter Davis, whose Halifax had been shot down near Rudnik nad Sanem, just north of Rzeszów, had been on the run from the Germans since the crash. He knew he was lucky to be alive and hoped for local support:

As I was creeping out of the forest, I saw an enemy Fieseler Storch aircraft overhead checking the crash area but it didn't see me. I had a compass from my survival kit and kept going in one direction, but my floppy leather flying boots were not great to walk in. As it became light, I came across a woman and young girl tending a grave. I drew a swastika in the soil and scrubbed it through with my boot so they knew I was friendly. They directed me on and after a while I came to the top of a hill and saw a village down below. We'd been taught to seek out the poorest house on the edge of a village – they had the least to lose by assisting an enemy of the Germans. The cottage dwellers took me in, gave me food and washed my bleeding feet and I slept there for forty-eight hours.

Then a man came to collect me in a pony and cart. He must have been an AK man as he took me to a new safe house in a village some miles away. And there I hid for five months. The local AK set me up as a farm worker with false papers and the family who looked after me gave me Polish clothes. The Germans were everywhere and to avoid contact with them, I slept in a haystack at night. Then finally in the summer, the Germans disappeared and the Russians arrived. It was terrible. They shot all the local AK officers, including the kind man who had moved me in his pony and cart. I made it out of there pretty quick and travelled towards Lwów, encountering two other British airmen from 148 Squadron who were also trying to get out. Eventually I reached Odessa and was put on a ship for home. I will never forget the kindness of those Poles who took me in and risked their lives for doing so.[56]

Although Flight Sergeant Davis's aircrew were unfortunate, the spring of 1944 had seen some very impressive flight statistics. In April, a total of 132 sorties were flown to Poland, of which fifty-five were carried out by Polish aircrews. During May, a total of 166 aircraft made the journey, with 121 aircraft from Polish 1586 Flight and forty-five from 148 Squadron. But there was always a bill to pay. Canadians from the Royal Canadian Air Force (RCAF), as well as British aircrews, flew with 148 Squadron, and suffered casualties. On 27 April, a Halifax flown by W/O N. Bruce of the Royal Canadian Air Force (RCAF) was shot down on the return flight over Albania, with all the crew posted as 'missing', while three days later another Halifax piloted by Flight Sergeant T.J. Makepeace (RCAF) was brought down over the Yugoslav border.[57]

Among the supplies dropped into Poland were a dazzling array of sabotage items, which were manufactured at Aston House, SOE's secret testing and production centre near Stevenage in Hertfordshire. Known as 'Station 12', the country estate was home to over 500 personnel who tested such devices as pencil fuses, limpet mines, pocket incendiaries, 'tyrebursters' and 'tree spigots' – all effective equipment for secret armies

in occupied Europe. Since 1941, the testing and experimental department, 'Station 9', in Welwyn Garden City had maintained its prodigious
output of inventions. Of particular use to clandestine operations in
Poland was the new silenced version of the Sten submachine-gun. The
'Welsilencer' was in fact designed by a Pole and, when attached to a Sten,
was used extensively in 1943–44 to quietly kill guards or sentries and
carry out assassinations.[58]

Other small arms which were widely used by agents were pocket
pistols. The 9mm short calibre handgun could be easily concealed but the
SOE Arms Section, 'Station 6', based at Bridehall in London, spent much
of their time procuring large quantities of these weapons from Spain or
Argentina – or anywhere but Britain – so that, if caught, the agent would
not be compromised. These materials were packed into cylindrical containers (originally designed by Harold Perkins himself), and attached to a
parachute for release through the aircraft's bomb bays. While some agents
were sent to 'Station 17', the industrial sabotage school, most Poles were
dispatched for training to SOE's 'Station 43' based at Audley End House,
near Saffron Walden in Essex – one of the glorious requisitioned country
houses that earned SOE the epithet, 'Stately 'Omes of England'. The base
had trained notable agents such as Elzbieta Zawacka, the only female Pole
to be parachuted into her homeland. But during 1944, with restricted
flights from Brindisi to Poland, only five out of the seventy Polish agents
trained at Audley were actually dropped into occupied territory.[59]

On 29 July 1944, just days before the Warsaw Rising, Major-General
Stanisław Tatar ('Tabor') asked for a meeting in London with Major-
General Gubbins, Colonel Keswick (Director of Mediterranean Group),
Lieutenant-Colonel Henry Threlfall and Major Mike Pickles. Tatar
quickly told the SOE officers that the Polish Government-in-exile in
London had now given the underground Deputy Prime Minister in
Poland and the GOC, AK in Warsaw, freedom to act and it was expected
that the Rising would occur within a few days. Furthermore, he
demanded that the Allies should bomb urban centres and that Polish
Mustang fighters should land in Warsaw together with elements of the
Polish Parachute Brigade. There was also an urgent request for an Allied
Military Mission to be sent to the AK headquarters inside Poland. The
senior SOE officers listened carefully to Tatar but some of his requests,
such as urban bombing for which US aircraft demanded at least 2,000
metres clearance, were clearly unrealistic.[60]

Although the SOE officers were all personally committed to the Polish cause, their despair at the dislocation of British efforts to help the Poles was evident in their memoranda. The AK had always hoped that any rising in Warsaw would have come about as part of the nationwide 'Operation Storm' ('*Burza*'), and that the AK would liberate the city in advance, or at least in conjunction with the advancing Red Army. Yet Soviet actions during their summer offensives had shown that 'cooperation' was not usually on their list of priorities. Nonetheless, Allied Chiefs of Staff, the British Foreign Office and SOE all knew about 'Operation Storm' and that a rising in Warsaw was about to erupt. However, none of these parties had much idea what the other was going to do about it. There was no concerted British response, and even an important memorandum about the SOE meeting with Tatar took several days to reach the British Chiefs of Staff Committee.[61] SOE's Polish Section stated on 18 July, 'the nature of the action is clear – there is to be an armed rising' and although the section surmised that 'because of the Soviet advances, we may be out of business in a month', they still agonised over the fate of the Poles and stated as much to Tatar.[62] SOE remained confused over what British policy was in the event of a rising, and were uncertain as to the motives of their political and military masters in London. An SOE officer despaired:

> A rising will come, and the Russians will find them [the Poles] with arms in their hands in some sort of control of their own country. For all we know this may by now be part of the Chiefs of Staff plan, and a PWE [Political Warfare Executive] directive dated 14 July, we have just received, looks almost as if it were, even though all the indications we have received on the subject of stores planning, indicate the contrary.[63]

Such comments from a senior and experienced SOE officer seem naïve in the light of what is known today. The PWE was, after all, charged with organising subversive propaganda and their brief was to 'massage' facts and promote rumour to demoralise the enemy. As far as the Poles were concerned, the PWE reached its apogee by organising leaflets to be dropped by the RAF over occupied Poland in order to incite rebellion – it was a feeble attempt and an insult the Poles never forgot. And Churchill remained unimpressed with PWE's accountability, especially in the run-up to D-Day, demanding that it be 'brought under close control.' Yet PWE did fulfil a useful role in establishing and supporting broadcasting stations such as 'Świt' that transmitted material to occupied Poland, as well as supplying copy for the country's clandestine presses; PWE's role in this radio base was so sensitive that the Foreign Office had to warn its Moscow diplomats that 'you should not (repeat not) volunteer any information about where the real control of the station lies or where it operates'.[64] Despite the prevarication in London by both the British and Polish Government-in-exile, events within Poland were moving at a rapid pace. As the AK command were finalising plans for the rising in Warsaw, they received news that the Soviets, who had recently occupied Wilno, had arrested the local AK commander and disarmed his troops. Although this was in territory claimed by Stalin, it was a foretaste of events in Warsaw.

NOTES

[1] For the troubled relationship between SIS and SOE, see Anthony Verrier, *Through the Looking Glass: British Foreign Policy in an Age of Illusions* (WW Norton, New York 1983), pp. 31–48.

[2] Minutes, War Cabinet Defence Committee, 14 January 1944, PREM 3/408/3, NA.

[3] For an overview of SOE's creation as well as other major themes, see, Mark Seaman, 'A New Instrument of War' in Mark Seaman (Ed.) *Special Operations Executive* (Routledge, London 2006). Also Sir Michael Howard, *The Mediterranean Strategy in the Second World War*, (Greenhill Books, London 1993), pp. 13–15. The Foreign Office was sometimes seen as an arbiter between the warring factions; see Lord Harvey to Lord Avon, 21 October 1964, AP23/36/35, Lord Avon Papers, UB.

[4] For the exploits of Christine Granville (Countess Krystyna Skarbek 1915–1952), see Patrick Howarth, *Undercover: The Men and Women of the SOE* (Phoenix Press, London 1980), pp. 65–71. She was tragically murdered by a spurned lover in 1952.

[5] It has been estimated that nine were killed during their drop; twenty-six were killed fighting German troops; twenty-seven were murdered by the Gestapo; eight died in concentration camps; ten committed suicide; eighteen were killed during the Warsaw Rising.

[6] For example, SOE was responsible for the Middle East, West and East Africa and India, while OSS looked after China, North Africa and the South Pacific; see Ian Dear, *Sabotage & Subversion: Stories from the Files of the SOE and OSS* (Arms and Armour, London 1996), pp. 14–19.

[7] David Stafford, *Britain and European Resistance 1940–1945* (Macmillan, London 1980), pp. 60–1.

[8] M.R.D. Foot, *SOE: The Special Operations Executive 1940–1946* (Pimlico, London 1999), pp. 275–6. For 'Bardsea', see Leo Marks, *Between Silk and Cyanide: The Story of SOE's Code War* (HarperCollins, London 1998), pp. 529–32.

[9] Hugh Dalton to Basil Liddell Hart, 31 August 1939, LH 11/1939/85. For Dalton's relationship with the Poles, see Terry Charman, 'Hugh Dalton, Poland and SOE, 1940–42' in Seaman, op. cit.

[10] Hugh Dalton, son of a canon of Windsor who was also a tutor of King George V, was educated at Eton and served as an artillery officer in the Great War. Roy Jenkins, a political confederate, paints an unattractive portrait of Dalton – 'his body ever more top-heavy and pear-shaped, with an increasing tendency to stoop, his bald dome more gleamingly polished'. See Roy Jenkins, *Gallery of Twentieth Century Portraits and Oxford Papers* (David & Charles, Newton Abbot 1988).

[11] Diary, 2 August 1944, Ben Pimlott (Ed.), *The Second World War Diary of Hugh Dalton* (Jonathan Cape, London 1986), p. 380. Dalton was not impressed by Selborne's tenure as Assistant Postmaster-General.

[12] Peter Wilkinson, *Foreign Fields: The Story of an SOE Operative* (IB Taurus, London 1997), p. 124.

[13] Included in Chiefs of Staff Committee report, 'Polish Resistance Movement – Assistance by SOE', 29 October 1943, PREM 3/408/3, NA.

[14] K. Sosnkowski to Lord Selborne, 21 October 1943, PREM 3/408/3, NA.

[15] 'Draft Memo, SOE to COS, 15 January 1944, HS4/144, NA.

[16] Sue Ryder, 1987, ref 10057, Sound Archive, IWM.

[17] Colonel David Keswick (AD/H) to Colonel RH Barry (D/Plans), 29 January 1944, HS 4/144, NA. Also *Intelligence Co-operation*, op. cit., pp. 108-17, 205.

[18] For SOE brief, see 'MP21' to 'MP1' (Major Boughey), 4 September 1944, HS4/146, NA. Also Minutes, War Cabinet Defence Committee, 14 January 1944, PREM 3/408/3, NA.

[19] Harold Benjamin Perkins OBE (1905–1965), Captain RE. After service heading the Poland, Czechoslovakia and Hungary Section of SOE, he was sent to Czechoslovakia in May 1945 to head the SOE Mission. After the War he was engaged in SIS activities covering Poland, Czechoslovakia, Albania and Palestine.

[20] G. Iranek-Osmecki, op. cit., p. 27.

[21] 64 Baker Street received a colourful and sometimes dangerous mix of operatives, including the future spies Guy Burgess and Kim Philby. The latter was appointed, as an instructor, to radio and propaganda operations.

[22] Massey debriefing, 7 October 1944, FO 371/39454, NA. Bickham Sweet-Escott was the first head of SOE's Polish Section. He wrote one of the early

SOE memoirs, *Baker Street Irregular* (Methuen, London 1965). Also Nigel West, *Secret War: The Story of SOE, Britain's Wartime Sabotage Organisation (Hodder & Stoughton, London 1992)*, appendices.

23 Quoted in Russell Miller, *Behind the Lines: The Oral History of Special Operations in World War II* (Secker & Warburg, London 2002), p. 3.

24 Harvey to Eden, 21 October 1964, AP23/36/48a, Lord Avon Papers, UB.

25 Ernest van Maurik to Author, 15 August 2007.

26 Stalin had also imposed a ban on any Allied aircraft, which had assisted non-Soviet partisans, landing on Soviet territory. Wilkinson, op. cit., 124–5.

27 Gubbins to SOE Polish Section Officers, 'Co-ordination of Anglo-Soviet Resistance Policy', 31 May 1943, HS4/142, NA.

28 Sue Ryder, 1987, ref 10057, Sound Archive, IWM.

29 Sue Ryder, *Child of My Love* (Harvill Press, London 1997), p. 106.

30 Sue Ryder, 1987, ref 10057, Sound Archive, IWM. Those Polish agents who parachuted into their homeland gained the prestigious parachute badge with garland.

31 PREM 3/408/1, ob. Cit., NA.

32 SOE Report on Sosnkowski, 19 September 1944, HS4/145, NA.

33 Jerzy Cynk, op. cit., p. 463.

34 Jerzy Cynk, op. cit., pp. 463–4.

35 David Williams, *Nachtjäger: Luftwaffe Night Fighter Units 1943–1945, Vol. Two* (Ian Allan Publishing, Hersham 2005), p. 117, 145.

36 Walter Davis to Author, 19 January 2007. A 'Mae West' was an airman's yellow life-jacket, so named because of its obvious pneumatic properties. Three of the seven aircraft bound for Zamość were successful with their drops. Of the remaining twelve drops, only one RAF Halifax was successful. See Cynk, op. cit., p. 465.

37 M.R.D. Foot and J.M. Langley, *MI9. Escape and Evasion 1939–1945*, (BCA, London 1979), pp. 190–4.

38 Dr Paul Latawski, 'The Polish Intelligence Contribution in the Second World War: Historiography, Issues and Controversies', paper given to British Commission for Military History, 6 May 2006.

39 Tessa Stirling, *Intelligence Co-operation*, op. cit., p. 10. This magisterial volume deals with, among other issues, the quest for the fate of the Bureau II files after the war. SIS material can be detected in the NA, using the 'CX' reference in documents and Polish to SIS using 'JX' source.

40 Gris Davies-Scourfield, *In Presence of my Foes*, (Pen & Sword, Barnsley 2004).

41 Michael Zylberberg, *A Warsaw Diary 1939-1945* (Vallentine Mitchell, London 1969), p. 146.

42 'MP1' to 'MP', 30 June 1944, HS4/301, NA. Also Ian Valentine, *Station 43: Audley End House and SOE's Polish Section* (Sutton, Stroud 2004), p. 163.

[43] Iranek-Osmecki, op. cit., p. 75.

[44] Telegram to Berne, 22 April 1944, HS 4/265, NA.

[45] Czerniawski later recounted his experiences of working with the *Interallié network* in France, in *The Big Network* (George Ronald, London 1961). For double agents, see JC Masterman, *Double-Cross System in the War of 1939-1945* (Yale University Press, New Haven 1972).

[46] The intention was that the 'Bardsea' teams should operate in the same way as the Special Forces 'Jedburgh' teams; see William Mackenzie, *The Secret History of SOE: Special Operations Executive 1940–1945* (St Ermin's Press, London 2000), pp. 579–80. Certain details of the 'Monika/Bardsea' operations during 1943–44 can be found in HS4/266, 267, 229, NA.

[47] Details of the 'black market' operations are still subject to censure. Most documents in the National Archives file HS4/219 ('Purchase of Reichmarks from SOE for the Polish Ministry') are retained under Sec 3 (4) Public Records Act 1958. See also Eugenia Maresch, 'SOE and Polish Aspirations' in *Intelligence Co-operation,* op. cit. and Stephen Dorril, *MI6: Fifty Years of Special Operations* (Fourth Estate, London 2000), p. 253. Also 'SOE Activities: Summary for the Prime Minister. April–June 1944', PREM 3/408/1, NA.

[48] 'SOE Activities April–June 1944', PREM 3/408/1, NA.

[49] 'MP21' to Major EPF Boughey (MP1), 4 September 1944, HS4/146, NA.

[50] 'Top Secret Memorandum, 'General Policy for Kensal', 4 September 1944, HS4/146, NA. See also 'Role of Polish Secret Army in Operation Overlord', HS 8/ 291, NA.

[51] 'MP.61' to 'MP' (Perkins), 28 June 1944, HS4/146, NA.

[52] 'Memorandum on Polish Situation', prepared by 'MP61', 18 July 1944, HS4/146, NA.

[53] Ibid.

[54] Ron Jeffery, op. cit., p. 153.

[55] Ron Jeffery, op. cit., pp. 258–66. Ron Jeffery was awarded the Polish Cross of Valour by Lieutenant-General Bór-Komorowski. However, his celebrity status in Britain soon evaporated and he was returned to his regiment. After the war he settled in New Zealand and died in Auckland in the 1990s.

[56] Walter Davis to Author, 19 January 2007. The AK Legalisation Department ('Agaton') issued over 1,000 false documents each month, including the identity card, *Kennkarte* and night pass, *Nachtauzweis*.

[57] The Polish Flight No. 1586 flew a further 42 missions to other occupied countries; Cynk, op. cit., pp. 465–7.

[58] Over one million Stens were supplied by SOE during the course of the war, see Paul Cornish, 'Weapons and Equipment of the Special Operations Executive', in Seaman op. cit.

[59] For a history of activities at Aston House see Des Turner, *Aston House Station 12: SOE's Secret Centre* (Sutton, Stroud 2006). For Perkins, see Peter Wilkinson and Joan Astley, *Gubbins and SOE* (Leo Cooper, London 1993), p.81. For 'Station 43', see Valentine, op. cit., pp. 110–11.

[60] 'Overlord action co-ordinated with Polish Secret Army', HS8/291, NA. Also 'Memo of Meeting 29 July 1944', Polish General Staff VI Bureau, HS4/156, NA and 'Assistance to the Poles', Chief of Staffs 272nd meeting, AIR 20/7983, NA.

[61] SOE Memo, 'General Rising by the Polish Secret Army in Warsaw Area', 29 July 1944, HS4/156, NA. This memo was not circulated to the Chiefs of Staff Committee until 31 July 1944.

[62] 'Memorandum on Polish Situation', 18 July 1944, HS4/146, NA. Also William Mackenzie, op. cit., p. 522.

[63] MP1 (Major Boughey) to MP (Lieutenant-Colonel H. Perkins), 20 July 1944, HS4/146, NA.

[64] E.D.R. Harrison, 'The British Special Operations Executive and Poland', *The Historical Journal*, 43, 4 (Cambridge University Press, 2000), p. 1073. For Churchill, see WSC to Anthony Eden, 6 June 1944, AP20/12/315, Lord Avon Papers, UB. For 'Świt', see Foreign Office to Moscow, 13 June 1943, HS4/142, NA; also David Garnett, *The Secret History of PWE* (St Ermin's Press, London 2002), p. 183.

Chapter Six

Soviet Onslaught

1944 was a momentous year on the Eastern Front. On 3 January, after an exhaustive campaign on Soviet territory, Red Army troops had finally crossed over Poland's old eastern borders and into the Volhynia region. That month also saw the collapse of the last German resistance on the River Dnieper. By the spring, Leningrad in the north had been liberated and in the south, the Red Army had closed in on the Romanian border. But a huge task awaited it, for the bulk of Axis forces, and in particular the German Army Group Centre, still held the important region of Byelorussia. The Wehrmacht was still too strong to buckle under a single Soviet attack, so in order to push on westwards through Poland to Berlin, the Soviet *Stavka* (Supreme Main Command of the Soviet Union) planned to unleash five massive offensives through the summer of 1944. They were to unfold along a line running from the Baltic in the north to the Black Sea in the south. Starting in the north against Finnish forces in early June (Karelian Offensive), the second and third offensives were to strike German positions around Minsk (Operation Bagration). The fourth offensive was planned to capture the Polish cities of Lublin and Lwów (Lwów-Sandomierz Offensive) and if this was successful, the fifth offensive was then designed to push through Romania in the south and capture its vital oilfields by late summer.[1]

On the political front, the beginning of the year had seen another round of declarations between the Polish and Soviet governments over Poland's eastern borders. Stalin continued to demand the territory broadly to the east of the Curzon Line which included the two important Polish centres of Wilno and Lwów. He hoped to coerce the Polish Premier, Mikołajczyk into accepting the Soviet claims and thereby split him from General Sosnkowski.[2] But while Mikołajczyk rejected any Soviet land grab, he was careful to leave room for negotiation on other issues. However, for Stalin, 'negotiations' were a sign of weakness and *Pravda*, the official Soviet newspaper, soon launched a barrage of insults against the Polish Government-in-exile, claiming it included 'Fascists' who 'live in a world of Nazi mirage'.[3]

It was strong stuff, but the British Government were nonetheless losing patience with the Polish stance and even Churchill, knowing that Hitler could not be defeated without a Soviet advance on the Eastern Front, reminded the Polish Premier that Poland would be compensated with territory in the west up to the River Oder as well as East Prussia.[4] In short, he told Mikołajczyk to accept Stalin's conditions 'with enthusiasm', as Poland's eastern borders would never be an issue that Britain would contest; and to confirm his government's stance, on 22 February Churchill announced to Parliament that he accepted Stalin's demands. Harold Nicolson, Principal Private Secretary to the Minister of Information watched the Premier's performance, noting in his diary, 'Winston is not of course as vigorous or as pugnacious as in 1940' but he was determined to state that the Curzon Line 'was reasonable and just.' The British press, including *The Times*, *Manchester Guardian* and *Spectator*, all rammed home the point that Soviet power in itself ruled out negotiations on the issue, while Lord Beaverbrook's *Daily Express* proffered that a relationship with the Soviet Union was more important than Anglo-Polish relations.[5]

Many senior figures in the Allied camp had little patience or sympathy with the Polish over their border issue. With little understanding of the wide social, including peasant, background of many in the Polish Government-in-exile, the US ambassador in Moscow, Averell Harriman described them as 'a group of aristocrats looking to America and Britain to restore their position in Poland and their landed properties and feudalistic system'.[6] Although Churchill had a personal empathy for the Poles, there were those in his Imperial War Cabinet who were not so inclined. The influential Field Marshal Jan Smuts, Prime Minister of South Africa was blunt in his criticism of the Polish stance; writing to Churchill in March 1944, he warned:

I have been following recent messages about the Russian attitude towards us, and feel some anxiety that a rift is developing and that your desire to assist Poland is largely responsible for this. It is clear that Stalin is most sensitive about this, and his offensive remark to Harriman that the Poles are following you is ominous. It would be calamitous if the Polish question were to sour Russian relations with Britain.[7]

The other burning issue in 1944, which might have soured British–Soviet relations was the reopening of the Katyn controversy. In January 1944, Moscow held a pseudo investigation into the atrocity, claiming that the Germans had committed the killings during their occupation after Barbarossa in 1941. Furthermore, this Soviet line was faithfully reported by a group of US journalists, including Kathleen Harriman, daughter of the US Ambassador, who were taken on a site tour of the supposed German atrocity. The journalists duly came back to *Time* magazine, commenting 'as far as we were concerned, the Germans had slaughtered the Poles.' Yet Polish journals and pamphlets knew the real culprits and credible British sources privately doubted the Soviet version.[8] In February 1944, the Savory Report concluded that 'the Polish Government was fully justified in demanding an impartial inquiry' and Foreign Secretary Eden confided to Churchill that the age of the young trees planted over the grave site could be determined at two/three years, putting the date of their planting at 1940. It was not conclusive, but it was very strong evidence that the massacres were carried out during Soviet occupation and before the German invasion. However, the British Government, still anxious to maintain a relationship with Stalin, did not pursue him over the question of the Katyn atrocity. They trod warily with the Soviet Premier, even to the point of banning the export of the Polish weekly paper, *Wiadomosci Polskie*, because of its 'violent attacks on the Soviet Government'.[9] And the British Government also showed signs of caving in to the Soviets over the right of the Poles to maintain their independent transmission stations. Stalin wanted these stations closed down or, at the very least, controlled by the British, which meant Allied access to the secret Polish cypher codes. While the Foreign Office showed signs of bending to this Soviet pressure, other agencies such as SOE strongly resisted. Lieutenant-Colonel Harold Perkins was furious at an FO paper suggesting it would be a good idea to control the cyphers:

I must honestly state that the attached paper fills me with horror in that it shows a complete lack of understanding of the Polish mentality by the Foreign Office. I can only assume that it has in some way slipped past the consideration of people such as Frank Roberts and Strang, who have a real knowledge of the situation. I suspect that its originator was our old friend ★★★★★★ who has in the past made many vain attempts to shoot down the Polish wireless network for one reason or another.

If this matter is really put to the Poles, and I have every confidence that this will not be the case, then all that we will have achieved is that we will completely alienate their already waning affections and gain nothing thereby.[10]

Fortunately, the British War Cabinet listened to SOE's Polish Section and on 3 February 1944, after much deliberation, they agreed to allow the Poles to keep control of their own cyphers and radio stations.[11] These were vital to Polish integrity, but the major sensitive issue remained the argument over the Polish/Soviet border. The Foreign Office felt that they, rather than the Poles, were best suited to settle the issue, with Eden advising the Prime Minister that 'we should be unwise to take the responsibility for informing the Polish troops of current developments in our discussions.'[12] Sue Ryder, always sympathetic to the Polish position, concluded:

The Poles had Bureau VI. They didn't trust the British, so all their signals were done by Stanmore, and their forging was done elsewhere in Hertfordshire. They didn't trust the British because they felt that incoming signals would be taken by the British and used against them. I think they had every right to believe that. They knew that they would be let down, that the Soviets really would take over. They never withheld things from us, but those things I was told by Poles, I would never ever repeat.[13]

For their part, the Poles felt constrained by Allied Command, especially over the issue of flights to Poland. At Brindisi, the momentum of successful relief and agent drops during April and May was abruptly halted in June, when MAAF diverted all missions away from Poland and redirected 1586 Polish Flight and 148 Squadron towards drops for partisans in the Balkans and Northern Italy. For Italy was again the scene of fierce fighting in late May and early June 1944, as the Allies finally broke out from the Anzio beachhead and advanced on Rome. It was a costly operation with heavy losses; Air Chief Marshal Lord Trenchard lost his step-son, Lieutenant-Colonel Patrick Boyle and wrote a remarkably stoic letter to Air Marshal Sir Jack Slessor, Deputy C-in-C MAAF:

> Mr Dear Slessor
> It is really tragic. We have lost three boys in the last five years and my other one is just ready to go overseas. But it is wonderful what the Air has done and what all the Forces have done. I only hope history will really be written. Excuse a disjointed letter. There is nothing more you can do, except I am trying to get out of the Regiment a photograph of the Anzio beachhead cemetery with my boy's name shown.[14]

Slessor himself was not immune to personal loss that summer – two of his relatives were airmen who perished in the Mediterranean theatre, one being shot down during a Ploesti oilfield bombing mission.[15] But while he knew only too well the pain of the casualty lists, as Deputy C-in-C of Mediterranean Allied Air Force, he was continually having to juggle his scarce resources and spread them over a number of pressing fronts. There is no doubt that he had to take advantage of the favourable weather conditions during April and May to support the Allied pressure in Italy, but it was also imperative that German troops remained tied down in Eastern Europe. For the opening up of a western front by a successful 'D Day' landing on 6 June meant that Germany's industrial heartland was under direct threat. The war on the Eastern Front would sap Germany's manpower, and eventually Soviet advances would threaten her oil supplies, but a new Allied front in the west would only be 300 miles from the industrial Ruhr. Therefore, in the run-up as well as the aftermath of successful landings in Normandy, a well-supplied AK was one important tool in occupying Wehrmacht and SS forces. Flights to Poland therefore resumed in July, with the first mission on the night of 3/4 July comprising five Polish and seven RAF aircraft. As usual, the mission was partly successful, with some drops on target, some into the hands of the enemy, and some aborted. But the cost was high, with three RAF Halifaxes shot down over Yugoslavia, resulting in the deaths of thirteen aircrew while eight survivors were captured.[16]

The British Foreign Office had, for some time, considered the Soviet Union the lesser of two evils. Anthony Eden thought that Stalin should be allowed credit for the Soviet sacrifices in the east, and that this credit would probably take the form of dominance over certain east European countries, such as Romania and Poland. This view was supported by most senior officials, including Sir William Strang, Assistant Under-Secretary of State until 1943, who admitted that it would be in Britain's interest to accept Soviet domination of Eastern Europe:

> If a victorious and dynamic Russia lays a heavy hand upon the peoples of Eastern, Central and South-Eastern Europe, I should not like to say that this would be to our disadvantage provided that the German menace to our own existence continued to be mastered. It is better that Russia should dominate Eastern Europe than that Germany should dominate Western Europe.
>
> The time may come when Russia will take the place of Germany as a threat to our world power or to our existence. But there are no signs that this will occur in any immediate future.[17]

Strang's views were endorsed by his superior at the Foreign Office, Sir Orme Sargent, and this view of an unstoppable 'Sovietisation' of Eastern Europe widely prevailed in many departments of state.[18] Sir Owen O'Malley, who became British Ambassador to the exiled Polish state from 1943 until 1945, believed that some form of Soviet dominated confederation in the region should be accepted. To usher this in, goodwill with the Soviets would have to be maintained and the relevant governments would have to 'soften up their anti-communist fronts'. Such goodwill also extended to Foreign Office officials passing selected extracts of Polish 'Sitreps', or intelligence reports, to their Soviet counterparts. Yet, these officials still professed irritation at Polish stubbornness over border issues, with one official complaining, 'I do wish the Poles would realise that no good can be done by continually attempting to stir up trouble in every possible quarter.'[19] Oliver Harvey, who replaced Strang as an Assistant Under-Secretary in 1943, saw Stalin operating at both the Moscow and Tehran conferences, yet continued with the line that Soviet intentions were understandable. Furthermore, he believed that the Poles were an obstacle in the way of a British-Soviet understanding, dismissing them as possessed of 'a somewhat Irish type of temperament who enjoy always being against somebody'. His views were reported in February 1944, in a memo to Major-General Gubbins of SOE:

They [the Soviets] feel they can really rely on nobody except themselves with safety. They prefer, in their own version of the Cromwellian maxim, 'to trust in God and keep their powder dry'. They feel they have been through quite enough and they want, like everybody else, to make perfectly certain that they will never be invaded and put to all this trouble again. Therefore, he [Harvey] thinks, that it is no longer their policy to bother to bolshivise the rest of the world but, in the spirit of nationalism evoked by this war, to surround themselves by neighbours on whom they can depend.

The USSR have shown themselves perfectly ready to come to terms with the bourgeois Czechoslovak Government. The Czechs have never been anti-Russian. They would be willing enough, Mr Harvey thinks, to reach a reasonable agreement with the Polish Government provided they could feel sure that the Poles would not continue their traditional anti-Russian policy.[20]

This report came into the hands of Colonel Perkins, who found Harvey's reported comments about the Poles 'in singularly bad taste'. He despaired that Soviet views seemed to dominate British thinking, while Polish views were suppressed. After all, it was not just the FO and sections of the British Press who lauded the Soviet Union. Ever since Stalin had joined the Allies in 1941, there had been a number of 'Anglo-Soviet' weeks staged in Britain every year. One such event in Coventry enlisted the support of local dignitaries, MPs and clergy, whose platform extolled the virtues of the Soviet way of life with numerous musical tributes to the Red Army. In February 1944, Britain celebrated the 26th Anniversary of the Red Army by tribute shows in Edinburgh, Belfast and in London's Albert Hall, where the 'Salute to the Red Army' was endorsed by a reading of the Poet Laureate's 'Ode to the Red Army'. Against such a background of pro-Soviet propaganda, SOE had good reason to believe they were a voice in the wilderness.[21]

The Soviet media also went onto the offensive. During the spring and summer of 1944 Soviet radio stations kept up an unrelenting diet of vitriol against both the Polish C-in-C, Sosnkowski and the AK, with broadcasts in support of their own sponsored Berling's LWP Army. The Soviets announced 'the increasing blows now being struck against the Germans by Polish patriots were being obstructed by traitors in Poland who take their orders from General Sosnkowski.' Soviet propaganda under the guise of 'The Voice of Free Poland' continued to attack the Polish Government-in-exile and tellingly, offered support to the 'ever patient British press' who 'repeatedly had to raise its voice in an effort to check the irresponsible pranks of Polish politicians.'[22]

As Stalin 'thrust and parried' over the border issue, he knew that events on the Eastern Front were moving inexorably his way. Although early contacts between the Red Army and local AK units in Volhynia had been violent, with the swift execution of the local AK commander and his lieutenants, Stalin gained time by publicly encouraging military collaboration against the common German enemy. However, in the swamps and deep forests of Western Byelorussia in eastern occupied Poland, there were any number of displaced and roaming bands of Poles or Russians, over whom there was no control. Jewish groups such as the Grynszpan band found sanctuary there, and although hunger often drove these refugees back to the towns and cities, it was estimated that twenty-seven Jewish partisan bands operated in the region occupied by the Red Army in 1944.[23] Partisan gangs could boast a wide range of members, from Jews or Ukrainians to Red Army deserters, and there was often internal fighting as well as pitched battles between the groups. There was also tension between partisans and local villagers, who were fearful of German reprisals, while there were a number of Polish 'forestmen' who themselves had been driven from their homes and had become looters or marauders, and who could also turn out to be informers. Yet although Jews were sometimes hounded and shot, at other times they were helped by a wide variety of individuals. One Jewess recalled assistance at various times from a German prostitute, a Polish aristocrat, two ethnic Germans, and members of a right-wing Polish resistance group.[24] In this ethnic melting-pot, cruelty was rife. One Polish resistance fighter, who was one of the 'unseen and silent' recalled the fate of an AK company in the Wilno region:

Our 1st Company was stationed at Derewno. That morning they had been treacherously attacked by one of the Soviet brigades; and after some of our men had taken to arms, ten of them were put against a wall and shot. The few who were wounded were finished off, but not before they had been hideously tortured. Some were kicked to death, others had their fingers and ears cut off. The rest with Lieutenant 'Jar', were taken to the forest under escort. The first news began to reach us from the forest. Frolow, a Soviet citizen married to a Polish girl, who had earlier refused to join the Soviets and had remained with us, had been hanged. The brothers Skrodzki had been killed in an appalling fashion. Their ears, cut off while they were still alive, were fried and they were made to eat them…and at the same time London instructed by radio: 'Units of the Home Army are to reveal themselves to the Soviet front-line commanders.'[25]

Such events were by no means untypical, and demonstrate the gulf between the public policy of cooperation with the Soviets and actual activities on the ground. Brutality was not just confined to SS or NKVD units, and soldiers from both the Wehrmacht and Red Army could act with the same casual cruelty in this 'racial' war on the Eastern Front. Many ordinary German *Landsers*, or infantrymen, keenly embraced the Nazi propaganda that saw the enemy as 'Asiatic hordes' or the soldiers of a 'Jewish–Bolshevik conspiracy'.[26] Consequently, few Soviet prisoners were taken, with some *Landsers* excusing themselves for the slaughter of prisoners by blaming the partisans for blowing up trains that could have taken POWs to the rear. As they retreated across Poland, Wehrmacht units committed many acts of savagery against the local population. One particularly wanton act involved the German 253rd Infantry Division who drove tens of thousands of people from their homes in the Osarishchi district of Soviet Byelorussia, slaughtered those who would not move and drove the others into camps without housing or sanitary facilities, where thousands died of hunger or typhus.[27] Unsurprisingly, the new Soviet conquest also saw numerous acts of revenge carried out by local partisans on recently captured German troops:

> A partisan, a small man, has killed two Germans with a stake. He had pleaded with the guards of the column to give him these Germans. He had convinced himself that they were the ones who had killed his daughter, Olya and his sons, his two boys. He broke all their bones, and smashed their skulls, and while he was beating them, he was crying and shouting: 'Here you are – for Olya! Here you are – for Kolya!' When they were dead, he propped the bodies up against a tree stump and continued to beat them.[28]

Red Army units had little time for the local inhabitants in villages and towns that they 'liberated'. Occasionally, a Soviet advance would be driven back and German soldiers would once again occupy villages they had held for four years. Günter Koschorrek, a German *Landser* who had witnessed his share of cruelty on the Eastern Front, was nonetheless appalled by what he found.

> Sometimes, their [Red Army] advance units ran into strong German opposition. Then they withdraw and leave behind masses of murdered women and children in the villages, hacked to death along the muddy roads and in the houses. Above all there remains an unremitting hatred towards the Germans and towards those who have served them during the occupation. They don't ask if those who have served have done so voluntarily or if they have been forced to do it; it's enough that they have lived under German occupation…these women, murdered by their own allies were really only normal everyday women. God knows, they didn't want to work for their occupiers: they only wanted to survive.[29]

There were many occasions when the Red Army came across large AK formations and, after formalities were dispensed with, dealt with them ruthlessly. The 27th Volhynian Division had played a significant role in helping Soviet forces breakout from the Koval district, to the east of the Pripet Marshes and had then withdrawn towards Lublin. Yet, when the Red Army caught up with them again at the city, they immediately disarmed them and broke up the division.[30] At the end of July, Colonel Władysław Filipkowski ('Janka') and units from the AK 5th Infantry Division assisted in the capture of Lwów, and were greeted by Soviet forces who arrived simultaneously, only to be disarmed by the NKVD. Those who then refused to join Berling's communist LWP were arrested and deported.[31]

Amongst all this social mayhem, Polish families were often torn apart, producing many orphans. Some herded together in cities, where they were taken under the wing of underground units, but others in distant rural areas had to fend for themselves. Consequently, some partisan bands operating in Polish forests found themselves followed by the *besprizorniki,* or homeless children, whose homes had been destroyed by German anti-Semitic or anti-partisan operations, such as those carried out by the infamous Kaminski Brigade. These feral children roamed the forests living off berries, mushrooms and nuts unless they were lucky enough to be taken in by a partisan group and used as couriers or observers of enemy troop movements. For the partisans, like those of the large Bielski

Band, it meant sharing precious food as well as increasing their risk of exposure to the enemy.[32] Many AK units also made efforts to help local Jews but as in the general Polish population, attitudes towards the Jews could be uneven. In Wołyń, Tarnapol and the Narotch forest, AK units made determined efforts to help Jewish refugees, but there were claims that other units in Wilno and the Białystok Forest colluded with the SS and thwarted relief efforts to the Jews.[33]

In a world away from the deprivations in eastern Poland, the political negotiations ground on. On 6 June, the Polish Premier, Mikołajczyk landed in Washington to seek support from President Roosevelt for his rapidly evaporating dialogue with Stalin. But the US President, unknown to Mikołajczyk, had already secretly conceded Poland's eastern borders to Stalin, a man who the President was happy to describe as 'a realist rather than an imperialist.' Furthermore, Roosevelt told the Premier that he thought a deal could still be struck and that a 'strong and independent Poland would emerge.' Roosevelt sent a personal telegram to Stalin in support of continued negotiations, but that was the extent of US help. Mikołajczyk returned to Britain empty-handed, but remained determined. On 20 June he met the Soviet Ambassador in London and there was again talk of a deal but this hope was dashed three days later by the sudden Soviet demand for the removal from government of Stalin's *bête noire*, General Sosnkowski and his Chief-of-Staff, General Marian Kukiel.[34]

The Soviet summer and autumn operations aimed to push the Germans back over a series of defensive river lines that ran through Poland. During 1943 and the spring of 1944, German forces had been forced back from the River Dnieper in old Soviet territory, so that by early June 1944, the frontline ran from the eastern borders of Estonia in the north to fifty miles west of Odessa, in the south. The Soviet advance had been particularly successful in the south, where the First, Second and Third Ukrainian Fronts had reached the edge of the Carpathian Mountains and were barely fifty miles from the southern Polish city of Lwów. However, in the top half of the frontline, adjacent to Warsaw and the Baltic states, the Wehrmacht Army Group Centre had stubbornly resisted and the Soviet line lay 150 miles further back. In order to push the Germans back to their next defensive river line on the western River Bug (also the eastern boundary of the German General Government sector), Army Group Centre would have to be dealt a crushing blow.

Even in the face of impossible Soviets odds, and much to the chagrin of senior German commanders, Hitler would not accept any plans for strategic withdrawals on the Eastern Front. Certain towns and positions were ordered to be held at all costs, with the result that large numbers of German troops were invariably cut off and captured. This idea of rigid defence was catastrophic for the German Army, when pitched against the offensives that the Soviet *Stavka* had planned for the summer of 1944. The concept of 'Elastic defence' was simply not acceptable to Hitler. It was a fatal mistake.[35]

On 22 June, the Soviet Army unleashed 'Operation Bagration', named after the Tsarist General, Peter Bagration, who died of his wounds after the Battle of Borodino in 1812. The sheer scale of this offensive was astounding. Marshals Zhukov and Vasilevsky co-ordinated the knockout punch involving four Soviet 'Fronts', which approximated in size to Army Groups, each containing up to nine infantry armies, three tank armies, two air armies, five mechanized corps, two cavalry corps, as well as artillery and engineer units. The Third Byelorussian Front (Army General Ivan Chernyakovsky) and First Byelorussian Front (Army General Konstantin Rokossovsky) formed the core of the offensive, with the First Baltic Front (Army General Ivan Bagramian) covering the offensive's northern flanks and the weaker Second Bylorussian Front (Army General Georgii Zahkarov) offering follow-up support. Ranged against them was the German Army Group Centre (Generalfeldmarschall Walter Model), which comprised four Wehrmacht infantry armies together with ancillary and support units – numbering nearly 800,000 men. Within two weeks, the Soviets had captured Minsk, 250 miles north-east of Warsaw and by 12 July they had cleared most of Soviet Byelorussia and with the assistance of AK units entered Wilno.[36] Byelorussia, the vast region to the east of Lublin had never been a single unified entity with its own borders. Before 1939, its western area, containing the towns of Brześć and Pińsk, had formed part of Poland, whilst the eastern part, with its regional capital Minsk, was incorporated into the Soviet Union.[37]

Skirting the south of the whole region were the Pripet Marshes, the largest area of swampland in the European continent. Fed by the River Pripet, a major tributary of the Dnieper, this vast area covered some 45,000 square miles, nearly the size of England, and its impenetrable forests, swamps and moors created a serious obstacle to any attacker. During Barbarossa in 1941, the Germans had attempted to bypass the marshes but found that they were home to bands of partisans who successfully harried and disrupted the Wehrmacht advance. Trying to pass through the flanking forest areas was equally impossible, especially for infantry. The areas comprised dense deciduous trees, many of which had rotted over the centuries and created a haven for thick, barbed undergrowth, harbouring mosquitoes.[38] To overcome the sodden terrain engineers constructed timber causeways.

The first phase of 'Bagration' saw the encirclement and destruction of Army Group Centre's command and the second phase saw the Red Army's rapid pursuit of broken German units. In fact this advance was the greatest of any army during the war and the sheer speed of the Soviet successes even surprised the *Stavka* command. But although credit is given to innovative Soviet tactics, the Red Army could not have moved at such a pace without material assistance from the West, including large quantities of US Studebaker trucks, supplied to them under the 'Lend-Lease' scheme. The Allies also assisted the Soviet offensives by keeping the pressure on Germany in the west with the Normandy landings coupled with strategic heavy bombing.[39]

Nowhere was this more evident than during the Lwów-Sandomierz Offensive, the second largest Soviet attack, which was launched on 13 July. The Soviet First Ukrainian Front (Marshal Ivan Konev), which was the biggest formation in the Red Army, had managed to convince the defending German Army Group North Ukraine (*Generaloberst* Josef Harpe), that any Soviet offensive would come south of the strategic city of Lwów. Consequently, the Germans felt it was safe to transfer II SS-Panzer Corps, together with its two crack panzer divisions, to the Western Front to face the Normandy landings. In the event, the main Soviet thrust came around the north of Lwów and pummeled the depleted flank of the German 4th Panzer Army. It then moved on westwards towards the next German defensive line on the Vistula, a broad river, which although not deep, extended to over 200 metres-wide in places. Meanwhile the Lwów German garrison broke out and retreated south-west towards the Carpathian Mountains, leaving the city to be occupied by Soviet forces on 27 July.[40]

On 18th July on the southern flank of the Bagration Offensive, the Soviet 8th Guards Army comprising three Rifle Corps and the 1st Polish Army (Berling), had deployed south of the Pripet Marshes and advanced to smash the German 4th Panzer Army. The 1st Polish Army under the command of General Zygmunt Berling, had developed into a formidable unit, despite its mongrel origins. It was nominally made up of communist and pro-Soviet Poles, but in reality comprised many Poles who had been captured during the Soviet invasion in 1939 and given the choice between a hard labour camp or military service. The force was bolstered in 1943 by the conscription of all Poles in Soviet-occupied territory between sixteen and fifty-five years-of-age. However, while the ranks comprised mainly Poles, Polish officers were in short supply. The massacres at Katyn and regular NKVD executions had greatly diminished the available pool, so recourse was made to recruit Russians, Ukrainians, Byelorussians and Jews – few of whom had ever been Polish citizens.[41]

On 24 July, Rokossovsky's First Byelorussian Front captured Chełm and Lublin, the first significant towns beyond the old Soviet borders. It was an important operation entrusted to one of the most capable and enduring Red Army commanders, Konstantin Rokossovsky. Born to a Polish father and Russian mother, he soon acquired impeccable Bolshevik credentials, joining the Red Army in 1918. By 1941 he was a General Major participating in defensive operations during Barbarossa and Stalingrad. He then played a successful role in the planning for the Battle of Kursk, and was moved to a critical role in the vanguard of the 1944 Soviet summer offensives. His swift acquisition of the two centres was a high priority for Stalin, for these gains enabled the Soviet-backed 'Lublin Committee' to be established first in Chełm and a week later in Lublin. Rokossovsky then moved on towards the Vistula River to the south of Warsaw. On 29 July, his 2nd Tank Army moved up towards Warsaw's eastern suburbs, with the intention that the Soviet 47th Army would cover its flank. But before this cover could arrive, *Generalfeldmarschall* Walter Model, Commander of the Wehrmacht Army Group Centre, ordered two German panzer corps to counter-attack and push back Rokossovsky's tanks.[42] The German counter-attack also involved infantry units, who took on the Soviet armour with incredible bravery. A German Grenadier recounted his uneven fight with a 26-ton T-34 tank:

> It had been planned that we should allow the first group of T-34's to roll over us. The grenade had a safety cap, which had to be unscrewed to reach the rip-cord. My fingers were trembling as I unscrewed the cap and climbed out of the trench. Crouching low, I started towards the monster, pulling the detonating cord and prepared to fix the charge. I had now nine seconds before the grenade exploded and then I noticed, to my horror,

that the outside of the tank was covered in concrete. My bomb could not stick on such a surface. The tank suddenly spun on its right track, turned so that it pointed straight at me and moved forward as if to run over me.

I flung myself backwards and fell straight into a partly dug slit trench so shallow that I was only just below the surface of the ground. Luckily I had fallen face upwards and was still holding tight in my hand the sizzling hand grenade. As the tank rolled over me there was a sudden and total blackness. The shallow earth walls of the trench began to collapse. As the belly of the monster passed over me I reached up instinctively as if to push it away, stuck the charge on the smooth unpasted metal. Barely had the tank passed over me when there was a loud explosion. I was alive and the Russians were dead. I was trembling in every limb.[43]

To combat the Soviet T-34 tank during the summer of 1944, the German Grenadier also had access to powerful rocket-propelled weapons. Apart from throwing satchels of explosives or Molotov cocktails at tanks, which meant leaving the cover of a slit trench, he could now employ a *Panzerfaust 30,* which fired a hollow-charge grenade. It was a one shot weapon, using a light disposable launch tube that discharged a grenade, which could penetrate 140mm armour. The absence of recoil meant a prolific expulsion of flame so it could not be fired in a confined space, but its strength was its simplicity. It took nerve to wait until a tank was within the 30m range, but with the weapon sighted, the safety pin extracted and striker cocked, all the operative had to do was press the release button.[44] Keeping a steady nerve in the face of a Soviet tank attack was not easy, as Grenadier Guy Sajer recalled:

We were all torn between wanting to weep and run away, and to scream and run out to meet the danger. 'No Bolshevik will ever tread on German soil.' But they were there by their thousands, crushing it with frenzy and jubilation – and there were eighteen of us to stop them… Then they appeared, ten of them at first, following the road guarded by our third group. The first tank was stopped some twenty yards from the two *Panzerfausts* in the third group. One of their projectiles burst on the tank's front apron scattering a shower of rivets and killing the monster and its occupants. The others were slowly manoeuvring, heavily attacking the incline of the bank, to make their way around the burning tank. I couldn't stop myself from whispering, 'they're coming for us'.

But the tanks – three to be exact – climbed back to face up to the threat. They hoped to frighten the anti-tank crew, counting heavily on their terrifying appearance – a calculation which almost worked. However, a second monster burst into flame. The tank behind it brushed past opening up a passage. It reached the German position, and broke its occupants' nerve. We saw our comrades jump from their hole and run like madmen. They were trying to reach the woods and began to climb the hill. The tank, which was following right behind them, drew so close it almost touched them before knocking them to pieces with the machine-guns on board.[45]

Apart from the *Panzerfaust,* the other heavier-duty weapon, which had only become available since 1943 was the *Panzerschreck* (tank frightener). Also known as the 'stove pipe', it was based on the US bazooka and had an open ended tube with blast shield, and weighed 11kg when empty. Its range was about 180m and its rocket-propelled grenade could smash through 200mm armour, thus making it capable of destroying most Allied armoured vehicles in one hit.

Another characteristic of warfare on the Eastern Front was the widespread use by both sides of rocket launchers. While the Red Army had the famous *Katyusha* rocket launcher, the Germans used the *Nebelwerfer,* originally named after the smoke rockets it fired. The rockets had an erratic trajectory, but the explosive or incendiary burst just above the ground so the force of the blast was not lost in the earth. Although the heavier 210mm rocket only had a range of ½ mile, the lighter 150mm projectiles could reach over three miles. Each *Nebelwerfer* could fire six rockets, so a conventional battery of six launchers could loose off thirty-six rockets in twelve seconds – a debilitating attack, as an 'Ivan' from the Soviet Army noted:

We had not taken cover but continued marching and then suddenly we saw sheets of flame coming from behind the German lines, then the smoke and then the howling again. This time the mass of smoke and flames roaring towards us seemed to cover the whole of the battalion front. The area in front of us and behind us as well as at intervals along the line was suddenly blotted out and what seemed to be hundreds of simultaneous explosions. Snow and earth clods were flung up obscuring visibility and then came the cry for medical personnel to help the wounded. Under this first mass bombardment we had gone to ground and thus, we were a stationary target. Within seconds, the second wave had come down and then a third. After that I lost count – it just seemed as if the whole sky was raining noise and explosive on us.[46]

As the Red Army swept on, it pushed the vast tide of refugees ahead of it. Retreating German soldiers, often starving and in rags, fought each other or civilians for scraps of food. In desperation, still heavily defended German supply depots were attacked by their own retreating men, while *Landsers* who were caught by their military police in possession of food, were strung up from trees with a sign around their neck, 'I am a thief and traitor to my country.'[47]

Despite ferocious German resistance, the Red Army rolled forward at a speed that surprised its western allies, eclipsing US plans for air attacks against German targets in central and Eastern Europe. These plans had started with a United States Military Mission to the Soviet Union, which had been established back in October 1943, and although its stated aim was co-ordination with Soviet forces, the real aim was to set up Army Air Force bases on Soviet territory. These were to be used to attack German oil installations or industrial units beyond the range of Britain or Italy. Alternatively, the bases could be used for shuttle missions, whereby Allied aircraft could take off from Britain, bomb targets or drop supplies in central Europe or Poland, then land at Soviet bases to refuel and re-equip. Further targets could then be bombed on their return to Britain or Italy. President Roosevelt had pursued the matter at the Tehran Conference in November 1943 and while Stalin was reported to have 'agreed in principle', he side-stepped any firm proposals. Eventually however, the Soviets conceded that US Eastern Command could establish three bases in the Ukraine – Poltava, Mirgorod and Piryatin, which became operational in the summer of 1944. Deploying air force units in these bases required huge resources and some 9,000 personnel, 3 battalions of anti-aircraft artillery as well as a squadron of night-fighters were installed by the US Eastern Command. To balance this presence in Soviet controlled territory, units of the Soviet Air Force were allowed access to an Allied base in Italy. One Soviet transport squadron employing Dakotas and one Soviet fighter squadron using Yaks came under the command of the British 334 Wing to assist Tito's partisans fighting in Yugoslavia. But Soviet contacts with British airmen or SOE officers based in southern Italy were very limited. SOE's Major E.P.F. Boughey was not impressed with the Red Air Force:

> The Russians are among us, but hardly of us. We see them about the place in Bari in their thick serge uniforms on the hottest days, but we have of course, no professional contact with them, and it has not happened that any of us have had any social contact with them either. As a matter of fact, very few people do…Our colleagues up the road are fed up with them because of their atrocious behaviour on the matter of Greece and the RAF are not awfully pleased with them either, since they do not think it really necessary to get themselves killed flying 850 miles because the Russians refuse to fly 20 miles.[48]

On 2 June 1944 the first US shuttle mission took place, using Soviet facilities. As part of 'Operation Frantic', 127 B-17s or 'Flying Fortresses' and 64 Mustangs took off and bombed the marshalling yards at Debrecen, Hungary. Two more missions against Romania followed and then on 21 June a similar sized force attacked synthetic oil facilities in Lower Silesia, stopping off at a Soviet base and launching an attack the following day on oil refineries at Drohobycz in Poland. But unknown to the task force, a Luftwaffe pilot had trailed them back to the Poltava base. It was not long before a seventy-five-strong Luftwaffe bombing group appeared and unloaded 110 tons of bombs onto the US aircraft standing on the ground at the Soviet base. Soviet anti-aircraft defences were sparse and the firing poor, with the result that the raid destroyed or damaged 69 B-17s and Mustangs on the ground, and killed over 100 Soviet personnel.[49]

The US responded by talk of increasing the manpower and facilities at the three US/Soviet bases, but Stalin's acquiescence in the 'Frantic' project was rapidly failing. Although July saw a small number of Lightening fighter missions taking off from the Soviet air bases to attack targets in Romania, the losses in aircraft were too numerous for any advantage gained. Furthermore, the Soviet Bagration Offensive had successfully captured large swathes of German occupied territory and thereby removed many of the former American targets. Three further Allied bombing missions were carried out in July but the Soviets were fast growing irritated by the presence of large numbers of American forces in the Ukraine. The Western press hardly helped, with lurid stories about the sexual prowess of American soldiers. But fear for the welfare of Ukrainian women probably came some way behind the fact that US bombing raids had largely become irrelevant to the course of the war on the Eastern Front.[50]

The scale of the summer Soviet offensives sweeping across Byelorussia was impressive. In the vanguard of the Red Army were the 'Guards Armoured Break-through Regiments', equipped almost exclusively with medium T-34 tanks, built with sloping armour which made them very difficult to knock out. Some units were equipped with the latest version, the T34/85, which had only come off the production line during the previous winter. Its main modifications involved replacing the earlier turret and 76mm gun with the turret and 85mm gun of the heavier KV-85 tank, giving it superior fire-power over the German Panther. Typically, each Soviet 'break-through' regiment comprised twenty-one tanks and two armoured reconnaissance cars, together with approximately 350 men. These high-speed units would drive forward after strong artillery preparation and air support in an attempt to probe and puncture weak German defences. Into any breaches would come 'Armoured Corps', whose heavier JS-2 tanks would be protected on the flanks by 'Mechanised Corps'. Then waves of rifle corps, each containing about three divisions of 6,000 men, together with the usual corps compliment of howitzers, assault-guns and signals units. In all, it is estimated that Operation Bagration mustered about 1.7 million Soviet troops – more than double the number of German defenders.[51]

German armoured units had great difficulty holding back such an onslaught. Units were invariably equipped with the Panther tank, with its 75mm gun, or the slower, heavier Tiger tank with its more powerful 88mm armament. Tank crews called the 23mph Tiger 'a furniture van', which was good for breaching Soviet lines, and while it may have been successful in Western Europe, its slow trundling pace was a great handicap in the vast spaces of eastern Europe. By contrast, senior German commanders, such as General von Manteuffel, commander of the elite *Grossdeutschland* Division in 1944, believed the Soviet Josef Stalin tank (designated JS-2), to be 'the finest in the world'. With its lower profile, heavy armour and powerful 122mm gun, its shells could penetrate or knock off enemy tank turrets or burst open infantry bunkers. However, as it only came into production in the spring of 1944, just eighty-five JS-2s were available to four Soviet regiments for the initial Bagration operations. Nonetheless, when employed, it was more than a match for the German Panther or Tiger tank, and von Manteuffel recalled that while his Tigers began to hit the Josef Stalins at 2200m, their shells could not penetrate the Soviet tanks until they had closed to half that distance. Effectively, the technical superiority of German armour that was so overwhelming at Kursk in 1943, had ceased to exist.[52]

The Soviets also made good use of cavalry, helped by the vastness of the front, and the resourcefulness of these units certainly impressed German commanders:

> The advance of a Russian army was something that westerners could not imagine. A Russian army was largely composed of mounted infantry on horses, and it was not dependent on supplies in the way that a western army was. The soldier had a sack on his back, in which he had nothing more than bits of bread and such raw vegetables as he could collect on his march. The horses got nothing except straw from the roofs of houses and turnips from the fields, supplemented by such scraps of food and fodder as could be found in the villages they passed through. During an advance the Russians were accustomed to carry on for as much as three weeks like this.[53]

While German commanders may have respected their enemy, some felt that a greater threat came from their own side. General Hasso von Manteuffel, who achieved success in June 1944 by slowing the Soviet advance into northern Romania, remained critical of his Commander-in-Chief's lack of military education:

> Hitler had a real flair for strategy and tactics, especially for surprise moves, but he lacked a sufficient foundation of technical knowledge to apply it properly. Moreover, he had a tendency to intoxicate himself with figures and quantities. When one was discussing a problem with him, he would repeatedly pick up the telephone, ask to be put through to some departmental chief and ask, 'How many so-and-so have we got?' And then he would turn to the man he was arguing with, quote the number and say, 'there you are'. He was too ready to accept paper figures, without asking if the numbers given were really available. It was always the same whatever the subject might be – tanks, aircraft, spades etc.[54]

Ahead of the advanced parties of the Red Army, communist partisan bands attempted combined operations with local AK units against German targets. A local AK commander, 'Mira' reflected that negotiations were usually protracted, with each side demanding concessions. He recalled that for one operation involving an attack on a prison 'the communists undertook to provide a detachment of unarmed men and two motor-cars, and to cover our retreat as far as Stolpce. In return they received from us arms for all the men they were to provide, and 10,000 Ostmarks.' However, treachery was imminent:

> The base from which the attack was to start was Katia's wooden house and the prison was about 500 yards away. The action was to begin at 7.00 am and the Communists and the cars were to arrive an hour earlier. We were betrayed. Instead of the Communists, a detachment of the Gestapo on foot, as well as a tank equipped with a flame-thrower, arrived at 6.30 am. We were not taken by surprise, as the delay had made us suspicious and we were keeping watch at the windows. Katia was not at home; she was supposed to have gone to Molodeczo to organise the cover for our retreat. We fired first at the approaching Germans. There was a short desperate fight. 'Tumry' was seriously wounded in the chest, 'Kazik' and 'George' were killed on the spot. The Germans lost three men, either killed or seriously wounded. The rest of them took cover behind the tank, which sprayed us with strong machine-gun fire and the blazing jet of its flame-thrower. Within a few seconds the house was a blazing inferno. 'Tumry', seeing that further resistance was impossible, ordered Big Ted and myself to escape through the loft…We knew when we left 'Tumry' that we'd never see him again.[55]

On the northern flank of the Soviet thrust, the First Baltic Front forced the German Army Group North back from the River Dvina towards Lithuania and East Prussia. German forces risked being encircled, pushed up into the Kurland peninsula and cut off. By the end of first week of July, Soviet forces were less than two hundred miles from Hitler's '*Wolfsschanze*' HQ at Rastenburg in East Prussia.[56] Senior commanders based at the 'Wolf's Lair' were becoming increasingly alarmed at Hitler's strategy. Generaloberst Kurt Zeitler, Chief of Army General Staff, felt himself side-lined by his C-in-C, who refused any suggestions or advice. Zeitzler, the son of a Lutheran parson was based at a battle HQ, some fifteen miles away from the *Wolfsschanze,* and had offered his resignation once before. On 7 July he attended the Führer's HQ for a further showdown, knowing that the other senior commanders, Keitel and Jodl would always support Hitler. Zeitzler later confided to the war correspondent, Chester Wilmot:

> I told Hitler that I could not be party to the encirclement of the Army Group Kurland [known as Army Group North before November 1944]. It would be lost to no purpose in the same way as the Stalingrad Army. This made him lose his temper. He became very loud and broke off the interview with the words, 'I bear the responsibility and not you'. I replied just as loudly, 'In the same way as you, my Führer, are responsible to the German people, I am responsible to my conscience. And nobody can relieve me of that responsibility. Not even you, my Führer'. He thereupon went pale with rage...I considered it my duty to tell him that it was impossible to win the war by military means. Something had to be done (I meant some political action). He then started roaring. He spoke of defeatism and railed at the General Staff.[57]

Not surprisingly, Zeitler recorded that it was the last time he saw Hitler. He subsequently had a nervous breakdown and was dismissed from his post, to be replaced by the legendary Panzer commander, General Heinz Guderian on 20 July – the very day that an attempt was made on Hitler's life. Guderian was a surprising choice. Although he was a famous pioneer of German armoured warfare and had enjoyed considerable success in Western Europe and the early months of Barbarossa in 1941, Hitler had sacked him in December of that year after the Wehrmacht advance had stalled in front of Moscow. However, despite his undoubted flair and imagination, even Guderian could not stall the Soviet onslaught. He was hardly in a position to influence events, for Hitler had already eroded the role of Chief of the General Staff, who was now just 'an executive who acted as the intermediary and telephonist between the Commander-in-Chief and the army group commanders.'[58]

The threatened collapse of the German front in the East had undoubtedly persuaded a circle of plotters around Count von Stauffenberg and General Ludwig Beck, to act swiftly against Hitler. At 1242 hours on 20 July, a bomb exploded in a conference room at the Rastenburg lair but failed to kill Hitler. Instead of acting decisively, the plotters faltered, their plan unravelled and nearly 5,000 of those implicated in the conspiracy were executed.[59] The plan failed because of bad luck, poor organisation and the unwillingness of the Army, Security apparatus and general public to support a rising against Hitler at this stage of the war. It appears that British intelligence knew little of the plot and although SOE had a German Section, there was no direct involvement with the plotters. In fact SOE representation inside the Reich was woefully inadequate, and even its US sister organisation, the Special Operations section of OSS had made little progress, as a secret OSS memo pointed out:

> There is at present no W/T operator working for SFHQ (Special Forces, HQ) in Germany. Attempts have been made in the past, but the agents sent in have never survived. The situation in Germany is not fluid enough to allow a more active exploitation of opposing elements, particularly in view of the power of the Gestapo and the absence of any indication that the opposition is prepared to come out into the open or to appeal to the Allies for help.[60]

Even allowing for the successful introduction of agents into Germany, SHAEF had already directed that SOE and OSS should act independently inside the Reich. Accordingly, OSS were allocated Poles for such work and following the Allied advances in Normandy during 1944, a number of Poles who had been pressed into the Wehrmacht were captured. From these German-speaking soldiers, twenty agents and twenty radio operators were selected and re-introduced into Germany to acquire intelligence. The emphasis was not on contacting those Germans who might assist the Allies. Instead intelligence was collected on those Nazis who might cause trouble during a future Allied occupation of Germany. Despite SHAEF's directive, OSS employed SOE to train these Poles at Aris Aig, near Inverness in Scotland, before their embarkation on 'The Eagle Project'. Beyond this, SOE's involvement in the Reich would remain sketchy. Major-General Gubbins realised that there were severe operational limitations, and for the rest of 1944 he settled for a joint SOE/Political Warfare Executive operation to engineer a fictitious anti-Nazi underground movement, designed to unbalance the German security apparatus.[61]

While operations inside the Reich remained uninspiring, events on the Eastern Front during July continued their extraordinary pace. 'Bagration' had delivered a crushing blow to the Wehrmacht. By the time it was over, Army Group Centre command was totally smashed and seventeen divisions were decimated, while over fifty other divisions were crippled. Army Group Centre had lost nearly 450,000 men and its strength had halved, yet an outraged Hitler saw only treachery and desertion and forbade higher decorations to any of the Group's officers. At the same time the cost to the Soviets had been huge, with the Red Army suffering 178,000 killed and 587,000 wounded in Byelorussia alone. During the Lwów-Sandomierz operations a further 65,000 Soviet troops were killed and 224,000 wounded.[62]

The Soviet advance had also elevated the profile of the communist sponsored 'Lublin Committee'. At 2015 hours on 29 July 1944, the committee broadcast from Moscow on Radio Kościuszko, announcing that the Red Army and Polish People's Army (LWP) were on the outskirts of Warsaw and exhorted the population to rise up and attack the German occupiers.[63] Rokossovsky's 1st Byelorussian Front was indeed near the city, having reached the east bank of the Vistula, and in certain places such as Magnuszew, thirty miles south of Warsaw, Soviet forces had secured a bridgehead. But speedy Red Army progress was by no means assured. On 28 July, General-Major Radzievsky's Soviet 2nd Tank Army turned north towards the city, but after five miles was suddenly attacked by the German 1st Parachute-Panzer Division Hermann Göring together with the 73rd Infantry Division. Radzievsky then split his forces, and while his 16th Tank Corps continued to engage German forces south-east of Warsaw, his 3rd Tank Corps and 8th Guards Tank Corps worked their way northwards to try and turn the German flank north-east of the city. They reached Wołomin, some ten miles outside Warsaw, where they were attacked by armour from the German 19th Panzer and Hermann Göring Divisions.[64]

The Germans were far from conceding defeat around Warsaw, yet the attitude among their troops within the city was nervous and trigger-happy. They were well aware that Army Group Centre had been effectively destroyed, the city garrison was depleted and German citizens were fleeing in large numbers, yet Warsaw was still the largest city that lay between the Soviet front and Berlin, 300 miles to the west. Many of Warsaw's buildings were battered from the 1939 German invasion and the Jewish rising in 1943, but the city still retained its moody atmosphere. Lance-Corporal Ron Jeffery, the British ex-POW on the run and living in Warsaw, recalled the city's network of alleyways and courtyards:

The centre of Warsaw, some few miles in extent, was a brooding and dis-
turbing part of the ancient city. It included the famous Stare Miasto, the
Old Town, an entrancing assembly of even more ancient and quaint buildings arranged in rickety squares and cul-de-sacs. Wandering the streets
and alleyways, I was much reminded of the old parts of Paris and some of
the inner City of London. The grimed heavy masonry with a multitude
of stonework entrances leading to secretive small courtyards with further
openings leading up silent flights of stairs.[65]

Though Soviet strategy resisted full-scale onslaughts on cities, it seemed
inevitable to the Governor of Warsaw, Ludgwig Fischer that a Soviet
attack was imminent. On 27 July he ordered 100,000 able-bodied
Varsovians to report the following day to dig defences around the city.
There was no response, so on 30 July Himmler himself issued a new
order for 200,000 to report. The AK knew that acceptance of this order
would deprive its army of the bulk of its manpower in the city, so compliance was out of the question. However, they also knew that when
the deadline passed, the Germans would exact terrible retribution on
a population who failed to respond, and this was one more reason for
those who argued for an immediate AK Rising. The underground was
certainly organised – and not only with just foot soldiers. Even young
teenagers, such as Hanna Czarnocka, were prepared and ready for action.
Before her mother Halina was arrested and sent to Auschwitz, Hanna
was introduced to the Polish Girl Guide network. She had joined the
1st Warsaw Female Scout Troup headed by Jola Wedecka and, after attend-
ing clandestine school classes (the Germans had shut-down all official
education) she was encouraged to form a new patrol with schoolfriends.
As an enthusiastic sixteen-year-old, she had developed a number of
useful skills.

We learned first aid and how to work as couriers, as well as lessons in
weapon handling. We also had to know our way around Warsaw and
how to use the secret passages. Our Girl Guides' patrol was known as 'the
fireflies', and we were part of the 'Grey Scouts' movement and used to
congregate in a bakery, which belonged to the family of one of our members. My brother, Bohdan and I were effectively orphans and there were
others – I had a friend whose mother was shot dead by the Germans. As
August approached, I was allocated as a courier and stretcher-bearer to

a medical unit based in the *Instytut Głuchoniemych I Ociemniałych* [Deaf and Blind Institute] in *plac Trzech Krzyży* [Three Crosses Square]. We had a doctor, Dr Burska and two professional nurses and were to operate as a dressing station. The prospects for any rising looked good to me because, although some Germans had stayed in Warsaw for the war and were healthy and fat, most we saw looked thin and haggard with very tatty uniforms from their time on the Eastern Front. They tended to go out on patrol in threes, machine-pistols at the ready and we thought that if we had to fight these men, we could win. We knew we were on our own and although you could hear the Soviet bombardment coming closer, that was no comfort to me as I knew they had sentenced my father to death.

The Germans started to get panicky. They regularly posted lists of persons held in captivity and confirmed that if any German was hurt the Polish prisoners would be shot. And they were. The poor people were lined up in streets and would shout 'Long Live Poland' just before they were executed. To prevent this, the Germans would stuff the mouths of the condemned with plaster just before shooting them.

Faced with this sort of barbarity, we had no option but to fight back. Then the Germans ordered that all men under sixty, in Warsaw, had to report to them. Therefore, if we were to rebel, we had to act quickly.[66]

It was a sentiment held by a majority of the AK leaders. Having already gained the unanimous consent from members of the underground parliament, the Council of National Unity, the AK's General Staff and senior commanders met for a final conference on 31 July. There, in a safe apartment in central Warsaw, the two deputy C-in-Cs, General Leopold Okulicki ('Bear Cub')[67] and General Tadeusz Pełczyński ('Gregory') argued for an immediate rising as the first Soviet tanks crossed into the eastern suburb of Praga. This option was supported by the chief of intelligence, Colonel Iranek-Osmecki ('Heller') and the head of Warsaw District AK, General Antoni Chruściel ('Monter'), who added that even if Soviet forces were delayed, his troops could capture the city and hold it until Soviet help arrived. These commanders were determined to seize Warsaw before the Red Army could, enabling them to greet the Soviets as 'Warsaw's rightful owners' who even had their own civil administration.[68] Furthermore, they wanted to prove to the outside world that they had defeated the Germans and thereby exacted revenge for five years of cruel occupation. The Germans were seen to be retreating and such was the momentum for action within the Polish community that unless a proper rising was instigated, sporadic and ineffective fighting might break out. These were forceful arguments for instant action and did seem to be supported throughout the rank and file of the AK as well as portions of the civilian population. However, the C-in-C of the AK, General Tadeusz Bór-Komorowski favoured a more cautious approach. He wanted to wait until the Red Army had secured a material advantage, either by capturing the eastern suburb of Praga or by encircling the city. Then, he argued, if some better communications could be established with the Soviets, a Polish rising might succeed. Overriding all these concerns was the fact that the AK did not have the heavy arms or artillery to combat German tanks and neither did they have anti-aircraft guns or indeed, any of their own air support; even General Chruściel conceded that the AK only had resources to hold out for five days.[69] Nevertheless, emotions were highly charged and the demand for action seemed unstoppable. Intelligence reaching Bór-Komorowski indicated that Soviet forces had reached villages only ten miles from Warsaw, and that local German garrisons were fleeing. An intercepted German OKW communiqué announced, 'Today the Russians started a general attack on Warsaw from the south-east.' It was enough to convince General Bór-Komorowski to strike. He ordered the Rising to commence at 1700 hours on 1 August.[70]

NOTES

[1] *Slaughterhouse*, op. cit., pp. 48–51. Also Erickson, op. cit., pp. 248–9; Dr Otto John, 'Germany's Eastern Front 1939-45' in *The Army Quarterly*, October 1950.

[2] Anthony Eden to Prime Minister, 5 February 1944, AP20/10/43, Lord Avon Papers, UB.

[3] *Pravda* extracts quoted in the *Manchester Guardian*, 14 February 1944.

[4] The Foreign Office felt that 'a large extension of Polish territory at the expense of Germany would probably so embitter [post-war] Polish–German relations that Poland would be forced into close relations with the Soviet Union'. See 'Foreign Office paper on post-war Soviet policy, 29 April 1944', in Graham Ross (Ed.), *The Foreign Office and the Kremlin: British Documents on Anglo-Soviet Relations 1941–45* (Cambridge University Press, Cambridge 1984).

[5] Messages #223 to #244, January, February 1944, *Stalin's Correspondence with Churchill and Attlee*, op. cit. Also Edward J. Rozek, *Wartime Diplomacy: A Pattern in Poland* (John Wiley & Sons, Boulder, US, 1958), pp. 187–90. For Churchill's

speech in parliament, see Nigel Nicolson, (Ed.), *Harold Nicolson: Diaries and Letters 1939–1945* (Collins, London 1967), pp. 352–3. For Beaverbrook, see Beaverbrook to Eden, 26 August 1944, FO 954/20, NA.

6 W. Averell Harriman and Elie Abel, *Special Envoy to Churchill and Stalin 1941–1946*, p. 291, quoted in Michael Peszke, op. cit.

7 Field Marshal Smuts to WSC, 8 March 1944, AP20/11/149A, Lord Avon Papers, UB.

8 For US journalists, see 'Day in the Forest', *Time* magazine, 7 February 1944. Also George Sanford, *Katyn and the Soviet Massacre of 1940: Truth, Justice and Memory* (Routledge, London 2005), p. 143.

9 For Katyn, see Eden to Churchill, 25 February 1944, AP20/11/99, Lord Avon Papers, UB. Also 'The Massacre of Polish Officers in Katyn Wood', AP14/3/37a, Lord Avon Papers, UB. For Polish newspapers, see *Hansard*, Fifth Series, 17 February 1944, Cols. 171–2.

10 Lieutenant-Colonel H. Perkins (MP) to Brigadier E. Mockler-Ferryman (AD/E), 15 January 1944, HS4/144, NA.

11 SOE Memo, 8 February 1944, HS4/142, NA.

12 Anthony Eden to Prime Minister, 13 March 1944, AP20/11/145, Lord Avon Papers, UB.

13 Sue Ryder, 1987, ref 10057, Sound Archive, IWM.

14 Lieutenant-Colonel Patrick Boyle was serving with 2/Royal Scots Fusiliers. Trenchard to Slessor, 20 June 1944, AIR 23/885, NA.

15 Flying Officer Clarke-Hall was navigator in a Catalina, which crashed in Spanish Morocco, 15 June 1944. Flight Sergeant Charles Hill was shot down near Bucharest on 9 August 1944. See Group Captain Morris to Air Marshal Sir John Slessor, ref 75a, AIR 23/885, NA. For an overview of the Italian campaign, see Major-General H. Essame, 'A Controversial Campaign – Italy 1943–45', in *The Army Quarterly and Defence Journal*, January 1968.

16 Cynk, op. cit., p. 468. Also Committee of the Polish Air Force Association, *Destiny Can Wait: The Polish Air Force in the Second World War* (William Heinemann, London 1949), p. 217.

17 W. Strang memorandum, 29 May 1943, FO 371/35261, NA. For Eden's view on the future of Romania, see Eden to WSC, 13 March 1944, AP 20/11/147, Lord Avon Papers, UB.

18 Lothar Kettenacker, 'The Anglo–Soviet Alliance and the Problem of Germany, 1941 – 1945' in *Journal of Contemporary History*, Vol 17, #3, July 1982.

19 For 'Sitreps', see Cypher from Moscow (Embassy) to SOE Polish Section and Polish Minorities Section, 3 March 1944, HS4/142, NA. For 'stirring up trouble', see hand-written memo to H. Perkins, 25 March, ibid. A superior had added 'very stupid of them'.

20 'K/POL' to 'V/CD' (Gubbins), 3 February 1944, HS4/142, NA.

[21] 'MP' (Perkins) to 'V/CD' (Gubbins), 8 February 1944, HS4/142, NA. For Soviet acclamation, see Sonya Rose, *Which People's War? National Identity and Citizenship in Wartime Britain* (Oxford University Press, Oxford 2003), p. 50.

[22] Memorandum, 8 May 1944, AP 20/12/248, Lord Avon Papers, UB. For Soviet press, see Bulletin of the Voice of Free Poland, ref. 595, PRM/154a, PISM.

[23] 'Jewish partisan units in the Parczew Forest', United States Holocaust Memorial Museum.

[24] Nicholas Stargardt, *Witnesses of War: Children's Lives under the Nazis* (Jonathan Cape, London 2005), p. 153.

[25] Testimony by 'Góra' in Iranek-Osmecki, op. cit., pp. 157–8.

[26] From 30 May 1944, German infantry regiments were re-designated as 'Grenadier Brigades'.

[27] Christoph Rass, *Menschenmaterial: Deutsche Soldaten an der Ostfront. Innenansichten einer Infanteriedivision 1939–1945* (Ferdinand Schöningh, Paderborn 2003), pp. 385–94. For a wider study of German infantryman on the Eastern Front, through letters and diaries, see Stephen G. Fritz, *Frontsoldaten: The German Soldier in World War II* (University Press of Kentucky, Lexington 1995).

[28] Quoted Rossiisky Gosudarstvenny Arkhiv Literatury I Iskusstva, Moscow, ref. 1710/3/47 in Anthony Beevor and Luba Vinogradova (Eds.), *A Writer at War: Vasily Grossman with the Red Army 1941–1945* (Harvill Press, London 2005), p. 276.

[29] Günter K. Koschorrek, *Blood Red Snow: The Memoirs of a German Soldier on the Eastern Front* (Greenhill Books, London 2002), p. 235–6.

[30] Davies, *Rising*, op. cit., pp. 223–4. Churchill agreed with Stalin in February 1944, the arrangements whereby the AK would assist Soviet forces; see Prime Minister to Marshal Stalin, 8 February 1944, AP20/11/73a, Lord Avon Papers, UB.

[31] Flight Sergeant John Ward, claimed rather surprisingly that in his experience 90% of the NKVD operating in Poland were Jewish and largely of Polish origin. See Report of interrogation of 542939, Sgt. John Ward, HS4/256, NA.

[32] Nicholas Stargardt, op. cit., p. 153.

[33] Michael Elkins, *Forged in Fury*, (Piatkus, Loughton 1971), p. 32.

[34] In addition, Stalin called for the removal of President Raczkiewicz and Stanisław Kot; Mikołajczyk, op. cit., pp. 65–75. See also Jonathan Fenby, *Alliance: The Inside Story of How Roosevelt, Stalin and Churchill Won One War and Began Another* (Simon & Schuster, London 2006), pp. 294–5. Also Erickson, op. cit., pp. 260–5.

[35] Basil Liddell Hart in conversation with Lieutenant-General Dittmar, 1 November 1945, LH15/15/149/12, Liddell Hart Papers, LHCMA.

[36] The extent to which the AK contributed to the capture of Wilno was hotly disputed; see *Sunday Times*, 16 July 1944 and *New York Times*, 16 July 1944.

[37] Byelorussia was a military, rather than a political entity, though its inhabitants varied in their allegiances. It later became a Soviet Republic and after the collapse of communism, was recreated as Belarus.

[38] James Lucas, *War on the Eastern Front: The German Soldier in Russia, 1941–1945* (Greenhill Books, London 1998), pp. 71–5. For the Byelorussia region, Janek Lasocki to Author, 20 January 2008; also see Norman Davies, *Rising '44*, op. cit., pp. 138–40.

[39] Professor Hew Strachan, xix, in Even Mawdsley, *Thunder in the East: The Nazi-Soviet War 1941-1945* (Hodder Arnold, London 2005). It has been estimated that between 1941and 1945, Britain and Canada shipped over 5,000 aircraft and 5,000 tanks to the Soviet Union. This support was dwarfed by the US whose supplies included 427,000 motor vehicles, 8,000 armoured vehicles, 35,000 motorcycles and 14,000 aircraft. See Albert Seaton, op. cit., Appendix A.

[40] Erhard Raus, *Panzer Operations: The Eastern Front Memoir of General Raus 1941–1945* (Da Capo Press, Cambridge, US), pp. 285–91. Also Steven Zaloga, *Operation Bagration* (Osprey, Oxford 1996), pp. 73–82.

[41] Material for Polish response to *The Times*, 17 April 1944, PRM 154b, Polish Institute and Sikorski Museum, London (hereafter PISM).

[42] Glantz, *Slaughterhouse*, op. cit., pp. 50–1. Model, a fervent disciple of National Socialism, was transferred to the Western Front in August and played a part in defeating 'Operation Market-Garden' at Arnhem. He committed suicide on 21 April 1945.

[43] James Lucas, op. cit., p. 159. For the single-handed destruction of an enemy tank a special badge was awarded to German soldiers, comprising a black metal tank on a silver lace backing. The badge was worn on the right upper sleeve.

[44] The longer range *Panzerfaust 60* was not available until September 1944. Further improved models were produced towards the end of the war, with ranges of 150m achieved during the defence of Berlin.

[45] Guy Sajer, *The Forgotten Soldier: War on the Russian Front – a True Story* (Cassell, London 1999), pp. 491–2.

[46] James Lucas, op. cit., p. 168.

[47] Sajer, op. cit., pp. 463–66.

[48] Major Boughey (MP1) to Lieutenant-Colonel Harold Perkins (MP), 14 September 1944, HS 4/146, NA.

[49] Richard C. Lukas, *Eagles East: The Army Air Forces and the Soviet Union 1941–1945* (Florida State University Press, Tallahasse 1970), p. 199. Also Mark J. Conversino, *Fighting with the Soviets: The Failure of Operation Frantic 1944–1945* (University Press of Kansas, Lawrence US, 1997), pp. 85–7.

[50] Mark Conversino, op. cit., pp. 127–9.

51 'Formation and Manner of Fighting of the Soviet-Russian Armoured Forces, 1 July 1944', LH 9/24/222, Liddell Hart Papers, LHCMA. Also Steven Zaloga, *Operation Bagration*, op. cit., pp. 27–34; Glantz, *Slaughterhouse*, op. cit., p. 300. See also Earle F. Ziemke, *Stalingrad to Berlin: The German Defeat in the East* (Center of Military History, Washington 1968), pp. 313–40.

52 General von Maneuffel to Basil Liddell Hart, 10 December 1945, LH 15/15/149/1, LHCMA. When von Manteuffel was given command of the *Grossdeutschland* Division in January 1944, his previous command, the 7th Panzer Division was given to General Major Adalbert Schulz. Schulz had survived 136 tank engagements only to be killed on the first day of his new command.

53 Von Manteuffel, op. cit.

54 Ibid.

55 Iranek-Osmecki, op. cit., pp. 93-4.

56 The complex, which was heavily dynamited when Hitler left in November 1944, is still very visible. Rastenburg, approximately 150 miles due north of Warsaw, was incorporated into Poland after the war and renamed Kętrzyn.

57 'Chester Wilmot's Notes on interrogation of General Kurt Zeitzler', Liddell Hart Papers, LH 15/15/150/3, LHCMA. See also 'FM Ewald von Kleist interrogation', Liddell Hart Papers, LH 15/15/149/13, LHCMA.

58 Albert Seaton, *The Russo-German War 1941–45* (Arthur Barker, London 1971), p. 452.

59 William Shirer, *The Rise and Fall of the Third Reich* (Secker & Warburg, London 1960), p. 1072.

60 'OSS Relations with SOE', Vol. 7, Reel 8, #0039, GB99, MF 204–211, LHCMA.

61 Ibid. Also *Gubbins*, op. cit., pp. 208–11. The Special Operations (SO) Branch of OSS, London was charged with conducting sabotage operations and providing support for resistance groups in occupied Europe. On 10 January 1944, a Special Forces HQ was set up to coordinate SOE and SO activities.

62 David Glantz and Jonathan House, *When Titans Clashed: How the Red Army Stopped Hitler* (Birlinn, Edinburgh 2000), p. 215, 298–9. During the summer offensives of 1944, the Red Army lost almost 2 million men killed, wounded or captured.

63 For a transcript of the broadcast, see Edward Rozek, op. cit., p. 235.

64 For Soviet broadcasts, see 'Union of Polish Patriots' transcript, 29 July 1944, PRM 154b, PISM. For Red Army/German operations around Warsaw, see Ziemke, op. cit., pp. 341–5.

65 Ron Jeffery, *Red Runs the Vistula* (Nevron Associates, Peterborough 1989), p. 67.

66 Hanna Kościa to Author, 22 September 2007.

[67] Colonel Okulicki had been dropped back into Poland on the night of 21-22 May 1944 by Halifax GR.E JP222.

[68] Lieutenant-Colonel H. Threlfall to Colonel Dodds Parker, 16 August 1944, HS4/157, NA.

[69] Interview with General Bór-Komorowski, 12 September 1944, in 'Radio Messages Received from John Ward', ref. 3.9.2.8.9., PUMST.

[70] 'Statement by General Okulicki to NKVD', following his arrest on 27 February 1945. Translated from Russian by Dr Polly Jones, www.war-sawuprising.com. Also Norman Davies, op. cit., pp. 231–2; Bór-Komorowski, op. cit., pp. 214–5; Overy, *Russia's War*, op. cit., p. 247. Professor Overy asserts that one compelling reason for the sudden Rising was the recognition and pact of friendship signed on 26 July 1944 between the Soviet Union and the communist Lublin Committee (as the Provisional Government of Poland).

Chapter Seven

Warsaw Erupts (August 1944)

As Warsaw woke on Tuesday 1 August, a light rain was falling across the city. Distant booming could be heard coming from across the River Vistula as German units dynamited railway installations around Praga. Civilians, still unaware that a rising was about to erupt, mingled with AK members on their way to work. Women bustled along pavements carrying bundles containing pistols and ammunition, while boys and girls shouldered rucksacks full of medical supplies and food and made their way to rallying points all over the city. All this passing activity was eyed nervously by German police units manning corner strong-points, while their three-man street patrols and armoured car activity was stepped up.

General Bór-Komorowski had over 25,000 potential AK fighters in the Warsaw district with thousands more auxiliaries, but the actual number who could be initially armed was only 3,500 men.[1] This shortage of arms was exacerbated by the AK policy that spread their limited weapons around the country in preparation for a national upris-ing. Consequently, until German armouries in the city were captured or artillery units overpowered, the armed Polish fighters would have to engage their occupiers with pistols, home-made flamethrowers and *Błyskawica* sub-machine guns. These light arms were supplemented by grenades, 'Molotov cocktails' and also a few mortars, machine-guns and anti-tank rifles, which were thinly spread over the AK platoons.[2] Facing them on 1 August was an existing German garrison of about 16,000 men, whose fighting strength comprised mainly SS and SD Police battalions together with a Cossack and an Azerbaijani battalion.

General Bór-Komorowski made his HQ at the Kammler Factory in the suburb of Wola and recalled that he was in position as zero hour came at 1700 hours:

> At any moment we could expect Germans from the nearby garrison to arrive on the scene. Brief orders were shouted and our platoon was swiftly posted at windows and gates. When I returned upstairs, I could see German soldiers in full equipment occupying the house opposite. Machine-guns from the two pillboxes sprayed both streets constantly. One burst crackled through our room, spattering a line of holes across the walls and ceiling. Glass flew and dust and plaster filled the air. The Germans in the windows of the house opposite were within a grenade's throw of us; high factory windows were no protection … In our narrow street a heavy German lorry appeared, filled with police armed with tommy-guns and grenades. Obviously, they did not realise the exact location of the fight. The Germans already on the scene gave warning signs and shouted to them to stop, but the men in the lorry did not grasp what was happening and drove on under our window. This was just what our men had been waiting for. From a window, another *filipinka* [hand-grenade] landed plumb in the middle of the lorry. It swerved suddenly, hit the wall opposite and burst into flames. In a few seconds, thirty-five enemy dead and the wreck of the lorry were all that remained in the road.[3]

The initial objectives of the AK were to capture key installations, as well as the six municipal districts of the City Centre, Wola, Ochota, Mokotów, Żoliborz and Praga. All would prove difficult but the taking of Praga, the suburb across the Vistula, would involve complex tactical manoeuvres. It was vital for the AK to capture the four bridges over the Vistula, especially the Kierbedź and Poniatowski bridges, in order to maintain contact with the eastern suburb. In the event, the AK spread their forces too thinly and tried to capture all four crossings at once. The Germans were determined to keep the roads that led to the Vistula bridges open and there was fierce fighting around Jerusalem Alley and Volska Street. Similarly, their strong forces in Praga crushed any early gains made by the AK and there were reports that German units had bound AK prisoners to the front of their advancing tanks or pushed them along in front, to fend off potential attacks.[4] The Germans, temporarily thrown off balance by the outbreak, were now determined to crush the revolt. Teenager Hanna Czarnocka was too busy to be terrified by her first time in action:

> We assembled just before zero hour on 1 August. I was very proud when the Commandant asked me to go to HQ to collect our red and white armbands. I walked, though I wanted to run, but couldn't attract attention. When I arrived I gave a code word, 'Warsaw' and a woman replied 'Freedom'. She continued, 'You know we start at 5pm'. I collected the armbands and by the time I arrived back at my base, I could hear shots. Soon there were tanks passing outside the Institute and we were protected by Murdek's platoon when our building came under attack. We had to jump out of a first floor window – we were surrounded and we could either risk breaking our necks or be killed by the Germans. The school on the corner was now on fire and we started attending to our casualties, carrying them out of the firing line. On Rozbrat Street I had a narrow escape when a German soldier, who was cutting the grass with a scythe in front of his bunker to increase his visibility, spotted me running past. We looked each other in the eye before he put down his scythe, collected his rifle and fired at me. I still managed to deliver my message.[5]

Holes were soon blown in party walls between the large tenement blocks so that the wounded could be evacuated and supplies passed on out of sight. The city's sewers provided an excellent, if unpleasant, means of communication and escape, but sooner or later the AK had to make assaults across open ground. One of their early successes was the capture of the power station, for the loss of seventeen killed and twenty-seven wounded. However, early objectives proved too ambitious for the number of armed AK troops available, and when a 100-strong unit of their 7th Regiment Lublin Lancers attacked the German police headquarters in Szucha Avenue together with the printing house on Marszałkowska Avenue, they suffered terrible casualties. Sixty-two were killed and all the rest were wounded.[6] Meanwhile, attacks on the city's two airports during the first days of the rising met with similar stiff resistance and German aircraft continued to land and take off with impunity. Yet, despite the confusion and erratic tactics of the AK, their passion and bravery for the fight soon brought dividends. By the morning of 5 August they had captured most of the City Centre, half of Żolibórz in the northern sector of the city and parts of Wola and Mokotów, together with important utility buildings. Across streets and squares that were AK controlled, barricades were thrown up and trenches dug; most tenements had a 'house commander', with snipers and twenty-four hour aircraft watchers on the roofs. Overall, territory captured was impressive but this belied a weakness; it was also disjointed, with pockets of strong German resistance in between, which frequently cut AK supply lines.

General Bór-Komorowski and his AK commanders had always believed that their resources could only hold out for days rather than weeks. So, when ammunition began to run out on 3 August, he sent an urgent request for help to SOE's Force 139 in Italy, hoping that British or Allied air-drops would sustain them should the Germans regain the initiative.[7] This hope also lived on with Polish commanders in London, such as General Tatar, but it was soon dashed by a message on 3 August from Lieutenant-Colonel Ryszard Dorotycz-Malewicz ('Hańcza'). The Polish commander at Brindisi air base (No. 11), the main send-off station for flights to Warsaw, confirmed that only flights by Polish crews were sanctioned:

> Group Captain Rankin [RAF], after studying General Gubbins signal, refuses to carry out dropping over Warsaw. His probable motives are that heavy losses should be expected and the result would be slight.
>
> Rankin leaves free hand for our flight. This has up to five aircraft. Today there are bad net conditions and it would be possible to send only three Liberators without guarantee of reaching target. Operations by our flight would have a purely symbolic meaning and would result in complete destruction of the flight.
>
> To obtain pinpoint dropping it is necessary not to fly above 1000ft. According to our airmen, this sort of flying has very little chance with existing light ack-ack. Dropping from a higher level does not give necessary accuracy.[8]

British caution was hardly surprising, for although secrecy was essential for any rising, it was unfortunate that the AK command in Poland had not entered into any forward planning with SOE for air support before the outbreak. One unsuccessful air mission had already been despatched by the British on the evening of 1 August – but this had merely high-lighted the problems of operating over Warsaw. Of the eleven Polish and RAF Halifaxes and Liberators that took off from Brindisi, three had to turn back because of technical difficulties. Out of the eight aircraft that crossed the Polish border, only half managed to make good drops, and one of those was shot down afterwards by an enemy night fighter. The Deputy C-in-C Mediterranean Allied Air Force, Air Marshal Slessor was prepared to allow further drops to AK units in Poland, but not to Warsaw itself. Accordingly, on the night of 4 August, a combined sortie of four-teen Polish and RAF aircrews from Special Duties 148 Squadron and 1586 Polish Flight took off for drops over rural areas and smaller towns in Poland. However, four of the Polish crews disobeyed the order and diverted to Warsaw, where they managed, with one exception, to make precise drops on insurgent positions in the city. One of their Liberators crash landed on the return, while a further four of the RAF Halifaxes, which had made good drops over their designated zones in Poland, were subsequently shot down by enemy night fighters or ack-ack guns on the return flight.[9] A total of thirteen RAF, seven RCAF (Royal Canadian Air Force) and one RAAF (Royal Australian Air Force) airmen were killed and a further seven RAF airmen were captured. Slessor could ill-afford these losses in aircraft and experienced airmen and he banned all further flights to Poland while there was a full moon.[10]

Hitler and Himmler at first welcomed the uprising as it gave them the excuse to destroy Warsaw as a lesson to other occupied coun-tries. It was also the catalyst for Himmler to display further acts of vengeance, such as his immediate order to the commandant of Sachsenhausen Concentration Camp to execute General Rowecki, the interned C-in-C of the AK. However, for all the posturing that went on at senior German command levels, the Rising had genu-inely caught the German Warsaw Garrison off guard. The commander of the garrison, Austrian, *Generaloberst* Reiner Stahel was initially cut off in his HQ in the centre of the city and the Chief of Police, Dr Ludwig Hahn initially failed to coordinate and rally his men for counter-attacks against AK positions. Help was not quick in coming from German forces outside the city. *Generalfeldmarschall* Model, who would shortly be sent to the Western Front, was occupied with stabil-ising his shattered Army Group Centre and holding other defensive positions along the Vistula.

With little Wehrmacht interest in defending the city, Himmler seized the opportunity to make its defence largely an SS operation. To this end, on 4 August he appointed *SS Obergruppenführer* Erich von dem Bach, as overall Commander of German forces in Warsaw. Other SS formations including the 5ᵗʰ SS-Panzer Division *Wiking* and 3ʳᵈ SS-Panzer Division *Totenkopf* arrived from Romania, together with the Luftwaffe-controlled unit, the Parachute Panzer Division Hermann Göring. These units were ordered in to protect Warsaw's eastern and northern approaches. For the first few days of August, these tough armoured units continued to rebuff Soviet forces approaching the city. The *Totenkopf*, were one of thirty-eight *Waffen*-SS divisions, originally recruited from SS concentration camp guards, while the Herman Göring Division was often described as an 'elite' unit, tracing its origins back to 1933, when it was formed by its namesake as a motorised police unit. During the war, it graduated from regimental to divisional status, acquiring panzer, armoured artillery and infantry in the process, as well as a bewildering array of unit titles including its latest one (its parachutes had not been used since 1939). The Herman Göring Division had fought well in Italy during 1943 and the spring of 1944 and although it had only arrived in Poland in late July, its tank compliment of Panzerkampfwagen IIIs, and IVs, and StuG IIIs were constantly in action.[11] The attacking Soviet 3ʳᵈ Tank Corps was crippled by this vigorous German defence, and it could expect little heavy support as the main Soviet vanguard comprised the 47ᵗʰ Army – mainly rifle corps units.

SS Obergruppenführer von dem Bach, a veteran of brutal anti-partisan operations, was given immediate reinforcements in the form of 2,700 officers and men from the Poznań Police Regiment, 1,300 from various Wehrmacht units, 900 from a battalion of the 'Dirlewanger' SS Penal Battalion and 1,700 non-German officers and men from the SS 'Kaminski' Brigade. In addition there were a number of units from the 111ᵗʰ Azerbaijani Regiment and various Cossack Battalions, many of who were drawn from Red Army POWs who were given the option by their German captors of 'freedom' if they fought against the Soviet Union.[12] This motley, but certainly fearsome collection of German forces arrived in the city shortly before von dem Bach and, under the command of *SS Gruppenführer* Heinz Reinefarth, were destined to spearhead a series of German counter-attacks to regain the initiative. The SS elements of this new force were made up of especially tough and feral individuals, few of whom fitted the model of Ayran correctness. Yet their anti-partisan experience was seen as essential for a contest with the Poles, who were always seen by the Germans as 'bandits and renegades'.

The idea of non-German volunteer units fighting on behalf of the Reich was not new. Auxiliary units were formed as far back as 1941 and by the spring of 1942, it was estimated that there were over 200,000 'volunteers' made up from Soviet deserters or ex-POWs working at the rear of the German lines. Though these 'volunteers' were formally grouped into a 'Russian National Liberation Army (RONA)', they rarely operated in anything larger than battalion size units, except in the case of the Kaminski unit. From 1941 this anti-partisan group was led by Bronisław Kaminski, the product of a Polish father and German mother, who had already gained a reputation for wanton cruelty. Originally a Bolshevik, he nevertheless enjoyed a spell in a Soviet labour camp. Disillusioned with the system, he subsequently attempted to form a Soviet Nazi Party, but when this came to nothing he settled for a German commission, and created mayhem with his 9,500-strong unit of Cossack and Red Army deserters in the partisan-dominated Bryansk Forest, to the east of the Pripet Marshes. Discipline was always a problem with the renegade and lawless Kaminski band and his personal brutal style of command made him infamous. In one reported incident, he quelled an attempted mutiny by landing his Feisler Storch at the headquarters of a rebellious commander; leaping from the aircraft, he berated the officer and then proceeded to strangle him to death in front of his own men. Such 'direct action' was not out of place when RONA was brought under the control of the SS in 1944 and accorded brigade status. At the outbreak of the Rising, the Kaminski Brigade was in the Polish General Government sector when it received the command to assist German police units in Warsaw, and dispatched a regiment comprising two battalions of some 1700 men. The regiment, commanded by Oberst Frolov was accompanied by four tanks, one SU-76 assault gun and two 122mm artillery guns.[13]

The renowned brutality of the Kaminski Brigade was easily matched by the other composite brigade commanded by *SS-Standartenführer* Oscar Dirlewanger, a sexual pervert and alcoholic. Despite his personal depravity – even Himmler described him as 'a bit of an oddity' – he had fought for Germany in four conflicts, was wounded seven times, and decorated for bravery in both the Great

War and the Spanish Civil War.[14] Protected and nurtured by Himmler, the Dirlewanger Brigade was drawn originally from game poachers but now comprised mainly ex-concentration camp German criminals and SS Penal troops.[15] While the armed AK insurgents engaged the enemy, the civilian population of Warsaw were to suffer terribly at the hands of these SS men.

At dawn on 5 August, *SS Gruppenführer* Reinefarth's 'Attack Group' moved into Warsaw's western suburb of Ochota. One of the early targets for the Kaminski Brigade was the Marie Curie-Skłowdowska Radium Institute, near Wawelski Street. When the drunken unit entered the hospital during the morning, the building contained about ninety cancer patients, together with eighty staff and associated family members. The staff and families were immediately driven out and anyone who protested was immediately shot. As the patients lay in their beds, the wards were ransacked and looted, while women patients were raped. The the violence abated when most of Kaminski's men left the building in search of further quarry. However, the following day they returned. Patients lying on the floor were dispatched with revolver shots and those in beds on the ground floor were burnt alive as their mattresses were set on fire. Meanwhile, some seventy patients and nurses had retreated to the upper floors of the hospital, while other German soldiers arrived with transport to carry away what was left of the laboratory and X-Ray equipment. For the moment, the remaining patients and nurses believed they might survive.[16]

Meanwhile, inhabitants from the neighbouring Wola and Mokotów districts were driven from their homes, in scenes reminiscent of the previous years clearing of the Warsaw Jewish Ghetto. Those not murdered on the spot were pushed out into the fields around Mokotów and left for days without food or water and were subject to random SS beatings or executions.[17] Meanwhile their homes were systematically pillaged and then burned. Maria Kietlicz-Rayska recalled her terror at the arrival of the SS troops:

The front doors of the house were smashed in by rifle butts, and a gang burst into the apartments. They wore German uniforms, spoke in Russian and were completely drunk. They demobilised the room in five minutes, seizing everything that was of value. Not content with that, they beat up everyone. They even wanted to kill our child, but the assailant was persuaded from doing so with the aid of a bottle of vodka. The house dog was killed with a bayonet, after which everyone was taken out 'to be shot'. Outside, there were already large crowds. Machine-guns were fixed, and the command given to form threes, after which the entire multitude was suddenly pushed into Grojecka Street. The German soldiers from the Academy building laughed, as though at a good play. The crowd of about 15,000 people were driven along the burning Grojecka Street for about 4kms, between burning houses, which after being left by their inhabitants were set on fire with hand grenades.[18]

On 6 August, the butchery in the district of Wola was stepped up. Any civilians who could be found were ordered by Dirlewanger's men to move to the Ursus factory at the corner of Skierniewicka Street and Wolska Street. There, men, women and children were executed in rows and their bodies piled up – a scene that greeted new groups of the condemned. In the surrounding streets, similar atrocities took place, including the assault and murder of pregnant women and young girls, while large groups of terrified civilians were ordered down into cellars and hand-grenades were thrown in after them. In another instance SS men drove civilians towards a picket fence, where each person was ordered to tear off a length of timber and line up with it. Then they were all mown down, row after row and fell in heaps with their pieces of timber. The victims never understood that the wood was to be used as tinder, but their executers soon poured petrol over the piles of bodies. In all, it has been estimated that the rampaging German units murdered over 30,000 civilians in the Ochota and Wola districts alone, in what was the most savage act of the Rising.[19]

The scale of destruction was increased over the coming weeks with the arrival of 2,500 reinforcements for Dirlewanger's unit, including 1,900 who came from the SS punishment camp at Matzkau, near Danzing. However, the effect of such enemy action only served to harden the resolve of AK fighters and no quarter was given to captured SS soldiers. After establishing which unit, and therefore which atrocity he had been involved in, any hapless SS man was swiftly tried by an AK court and executed. Others were shot out of hand.[20] As both sides raised the stakes, von dem Bach attempted to rein in the activities of the Dirlewanger and Kaminski brigades. This was not through any act of decency, as the SS Commander would later protest, but because he knew the war was lost and was fearful of later Allied reprisals. He also knew that barbaric acts would never compel the AK to surrender, but restraining these two commanders once they had been unleashed, was no easy matter. Dirlewanger, in particular, believed that he was only responsible to Himmler and soon fell out with his immediate superior *SS Gruppenführer* Reinefarth, even challenging him to a duel. For good measure, he also threatened to kill von dem Bach's Chief of Staff, *SS Standartenführer* Golz.[21]

Having devolved the control over the timing of the Rising to the underground in Warsaw, the Polish Government-in-Exile in London was gripped by inertia. It was true they had pressed for military aid from the Allies, including approaches to Washington for the use of US aircraft based in Europe, but their contact with the fighters in Warsaw was lamentable. In the immediate weeks before the Rising, messages coming out of London from the Polish leadership were disjointed and sometimes contradictory. This was hardly surprising, given the fact that the Polish Premier, Mikołajczyk and the Commander-in-Chief, Sosnkowski were both temporarily out of Britain at the end of July. Mikołajczyk had flown to Moscow to seek some accommodation with Stalin and by the time he was allowed an audience with the Soviet Premier, the Rising had erupted. Stalin promptly feigned ignorance of the AK actions in the city. Warming to his role as 'honest broker', Stalin then told the Polish Premier that it was up to his Polish government to come to an accommodation with the communist Lublin Poles and to this end, meetings would be arranged.[22]

However, as Mikołajczyk expected, the subsequent talks with the Soviet-backed 'Lublin Committee' were fruitless. The diverse collection of communist and socialist Poles headed by Bolesław Bierut, a former NKVD agent, regarded themselves as the 'sole legal source of authority in Poland' and had already declared their support for the Curzon Line. Mikołajczyk, who knew that it was political suicide for him to concede Lwów and the oilfields of Eastern Galicia, was also aghast at the derisory offer of four seats in the communist's proposed future cabinet. With their total disregard for the London Polish Government, the Lublin Committee had clearly no interest in negotiations, especially as Stalin held all the cards. The sham, while not convincing Churchill, seemed to have eased his conscience. In a telegram to Stalin he submitted, 'I am very glad that you brought both sides together. Undoubtedly, an advance has been made towards our common goal.'[23]

While Mikołajczyk was being stalled in Moscow, the Polish C–in–C, General Sosnkowski was touring Allied positions in Italy, to bolster morale among General Anders' II Polish Corps. He did not return to Britain until 7 August, by which time the Soviet press had the world stage to themselves, with broadcasts declaring that the only Varsovians fighting the Germans in Warsaw were members of the communist *Armia Ludowa*.[24] Although orders were not coming from London, Warsaw had managed to make contact with London by the second day of the Rising. The main transmitter, under the direction of the Chief of Civil Resistance, Stefan Korboński, was moved to a larger apartment and although the operatives came under withering enemy fire, they managed to drape the aerial over a neighbouring roof and achieve a decent reception.[25] However, this communication only travelled one way, and for the first ten days of the Rising virtually no bulletins or advice was forthcoming from London. On 10 August, the AK command in Warsaw sent yet another desperate plea for help to the Polish Government-in-exile:

10th day. We are conducting a bloody fight. The town is cut by three routes: (1) Poniatowski Bridge, Jerusalem Alley, Grojecka Street. (2) Theatre Square, Elektoralna Street, Chłodna Street, Wolska Street. (3) Żolibórz Viaduct, Gdańsk Railway Station.

Praga is cut off. All these routes are strongly held by German tanks and their crossing is extremely difficult (all the buildings along are burnt out). Two armoured trains on the railway line from Gdansk Station to West Station and artillery from Praga fire continuously on the town and are supported by air force.

In these conditions the fight continues. We received from you only once a small drop. On the German-Russian Front, silence since the 3rd. We are therefore without any material or moral support. With the exception of a short speech from the Vice [Deputy] Prime Minister from London, which took place on the 8th only, we have not had from you even an acknowledgement of our action. The soldiers and population of the capital look hopelessly at the skies, expecting help from the Allies. On the background of smoke they see only German aircraft. They are surprised, feel deeply depressed and begin to revile.

We have practically no news from you, no information with regard to the political situation, no advice and no instructions. Have you discussed

in Moscow help for Warsaw? I repeat emphatically that without immediate repeat immediate support consisting of drops of arms and ammunition,
bombing of objectives held by the enemy and air landing, our fight will
collapse in a few days.[26]

Lord Selborne was immediately notified of this message and contacted
Churchill. The SOE Minister made an impassioned plea for Allied air
support, reminding the Premier of the past loyalty and support of both
the Polish Army and Air Force and stressing, 'they have been fighting 10
days and we have so far given them only eight sorties with their own aircraft'.[27] This was strictly inaccurate, as RAF crews had also been involved
in relief flights, but this did stop General Sosnkowski from sending a
blistering telegram to the British Chiefs of Staff on 8 August, attacking
the ineffectualness of the British/Polish Alliance:

> Our alliance with Great Britain has resulted only in bringing her our
> assistance in 1940 in repelling the German attack against the British Isles,
> in fighting in Norway, in Africa, in Italy and on the Western Front. We
> request you to state this fact before the British in an official démarche – it
> should remain as a document. We do not ask for equipment. We demand
> its immediate despatch.[28]

Sosnkowski followed up his assault by demanding that Air Marshal
Slessor should order the Commander of the Polish Special Duties Flight
'to carry out operations regardless of weather conditions'. Not content
with this channel, Sosnkowski by-passed the British and sent similar
instructions through Polish networks to Brindisi. Slessor was furious at
this action, which he saw as undermining his authority. Yet, there continued to be conflicting signals from the British side, with SOE pressing for
relief flights, while Slessor and the Chief of Air Staff, Sir Charles Portal,
argued for caution. 'It appears', reasoned Portal, 'that the Poles are trying
to pass on to us the responsibility for any failure of the operations of the
Polish Secret Army, which might result from these forces having undertaken open warfare prematurely'.[29] It was an uncharitable view but one
that had some currency.

Meanwhile, the Chiefs of Staff attempted to persuade General Ira Eaker,
Commander-in-Chief, Mediterranean Allied Air Force to use his US
Fifteenth Air Force, based at Bari, to support the relief effort. But Eaker

was not keen to employ his aircraft to drop supplies into such small zones within Warsaw, where they were likely to fall into enemy hands. AK positions in the Kampinos Forest outside Warsaw offered a possible alternative, but even then, it was ten miles outside the city with enemy forces holding ground in-between.[30] There remained deep concern within the British Air Ministry and among senior RAF commanders that dropping supplies to relieve the AK inside Warsaw was still far too dangerous, and although they had little intelligence about the shrinking territory of the AK, they knew that control of drop zones in certain streets and squares could change by the hour, with the increasing possibility that supplies would be captured by the enemy. They did not believe the contention of certain Polish leaders that there were no German anti-aircraft defences around Warsaw. Nonetheless on 8 August Air Marshal Slessor relented and at least allowed volunteer Polish crews to fly to Warsaw.[31]

Over the next few nights, these Polish crews in Liberators and Halifaxes made good drops over Warsaw and the nearby Kampinos Forest, without losses. Then after several nights of bad weather the flights resumed on 12 August; this time including the RAF. Five aircraft from 1586 Polish Flight and six from 148 Squadron flew the gauntlet of ack-ack fire to drop supplies on the city. It was also agreed to divert two Liberator squadrons from the invasion of southern France to the Warsaw operation. Consequently, 31 Squadron SAAF (South African Air Force) and 178 Squadron of 205 Group were brought in to assist 1586 Flight and 148 Squadron.[32]

It was also unfortunate timing that Churchill left Britain in early August for a tour of Allied forces in Italy, though Foreign Secretary Eden did his best to convince the Polish Government-in-exile that the British were taking measures to help Warsaw and had already made sacrifices:

> I understand that on the night of 13/14 August, twenty-eight aircraft were dispatched, of which a considerable proportion accomplished their mission successfully, for the loss of three aircraft. Unfortunately, on the night of 14/15, out of twenty-six aircraft despatched to Warsaw, eight aircraft are missing and eleven only were successful.
>
> In the circumstances the Prime Minister wishes me to warn you that, although we shall not relax our efforts to send help for as long as the crisis in Warsaw persists, the heavy losses sustained by the squadrons involved may make it impossible to continue assistance indefinitely on the present scale.[33]

In fact, Eden was talking-up the success of the Allied missions. For during the two consecutive nights, fifty-four aircraft from 148 and 178 Squadrons, together with 31 Squadron (SAAF) took off for Warsaw. However, despite the bravery of the crews and the undoubted morale boost for the Varsovians, the missions were an example of everything the British Air Ministry had warned about. As the aircraft approached Warsaw, they came into heavy flak. Their drop zones were indicated by the AK on the ground as 'small yards' or street intersections and as the aircraft were picked out in the glare from over fifteen powerful search-lights, they had to rapidly reduce their height to 150ft to stand any chance of dropping their canisters near the zones.[34] Large parts of the city were obscured by fire and smoke and visibility was appalling. Consequently, only about fifteen drops were successfully made to AK units, at a total cost of eleven aircraft, with more damaged beyond repair. Again, the losses of airmen were heavy. Five RAF, five SAAF and one Polish crew were lost, amounting to the deaths of over fifty airmen. These desper-ate air missions were repeated on successive nights with a further four aircraft shot down by enemy night-fighters and two more by ack-ack fire. The losses were enough to compel 178 Squadron and 31 Squadron (SAAF) to withdraw from Polish operations, leaving 148 Squadron and 1586 Polish Flight to struggle on.[35]

By 12 August, von dem Bach's forces had taken back the western areas of the city but it was vital for them to secure the areas along the western riverbank to keep open the lifeline to German units across the Vistula bridges in Praga. Their tactics were witnessed first-hand by the British ex-POW, Sergeant John Ward, who not only reported on the fortunes of the Rising, but also took his place behind the barricades:

> The German tank forces during last night made determined efforts to relieve some of their strong-points in the city. This is no light task. On the corner of every street are built huge barricades mostly constructed of concrete paving slabs torn up from the streets especially for this purpose. In most cases the attempts failed, so the tank crews vented their disap-pointment by setting fire to several houses and shelling the others from a distance. In many cases they also set fire to the dead, who litter the streets in many places. The enemy had begun to have great respect for the Polish barricade, for they know that behind each one wait determined AK troops with petrol bottles.[36]

At the outbreak of the Rising there were a number of escaped British POWs hiding in Warsaw, though most managed to flee in the early days. However, Ward had joined the AK, received a commission and decided to remain in the city and help his Polish comrades. The first occasion that London heard from 'Lieutenant' John Ward was when he broadcast an incident in Pius Street, where Polish women were driven along in front of several German Tiger tanks in an attempt to stop the insurgents attacking the formation.[37] The women had eventually broken free to reach the Polish lines and mindful of the need to broadcast such a strong story, Stefan Korboński later took Ward to a hospital where the women were recovering. There, the airman, 'a young man of middle height, snub nose and pleasant face', interviewed the exhausted women. His tolerable Polish was delivered in a 'strong foreign accent' but he nonetheless made himself understood and faithfully reported the incident, sending a telegram to London with his name and service number.

That evening, the BBC broadcast the news from his telegram and the British newspapers picked up this report the following day. In the light of an almost total lack of first-hand intelligence from Warsaw, SOE became very interested in Ward's possibilities. At their base in Monopoli, in Italy, SOE's Lieutenant-Colonel Henry Threlfall, still commanding 'Force 139', placed great store on Ward's dispatches and passed them on to interested parties.[38] At the same time in London, Colonel Harold Perkins, swiftly sent a telegram to the AK requesting the young airman to submit further details about himself. Ward complied and furthermore, suggested that he could send regular bulletins on the course of the fighting to London, via an AK transmitter. This news reached a clearly delighted British Secretary of State for Air, Sir Archibald Sinclair who personally telegrammed Ward to congratulate him on his initiative, while another telegram soon arrived from *The Times*, asking him to be a regular correspondent who could supply a daily bulletin on the fighting. The AK duly supplied Ward with all the secretarial support he needed. For these authentic reports, coming from a British serviceman, could carry the exploits of the Rising to a worldwide readership. He was also in the unique position of advising members of the British Government as to weapons required, which weapons already dropped had proved most useful and which enemy strongholds should be bombed.[39]

The AK meanwhile, consolidated their remaining positions within the city – Żolibórz in the north, the city centre and adjacent Old Town, together with part of Mokotów in the south. Their stocks of arms and ammunition had run extremely low, so there was much jubilation when a German stronghold was captured, yielding 11,600 rifle rounds, 8,500 pistol rounds, five machine-guns, thirty anti-tank mines and three motor cars.[40] In the suburb of Stawki, a large store of Wehrmacht and Waffen-SS uniforms and equipment was raided, providing the AK with helmets and camouflaged kit. The uniforms were immediately doctored with Polish national emblems and those fighters lucky enough to secure the distinctive M1942 helmet, soon painted on it a white and red band or the white Polish eagle. Camouflaged smocks, or *panterki* were popular wear for the ranks, coupled with the compulsory white/red arm bands, which sometime bore the initials 'WP' (*Wojsko Polskie*, or Polish Army), while most officers and NCOs wore their own full Polish Army uniforms.[41]

For Polish agents anxiously hoping to be dropped into their mother country, the events unfolding in Warsaw were agonising. Sue Ryder recalled their mood:

> The whole city was enveloped in smoke. The Poles viewed the time as desperate and there was never any question that Warsaw should not rise up – they thought their honour was at stake. We discussed it with them and I have never met a Pole who thought it was unwise. They simply had to show the world that they were going to rise against the Germans. They knew the Russians would never help. In a way, they hoped this would show the Allies what the Soviets were really like. But they would ask, 'is no-one going to come to our aid. What about the Polish Parachute Brigade?'[42]

The fortunes of the brigade were indeed a difficult issue. The Polish C-in-C, General Sosnkowski constantly lobbied the British Chiefs of Staff to use the Polish Parachute Brigade in the fight for Warsaw. But the brigade was under the control of Supreme Headquarters Allied Expeditionary Force (SHAEF) and it was unlikely that the HQ's commander, General Dwight Eisenhower would release resources already marked for north-west Europe. Even if such troops were released, it was estimated that it would take 125 Stirlings or over 200 Halifaxes (or a larger number of armed Liberators) to move the 1,500-strong force from bases in England, via Sweden to Poland.[43] And, as Józef Garliński surmised, the journey would be a nightmare:

> The vast fleet of Liberators, extended over many miles, takes-off from British airfields and advances eastward. Over the North Sea it is intercepted by German night-fighters and suffers its first losses. It flies on in a looser formation as far as Sweden, where it turns south over the Baltic to the Danzig area. In a storm of flak and harried by fighter aircraft with quick-firing guns, the fleet moves southward along the course of the Vistula. By now several planes have been lost in the North Sea and Baltic, some have been shot down in Poland, others have had to turn back with engine trouble and others again have strayed off course in the dark. At last, far below, the flames of the burning city come into view. The planes come down to a low altitude, since otherwise the paratroopers will be dispersed and unable to act as a unit. A fresh barrage of flak shoots up to meet them.[44]

Those paratroopers who managed to avoid the perils of landing in a built-up area, or indeed accidental landings in enemy areas, would only have had one day's ammunition reserve. Most would be unfamiliar with the myriad alleys and tunnels, so necessary for the successful defence of various quarters of the city. Yet, although the British Chiefs of Staff dismissed the idea of dropping paratroopers, they did undertake to review the possibility of further supply drops. However, they remained adamant that because the AK were unlikely to come into contact with 'Anglo-American armies', they were not worthy of having Allied Liaison Officers at their Headquarters. Considering that the British lacked up to date intelligence on events in Poland, this seems remarkably short-sighted.[45]

After the heavy losses in aircrew and aircraft from the missions of 13-16 August, SOE changed its supply dropping tactics. Under Lieutenant-Colonel Henry Threlfall's direction, supplies were now being dropped a little way outside the city into larger AK-controlled rural areas with fewer enemy ack-ack batteries, so that arms and equipment could be filtered in by foot.[46] These smaller scale operations flown by Polish volunteer crews enjoyed some success and during the week ending 25 August, twenty-six sorties were flown, which achieved seventeen drops on target without any loss of aircraft. But this was only temporary good fortune. As August drew to a close, four more Halifaxes from 1586 Flight were shot down by Messerschmitt Bf109 night-fighters. As the Rising reached its grim final phase, 148 Squadron took stock of its losses. Since the move to Brindisi in January, the squadron had lost nineteen Halifaxes and almost as many crews in its sorties to Poland.[47]

Sergeant John Ward was still the only British contact in Warsaw who could inform the RAF of desired drop zones for supply canisters. The AK only had one telegraphist and she was allocated to Ward, relaying his messages on her transmitter, sometimes for eighteen hours a day.[48] Despite being hit in the leg by a sniper while crossing Pius Street, Ward continued his detailed reports:

> The people of Warsaw call the German mine-throwers 'moving cupboards' on account of the fact that it gives out a sound like that of a heavy piece of furniture being moved, followed a few moments later by a number of terrific explosions. The Prudential building on Napoleon Square, the highest building in Warsaw was hit three times by mines and once by bombs. It is completely burnt out. The pavements in Warsaw have been turned into graveyards. In many places one cannot walk on the pavement without walking on fresh graves.[49]

On 19 August Hitler found himself challenged by another Rising, nearly 1,000 miles away in Paris. Again an insurgency, involving some 20,000 armed fighters, had erupted as Allied liberating troops were within sight of the French capital. However, a decision was made for Allied troops to skirt the city rather than attempt a direct assault that would have resulted in widespread destruction. No such sensibilities surrounded the city of Warsaw. On that same day, the Germans launched a massive assault on the Old Town district with ten battalions of troops and police, a company of nine Tiger tanks, together with 88mm guns, assault guns, howitzers and fifty Goliath mine tanks. This awesome firepower came to bear on the square mile of the Old Town and for the next two weeks until 2 September, an estimated 4,000 tons of shells fell on the defenders, as well as bombs from six daily aircraft sorties.[50]

Thirty miles south-east of Warsaw, the Soviet 8th Guards Army, reinforced by Berling's Polish Army 1st and 2nd Rifle Divisions, were holding onto their bridgehead on the western side of the Vistula, at Magnuszew. On 8 August, the German 45th *Volksgrenadier* and 17th Infantry Divisions were joined by the 19th Panzer and Hermann Göring Divisions, who were rushed down from defending Warsaw to counter-attack the Soviet bridgehead. Magnuszew soon became the centre of attention for Soviet operations even at the expense of entering Warsaw, and as the situation around the bridgehead became critical a Soviet tank corps from the 2nd Tank Army outside Warsaw was sent down to bolster the defences. Luftwaffe aircraft strafed and bombed the Polish 1st Army Rifle units coming across the Vistula in small craft to reinforce the west bank, but gradually the Red Army widened and consolidated their bridgehead.

On 8 August, despite being heavily outnumbered, Model's divisions, which included the recently arrived elite *Grossdeutschland* Division, launched a series of counter-attacks against the Red Army that succeeded in stemming their advance. On 10 August, the Soviets started to lever away the German grip on territory to the north of Warsaw. They unleashed a massive assault against German Army Group North, 200 miles northeast of Warsaw, with the hope of breaking through Latvia and into East Prussia. As the Soviet Third Baltic Front, together with the Second Baltic Front broke through the German positions, the Army Group Commander *Generalfeldmarschall* Ferdinand Schörner attempted to stiffen the resolve of his men, issuing one order to a subordinate to 'report by 2100 hours which commanders he has shot, or is having shot, for cowardice.'[51] Little could be done to halt the Soviet advance through the Baltic states, and by late August the Red Army were close to the East Prussian border; they were thus about to finally enter German territory.

Nonetheless, Army Group North still managed to hold onto a fifty mile-deep coastal strip running through Lithuania, Latvia and Estonia to the Gulf of Finland, which was reinforced for the time being, through an eighteen-mile corridor. Senior German commanders, including *Generaloberst* Georg-Hans Reinhardt (who, on 16 August replaced Model as Commander, Army Group Centre) recommended evacuating the remaining German forces from the Baltic States.[52] But Hitler would have none of it, and on 27 August he ordered a panzer division to be transferred to the beleaguered Army Group North. German forces then enjoyed a brief respite as an exhausted Red Army refitted and reinforced for the next round of offensives in the autumn. Forward Soviet units still lay twelve miles away from Warsaw's suburb of Praga and were to remain there for nearly another month. Their air force similarly held back and let the Luftwaffe dominate the skies over Warsaw.

Air superiority was vital to the Germans, but bombing and strafing AK positions could not winkle out all the Polish fighters – Warsaw had to be taken back, tenement by tenement, cellar by cellar. Accordingly, German pressure on AK-held territory in the Old Town was stepped up from 14 August. Barricades thrown up by the insurgents offered little protection against German armour, especially the new remote-controlled Goliath and B-IV mine vehicles. The Goliath was expendable and would be destroyed along with its target. The B-IV however, was twice the size of a Goliath and would normally be guided by a driver who would dismount once the vehicle was on target; the B-IV would then drop its mine at the target and reverse out of the destruction zone so it could be used again. On one occasion during the Rising, the Germans left a B-IV beside a Polish barricade. In an attempt to use the vehicle as a transport, AK soldiers pulled it inside their lines, where its massive mine suddenly exploded, killing or wounding 200 soldiers and civilians. Such large casualties were a heavy blow to the underground, and recovering and caring for the regular stream of the wounded placed a heavy burden on its resources. It was important but exhausting work, and willing Girl Guides like Hanna Czarnocka constantly scrambled back and forth across the ruins in search of those who could be saved.

Someone reported a wounded girl in the grounds of the Institute. The shots had come from the nearby IMKA (YMCA) building and the wounded girl lay in the bushes but was quite visible because of her bright blue coat. 'Koza' and I took a stretcher and began to pull her towards it. She was still bleeding in my arms when she was hit by another bullet in the shoulder. There were German snipers in all the tall buildings. Her commander, who was also wounded and lying in the bushes nearby, called out to us to leave him until night-time. We got the girl, who had been carrying important information about the names of German spies, to our sick-bay but it was too late to save her. As for the commander, when he was recovered his hair had gone completely white and I had seen him that morning with jet-black hair.

It was sometimes difficult to identify our own soldiers as they had stolen German equipment, including helmets. At least they had painted a red and white band around the helmets and usually wore civilian clothes, but from a distance it was confusing. We soon ran out of disinfectant and bandages and as the Germans had recently evacuated St Lazarus's Hospital, Dr Burska ordered us to get into the stores and retrieve supplies. However, as the Germans were still patrolling in the streets around the hospital, I was sent with a nurse and a boy armed with a gun. We managed to climb into the building under fire and crawled on our stomachs into the infirmary and my nurse knew exactly where all the supplies were. We quickly stuffed a quantity into our sacks and crawled out again under fire. Waiting for us was one of our brave insurgents, Witeź armed with a *Błyskawica* who escorted us away. We suffered no wounds but one of our sacks was full of bullet holes.

We also ran out of meths and we knew there were quantities in the Polytechnic. It was some way off and we had to cross barricades and many buildings. Other civilians were a great help as they knocked through cellars so we could travel underground some of the way. I managed to pick up ten bottles and as I was running back, the Germans shelled a building next to me. Before the smoke had cleared, people had rushed forward and were digging in the ruins for survivors. I had a backpack full of meths bottles and suddenly a German with a flame-thrower appeared. He put out a burst of flame and I could feel the heat on my legs, but amazingly, although it was leaking, the meths didn't explode on my back. When I arrived back at my base they complained that one of the bottles had leaked.

We took all our wounded to a makeshift hospital and when it had filled up, we stacked them outside. At first we had anaesthetic but then it ran out. However, the doctors and nurses were very skilful and carried out emergency operations under basic conditions. Our old caretaker was a courageous man who organised our collections of the wounded. I was so lucky to escape injury, such as the time I was crossing open ground with the Germans entrenched on one side. We were carrying a wounded man and a grenade was thrown at us but miraculously my sleeve was torn but we were all unharmed.

There were also deaf and blind units, with a priest in charge, helping us. I had a deaf man to help with our stretcher. One day we picked up a boy who was bleeding badly and had to carry him back over some high debris. I was using deaf signs to communicate with my assistant. Then suddenly, for the first time in his life, the deaf man heard sounds. It was the nearby anti-aircraft guns and he got so excited that he dropped the stretcher, shouting, 'I can hear. I can hear.'[53]

As the daily struggle ground on amidst the ruins of the city, the contest outside was every bit as fierce. It was always an AK assumption that Stalin wanted to capture Warsaw in August, but the commander he had entrusted with the role was showing little interest in the city. By the end of the month, Marshal Rokossovsky's First Byelorussian Front had managed to push back the German Army Group Centre to the River Narew, which ran just north of the city. Rokossovsky later excused his failure to enter Warsaw's eastern suburb of Praga, by stressing the importance of diverting his troops to the bitter struggle at the southerly Magnuszew bridgehead as well as the contest to control the crossings of the strategically important River Narew, to the north of the city.[54] Certainly, a bridgehead at the Narew was important as a precursor to any future Soviet sweep towards Berlin, while the Magnuszew bridgehead was an important breach in the German's Vistula defences. It was also true that the Red Army was determined not to stretch its lines of communication and to refit before resuming the next round of offensives. But it was clear that Stalin was playing a waiting game with the Polish capital. He was certainly not going to help the Allies with their efforts to airlift supplies to the AK. Molotov's deputy, Andrey Vyshinskii told the US Ambassador that Soviet airfields were not going to be available for Allied aircraft – even transports – to land for refuelling after drops on Warsaw. And neither would the Red Air Force take part in bombing German positions in the city, especially if it meant assisting, in Vyshinski's words, 'the work of adventurers.'

In a mood calculated to ratchet up opposition to the AK, the Soviet press mounted a vilification campaign against Polish political and military leaders, such as Generals Sosnkowski and Anders, who were lampooned in crude cartoons.[55] In a cypher to Churchill and Roosevelt, Stalin hammered home his objections, warning that 'sooner or later the truth about the group of criminals who have embarked on the Warsaw adventure in order to seize power will become known to everybody.'[56] The British response to the Soviet attitude was feeble. The Soviet Ambassador, F.T. Gousev was called to the Foreign Office and told that the British public would not understand Stalin's attitude, as the military situation in Warsaw was critical and the AK needed urgent help. Gousev feigned ignorance of the dire situation in the city, claiming that the military impact of the Rising was overstated. Sergeant John Ward's reports were even read out to Gousev to appraise him of the scale of the fighting, but he brushed these aside.[57]

In southern Poland, the Soviet First Ukrainian Front had made startling progress with its Lwów-Sandomierz Offensive. Since capturing Lwów in late July, it had pushed the opposing German Army Group North Ukraine back over the River San and into the Polish General Government territory. On 18 August, the Red Army had captured Sandomierz and by the end of the month had taken Rzeszów, Dębica and with it, the German V-2 testing site at Blizna. All 'liberated' towns were issued with Soviet-made loudspeakers in public places, and from 10 August local populations were subjected to six-hour broadcasts by 'Polskie Radio', the mouthpiece of the provisional Lublin government. Details of the Soviet advance, together with the progress of the Moscow-sponsored government, blared out continuously, accompanied by much derision of the AK actions in Warsaw.[58]

Inside the city, the Germans were impatient to crush Polish resistance. On 13 August the Gestapo herded together the remaining thirty prisoners in Pawiak jail, including a battered and bloodied Antoni Kocjan, and shot them all. Then on 19 August, men from the Kaminski Brigade returned to finish their work at the Marie Curie Institute. Mounting the stairs to the upper floors, they ordered the nurses to carry out the remaining 70 patients and killed those who were too sick to move. The desperate party was then ordered into the nearby Health Centre building, where a German officer was waiting for them. He calmly moved amongst them, shooting each in the head with a revolver. Petrol was then brought in, splashed over the bodies and ignited.[59] Meanwhile Dirlewanger's units made short work of clearing buildings. If a German police or Wehrmacht squad could not expel AK fighters from a tenement, they invariably called in the *Sonderkommando*, as one German soldier vividly recalled:

> That's when the Dirlewanger crowd was thought of. The 'crowd' arrived, took a look and stormed in. About 50 men rushed across the street. Approximately 30 men remained lying there and did not move anymore. The remainder vanished into a house and during the next ten minutes, both corpses and living people flew out of the windows of the fourth and fifth floor. The Dirlewanger people did not stop by giving long speeches. This is how the houses of Warsaw were cleaned up.[60]

According to AK sponsored radio stations, German forces did not hold all the initiative. On 24 August, 'Radio Lightening' broadcast an account of a fight around the German Police headquarters:

> It was necessary to fight for the church. The Holy Virgin Chapel had to be taken by grenades. The Germans were beaten to their knees there. At the same time the ring around the Police HQ was tightened. There, the Germans had six machine-guns with which they swept all our positions with fire, and the road of retreat was cut off. We shot the Germans like rabbits. Through the open door the Germans shot salvos from guns. All around the houses burned. Our fire defence and the civilian population immediately went into action and put out the fires. About noon the first group of German prisoners showed themselves. Finally it was over. One of the prisoners said 'Lt. Kutcher fled like a crazy person, he got a bullet in the stomach.'[61]

Stalin repeatedly turned down Polish appeals for help, dismissing the rising as 'a thoughtless brawl'. Both Churchill and Roosevelt tele-grammed Stalin with similar requests for assistance and on 20 August they sent a joint appeal requesting the use of Soviet airfields for US aircraft which had flown from Britain, to refuel after drop missions over Warsaw. Predictably, Stalin ignored the request, denigrating the AK as a 'handful of power-seeking criminals'. Even for those willing to excuse Stalin's failure to assault Warsaw because of strong German counter-attacks, now realised that the dictator wanted the Rising crushed. Churchill how-ever, was minded to test Stalin's resolve and suggested to Roosevelt that the aircraft land on Soviet airfields without advanced permission. They might just be refuelled without referral to higher Soviet command. But the US President would have none of it, so SOE had to resort to the continued use of small sorties from Brindisi to re-supply Warsaw.[62]

However, despite the problems of long distance missions to Poland, the RAF did engage in other operations of a similar distance. On the night of 28/29 August, 402 Lancasters attacked the Baltic port of Stettin, while 189 Lancasters made for Königsberg. Both raids were in support of Soviet offensives and although successful, the losses were high – thirty-eight bombers were shot down. Immediate questions were raised by the Polish Air Force as to why this volume of bombers could not be used for Warsaw. It proved a sensitive enough issue to warrant a meeting the following morning at 1030 hrs in the office of the Deputy Chief of Air Staff, Air Marshal Sir Norman Bottomley. The Deputy Chief defended the raid, stating that the Lancasters could only fly that distance if they maintained a height of 20,000 ft. This was a suitable level for bombing, he argued, but certainly not for dropping supplies by parachute into closely defined zones within the Warsaw suburbs. To descend to the extremely low level required for drops and then to ascend back to a safer height would expend large quantities of fuel, for which Lancasters simply did not the capacity. Air Vice Marshal Mateusz Iżycki, Air Officer C-in-C, Polish Air Force pursued the matter of the extra fuel tanks and was told that there were none available to fit Lancasters. Furthermore, although the RAF had suffered losses, they only equated to 6% of the aircraft employed on the raids. Königsberg was a 'fringe' target requiring very little land penetration, while flights to Warsaw were deemed far more costly – they involved flying over land for a long distance, enough for the enemy to plot the aircraft and vector night-fighters in to attack.

SOE, at last, seemed to be having some impact on the mindset of the British Chiefs of Staffs. The Chiefs received an SOE report confirming that due to losses, there remained only four serviceable aircraft available to 1586 Flight. In response, on 23 August the Chiefs sent a bullish cable to General 'Jumbo' Wilson, Supreme Allied Commander Mediterranean, requesting:

> That the Polish crews should be allowed, indifferently of losses sustained, to fly to Warsaw and Poland and should be used exclusively for operations to Poland. That the Polish Flight should be supplied with sufficient number of aircraft to enable them to fly 14 sorties every flying night. That the British crews and aircraft of 148 Squadron should continue their assistance – in spite of Polish crews being used for Poland alone – by carrying out operations to southern Poland.[63]

By late August, the front to the south of Warsaw had stabilised. The Vistula River snaked down for 100 miles before turning back westwards and it was along this natural obstacle that the Soviet and German forces faced each other. AK soldiers caught in the middle could either be disarmed, drafted into Berling's communist Polish 1st Army or simply melt away to await orders. Lieutenant Mieczysław Wałęga who had been involved in running the AK's Rzeszów District moved out when it fell to the

Red Army in early August. As he made his way westwards, he observed his old enemy retreating:

> Even though we hated them, you had to concede that the Germans were excellent fighters and their sense of direction was superb. Even in retreat they seemed to know exactly where they were heading. Their officers, even towards the end, maintained discipline.[64]

German units were ordered to stand fast when they reached the River Vistula. An exhausted nineteen-year-old Günter Koschorrek and his unit had dug in near the river. He nervously awaited the next Soviet onslaught:

> I know that our lives are now worth less than the straw we are standing on. I have been on the front long enough to be able to size up a situation correctly and to know that belief in luck is a very weak subterfuge. Here only a prayer can help us – to ask God that he will be with us in this bitter hour of our wretched lives. Unlike me, Dorka is a Catholic: while I pray silently, he crosses himself and prays with trembling lips.
>
> …As the wind removes the last vestiges of fog in front of us we are staring directly into the barrels of four guns. The range is about 100 metres. They must have discovered our positions or else just fired first where the sheaves of corn are stacked up. As the muzzles flash, we feel the blast in our faces – that's how near they are. There is a sharp explosion, the sheaves are blown into the air and our machine-gun is now in the open.
>
> 'Anti-tank guns!' yells Dorka, thunderstruck, and crosses himself. At the same moment a second shell hits the mound and shatters the HMG [heavy machine-gun] to pieces. Dorka yells and clutches his throat. He looks dumbstruck at his bloody hand and presses it against his wound. Panic-stricken, he jumps out of the hole and runs up the field towards the village. Right behind him another round explodes and rips off both his legs. His backside is thrown into the air and falls, covered in blood, on to the ground.[65]

Until the night of 27/28 August when Air Marshal Slessor called a halt to flights to Warsaw, a total of 161 sorties had been flown from Brindisi. Of these, eighty had been successful but twenty-seven aircraft and most of their crews were lost. It was true that seven of these had been shot down between Kraków and Tarnów, but they were nevertheless on Warsaw missions. It was now apparent that the losses of aircraft increased sharply with the number of machines dispatched, for the enemy were not sending up night-fighters to engage missions unless there were a large number of aircraft heading towards Poland. With regard to the actual supplies dropped, only fifty-two tons of supplies (against 500 tons requested by the AK) fell into Warsaw itself and of these supplies it was estimated that only thirty tons were collected by the AK, the rest falling into enemy hands.[66] After four weeks of organising these ever more desperate relief flights, a weary Harold Perkins wrote to his chief:

> Recent operations, even to the Warsaw district, have proved disastrous and we have on two occasions lost two out of the four or five machines dispatched. It is my confirmed opinion that we must put aside heroics and the honour and glory of Polish crews dying for their capital, for Warsaw cannot be rationally sustained in this manner.[67]

On 29 August the Soviet *Stavka* ordered its main forces in Poland (Third, Second and First Byelorussian Fronts, together with First and Fourth Ukrainian Fronts) to switch to the defensive. At the same time, those forces covering the northern flank in the Baltic States (Third and Second Baltic Fronts) and the southern flank inside Romania (Second and Third Ukrainian Fronts) were ordered onto the offensive.[68] Marshal Rokossovsky still awaited orders from the *Stavka* about an advance into Warsaw.

NOTES

[1] General Tatar estimated the AK strength in Warsaw at '43,000 men', but this is almost certainly an exaggeration and may have included auxiliaries, messengers, 'Grey Ranks' etc. He also stated that they were all armed. See SOE Memo, 'General Rising by the Polish Secret Army in Warsaw Area', 29 July 1944, HS4/156, NA.

[2] Marek Ney-Krwawicz, op. cit., pp. 74–5. It is estimated that at the start of the rising, the AK had an arsenal comprising 44,000 grenades, 4,000 pistols, 650 automatic pistols and 12,000 Molotov cocktails. Such reserves could only last days.

[3] Bór-Komorowski, op. cit., pp. 219–20. The *filipinka* was a home-made Etwz40 hand-grenade.

4 Report from GOC, AK, 5 August 1944, HS 4/157, NA.

5 Hanna Kościa to Author, 22 September 2006. Mailboxes, used for messages during the Rising, were normally emptied twice a day by members of the scouting movement.

6 Richard Lukas, *The Forgotten Holocaust*, op. cit., p. 190. Also 'Radio Messages Received from John Ward', 13 August 1944, ref. 3.9.2.8.9., PUMST.

7 Lieutenant-Colonel H. Threlfall to Colonel Dodds Parker, 16 August 1944, HS4/157, NA.

8 Colonel Hańcza to General Tatar, 3 August 1944, HS4/157, NA.

9 The mangled remains of one of the Halifax II Bs, piloted by Flight Lieutenant A.R. Blynn, were found in a field near the Polish town of Dabrowa Tarnowska in 2006. Aircraft JP276 FS-A had been detailed to make supply drops to the Skierniewice region.

10 Jerzy Cynk, op. cit., pp. 473–4, and Garliński, *Poland, SOE and the Allies*, op. cit., p. 189–90. At this stage, a full moon was needed to assist navigation. Later flights had to be made in complete darkness.

11 The Panzer IV medium tank remained in production through the war and was a staple of German armoured divisions. The Sturmgeschütz III, known as the StuG, was a tank destroyer/assault gun with a fixed 75mm gun. It was much cheaper to produce than a turreted tank, with perhaps four StuGs costing as much as one Tiger tank.

12 Cossacks who fought for the Wehrmacht increasingly comprised civilians from Cossack lands who had suffered at the hands of the Soviets. When the Germans occupied these areas in 1942, they were often greeted as liberators.

13 For RONA units, see 'Eastern Volunteer Formations' in General Władysław Anders, *Hitler's Defeat in Russia* (Henry Regnery Company, Chicago 1953), pp. 173–203. For Kaminski, see Antonio J. Muñoz, *The Kaminski Brigade: A History 1941–1945* (Europa Books, New York 2003).

14 Full details of Dirlewanger's career, together with the exploits of his unit can be found in French MacLean, *The Cruel Hunters: SS-Sonderkommando Dirlewanger. Hitler's Most Notorious Anti-Partisan Unit* (Schiffer Military History, Atglen, US 1998).

15 Although Dirlewanger was himself a member of the SS, his brigade did not formally belong to the *Waffen-SS* (armed SS). The unit could best be described as *Allgemeine SS* (general SS). At the start of the rising they comprised 5% poachers; 10% foreign troops; 40% SS & Army penal troops; 40% criminals from concentration camps; 5% others; see MacLean op. cit., p. 282.

16 Nuremberg War Crimes Record No. 45/11, quoted in Muñoz, op. cit., pp. 65–7. Also 'Radio Messages Received from John Ward', 13 August 1944, ref. 3.9.2.8.9., PUMST.

17 Ward Reports, op. cit., 20 August 1944.

[18] Maria Kietlicz-Rayska was the daughter of Colonel Björkland, the former Finnish Military Attaché in Warsaw. Her account was related on 29 September 1944; see 'Situation in Warsaw at the beginning of August 1944', HS4/146, NA. For other accounts of the expulsions, see Richard Lukas, op. cit., pp. 198–203.

[19] Because of lack of documentary evidence, estimates of the massacre vary widely and are calculated on the basis of witness testimonies. Joanna Hanson, in her study, *The Civilian Population and the Warsaw Uprising of 1944* (Cambridge University Press, Cambridge 1982), pp. 89–90, has put deaths at between 30,000 and 40,000.

[20] For Dirlewanger, see MacLean op. cit., p. 179; for AK, see Korboński, op. cit., p. 374.

[21] MacLean, op. cit., p. 187–8.

[22] For a detailed account of the meeting with Stalin, see Rozek, op. cit., pp. 237–42.

[23] Telegram no. 316, 10 August 1944, *Stalin's Correspondence* op. cit., p. 251. The Lublin Committee comprised three main communist groups; the Polish Communist Party, the National Council of the Homeland and the Union of Polish Patriots. See MK Dziewanowski, *The Communist Party of Poland: An Outline of History* (Harvard University Press, Cambridge US 1976), pp. 148–50.

[24] Peter Wilkinson, *Gubbins*, op. cit., p. 207. For Sosnkowski's trip, see 'Note by General Ismay', COS (44) 711, 8 August 1944, AIR 20/7983, NA. Also, Ward Report, 9 August 1944, op. cit.

[25] Stefan Korboński, op. cit., pp. 357–8.

[26] Translated AK cypher message no. 6642, 10 August 1944, HS4/157, NA. See also cypher, 'JSM Washington to AMSSO, 12 August 1944, HS4/156, NA.

[27] Lord Selborne to Prime Minister, 11 August 1944, HS4/156, NA.

[28] Sosnkowski telegram attached to 'Note by General Ismay', COS. (44) 711, 8 August 1944, AIR 20/7983, NA.

[29] COS, 262nd Meeting, 7 August 1944, AIR 20/7983, NA.

[30] Minutes of Chief of Staffs 273rd Meeting, 12 August 1944, AIR 20/7983, NA. Before taking any action in the European theatre, the United States Army Air Forces required directives from the Combined Chiefs of Staff.

[31] General Ismay to Foreign Office, 7 August 1944, HS4/157.

[32] Hilary St George Saunders, *Royal Air Force 1939–1945, Vol. III: The Fight is Won* (HMSO, London 1954), p. 240.

[33] Anthony Eden to Władysław Raczkiewicz, 17 August 1944, HS4/157, NA.

[34] In daytime, the AK advised the relief flights that there might be no signals from the zones; Memo, 'GOC Warsaw to Polish General Staff', 3 August 1944, HS 4/157, NA.

[35] For full details of crews and aircraft lost, see Jerzy B. Cynk, op. cit., pp. 474–6.

[36] Ward reports, op. cit., 11 August 1944.

37 'Radio Messages received from John Ward', 7 August 1944 transmission, ref. 3.9.2.8.9, PUMST.

38 Lieutenant-Colonel Threlfall to AOC, Balkan Air Force, 13 September 1944, HS4/146, NA.

39 Korboński, op. cit., pp. 358–61. Also Ward MI9 Report, 22 March 1945, HS4/256, NA. Ward sent 'shopping lists' of weapons to SOE's Colonel Perkins, as well as to Sir Archibald Sinclair. See Ward Reports, op. cit., 28 August 1944.

40 Ward Reports, op. cit., 13 August 1944.

41 Warsaw Dispatches, Polish General Staff VI Bureau, 12 August 1944, HS4/156. Good colour examples of these irregular outfits can be seen in Steven Zaloga, *The Polish Army 1939–45* (Osprey, Oxford 1982).

42 Sue Ryder, 1987, ref 10057, Sound Archive, IWM.

43 'Assistance to the Poles' in 'Conclusions of Chiefs of Staffs 267th Meeting', 9 August 1944, HS4/157, NA.

44 Garliński, *Poland, SOE and the Allies*, op. cit., p. 180.

45 'Employment of Polish Independent Parachute Company', 9 September 1944, AIR 20/7984, NA. Also 'Draft Letter to General Kukiel', undated, HS4/156, NA.

46 Lieutenant-Colonel Threlfall, 'Stores dropping to Poland', 16 August 1944, HS4/157, NA.

47 For a detailed list of aircraft losses, see David Waters, *The History of 148 Bomber Squadron* (privately printed, 1998).

48 Korboński, op. cit., p. 361.

49 Ward Reports, op. cit., 19 August 1944, NA.

50 Lukas, op. cit., p. 209–10. Also Ward Report, 20 September 1944, op. cit.

51 Ziemke, op. cit., p. 342.

52 Reinhardt was eventually captured and tried at Nuremburg. He was sentenced to 15 years, but released in 1952.

53 Hanna Kościa to Author, 22 September 2006.

54 K. Rokossovsky, *A Soldier's Duty* (Progress Publishers, Moscow 1970), pp. 258–9.

55 Foreign Office to British Embassy, Moscow, 25 August 1944, HS4/142, NA.

56 Cypher, 'Premier Stalin to Prime Minister Churchill and President Roosevelt', 23 August 1944, CAB 121/310.

57 Cypher 'From Moscow to Foreign Office', 15 August 1944, HS4/157, NA. Also telegram, Foreign Office to Moscow, 18 August 1944, HS4/157, NA.

58 BBC Monitoring Service, 'Radio Growth in Liberated Poland', PRM 154/ part II, Polish Institute and Sikorski Museum, London.

59 Muñoz, op. cit., p. 67.

60 Rolf Michaelis, *Die Grenadier Divisionen der Waffen SS* (Michaelis, Erlangen 1995) p. 173.

[61] Transcript, Radio Lightening, 24 August 1944, HS4/156, NA.
[62] Rozek, op. cit., pp. 251–2. For 'criminals', see *Stalin's Correspondence*, op. cit., 22 August 1944.
[63] Air Ministry Special Signals Office (AMSSO) to Allied Forces HQ, Italy (AFHQ), 23 August 1944, AIR20/7983, NA.
[64] Colonel Mieczysław Wałęga was awarded the Commander's Cross with Star (Rebirth of Poland) – the highest rank within the order – for his outstanding war service.
[65] Günter K. Koschorrek, *Blood Red Snow: The Memoirs of a German Soldier on the Eastern Front* (Greenhill Books, London 2002), pp. 284–5.
[66] Minutes of Air Ministry Meeting, 31 August 1944, HS4/156, NA. Also Cynk, op. cit., p. 477.
[67] Lieutenant-Colonel Harold Perkins (MP) to Major-General Colin Gubbins (CD), 29 August 1944, HS4/156, NA. Also 'Draft Minutes of Air Ministry Meeting', 31 August 1944, AIR 20/7984, NA.
[68] Evan Mawdsley, *Thunder in the East: The Nazi-Soviet War 1941–1945* (Hodder Arnold, London 2005) p. 329.

Chapter Eight

Warsaw in Flames
(September 1944)

At the beginning of September, the situation in the Old Town had become critical for the AK. Over half the buildings in the sector were destroyed and the constant German artillery barrage had driven most fighters underground into cellars and sewers. Those who remained underground were invariably buried alive by falling masonry or by enemy aerial bombardment. The sewers however, proved a sanctuary that allowed over 1,500 exhausted insurgents and civilians to escape, either north to the AK-controlled pocket in Żolibórz, or southwards into the city centre. Some were overpowered by the stench or dragged out of the sewers by the Germans, but most made it to friendly territory. On 2 September, with most AK positions in the Old Town evacuated, German forces closed in. A beleaguered AK wireless station sent a final message:

> The rising in the Old Town is nearing its tragic end. The Home Army with-
> draws from the Old Town. Germans complete the burning down of houses in
> the following streets – Pańska, Śliska, Sienna, Złota, and the sector of Chmielna
> between Żelazna and Marszałkowska. Next will be burnt the quarter round
> Napoleon's Square and Powiśle, which are continuously bombed from the
> air. We cannot fight the fires any longer because of lack of water and anti-fire
> equipment. The Germans are compressing us more and more.[1]

Although the AK-controlled areas in the city were now down to half that of the high point of the Rising on 5 August, the resistors grimly held on despite German attempts to prise them away from the key river bank positions. In fact, by the beginning of September, German losses had reached 191 officers and 3,770 men and over the next two weeks, they suffered a further 5,000 casualties.[2] High casualty rates were seen particularly among German police units, who were still very much to the fore of the action and in combat would have appeared almost identical to their comrades in the Wehrmacht or SS. Police troops operating as rifle battalions were issued with the same 'dot' or 'pea-pattern' camouflage uniforms and those police fighting in armoured units wore black uniforms similar to Panzer crews. Warsaw was seen by the Germans as very much a police operation and although Wehrmacht and SS units were employed, a high-profile role was taken by *Motorisierte Überfallkommandos* (riot squads) to quell what they deemed to be a 'bandit' uprising. These units were often equipped with obsolescent captured armoured cars, but nevertheless proved themselves a formidable fighting force.[3]

During the nights of 29, 30 and 31 August Sir Charles Portal, Chief of Air Staff had banned all Special Duties flights to Warsaw, including volunteer missions, informing the Prime Minister:

> The longer the Poles continue to volunteer and suffer these valueless losses, the more we are putting the British crews into an invidious position which is unfair to them and to the Royal Air Force. They too would doubtless all volunteer to go but, since the task is on military grounds not worth the risk entailed, we refuse to let them go.[4]

This enraged the C-in-C Polish Armed Forces, General Sosnkowski, who fired off a missive directly to AK forces in Poland, berating the Allies for their lack of air support, considering that they had at their disposal, 'tens of thousands of aircraft'. It was a wild and inaccurate statement, however passionate, which the British could never forgive. They began to work actively for Sosnkowski's dismissal.[5] However, regarding the suspension of flights to Warsaw, less volatile Polish voices such as General Kopański rightly reminded the Air Ministry that so far the Poles had incurred heavier losses in the defence of Britain than in flying to Warsaw. Such arguments found favour with the Air Staff, who conceded that Polish volunteer crews could restart their missions on the night of 1/2 September. Meanwhile, senior Polish Air Staff, including Air Vice Marshal Iżycki, approached Air Chief Marshal Sir Arthur 'Bomber'

Harris to see if he could wield any influence. At a meeting at Bomber Command HQ on 1 September, the Polish airmen tackled him on the feasibility of re-opening the northern Europe route to Poland. Harris was sympathetic but reminded them that while the logistics were possible, the planning of operations was not his responsibility – that lay with SHAEF – and his job was only to 'establish priorities and plan the technical side of operations'. Furthermore, he warned them that Allied relief aircraft would face a formidable foe because 'the German fighter command is about the only efficient force still left in Germany.'[6]

Harris's cautious advice was then countered by more optimistic news coming in of the possibility of a massive daylight drop by US aircraft. They would have to fly at about 10,000 ft to avoid ground fire around Warsaw, and although it was estimated that only 10% of the containers would hit their target from this drop height, the US Army Air Force was prepared to carry out the mission. But first, a refuelling stop would have be negotiated on Soviet-held territory.[7]

Meanwhile, SOE officers persevered in trying to make their operations to Poland more effective. In an effort to cut down on unnecessary weight and bulk for the long trip to Poland, Squadron Leader Jacko Allerton and Major Alfgar Hesketh-Prichard visited the Handley Page factory at Radlett, Hertfordshire, to discuss modifications to the Halifax being used for special duties. The aircraft being used were originally fitted out for service in the North African and Mediterranean theatres and consequently had tropical cooling and sand extractors – hardly useful in a cold east European winter. The other issue which concerned SOE planners, and for which there seemed no solution, was how to drop containers accurately without compromising the safety of the aircraft. If an aircraft dropped containers by parachute from the safer height of 10,000 ft above Warsaw, even with a light wind, they were likely to drift some five to ten miles away from the target. To obtain any sort of accuracy, the crew would have to know not only the wind speed at the height of the aircraft, but also the wind speed at heights all the way down to the target. This was clearly impractical, but the losses suffered from enemy ack-ack fire at much lower levels were unsustainable.[8]

With the embargo on Polish flights now lifted, on the night of 1/2 September Polish volunteer crews took off from Brindisi in two Liberators and five Halifaxes. The Liberators were bound for the Kampinos Forest, near Warsaw, while the Halifaxes were dropping supplies to AK units in the Radom-Kielce region. Although the Kampinos drops went well, disaster struck the Halifaxes; four were shot down on the return journey with the loss of most of the crews. SOE became increasingly frustrated that these costly relief efforts were going unmonitored; British intelligence had so far failed to put any agents into Warsaw to verify whether the AK were actually receiving the supplies. Lieutenant-Colonel Perkins warned his superior, Major-General Gubbins:

> This lack of intelligence has become increasingly apparent in connection with the efforts recently made to supply the city of Warsaw by air from the base in Italy. It is possible that if competent British observers had been within the city, not only might the severe aircraft losses have been decreased, but we should have obtained concrete evidence as to the value or necessity of our assistance. It is to be noted that Marshal Stalin insisted upon the despatch of a Russian observer to the city before any Russian assistance was forthcoming.[9]

Perkins wanted two of his SOE officers, Lieutenant-Colonel Bill Hudson and Major Peter Kemp to be sent to Poland immediately to act as liaison officers with the AK. Frustratingly, his request was denied and five weeks into the fighting, Flight Sergeant John Ward remained about the only British intelligence asset inside Warsaw. Ward, largely on his own initiative, confirmed that morale amongst the AK was faltering due to the huge strain on its resources. Nonetheless, in a despatch to *The Times* he was still amazed at what the Poles could achieve:

> The AK is a queer mixture. Fighting in it are young boys of 16 years and old men of 70 years. There are weapons for about one man in a hundred. Weapons are varied; they range from the small automatic 65 calibre pistols to rifles. There are also a few heavy machine-guns, but these are only used in an emergency, as they use too much ammunition…Very few military formalities are observed. In fact it is impossible to enforce any large amount of discipline in any army that is two thirds untrained and has no uniform. There are colonels fighting as simple soldiers under the command of young lieutenants.
>
> Weapons are being constructed. Hand grenades have been made from old glass pipes filled with some explosive mixture. These grenades one must light with a simple match before throwing them. Flame-throwers are

in use that have been hurriedly constructed in small workshops. Perhaps the most ingenious weapon of all was used two days ago. I personally saw ten of them explode. In an old German store were found 120-80 pound artillery shells; at first it seemed they were useless, until a sapper, since killed, put two detonators inside each of them, and attached a 25 seconds fuse. When the order for action was given, these shells were thrown from a second floor window as near to the German positions as was possible, and then the company of AK fled to such cover as was obtainable. The effect was considerable.[10]

On 5 September, Mikołajczyk again beseeched Lord Selborne to put pressure on the Chiefs of Staff to allow the Polish Independent Parachute Company to be dropped into Warsaw. The highly trained Polish 'Bardsea' parachutists, in particular, had found themselves redundant after the swift Allied advance across France and the Low Countries had rendered their operation obsolete, and they were desperate to see action. Consequently Lord Selborne passed the matter to Major-General Gubbins, who outlined the Polish case to the Chiefs of Staff. But on 9 September the idea was again rebuffed and Mikołajczyk was told that 'the Chiefs of Staff consider there is no military advantage to be gained from this operation.' No mention was made of the prevalent fear that the use of such Special Forces in the face of advancing Soviet troops would inflame Stalin.[11] The speed of the Soviet advance was the constant reason put up by the Foreign Office for not authorising an SOE operation to put their own agents into Poland. While Churchill was minded to allow such an action, Anthony Eden and the Foreign Office constantly warned against it. 'It will be bad enough', the Foreign Secretary advised, 'if the Polish Underground Movement are going to be liquidated by the Soviet authorities, but it would be worse if British liaison officers were there when this happened'.[12]

As the Rising went into its second month, SOE's attitude towards the Red Army and Berling's Polish Army became almost benign. Colonel Harold Perkins, no stranger to the complexities of Eastern Europe, reported to Lieutenant-Colonel EPF Boughey:

Their [Soviet] ideas of the sanctity of life are peculiar, and therefore such chaps who do not fancy Berling's army are packed off to Siberia or face a second Katyn, and if one reads Russian mentality right, the Soviet

Government does not really care two hoots what happens to them as long as they do not cause a nuisance.

Mik [Mikołajczyk] is perfectly happy about Berling's army and is willing to play with them one hundred per cent; he was impressed by their pure Polish nature. I am very surprised myself that the Polish Government [in exile] has not already issued orders to the Resistance Movement that when overrun they should volunteer for Berling's army; such an order would go a long way towards alleviating the present miserable position.[13]

The problem for the Poles, who took no part in the fighting, was that the Soviets would not leave them alone. 'Causing a nuisance' had not been the reason why thousands of Varsovians were pushed out of the city and into the misery of the vast transit camp at Pruszków. Starvation was a real problem and because the Rising had not been expected to last beyond a week before outside help came, the AK had done little planning to provide for food and water relief from supporters outside the city. There were also other ambivalent voices in SOE; one officer dismissed the agony of the Rising, arguing, 'My personal view is that there has been too much fuss made about General Bór and the defence of Warsaw.'[14]

The harder the situation became for the AK, the less the British press seemed to cover the story. Although British newspapers filled column space about the other resistance movement, the French *Maquis*, very little copy was devoted to the Polish Home Army for fear of upsetting Stalin.[15] Editors no doubt believed that Stalin, outraged by British publicity for the AK, would provoke a very public slanging match. It would be difficult to explain to a British public, fed on a diet of 'Uncle Joe Stalin' and the sacrifices of the Soviet Union since 1941 that, after all, he was a cruel dictator who had to be checked. This press policy was also evident in the US, where newspapers such as the *New York Times* trumpeted the progress of Berling's Polish Army at the expense of their non-communist rivals:

A number of generals and other high officers of the Red Army have joined the Polish Army [Berling's] either because of Polish birth or parentage. Other Poles from east of the Curzon Line are flocking to the Polish standard, entering training centers at a rate which sometimes reaches 1,000 a day.[16]

US newspapers took their lead from the top. For advice on Soviet affairs, Roosevelt relied heavily on his Soviet advisor, Harry Hopkins. The influential 'Harry the Hop', as he was known by the President, had been made administrator of the US 'Lend-Lease Programme', which saw over £11 billion in vehicles, aircraft and weapons provided to the Soviet Union. Seen by some as a misguided liberal and by others as possibly a Soviet agent, his pro-Soviet stance was undisputed and he considered Stalin 'not a communist but a Russian nationalist.'[17]

Even if Poles were flocking to Berling's standard, as US newspapers reported, they were not going very far. According to Marshal Rokossovsky, his First Byelorussian Front had stalled in front of a solid German defence around Warsaw. A protective shield formed by units of the 5th SS Panzer Division *Wiking*, 3rd SS Panzer Division *Totenkopf*, 19th Panzer Division, as well as two further infantry divisions kept the Soviets at bay. Rokossovsky, in his memoirs, later maintained that his First Byelorussian Front did not have the capacity to attack this shield until 11 September and even then, it took three days of hard fighting for his troops to enter the eastern suburb of Praga, only to find most of the bridges connecting Praga to the western bank had been blown up.[18]

Further south, by early September 1944, the Red Army advance had taken their units to within 100 miles of Auschwitz. Liberation was still some way off and yet the Auschwitz camps had already had direct contact with the Allies. However, as Brian Bishop a British POW interned near Auschwitz III recalled, it was not the type of contact that he wanted:

On 20 August 1944, the POW camp next to Buna-Werke was bombed by the Allies and thirty-eight British prisoners were killed. On that day I was confined to the camp infirmary with para-typhoid. Suddenly there were explosions nearby and one of our sergeants staggered into my room with his scalp hanging off. I got out of bed and someone gave me Red Cross parcels to help the wounded in any way I could. Thirty-eight of our men were killed in the bombing raid that day. Most had taken shelter in the slit trenches on the edge of our camp nearest to the Buna camp.

In September 1944, there was another bombing raid. The factory radio warned us of an incoming radio and everyone had to clear the building. I wasn't quick enough and had to hide in a 3 ft pipe. None of the bombs hit our part of the factory, but the explosive force of those that landed outside, lifted the pipe. It was an extremely close shave.[19]

Bishop's close encounters had been the result of US bombing raids on the IG Farben and Monowitz complex near Auschwitz. The luckless British POWs who were killed in the US bombing raid in August, had been on an outdoor sports activity inside camp E715 and although there were air-raid shelters within the IG Farben complex, there was no provision within the POW camp. The dead were buried in a mass grave within the camp, but bombs from the raid on 13 September 1944 fell on the grave and the prisoners' remains were destroyed.[20] The bombs fell from 20,000 ft and inevitably many landed outside their target area, including some that were dropped 'by mistake' on Birkenau, killing and wounding a number of SS guards.[21] It was not by design, for not only was Birkenau less than three miles from the industrial site, but US intelligence were still treating the three Auschwitz camps as penal centres, to be side-lined in the priority to destroy industrial targets. Yet, by this time the West was already learning the horrific secrets of the concentration camp system. By the beginning of September 1944, readers of *The New York Times* were under no illusions as to life in these camps. The journalist William Lawrence had followed Soviet forces into the liberated camp at Majdanek and as the Soviet-sponsored Lublin Committee quickly set up hearings into the atrocities, he penned his report. This was followed, several weeks later, by a gruesome account in *Life* magazine, written by Richard Lauterbach, another journalist who witnessed the testimonies of SS guards and 'Capos' stationed in Poland:

> A tall, grisly character named Staub who had been a trusty at Majdanek followed the first of the German witnesses on the stand. One day, he testified, he saw a truckful of prisoners arrive. They were told to undress. One Polish girl, 28 or 29 years old, refused. Mussfeld, one of the camp's *Oberführer,* began to beat her. She scratched him, yelling 'Why am I to die?' Enraged, Mussfeld roared, 'I shall burn you alive!' He called two assistants. They grabbed the girl and bound her hands and legs. She was carried to the crematorium, where they put her on one of the iron stretchers and slid her into an oven. Staub recalled calmly, 'There was one loud scream. Her hair flared up in the flames momentarily. Then I could see no more.'[22]

The details of the terrible day-to-day actions of SS functionaries in the camps were reported by journalists but were suddenly overshadowed by dramatic events unfolding in Britain. SS General Hans Kammler, now answerable directly only to Himmler, had assumed control of not only rocket production but also tactical deployment of the V-2 rocket. On 5 September he was authorized to unleash the V-2 rocket offensive and accordingly, the 8,000 men of his newly organised *Division zur Vergeltung* (Vengeance Division) were deployed around The Hague, on the Dutch coast. Their orders were to bombard London, while units on the German border were detailed to launch rockets against Lille and Paris. But technical faults and partisan actions delayed firings. In London, there was a mounting belief that due to the success of RAF bombing raids and Allied advances in Western Europe, the rocket menace had been defeated.

On 6 September, the Vice-Chiefs of Staff advised Duncan Sandys that the threat was over and the following day, he announced at the Air Ministry HQ that 'the Battle of London is over.' Indeed, the majority of V-1 attacks had now ceased and on 8 September British newspapers headlined Sandys' triumphant speech. But as Londoners came home from work the same day, they were in for a shock. At 1806 hours, Kammler's Battalion 485 launched two V-2 rockets from the unlikely site of a road intersection in a leafy suburb of The Hague. Five minutes later, the first rocket slammed into Chiswick killing three people and seriously injuring another fifteen. The second rocket landed harmlessly beyond Epping, but it signalled the beginning of a campaign that was to see 1,403 V-2 rockets fired at the British cities of London, Norwich and Ipswich, killing 2,754 and seriously injuring 6,523 civilians. The warhead, which had been confirmed by R. V. Jones the month before at one ton, may have delivered a relatively small explosion, but the impact of the rocket itself, striking at over 3,000 ft per second, was considerable.[23]

With one eye on post war missile development, both the Allies and Soviets were keen to be the first to examine what remained of the German rocket-testing site at Blizna, in Poland. In August a British and US delegation, under the command of Colonel T.R.B. Sanders had flown to Moscow, hoping to gain permission to access the Soviet-controlled site; unsurprisingly they were held up for some weeks while Soviet scientists examined the remains of the installation. Finally, on 2 September, the nine British and three US members of the mission left Moscow and travelled in Red Air Force aircraft via the American advanced air base at Poltava, to Rzeszów. There they were filled with vodka and then transported by armed convoy to Blizna. The Mission, which included Captain L.M. Massey, Intelligence Officer for SOE's

Polish Section, also visited the V-2 crash sites in the north of Poland, near Sarnaki, but they were closely watched by NKVD agents at all times and were not allowed to speak to local Poles without an 'interpreter' present. The mission descended into farce, for while Varsovians starved during the Rising, the mission was almost force-fed by their Soviet hosts, with vast quantities of sausage, sardines and salmon, together with lashings of vodka and champagne. Everywhere they went they sat and waited for hours on end, bleary-eyed and groaning with indigestion, waiting to see some sign of rocket debris, as one day's diary entry reveals:

> We arrived after one hair-raising flight at tree-top level, 45 minutes later. On landing we were informed it was the wrong airfield, so we took off again and searched for a considerable time for the appropriate land-ing ground. Eventually we came back to our starting point and were informed by our pilot that he had found the place but as there were some cows on it, and it was too short to take our aircraft, he decided to return. After unloading our luggage again, we were led into a tiny room where we sat from 18.00 to 23.00 hrs, with no explanation of any sort…we were then taken to the Town Mayor's office. After a long wait outside in the bitterly cold cars, we were invited in as 'the Town Mayor wished to see us.' Actually, he never turned up at all and we sat in his office until 0330 hours.[24]

Despite the crippling restrictions, SOE's Captain Massey did manage to report on local conditions in occupied Soviet areas. He observed that all Polish males between the ages of twenty-four and thirty-three were now conscripted into the communist PLA and many were being held at the recently liberated Majdanek concentration camp. He was able to report on the conditions of the buildings, roads and railways and everywhere he went, he was 'told that if it had not been for American 'Lend-Lease' transport, the Red Army could not have advanced at all.'[25] Local cra-ters around Blizna yielded surprising numbers of rocket parts and the British Mission members managed to shake off their Soviet minders for long enough to find a burner unit, warhead shield and fuel supply parts – in fact enough to fill two one-ton crates for transport to London and Moscow. London eagerly awaited the contents.

On 9 September, von dem Bach approached the Polish Red Cross, offering to open negotiations with the AK for the surrender of Warsaw.

He also offered the rights of POW status to any surrendering fighters. With the surviving population now on the point of starvation and material help from the Allies still absent, General Bór-Komorowski was minded to enter into talks. But pressure from the Polish Government-in-exile, who still held out hope of a Soviet change of heart, persuaded the C-in-C to hold out. Bór-Komorowski stretched out his negotiations with von dem Bach and then, on 10 September, extraordinary developments took place across the Vistula River in the eastern suburb of Praga. In a serious setback for German forces, they lost nine tanks in the city – all knocked out within a matter of hours – while the Soviet 47th Army finally moved into Praga and attacked the German 73rd Infantry Division defending bridgeheads on the Vistula.

Meanwhile, further British attempts at air relief were dogged by mechanical problems. Excitement at the prospect of the arrival of eighteen new Special Duties Halifaxes, (released from operations in western Europe with 158 and 161 Squadron) was soon dampened when it was found that their engines were unsuitable for use in the Mediterranean. MAAF refused to accept them and sent fifteen of the aircraft back to Britain for replacement engines, resulting in a crucial shortage of aircraft at a desperate time.[26] As a result, other squadrons had to be called upon. On the night of the 10/11 September, the last combined Polish/Allied operation left Italy and this time the mission included Liberators from two South African Heavy Bomber squadrons, 31 and 34 Squadron (SAAF), together with aircraft from 178 Squadron. The eleven aircraft from these three squadrons set off from Celone Air Base, Foggia, and were joined by nine remaining aircraft from Polish 1586 Flight and 148 Squadron coming up from Brindisi. As the aircraft passed over the Yugoslav border, Pilot Officer Stanisław Franczak's Liberator was shot down, followed soon after by a Halifax from 148 Squadron. Then, as the remaining aircraft came within sight of Warsaw, two who were detailed to drop supplies in the Kampinos Forest, crossed over Soviet-controlled territory and were fired on by Soviet gun positions. Visibility was poor and as the aircraft came in low over the city, smoke obscured their target zones. Canisters dropped from the aircraft, fell everywhere and the AK could only retrieve some of them. Then, as the aircraft returned over Hungary, Pilot Officer Tadeusz Lach's Halifax was shot down by night-fighters with the loss of all the crew. As the survivors of the mission crossed over Yugoslavia, one Polish Halifax and a Liberator from

34 Squadron (SAAF) ran short of fuel and crashed. Three nights later, 1586 Polish Flight made its last mission to Warsaw and lost Pilot Officer Edmund Rygiel's Liberator, shot down over Hungary.[27]

In Warsaw the numbers of unburied dead, mounted during September. At the same time, several hundred thousand civilians crowded into the shrinking AK controlled territory and an epidemic loomed. John Ward reported the depressing situation:

> On every conceivable little piece of ground are graves of civilians and soldiers. Worst of all however, is the smell of rotting bodies, which pervades over the whole centre of the city. Thousands of people are buried under ruins. It is at the moment impossible to evacuate them and give them a normal burial. Soldiers defending their battered barricades are an awful sight. Mostly they are dirty, hungry and ragged. There are very few who have not received some sort of wound. And on and on, through a city of ruins, suffering and dead. The morale of the soldiers is also going down in many cases.[28]

As the fortunes of the AK ebbed, so the German police units became more confident of victory. An SS war correspondent reported the actions of his armoured unit as they winkled out pockets of AK fighters:

> We reach a block of flats in which many insurgents were still defending themselves. Fire from hundreds of rifles welcomed us. There was no need for us to fly for cover, for the bullets bounced off our armour like peas. We picked a target. We gave it a burst of 100 shots of machine-gun fire. The weapon spat savagely into the chosen window. The one among us who saw it first, exclaimed 'knocked out'. We just saw a rifle falling on the pavement from the windows under our fire.
>
> Then suddenly, the air shook. With a crushing blow, the first bombs of our fighters wiped out a nest of resistance somewhere behind the Citadel. The other weapons were silent for a moment, as if they had to pause while the bombs did their work. But soon it was there again. The unrelenting fire screamed and whistled. Mortars joined in, their muzzles pointing at the target. They did not wait until the missile was on its steep curve, but followed shot after shot, in the quickest possible succession straight onto the target. Two men with white and red armlets tried to escape. The machine-gun barked at them. For them, all is now over. The street was

now lifeless. Burnt-out windows looked down, blackened by fire. Very occasionally, one saw an undamaged house. Bedding, furniture and a pram lay on the ash-grey pavement.[29]

On 11 September the Red Army continued its sweep into Praga, shelling German positions, while its air force once more engaged the Luftwaffe in aerial combat. A week later Praga fell and German forces fled across the Vistula bridges, thereby reinforcing von dem Bach's forces in the Old Town and City Centre. These German units then launched fierce attacks against AK positions adjacent to the river, to prevent the Soviets establishing bridgeheads. By now, Soviet troops in Praga had been replaced by Berling's 1st Polish Army, some of whom attempted a river crossing on 17 September in an effort to reach the City Centre. But German troops vigorously repelled their landing, slaughtering most of Berling's men just after they had scrambled up the riverbank and into the Czerniaków area. Berling then attempted another river crossing – this time across to Żolibórz, and inexplicably, without co-ordinating with the AK. It ended in disaster and the loss of 2,000 of his men. This may well have been a weak gesture by Stalin, using expendable Polish troops, but it was the last attempt by Soviet controlled forces to cross onto the western side during the Rising.

On the city side of the river, Dirlewanger's brigade was again to the fore of the German assaults, especially around the bridgehead areas. Numerous atrocities were reported as the SS men forced their way into the Powiśle district between the two central bridges. In an effort to leave their own grim trademark, they entered the remains of the local hospital, killing those patients who were too ill to move, and driving others outside and into shell-holes where they were instantly dispatched by machine-guns. On 13 September the Germans blew up the central railway bridge and the Poniatowski Bridge over the Vistula, leaving only the old and narrow Kierbedz Bridge and the northern railway bridge.

In mid-September, clear skies over northwest Germany and Holland as well as over Poland, offered the chance of Allied air operations. In the west, the ill-fated Operation 'Market Garden' commenced on 17 September, which aimed to seize strategic bridges over the Lower Rhine, Waal and Maas rivers, and thereby outflank German positions. To the east, over Poland, the break in the weather also allowed a resumption of US 'Operation Frantic' missions. There had already been two

'Frantic' missions on 11 and 13 September, against targets in Germany and Hungary, the former successfully knocking out a factory producing all the engines for the Tiger and Panther tanks. But on 18 September, a massive relief mission of 110 B-17 'Flying Fortresses' was on its way to Warsaw. Three US Army Air Force bombardment groups (95th, 100th and 390th) from 13th Combat Wing left their bases at Framlingham and Thorpe Abbotts, Suffolk on the daylight mission; they were accompanied by seventy-three P-51 Mustangs as fighter escorts.[30]

At about midday, German fighters from Luftwaffe Central (*Weissrutenische*) Detachment were scrambled from their base at Radom to meet the incoming US aircraft.[31] Squadrons of Messerschmitt Bf 109s and Focke-Wulf FW 190s closed on the Fortresses, as they were still ten minutes away from their target drops in Warsaw. *Oberleutnant* Günther Josten, already a recognised ace in his squadron 3/JG 51, circled around the edge of the formation in his FW 190A and as the silver Fortresses dropped to 15,000 ft in preparation for emptying their loads, he dived in to attack. A B-17, piloted by Lieutenant Francis Akins, came within his sights. The heavy bomber, veteran of ten missions and known by her crew as 'Til we meet again', cruised at 200mph on the edge of the formation. Josten released a two-second burst from his 20mm cannons, which ripped through the bomber's cockpit. Akins caught the burst full in the face and was killed instantly. His blood covered the cockpit and as his screaming co-pilot tried to prize Akins fingers off the joystick, the aircraft started to loose height. As it fell out of formation, other enemy fighters closed in for the kill, shredding it with machine-gun fire. Miraculously, two of the crew parachuted out of the struggling aircraft before it was hit again by flak and crashed, killing the remaining seven airmen.[32]

Meanwhile, two of the escort Mustangs were shot down and eighteen other B-17s were damaged by enemy fire, but the bulk of the mission flew on and dropped 1248 containers over Warsaw. Down in the battered streets and courtyards, people braved the flying shrapnel and came out to get their first daylight view of the Allied formations overhead. Elation soon turned to despair, as most of the canisters fell into the more numerous German controlled sectors of the city. Other canisters drifted, caught in the crosswinds and were carried beyond the suburbs; it was estimated that only about 10% of the supplies were collected by AK units. The B-17s then flew beyond the burning city and landed at their

Eastern Command Ukrainian bases at Poltava and Mirgorod. One further 'Frantic' mission took off the following day for Hungary, but that would signal the last operation. Bad weather, Soviet obstruction and a less than enthusiastic US political will, conspired to prevent further 'Frantic Missions' to aid the Warsaw Rising. Even the US Commanding General, 8th Air Force, General Jimmy Doolittle, who had conceived the shuttle idea, conceded that the operations were not a success.[33]

Some food had come down inside AK lines, but it was not nearly enough. General Bór-Komorowski cabled London about the desperate situation:

> The food situation of the Army and Civilian population is catastrophic. All have been under-nourished for a long time now, and within a few days our last reserve will be finished. This means exhaustion, epidemics and finally starvation. Clothing and in particular, coats and boots are urgently needed, both for the Army and Civilian population. The mortality of children is sharply rising; also cases of death from hunger among adults. The Rising will collapse for lack of food. Only Allied flights with concentrated food, and later clothing, can bring relief.[34]

Water was only available to the Polish civilians if they stood in queues under fire for hours at a time, and food was just as scarce. Soldiers at the barricades only had about four ounces of boiled barley each day and bread was unheard of. It was agonizing for the Poles to realise that their food reserves were now buried in cellars under tons of fallen masonry. In desperation, they looked to the Soviet Union for help. The Red Air Force had started to make occasional supply drops over the city, but they were made without parachutes and often the containers were dashed to pieces as they hit the ground. The Soviet food, when it was recovered, consisted of more barley and coarse grain, which required scarce water and heat before it was edible; and any dehydrated food that was dropped had hardly any nutritional value. This poor quality food was matched by inadequate Soviet arms and ammunition, and canisters that contained weapons were usually full of Red Army rejects with awkward calibres.[35]

Soviet forces still held back from direct assistance to the beleaguered Poles. The AK had sent messages to Rokossovsky during August and early September, asking for immediate assistance and for provisions, but received no replies. However, on 18 September a small AK deputation met with General Berling just outside Praga, but the Polish communist seemed more interested in enticing AK men into his 1st Polish Army than offering help. The AK then received a telegram from Rokossovsky requesting details of how the AK would co-operate with a Soviet entry into Warsaw. Minimum details were supplied but again Marshal Rokossovsky failed to further the communications. Then on 21 September, signs of co-operation looked encouraging as several Soviet officers were parachuted into AK positions in the City Centre. However, they had been dropped in the wrong place (they were aiming for positions held by Berling's Army), and their brief was confusing. They were taken to AK headquarters, where they met the Home Army commander, and although an exchange of information took place, neither side gained from the event.[36]

However, elsewhere, sporadic Soviet help was having some effect. German positions in the city had been bombed by Soviet aircraft, as had the airfield at Okęcie, to the south of the city, where German planes and hangers were destroyed. But once again, British and US support faltered. Because there was no British liaison party with the AK, SOE received little direct feedback on how much material had reached the AK, through Operation 'Frantic'. Critically, the only other contact, John Ward, was wounded again on 23 September, when he was hit in the right knee by a bomb splinter and confined to bed for ten days.[37] Consequently, it was assumed that the large US airdrop had taken the pressure off supplies to Warsaw, and the Special Duties Squadrons took the opportunity to clear the backlog of drops due to the AK in other parts of Poland. The South African squadrons in particular, took a large share of the burden of these missions.

Collapsing Polish morale was bolstered by the unshakeable religious faith of Warsaw's inhabitants. It is impossible to overestimate the role of religion in Polish defiance, for the Catholic Church permeated all areas of Polish life. As Varsovians faced annihilation, their faith and determination grew, and was sustained often by the example of the city's clergy. Priests, monks and nuns played a significant part in not only sheltering the local population, but also in nursing the wounded and giving succour to the dying. Many priests were executed, while nuns who had protected fighters or concealed orphans, were subjected to rape or casual slaughter by the SS.[38]

Another weapon in the hands of the faltering resistance was the underground press. Newspapers such as *Barykada Wolnosci* (Barricade Freedom) and *Biuletyn Informacyjny* (Information Bulletin) helped maintain morale, especially when further US relief flights failed to appear. Ignoring Stalin's main motive, the newspapers announced that the delay in Soviet help was only because the Red Army had struggled against a determined German defence to reach the city. Even in the latter part of September, they declared that the AK rising was about to reach its final, victorious stage.[39] Nevertheless, news seeped into the city that the precious Polish 1ˢᵗ Independent Parachute Brigade had been squandered at Arnhem. Because of adverse weather, the Brigade had only been allowed into action on 21 September, but it was a terrible blooding. The unit was dropped into the enemy occupied village of Driel, near Arnhem and south of the river, beyond which lay the beleaguered British 1ˢᵗ Airborne. By the time the Polish paratroops were allowed into action, most of the British paratroopers were either dead or captured, and it was a hopeless task to expect even elite Polish troops to establish a link across the Lower Rhine. Cut-off from their supplies, the Poles still put up a ferocious fight against crack German forces, but in the end they were ordered to withdraw, having suffered 372 casualties.

On 24 September, the Germans attacked Warsaw's southern suburb of Mokotów, capturing it within three days. One glimmer of hope was an amnesty that allowed 8,500 civilians to be evacuated during the fighting. As the suburb finally fell, AK soldiers who surrendered were accorded POW status. For those who carried on the fight beneath the ground there was no amnesty, and many of the armed insurgents who were dragged out of the sewers in SS-held sectors did not fare so well.

As the final days of the Rising were played out, the British Government positioned themselves alongside the Soviets. During a debate in the House of Commons on 28 September, Churchill declared:

> Territorial changes on the frontiers of Poland there will have to be. Russia
> has the right to our support in this matter, because it is the Russian
> armies which alone can deliver Poland from the German talons; and after
> all the Russian people have suffered at the hands of Germany they are
> entitled to save the frontiers and to have a friendly neighbour on their
> western flank.[40]

Stalin no doubt drew strength from these sentiments, but his mood was further enhanced several days later by news that the Polish Commander-in-Chief, General Sosnkowski, had been dismissed. For some months, in response to Soviet pressure, the British Government had been pressurising Mikołajczyk and the Polish President, Raczkiewicz to remove 'the impossible Sosnkowski'. The embattled and cavalier commander was always a thorn in Stalin's side, but it was his toleration of anti-Government-in-exile elements within the Polish armed forces that finally prompted his sacking by Mikołajczyk. Furthermore, there was disquiet at reports that Sosnkowski had failed to give his junior commanders in the AK sufficient guidance during the Rising. Somewhat naively, senior British officials believed that the removal of Sosnkowski and his two closest colleagues would usher in a new agreement with Stalin.[41] Meanwhile, Hugh Dalton the former Minister for Economic Warfare, was still intriguing with Retinger and his Polish Socialist friends. He confided over a lunch at the 'Bon Viveur' in London that they should just 'content themselves with getting rid of Sosnkowski'.[42] Although Dalton still liked to maintain that he could affect the make-up of the Polish Government-in-exile, that was about the limit of his political influence. He and other senior British politicians failed to understand that Stalin would never make concessions over Poland. These figures, according to Sue Ryder, included the British Premier:

> He [Churchill] never seemed to give credit to those Poles who knew what the Soviets were up to and kept warning him. He seemed to have blind-spots like this, according to SOE people who attended meetings with him.[43]

Sosnkowski's departure would have little effect on the outcome inside Warsaw. Now that the suburb of Mokotów had fallen, the Germans mounted an all-out panzer assault on the northern district of Żolibórz on 28 September. The AK commander in the district, Lieutenant-Colonel Niedzielski, considered an offer from Berling's 1st Polish Army, sitting across the Vistula in Praga. They would provide boats to allow the AK men to escape to the eastern side, but just as the plan was discussed, the Rising finally ended. With all lifelines cut and starvation threatening all remaining AK sanctuaries, General Bór-Komorowski ordered a general surrender. The first round of talks commenced on 29 September and a truce finally came into force on 1 October. The terms of capitulation were signed in the early hours of the morning of 3 October at von dem Bach's HQ.

The fight on which the AK leadership had waged their all, was over. Out of an estimated 35,000 Home Army soldiers and auxiliaries inside the city, over 15,000 were dead or wounded. Furthermore, the civilian population was decimated. Nearly a quarter of Warsaw's one million inhabitants were killed. The Germans had also paid a heavy price for their control of the city with an estimated 10,000 killed and more than 16,000 wounded or missing. But the destruction they wrought was on an industrial scale and it is estimated that 70% of the capital was destroyed during the Rising and immediately afterwards.[44]

Those Varsovians who survived, fared better than expected. General Bór-Komorowski negotiated POW status and thus 'Geneva Convention' protection for those AK soldiers surrendering within the confines of the city. Over 12,000 officers and men of the AK were taken prisoner, while several thousand others melted into the general population. The AK had finally been accorded POW status by the Germans, in accordance with combatants' rights, but it had been a long struggle for the Poles even to secure this. They had persistently lobbied the Allies to be allowed the same status as that of the other underground army within the Allied camp – the 'French Army of the Interior'. But the Allies were unwilling to upset the Soviets, and dragged their feet over this issue, only granting 'Combatant Status' to the AK on 31 August.[45] An orderly withdrawal of the civilian survivors was also negotiated, as well as an agreement that the Wehrmacht, rather than SS units should guard AK prisoners. With one eye on the inevitable defeat of Germany, von dem Bach ensured that Bór-Komorowski and his aides were treated correctly. The SS Commander also hoped that similar leniency would be accorded to the recently formed German *Volkssturm* (Home Army) who would surely be captured during the fallback through the Reich.[46] These were measures von dem Bach hoped would 'buy him currency', as Bór-Komorowski and his aides were taken away for internment at Gansenstein.[47] While the non-combatants were hardly treated amicably, the butchery and atrocities carried out against civilians during the Rising were not repeated on anything like the same scale. Of the 200,000 civilians forced out of the city after the surrender, a quarter were dispatched to concentration camps, while the remainder were sent to forced labour camps in Germany. Like other resisters, Hanna Czarnocka heard stories of the German atrocities and believed that they would all be executed once the Rising collapsed:

> It was a great surprise when we were treated as POWs. But then the Germans knew they were losing the war and they certainly respected our bravery. A friend said, 'Let's disappear and pretend we're civilians.' But I felt I had to be loyal to my own unit so I was taken as a POW, and we were all marched out of the smouldering ruins, under a Wehrmacht guard. As we marched out, civilians lined the streets and some were crying, some singing and some threw us bread. We were then transported to Germany where we were interned at Oberlangen until the Polish 1st Division liberated us. It was then that I learned that my father had died in Soviet Russia.[48]

The Soviets kept a close eye on developments inside Warsaw and their sponsored Polish government wasted no time in pronouncing on the surrender. The leader of the Lublin Committee, Edward Osóbka-Morawski soon declared General Bór-Komorowski 'a criminal, who should be arrested, tried and sentenced for prematurely ordering the Rising.' However, the C-in-C AK was soon beyond their reach when the Germans moved him to Oflag 73, near Nuremberg. At the same time, command of the AK devolved to General Leopold Okulicki ('Bear Cub'), with General August Emil Fieldorf ('Nil') stepping in as Deputy Commander.[49]

As the city of Warsaw lay in ruins, Britain could do little except offer platitudes over the airwaves:

> This is London calling…we have to deplore the tragic fate of the Poles in Warsaw, after a heroic resistance to which our Prime Minister has paid an eloquent tribute on behalf of all of us.[50]

There followed recriminations against Britain by certain Polish commentators. SOE reflected on the sorry events in Warsaw but defended themselves against the 'familiar abuse' aimed at them by Polish broadcasters:

> The tragedy of the capital was a direct result of the contradiction between FIELD [AK] policy and that of the Chiefs of Staff. This must not recur.

We cannot allow ourselves to be faced by the operational blackmail of a sudden uprising of which only DULWICH [Soviets] will reap the benefit. Our policy must be to preserve the existing strength of the remaining units and prevent them from making more sacrifices as a political gesture. This time a liaison officer must explain the limitations of the air effort rather than its possibilities. Recent changes in the staff of the VI Bureau [Polish Bureau of Information and Propaganda] suggest that the KENSAL [Polish] General Staff cannot be trusted to do this honestly.[51]

Meanwhile, there were conflicting opinions about the role of General Bór-Komorowski among returning British POWs, who had been on the run inside Poland during the Rising. Lieutenant-Colonel Boughey thought that the Poles 'genuinely felt that this [Warsaw Rising] was a great mistake, largely due to the personal ambition of General Bor'. Yet Pilot Officer H. Brooks, a fluent Polish speaker, found that the Poles 'knew that General Bór was acting upon instructions from London'. However John Ward, who had spent so long amongst the Polish underground, was in no doubt where the blame lay. 'The failure of the Warsaw Rising is put on the Russians', he confirmed. 'The people think that Russia could have liberated Warsaw, and in any case could have given bases to Allied aircraft.'[52] As for the liberation of Warsaw, Stalin had claimed in his meeting with Mikołajczyk on 3 August that he had initially hoped to take Warsaw several days later but due to the tough German resistance, 'there would be a small delay in capturing the city'.[53] It would have been consistent with Soviet strategy to at least capture the suburb of Praga, and thereby secure the eastern bank of the Vistula. Even if a bridgehead on the western bank could not be achieved in August, this would have at least tied in with operations above and below the city to secure positions on the banks of the Vistula and Narew rivers. In the event, the Soviet attack on Praga was weak and ineffective.

Throughout the Rising, and despite the desperate odds and grim flying conditions, the relief aircrews never buckled. The British Air Ministry did not have to apply the cruel 'LMF' stamp (Lack of Moral Fibre) to any airman's service record for failure to face operational risks.[54] Yet those risks were high and a special duties aircrew would find they could be dispatched to any one of ten countries of southern, central or Eastern Europe. In fact during September, the largest recipients of aid were Yugoslavia (855 tons), Greece (126 tons) and Italy (90 tons), while Poland languished at the bottom of the list with just 11½ tons of supplies. This disparity also applied to personnel dropped into these countries. During September, the Polish Special Duties Flight found themselves transporting many of the 2,635 agents up to the Balkans to drop them off in support of the local partisans, while there were no personnel drops into Poland.[55] Even allowing for the best endeavours of the pilots, sometimes the missions went wrong. Heinz Spanglet, ('Stephen Dale') was a German Jew who was dropped into what he thought was friendly country:

> I was told that the Polish pilots had done great service during the drops over Warsaw, so I thought all would be well as we took off from Brindisi. As we flew north there was a lot of flak over Venice at 10,000ft. Then soon after, I jumped with four others and I landed on a patch of grass on a river-bed. I saw a torch and went towards it but heard German and Italian voices – I then realised we had been dropped in the wrong place. I was immediately arrested and they lined me up against a mound and stood around me in a semi-circle, cocking their weapons. I thought I was to be shot. But they strip-searched me and took me to a holding prison. I wore a British uniform and only gave them my name, rank and number.
>
> They bullied me with aggressive questions about what I was doing there and who I really was. I spoke German to the SS. I was moved to another jail for detailed interrogation, which took place each day. It was usually two different SS each day who came into my cell to interrogate me. Each session lasted about two hours.[56]

Although the move of SOE controlled operations to southern Italy had been of more direct assistance to events in northern Italy and the Balkans, Poland did benefit. The final tally of air support from both Tempsford in England and Brindisi in Italy showed a total of 485 drops of supplies and agents were made into Poland, including 192 during the Warsaw Rising. During 1944, 1586 Polish Flight had suffered losses of 37 officers and 107 airmen, including 30 officers and 79 airmen killed.[57] The other main Special Duties unit, 148 Squadron had also suffered heavy losses. Since the move to Brindisi in January, the squadron had lost nineteen Halifaxes (including three on loan to 1586 Flight) in its sorties to Poland and numerous crews were killed, missing or taken prisoner. Other RAF squadrons also shouldered the burden. 31 Squadron lost eight Liberators, 178 Squadron, five Liberators and 34 Squadron, a further Liberator.[58] Some airmen were fortunate to survive as POWs but many British, South African, Canadian and Australian crews from these squadrons were killed as their flaming aircraft came down into ice-cold mountain lakes or smashed into the snow-capped Tatra Mountains. The city they had sought to save lay in ruins. Maria Fiderer, a Polish editor and AK member who had only recently returned to Warsaw, lamented its pathetic state:

> The city is almost as complete a ruin as Stalingrad, so that one or two tall buildings stand out very clearly, with everything around them destroyed...people were anxious for an uprising in the early days and Bor was supported by almost everyone. Then they expected the Red Army to take the town quickly. Afterwards, when the Red Army failed and when no supplies were dropped by plane, they believed Bór and the London Government, who blamed the Red Army for this. Then no help arrived from British and American planes for weeks and they lost faith in that promise too.[59]

As far as Stalin was concerned, promises were never an issue. The failure of the Soviet First Byelorussian Front to move decisively into Warsaw in the first weeks of the Rising, has been excused by Soviet sources, citing stretched supply lines, exhausted troops and unexpectedly strong counter-attacks by panzer divisions north-east of the city.[60] All these factors were certainly a problem for the Red Army and coupled with their inability to maintain multiple bridgeheads over the Vistula, caused their momentum to falter. Stalin could certainly have committed more troops and armoured units to break through the important Vistula-Narew line north of the city, but this would have done more to assist his drive towards East Prussia than relieving Warsaw. While the Red Air Force made some efforts in September, their attempts at achieving air superiority in August were negligible. In short, Stalin attached little strategic value to Warsaw and it suited his purpose to let the Germans be tied down in the city for two months. There were other strategic opportunities opening up for him that autumn, such as the thrust through Romania, Bulgaria and Hungary, as well as advances through the Baltic States to the north. The Red Army would not march into Warsaw until January 1945, as part of a *Stavka* offensive plan to thrust through central and northern Poland towards Germany. In the meantime, the Germans had decisively crushed the military strength of the Polish Home Army. Now, in order to control his western neighbour, Stalin had to finally crush the political will of the Polish underground.[61]

NOTES

[1] Message from Warsaw, received 2 September 1944, AIR 20/7984, NA.

[2] Lukas, op. cit., p. 211.

[3] During the Rising many policemen were awarded the *Bandenkampfabzeichen* (Anti-Partisan War Badge), instituted by Himmler in January 1944. For details of armoured police units, see Gordon Williamson, op. cit., pp. 12–13.

[4] Sir Charles Portal to Prime Minister, 29 August 1944, AIR 20/7984, NA.

[5] Jerzy Cynk, op. cit., p. 477.

[6] Memorandum of Meeting with Air Chief Marshal Harris at Bomber Command HQ, 1 September 1944, HS4/156, NA.

[7] D.C.S. Evill, Vice CAS to Prime Minister, 1 September 1944, AIR 20/7984, NA.

[8] 'Minutes of Meeting held in DCAS Office', 29 August 1944, AIR 20/7984, NA. Also Patrick Howarth, *Undercover* (Phoenix Press, London 2000), p. 45.

[9] Lieutenant-Colonel Perkins (MP) to Major-General Gubbins (CD), 21 August 1944, HS 4/156, NA.

[10] Ward Reports, op. cit., 24 August 1944.

[11] Mikołajczyk to Selborne, 5 September 1944; Gubbins to Chiefs of Staff, 7 September 1944; Gubbins to Mikołajczyk, 9 September 1944, all HS4/156, NA. Also MRD Foot, op. cit., p. 276.

[12] Anthony Eden to Prime Minister, 30 August 1944, AP20/11/593, Lord Avon Papers, UB.

[13] Perkins (MP) to Boughey (MP1), 29 August 1944, HS4/146, NA.

[14] AD/H to Major-General Colin Gubbins, 15 September 1944, HS 4/156, NA.

[15] Davis, op. cit., p. 370.

[16] *New York Times*, 23 July 1944.

[17] There has been much controversy over Hopkins' true loyalty. The publication of details from the 'Venona' spy cables, originally intercepted by the US in the 1940s has led to many sources condemning him as a Soviet agent. He died in 1946.

[18] Rokossovsky, op. cit., pp. 260–1.

[19] Brian Bishop to Author, 10 January 2007.

[20] Bernard Williamson, 'Holocaust: The Count of Auschwitz' in *MQ Magazine*, April 2006

21 The 1972 US Democratic nominee for US President, George McGovern was a B-24 bomber pilot who took part in raids targeting the Monowitz industrial plant. For Threlfall, see Lieutenant-Colonel Threlfall to AOC Balkan Air Force, 22 October 1944, ref. 75, file 3.10.3.1, PUMST.

22 Richard Lauterbach, 'Sunday in Poland' in *Life* magazine, 18 September 1944, PRM 154 Part I, Polish Institute and Sikorski Museum, London (hereafter PISM).

23 Of these launchings, 1,115 fell in the UK, including 517 in London, 378 in Essex and 64 in Kent. See, Basil Collier, *The Defence of the United Kingdom* (Imperial War Museum, London 1957), pp. 405–7, 527–8. Also T.D. Dungan, op. cit., pp. 115–19, 217, and R.V. Jones, op. cit., 575–79.

24 'Report on visit to South and Eastern Poland', September 1944, HS4/146, NA.

25 Frank Roberts, Foreign Memo, 13 October 1944, FO 371/39454, NA.

26 The Merlin XX engines were to be replaced with Merlin XXIIs. Ref 12 (iii), 'Summary of Negotiations and Measures Taken for Air Supply to Warsaw', September 1944, CAB 121/310, NA.

27 Cynk, op. cit., p. 478.

28 Ward Reports, op. cit., 10 September 1944.

29 *The Times*, 13 September 1944.

30 For an overview of the 'Frantic' operations, see the autobiography of the Commanding General 8th Air Force, England, General James 'Jimmy' Doolittle, *I Could Never Be So Lucky Again* (Bantam, New York 1991), pp. 380–1.

31 Although Radom lay due south of Warsaw, the First Byelorussian Front did not overrun it until 16 January 1945, during the next series of Soviet offensives.

32 Akins' B-17 was part of 568th Bombardment Squadron, 390th Bombardment Group. This unit was part of the larger 3rd Air Division in the US Eighth Air Force. In OKL Fighter Claims, Leutnant Kurt Dombacher also claimed the kill, which he engaged at 13,000 ft; see 'OKL Fighter Claims: Reich, West & Südfront, Aug-Sept 1944', film C, 2027/11, #429, and 'Combat Chronology of the US Army Air Forces, September 1944'. Also Conversino, op. cit., p. 150 and William Green, *Warplanes of the Third Reich* (Macdonald & Co., London 1970), pp. 206–7.

33 Conversino, op. cit., p. 157. Also Doolittle, op. cit., pp. 379–81.

34 GOC & Delegate to the Prime Minister and C-in-C, in SOE report 'Further Assistance to Warsaw', 28 September 1944, HS4/156, NA. Also Ward Report, 20 September 1944, op. cit.

35 Ibid.

36 Norman Davies, *Rising 44,* op. cit., pp. 385–9.

37 Ward MI9 Report, 22 March 1945, HS4/256, NA.

38 Norman Davies, *Rising '44,* op. cit., pp. 402–6.

39 During the Rising there were 130 underground newspapers, journals and periodicals; see Joanna Hanson, *The Civilian Population and the Warsaw Uprising of 1944* (Cambridge University Press, Cambridge 1982), p. 169, 240–9. *Biuletyn Informacyjny* was the official underground newspaper, run by Michał Wojewódzki. He later became deputy chief editor of *Express Wieczorny,* Poland's popular afternoon newspaper, and author of *Akcja V-1, V-2,* the book detailing Poland's role in defeating the rocket menace.

40 *Hansard's Parliamentary Debates* CDIII, 1944, p. 489.

41 Sir Archibald Clark Kerr to Foreign Office, 17 September 1944, HS4/145, NA. Also John Harvey, (Ed.), *The War Diaries of Oliver Harvey* (Collins, London 1978), p. 357. Also Colonel H. Perkins to GW Harrison, 19 September 1944, HS4/145, NA.

42 *Diary of Hugh Dalton*, op. cit., 1 November 1944.

43 Sue Ryder, 1987, ref 10057, Sound Archive, IWM.

44 Estimates vary and the figure for those missing is hard to substantiate; see Rozek, op. cit., p. 256–7 and Professor Wojciech Rojek, 'The Polish Underground State in the Final Phase', see www.polishresistance-ak.org. Also, Ney-Krwawicz, op. cit., p. 82; also, Richard Lukas, *Forgotten Holocaust* op. cit., p. 219.

45 Major-General Kopanski to Lord Selborne, 1 August 1944, HS4/156, NA. See also E.D.R. Harrison, op. cit., pp. 1084–5. In trying to convince the War Cabinet to allow the AK combatant status, Eden had encountered opposition from two of Churchill's friends, Lord Beaverbrook and Brendan Bracken; see Elisabeth Barker, *Churchill and Eden at War* (Macmillan, London 1978), p. 255.

46 Bór Komorowski, op. cit., pp. 369–75. For an account of the meeting after the official surrender, see Iranek-Osmecki, op. cit., pp. 267–93.

47 Von dem Bach was not successful in obtaining a countrywide surrender of the AK.

48 Hanna Kościa to Author, 22 September 2006.

49 Foreign Office to British Embassy, Moscow, 3 October 1944, HS 4/145, NA.

50 International radio broadcast transcript, 13 October 1944, 7/1/30, Kirke Papers, LHCMA.

51 'Top Secret. General Policy for Kensal', 4 September 1944, HS4/146, NA.

52 'Foreign Office report on interrogation of returned Allied POWs', 17 April 1945, HS4/145, NA.

53 Mikołajczyk, op. cit., p. 74.

54 Amongst aircrews from Bomber Command, it was established that the first two sorties were critical in creating 'nerve'. A waiverer could be pushed on but would face a further psychological hurdle after 12 sorties. For a study of 'LMF' see John McCarthy, 'Aircrew and Lack of Moral Fibre in the Second World War', in *War & Society,* Vol. 2, No. 2, September 1984.

[55] 'MAAF Group Operational Figures for Quarter', CAB 121/310, NA.

[56] Stephen Dale, ref. 14582, IWM Sound Archive, London.

[57] *Destiny Can Wait*, op. cit., 226.

[58] For a detailed list of aircraft losses, see David Waters, *The History of 148 Bomber Squadron* (privately printed, 1998).

[59] 'Memo for H.E.', 29 September 1944, FO 371/39454, NA.

[60] Rokossovsky, op. cit., p. 252 and *Stalin's Correspondence*, op. cit., Stalin to Churchill, 5 August and 22 August 1944.

[61] Evan Mawdsley, op. cit., pp. 331–3.

Chapter Nine

Chaos and Collapse

As German forces fell back across Poland, AK units often moved in, only to find themselves increasingly overrun by Soviet forces. NKVD officers then swiftly disarmed them and frequently shot their local commanders, while junior AK officers and men were dispatched to Soviet labour camps. Many of the AK ranks were pressed, under pain of imprisonment, into Berling's Polish Army, while civilian supporters and officials of the underground state were identified by NKVD officers and arrested or executed.

As a commissioned officer in the AK, the British ex-POW John Ward was fortunate to escape with his life. Prior to the Warsaw surrender, General Bór-Komorowski had arranged for him to be sent to Kielce, picked up by aircraft and flown to Britain. Consequently, on 4 October Ward was helped to the outskirts of Warsaw by two Red Cross nurses, and although he was robbed by Ukrainian troops on the way, he arrived safely in the Kielce region a week later. Because of his invaluable work during the Rising, contacts were swiftly arranged and he was soon introduced to the local AK commander, Colonel 'Wojtek', whose 7th Polish Division were still engaged in operations against the Germans. Ward lost no time in transmitting to London cyphered news of conditions outside Warsaw, noting, 'medical supplies are very short. All people who are badly wounded, mostly lying by roadside. Tens of thousands of people sleeping in open fields.'[1] Ward also kept in regular contact with Major Mike Pickles, head of the SOE's Polish Section, who was arranging the next 'bridging operation' (Wildhorn IV), which could collect

Ward. A Dakota aircraft would also pick up senior figures involved in the Warsaw Rising, including 'Zych', 'Gromoski', 'Jaworski' and 'Adam', but Pickles stressed to the British Air Ministry that bringing out Ward was a priority – authorised at the highest level:

> We are very shortly hoping to have one of your very rare pick-up operations into Poland. It is hoped to bring out high-ranking staff officers who were concerned with the Warsaw Rising, a highly placed Polish Government delegate, and also Colonel Rudkowski, who was dropped into the country a short time ago to investigate the situation for the Poles. Since the fall of Warsaw, Polish affairs have been very confused and it is extremely important that the Polish Government here has first hand reports from the country. In addition to the above, this pick-up operation will bring out Sgt. J. Ward, RAF, whom you may remember sent back a long series of messages from Warsaw during the siege. This man has been asked for, both by the Prime Minister and the Foreign Secretary.[2]

However, arranging the 'Wildhorn IV' operation was becoming very difficult. Actually finding a decent landing strip, unoccupied by either German or Red Army forces seemed impossible. Relief air-drops to rural Poland were however still feasible, so at a conference with the Polish General Staff on 5 October, Air Marshal Slessor agreed to thirty sorties per night to Poland.[3] Consequently, thirty-three aircraft were scheduled for Poland for the night of 8/9 October, but foul weather again intervened and the mission was cancelled.

Since the Soviet summer offensives, the German-controlled areas of Poland had contracted and consequently the available safe drop zones had become more limited, particularly in southern Poland. So the option of assisting the AK in northern Poland was considered, but only if the old northern routes (Tempsford via Sweden or Denmark) could be re-opened. Lieutenant-Colonel Perkins pursued the issue with the Air Ministry in early November, suggesting that Stirling bombers from 138 and 161 Squadrons might be used. But this idea was soon squashed when Perkins was informed that German night-fighter squadrons had been recently reinforced in Denmark and consequently, enemy air defences were now far stronger in the north. Meanwhile, the southern routes from Italy were given a fillip by the announcement that a further twelve new Liberators were secured for 1586 Polish Flight. This was all very well, but with the collapse of Romania and the swift advance of Soviet forces into parts of Hungary and Slovakia, it was becoming very difficult to avoid crossing over Soviet-held territory during flights to Poland. The alternative was to fly on a long diversion through Austria and even then, Polish flights would have to run the gauntlet of very strong German defences around Vienna. Again Air Marshal Slessor sought permission from the Soviets to fly over their territory, and again his request was flatly refused.[4] Even if British missions were sent in unannounced, Soviet batteries or aircraft would certainly fire on uni-dentified targets.[5] With fading hope of any further bridging operations, Ward had to remain with the AK 7th Division in the Kielce region until further notice.

In the autumn of 1944, the near proximity of Soviet forces to Auschwitz did little to temper the activities of the SS, who proceeded to murder a further 33,000 Jews during October. However, the SS had become anxious and were preparing to kill the *Sonderkommando* at Birkenau, who had witnessed and assisted in the disposal of hundreds of thousands of corpses. This new policy prompted an unexpected reaction from these inmates, who had always believed that they could cheat death by being useful to their captors. On 7 October 1944, having discovered the intentions of the SS, they overpowered their guards and captured their weapons. Then, using explosives supplied by women prisoners working in the camp's Krupp munitions factory, they managed to blow up one crematorium and disable some of the others. A breakout followed, which was initially successful with nearly 250 prisoners managing to escape, but the SS soon caught up with them in a nearby forest. Most of the fugitives were immediately slaughtered, but an Allied air raid momentarily diverted attention and allowed twelve prisoners to flee. Their escape was short-lived and SS guards with dogs later found them in a barn, which was then torched. Many of the bodies of the escapees were taken back to the camp and displayed, while a further 200 *Sonderkommando* who had assisted in the escape, were summarily executed. With their usual scrupulous attention to detail, the camp authorities then proceeded to torture and interrogate those women who had supplied the fuses for the operation. Surprisingly, it took only a week for details of this upris-ing to reach London, via two cyphered reports from the AK's Kraków District, which also listed the names of the SS from the camp, including Krammer, who participated in the suppression of the revolt.[6] Alarmed by the rapid Soviet advance, Himmler ordered the demolition of the crematoria and gas chambers at Birkenau at the end of October. SS officers started the dismantling at the beginning of November and the last crematorium – No. 5 – was blown up just days before the Soviets entered the camp on 27 January 1945.

Elsewhere, Hitler had decided on the obliteration of another scene of German oppression. For their temerity in rising against German occupation, Hitler decreed that the Varsovians should lose what remained of their city. Despite the heavy pressure on the regime's resources, Warsaw was to be razed to the ground as an object lesson to the inhabitants of other occupied countries. Accordingly, during October and November, Wehrmacht demolition teams moved in and, district by district, methodically blew up any remaining buildings.[7] As Red Army observers in Praga watched the beginning of this destruction through their binoculars, 600 miles away in Moscow, another section of Polish territory was about to disappear. At 2200 hours on 9 October Churchill began his opening meeting in the Kremlin with Stalin to decide post-war East European boundaries. The Balkans were first on the agenda and the carving up of territories began with little ceremony. The two leaders swiftly bargained with each other over the percentage control of Romania, Greece, Yugoslavia, Hungary and Bulgaria. Pushing a piece of paper backwards and forwards, Churchill scrawled each suggestion on a half-sheet of paper and after thinking about it, Stalin leant forward and ticked it. They settled on a 50/50 split in Hungary and Yugoslavia. Greece achieved a 90/10 ratio in favour of the west, while Romania and Bulgaria were to be totally dominated by the Soviet Union. However, this 'naughty document', as Churchill called it, did not include any deal on Poland. She was to be the subject of a further meeting.[8]

Four days later, on 13 October, the Allied leaders and representatives convened again. On one side Stalin sat with his Foreign Commissar Molotov, together with Bierut and the Lublin Poles. On the other, Churchill, Eden and the US Ambassador, Harriman sat together with Mikołajczyk and representatives of the Polish Government-in-exile. As usual, Stalin would neither move on the border issue nor support for his Lublin Poles, while Mikołajczyk refused to budge on his position. Churchill pulled the Polish Premier away for a private meeting, arguing furiously with him that he would be only sacrificing Ukrainians, not Poles. 'Unless you accept the frontier', he shouted, 'you're out of business forever.'To an exasperated Churchill, trying to get through to the Polish Government was 'like being in a lunatic asylum.'

Then, to add oil to the fire, the calculating Molotov told Mikołajczyk that at Tehran the previous year, Stalin, Roosevelt and Churchill had accepted that the Curzon Line should form the border between Poland and the Soviet Union. This was a devastating blow to the Poles who retorted that 'Allied policy towards Poland had been neither loyal nor honest.' In something of an understatement, the Polish Interior Minister, Władysław Banaczyk uttered, 'It is, even in international politics, rather a novel procedure to partition the territory of an ally on behalf of another ally, and without even consulting the victim.'[9] The Polish Premier sunk further into the gloom but refused to revise his position. He returned to London and spent the next month in a joyless search for US and British support. He could not even bargain over Lwów, which Stalin cynically claimed he had to keep, 'to avoid betraying my Ukrainians'. Yet, Churchill's Chief of Staff, General Sir Hastings Ismay recalled that Lwów was 'In Polish eyes, a sacred shrine, for which 99 out of every 100 Poles would gladly have gone to the stake.'[10] The conference was a disaster for the Poles, and particularly Mikołajczyk, whose reserves were virtually spent.[11]

Having accepted Stalin's writ over Poland, Churchill was nevertheless keen to monitor events within the country and on his return to London, he immediately chivvied Lord Selborne to put as many agents into western Poland as SOE could manage. Ignoring the almost impossible odds, Selborne chased Sir Archibald Sinclair to resume flights to Poland.[12] However, the whole exercise seemed a façade to many SOE officers, who knew that when good flying weather came, bombing missions always had first call on available aircraft. On 16 October, one last effort was made, but although thirty-three aircraft were allotted to Poland, only fourteen could be mustered, using eight from No 1586 Polish Flight and six SAAF crews from No 34 Squadron. The mission was not a success and two SAAF Liberators were shot down, with two more badly damaged.[13]

SOE had also consistently pressed for a British Military Mission to be placed with the AK, precisely for the reason that Churchill was now using – to obtain intelligence on the Soviet takeover of Poland. In the past, SOE's request was always turned down because the Allied Chiefs of Staff felt that they should not 'encourage the Polish Home Army to believe that sufficient arms and supplies will be forthcoming for a general rising'. Furthermore, Allied Liaison Officers were forbidden to operate alongside a resistance army, which had still not been granted official 'combatant rights' by the Allies. This was bizarre, given that the 'French Army of the Interior' had for some time, been recognised as a proper component of the Allied fighting forces. The timing of the eventual Allied recognition of the AK as an army was ironic – coming only after the AK had been effectively destroyed in Warsaw. It was clear to the remnants of the Home Army that following the collapse of the Warsaw Rising, material British support would never be forthcoming.

However, there were still approved SOE operations waiting to be carried out inside Poland, such as sabotage attacks against German-controlled Polish shipyards, which assembled submarines in Gdynia and Danzig. While the speed of the Soviet advance might rule out such operations, SOE were determined that at the very least, a military mission should be sent to Poland. They believed the next round of Soviet offensives would certainly carry the Red Army into Warsaw as well as deep into Slovakia – Pickles predicted from his SIS contacts that such actions could happen by the end of November. So Colonel Perkins, as head of SOE's Czechoslovakia, Hungary and Poland Department was dispatched to Prague to organise pro-Western support among partisan groups. Meanwhile, SOE's Colonel Threlfall flew from Bari to Slovakia to head off Soviet influence in an emerging provisional government. But while Poland was considered a lost cause, SOE still felt that a British military mission should be its 'swan song'. 'This may lead to nothing', Pickles argued, 'but it is an essential end to our policy. We surely have not sacrificed so many crews and aircraft merely to send men that should be helped, to exile and prison.'[14]

While the issue of a British Military Mission to Poland continued to bounce around Whitehall and Baker Street, the other British asset in Poland – The Sanders V2 rocket party – arrived back in Britain in early October. By the time that Colonel T.R.B. Sanders and his team had returned from the V-2 testing site at Blizna, Britain had already been hit by a large number of rockets, and burnt out parts were commonplace. Nonetheless, the Royal Aircraft Establishment at Farnborough still awaited the crates of V-2 parts that the Sanders Party had recovered, for confirmation of the propulsion mechanism. These had been packed up in September and dispatched to Moscow, where the Soviets were to arrange for onward transmission to London. Logistics meant there was no alternative but to trust the Soviets, and it was no surprise therefore, when the crates finally arrived in London and were found to contain nothing more than old aircraft pieces. Moscow's scientists had substituted rubbish for the V-2 parts.

Although the collapse of the Rising had removed much of the rationale for a military mission, the British still required urgent inside intelligence on how long the estimated 100,000 AK survivors could maintain their formations west of the Vistula. SOE finally managed to get sanction to send a team, code-named 'Freston' into Poland. The leader of the team was an old Yugoslavia hand and a former SOE Liaison officer in Cairo, Lieutenant-Colonel Bill Hudson. His second-in-command was an AK reception officer and former prisoner of the Gestapo, Lieutenant-Colonel Alun Morgan (real name Szymon Jan Zaremba). Major Peter Solly-Flood, a quick-witted Irish diplomat acted as Intelligence Officer, while Captain Tony Currie (real name Antoni Pospieszalski) filled the job of interpreter. Finally, Sergeant-Major Donald Galbraith was co-opted as wireless operator. In addition there were to be the three sub-groups under the control of 'Freston', each consisting of two British officers and a wireless operator.[15] As the mission would enter Soviet-controlled territory, permission was applied for, but as usual, was turned down. Nevertheless, Major-General Gubbins was persuaded to dispatch the party and they were duly briefed by Lieutenant-Colonel Perkins not to engage in any offensive combat, but merely to observe and report. Accordingly, they drew US semi-automatic carbines for their protection from Baker Street and were issued with 'L' suicide pills, in the event of their capture. Towards the end of October the group flew to Brindisi for the onward flight to Poland, but their luck soon deserted them. On the flight to Poland, the dispatcher on the aircraft was inexperienced and as he prepared one of the agents who was to be dropped with the team, he incorrectly hooked up his static line. As the agent jumped from the aircraft, the line caught under his chute and he was trapped in the slipstream. He remained hanging there while he froze to death.[16] The mission was aborted.

Lord Selborne, writing to Sir Archibald Sinclair on 22 November, pleaded for more flights to Poland stressing that 'Poland put her shirt on Britain in 1939. Have we not a debt to repay?'[17] Two days later, he wrote to Churchill reporting that since the end of the Rising there had only been eight successful sorties to Poland, resulting in a pathetic ten tons of supplies. He summed up a situation, which was always apparent to the Prime Minister:

> However impractical Polish politicians may be, their Services have fought with us with the utmost gallantry on many fronts, and I fear that if we do not make more strenuous efforts to help them, even at some loss to ourselves, the Polish people will feel, not without cause, that we have let them down.[18]

Help to the Poles was now unlikely to come by airlifts. The crisis in the Polish Government-in-exile at the end of November ruled out further flights to Poland by either 1586 Polish Flight or any RAF Squadrons. In fact, the last few remaining sorties to Poland by the Polish Flight would revolve around another attempt at the 'Freston' operation in December. After that, it was all over.

In the hard opportunism of Allied planning, AK operations inside the dwindling German-occupied parts of Poland had lost their interest. Attention was, instead, being diverted to the ways in which the Poles could operate inside the Reich. As Allied troops moved eastwards towards Germany during late 1944, thought was given as to how Poles, forcibly conscripted into the German Army or into the labour (TODT) organisation, could help to ferment disruption inside Germany. Indeed, it was seen as vital work to disrupt the German industrial machine, and as about half the foreign workers inside the Reich were Poles, they could only be contacted via Poland. So SOE devised 'Operation Dunstable' to organise and train Poles to contact their compatriots inside Germany.[19]

At the same time SOE set up two other operations, 'Flamstead' and 'Fernham', which aimed to use agents to contact POWs inside German-controlled camps in Poland. It was feared that due to the threat of the Soviet advance, the Germans might slaughter the inmates of these camps. However, after much deliberation, it was decided that the two SOE trained teams should operate as 'sub-groups' of Operation Freston and should be dropped into Poland just after the Freston team, to liaise with local AK bands. But the Soviet advance had already pushed these bands into outlying forests and mountains and without proper Polish contacts, SOE decided to postpone the dispatch of the 'Flamstead' and 'Fernham' teams.[20]

Meanwhile the turmoil in Polish exile circles continued apace. At odds with his own cabinet, who refused to cede any eastern territory, Mikołajczyk finally resigned on 24 November and was replaced with the elderly socialist Tomasz Arciszewski. The new Premier had common cause with the immovable Polish President, Władysław Raczkiewicz and refused to make any new concessions to Stalin. The prospect appalled senior officers in SOE, who felt that all their efforts would now be thrown away. They made their concerns clear. At 1730 hours on Monday 27 November, Major-General Gubbins held his usual meeting with the SOE country sections, when the Polish Section leader, Major Mike Pickles stood up and announced that the Polish President and Prime Minister had picked a motley Cabinet who would 'drive themselves out of power and the Lublin Committee into power as fast as possible'. The new Cabinet included members of the right-wing *Narodowa Demokracja,* a party highly likely to inflame Soviet sensibilities, as well as, Pickles noted, 'dear old Kukiel – another *persona non grata*'. 'How is it possible', he continued, 'for these Poles to be such fools. The whole thing is, of course, utterly impossible.'[21]

The Foreign Office, as well as SOE felt the new government couldn't be trusted and the following day Polish intelligence were ordered to hand over their previously sacrosanct cypher codes for all messages transmitted to Poland. Diplomatic cyphers were excluded from the order, but all messages transmitted to the VI Bureau and the Ministry of the Interior were no longer for Polish eyes only. Furthermore, the Foreign Secretary stopped all future flights to Poland, with the exception of the proposed 'Wildhorn IV' operation. This escaped the axe only because it was part of a bizarre plan to reinstate Mikołajczyk as a Premier who would be acceptable to both the British and Soviet governments. Major Pickles optimistically believed that although Mikołajczyk had resigned, he would come back to power, 'stronger, bigger and better than ever', if only the frontier question could be put to one side. But first, something would have to be done about the Polish President, Władysław Raczkiewicz, seen as the major obstacle to better British/Soviet relations.[22]

Pickles and other senior SOE officers believed that President Raczkiewicz was controlling the new Polish Premier, Arciszewski and entrenching the policy of non-negotiation on the eastern borders. Pickles reasoned that if Raczkiewicz could be removed from office, and replaced with another more malleable politician who could accept Stalin's dictate, then Poland might just achieve a working relationship with her Soviet neighbour. A fourth 'Wildhorn' bridging operation could collect a likely successor from Poland and deliver him to Britain. With advice from ex-Premier Mikołajczyk, SOE identified Andrzej Witos, an ex-member of the Lublin Committee, as a likely contender. Witos was one of the few non-communist members of the Soviet sponsored committee, who as 'Minister of Agriculture' had been sacked in October on grounds of 'ill-health' (the real reason was his failure to re-distribute land quickly enough).[23] However, while SOE plotted and the Foreign Office withdrew diplomatic representation to the new Polish Government-in-exile, Churchill worried that it was all going too far. Rather than dramatic gestures such as withdrawing recognition, Churchill favoured leaving the Polish government 'severely alone'. He also reminded Eden that 'we cannot forget that we have 100,000 Poles fighting with us very bravely, both in Italy and France. These men's legal attachment is to the President of Poland.'[24]

Mikołajczyk's resignation on 24 November effectively sealed the fate of the AK. For the day after, SOE's Lieutenant-Colonel Perkins told the Polish Deputy Chief of Staff, General Tatar that the Polish underground could no longer expect help from the British. Perkins was taking his cue from the Foreign Office, but it was still a bitter pill for the Poles to swallow. SOE had been a friend, though not always a steadfast one, who now implemented a ban on further relief flights to Poland. The AK were to be deprived of arms, ammunition, wireless kit and medical supplies, while shipment of money was also prohibited. It was also another excuse to postpone the ill-fated British Military Mission to Poland.[25] Writing to Churchill on 14 December, Selborne protested:

> I hope you will decide that British sorties to the Polish Army of Resistance shall continue. I do not see how we could stop these without violation of the Anglo-Polish Alliance of 1939, nor without grave repercussions on the morale of Polish Forces fighting with HM's Forces.[26]

But the ban on RAF crews flying to Poland remained. There was still a possibility of dropping a British military mission into Poland, but at this stage it was hardly going to help the AK. It was supposed to be an aid to intelligence gathering, though Anthony Eden believed it could prove counter-productive. Writing to Churchill in early December, he was keen to quash the idea rather than promote it:

Our original intention to send them in was based on the assumption that they would be attached to an army under Monsieur Mikołajczyk's control. The Polish Underground Army is now controlled by a government in whose political attitude, we have no confidence, and the presence of British Liaison Officers in Poland might well prove a source of embarrassment to us. The Russians would also wonder why we had waited until the emergence of a less friendly government before making this marked gesture of support for the Polish Home Army. Finally, there is the practical consideration that the despatch of British liaison officers would presuppose the continuance on an undiminished scale of our material support for the Polish Home Army. This may however, no longer be practical.[27]

Eden need not have worried. Churchill was of the same mind, confirming to his Foreign Secretary on 14 December, 'I do not want to disturb Stalin before we are round the corner on Greece.'[28] Then, with some regard to Polish sacrifices, the Prime Minister urged Eden to 're-assure these men who have fought in the Polish Divisions that whatever else happens to them, the British Empire will find them a home.'[29] Churchill and SOE were full of admiration for Polish servicemen, but now had little time for the antics of Arciszewski's Government-in-exile. Furthermore, it seemed that US diplomats, the British Foreign Office and the British press, only added to the problem. When Major Mike Pickles came away from a British Parliamentary debate on 20 December, he was profoundly depressed:

The Old Man's [Churchill] speech was extremely unimpressive and rather gave one the impression that he was thoroughly fed up with these tiresome Poles…It cannot be said that the Americans are being too helpful. Mr Stenninius [US Secretary of State] puts his foot right in his mouth the first time he opens it…I suppose we in SOE are charged with the duty of implementing HMG's policy. I do not think, however, that this absolves us from the duty of criticising that policy if we think it wrong. I cannot think that the FO have been clever on the subject of Poland, and thinking back to that day on October 2nd, the day that Warsaw fell, it is obvious to me that had the decision to put missions into Poland been taken three months before that date, many of our present difficulties would never have arisen. We are now placed in the position of seeing all the messages, which pass through but being unable to influence them in any way whatsoever. I think Hudson and all his boys should definitely read the Hansard Report and should realise now that they are going into Poland with a major political role…It is difficult to understand why the FO have ever allowed themselves to be jockeyed into the position which they find themselves today, namely that of always singing in a minor key when the tune is conducted by Russia.[30]

Oliver Harvey, Assistant Under-Secretary at the Foreign Office was summoned to a meeting with Churchill and Eden, late at night on 20 December:

We met in the bowels of the earth in the Defence Map room. PM in his boiler suit rather sizzled, AE in his bottle green smoking coat, Portal, Archie Sinclair and Selborne. PM bellicose and repetitive, repeating snatches from the long speeches to the Poles that we heard in Moscow, very anti-Polish Govt. in London, but equally anti-Lublin Committee. It was decided to check the former's communications still more, to reduce their funds, and to send liaison officers into German Poland to see what is going on.[31]

While the Foreign Office dithered over sending the 'Freston' mission, Hudson and his men waited anxiously in Bari for the final go-ahead. Then, after a further month's wait, the exasperated group were suddenly allowed to set off for Poland. Their Liberator reached the Carpathian Mountains but ran into impenetrable mist and had to turn back. Two more tortuous and freezing flights had to be endured, before the weather improved and allowed the exhausted men to be dropped on 28 December. They parachuted down, landing near the town of Żarki in a thickly forested area, thirty miles north of Katowice and fortunately soon encountered the local AK committee. The following night they trekked through the freezing forests to their next *rendezvous*. However, their heavy wireless and generator were already lost and they had to resort to passing messages to Britain through their AK hosts.

Their difficulties were compounded by the fact that they all wore British military uniforms and were so conspicuous that they could never move without an AK escort. This really restricted their role as observers and, unable to move of their own accord they could never really judge the strength of the Home Army. Even the Germans were monitoring the 'Freston' group's movements, and on three occasions, attacked the house where they were staying.

One small success, however, was a meeting with the new AK C-in-C, General Okulicki, who had taken over from General Bór-Komorowski and appeared, in Peter Kemp's words to be 'a deferential but self-confident commander, who could always be relied on to put his men first.'[32] This was some comfort to SOE, who had received news that following the capture of General Bór-Komorowski the AK had been 'disorganised' for some time. There were also signs that the AK had now regrouped in their remaining strongholds within German-occupied Poland.[33] Units in Radom, Kielce, Kraków and Łódź were now in control of the surviving organisation. Indeed, it was with the AK 7th Division near Kielce that John Ward had seen recent action against the Germans. Even when the 7th Division were disbanded in December, Ward continued at his post with a radio receiver, remaining in regular radio contact with Major Pickles and had to co-ordinated the arrival of the 'Freston' team.

In early January 1945, while Hudson and his team were led from one safe house to another, news was brought to them that the local AK unit had made contact with Red Army forward scouts. These encounters heralded a massive new Soviet assault on 12 January, westwards towards the River Oder, involving nearly four million men with the main effort concentrated along the Warsaw–Berlin axis. The 'Vistula-Oder Operation' included the Second Byelorussian Front, commanded since November by the newly elevated Marshal Rokossovsky. This formation moved through East Prussia, enabling the First Byelorussian Front, now commanded by Marshal Georgii Zhukov, to execute a fast sweep through central Poland. Meanwhile, Marshal Ivan Konev's First Ukrainian Front tackled the southern Polish flank, capturing Kraków on 19 January.[34]

In the first week of the offensive, the Soviet 47th and 61st Armies (First Byelorussian Front) flanked Warsaw, crushing the panzer units of the Wehrmacht 9th Army. The smoke and din of the offensive skirted the broken city. Inside, Warsaw was an eerie wasteland awaiting Soviet occupation. Virtually all life had vanished. Yet, here and there odd survivors eked out a pathetic existence. Władysław Szpilman, a well-known Polish concert pianist and composer, had survived the 1943 Jewish Ghetto uprising as well as the 1944 Rising, and after a miraculous encounter with a compassionate German officer, found himself free in the winter of 1944/45. He staggered through the rubble towards the Soviet lines:

> I was going east towards the Vistula to Praga – it used to be a remote, poor suburb, but it was now all there was of Warsaw, since the Germans had destroyed what was left of it.
>
> I was walking down a broad main road, once busy and full of traffic, its whole length now deserted. There was not a single intact building as far as the eye could see. I kept having to walk around mountains of rubble, and my feet became entangled in a confused mess of ripped telephone wires and tramlines, and scraps of fabric that had once decorated flats or clothed human beings now long since dead.
>
> A human skeleton lay by the wall of a building, under a rebel barricade. It was not large, and the bone structure was delicate. It must have been the skeleton of a girl, since long blond hair could still be seen on the skull. Hair resists decay longer than any other part of the body. Beside the skeleton lay a rusty carbine, and there were remnants of clothing around the bones of the right arm, with a red and white armband where the letters AK had been shot away.
>
> I went on my way. A stormy wind rattled the scrap-iron in the ruins, whistling and howling through the charred cavities of the windows. Twilight came on. Snow fell from the darkening, leaden sky.[35]

On 17 January 1945 the Red Army, including the 6th Infantry Division from Berling's 1st Polish Army, finally entered the ruins of Warsaw. As they came across the Vistula at Bielany and Siekierki, there was some skirmishing with isolated German units, but the bulk of the occupying force had slunk away. Two days later, the Red Army occupied Łódź to the west and Kraków to the south, the capital of the old German General Government sector. As the vast armoured and rifle units of Konev's Front swarmed around Kielce and Kraków, their advanced scouts came across Bill Hudson and his party, still near the village of Żytno. At first relations were cordial, even hospitable, as the Red Army soldiers produced heroic quantities of vodka. The Soviets did not quite know what to do with the British party and the next few days were spent under house arrest – a tedious time, according to Peter Kemp, which was punctuated by explosive Soviet hospitality:

Jauntily I raised my tumbler and poured the contents down my throat: a moment later, if I had had any voice left I would have screamed. Mr P.G. Woodhouse once described a certain drink as having an effect 'as though someone had touched off a bomb in the old bean and then taken a stroll through the stomach with a lighted torch'. That is a fair description of what we had just swallowed; it burned like molten lead and tasted strongly of petrol. It was in fact a neat spirit used as the basis of vodka, and the petrol with which they drove their tanks, camouflaged with fruit juice.[36]

Then the mood darkened. The British party were taken to a Polish house requisitioned by the Soviet 60th Army, and interrogated by NKVD officers in squalid conditions. Peter Kemp remembered a scene of wanton destruction as Red Army soldiers stamped their mark on all the rooms by destroying furniture, urinating and defecating everywhere and, as excess vodka took its toll, vomiting over every surface. This was, he thought, the true picture for the Poles of Soviet 'liberation', rather than the 'glorious deliverance' trumpeted in the western press.[37] Despite their protests that they were operating with the consent of Moscow, Bill Hudson and his party were then carted from village to village in Soviet trucks, while local NKVD officers decided what to do with them.[38]

Even after the Red Army had overrun AK-controlled areas, 'cavalier' clandestine operations kept going. General Tatar, concerned that the Polish Government-in-exile were fast losing control of all aspects of underground activities, informed SOE that a number of secret wireless stations were already established in Lublin, Wilno and Lwów, and were making regular contact with Britain. On the surface, SOE were anxious to avoid association with these radio stations, but important information on Soviet troop movements and political activity filtered back to British intelligence.[39] No doubt, SIS felt their position all the more secure since the December directive, which compelled all Polish cyphers to be controlled by the British Foreign Office.[40]

As the January Soviet offensives rolled across Poland, John Ward prepared for an inevitable meeting with Red Army troops. Hiding in a safe house, he watched and heard reports of how the Soviet occupation was taking shape:

On approximately 18 Jan 1945, the first Russian forces appeared, who were a Tank Corps, and both officers and men were very drunk. On arrival they proceeded to act as though they were masters of the earth. I did not report myself to them.

Within a few days the Russians had raped every female in the district over fourteen years of age. They exchanged petrol, food, paraffin, tea, sugar, tobacco etc. for vodka, but more often took the vodka without payment. They appeared to beat Polish men without provocation and some were shot. All livestock on farms were stolen and taken to other villages, where they were exchanged for vodka. A few days later a Russian Commissar arrived and all livestock in the area were confiscated. The cattle were slaughtered and their carcases taken away.

I was in the stockyard of a farm where I was staying when a horse-drawn sledge arrived at a spot about eighty yards away from me. The sledge contained four Russian soldiers, who stood up in the sledge, shouted and then fired their rifles in my direction. I heard the whine of the bullets. I threw myself on my face in the snow and lay still. The Russians shouted again and then drove off.[41]

Wherever the Red Army gained new Polish territory, the NKVD followed closely behind. Curfews were enforced between 2000 hours and 0500 hours and this enabled Soviet security officers to move in and arrest all AK members or fellow political supporters in their own homes. For many, the contact with the NKVD was all too brief, as an escaped POW, Sergeant F.R. Smith, US Army, witnessed:

At 2 am a knock came at the door of the house I was stopping at, and a voice demanded in Polish, 'Does Mr X live here?' The answer was given that he lived next door. They went away. In the morning we found the body of the man they were looking for the previous night. He had been shot three times, all from the back. Fourteen others were killed that night.[42]

It was estimated that 80,000 NKVD agents were operating inside Poland by the winter of 1944/45 – approximately the same number as the previous Gestapo presence. But their techniques were very different. When the Gestapo were making arrests, they tended to roar through the streets with sirens blaring, but the NKVD called quietly at houses in the night, dressed either in an ordinary infantry officer's uniform or in civilian clothes. Moreover, unlike the Gestapo, they operated without an official

HQ, preferring to live together in small groups in a house with a basement, which was used as an interrogation centre. No-one could ever find out what had happened to an arrested person.[43]

Soviet advisors and controllers moved into all aspects of a community's life, though their first job was to strip Polish assets. There was little effort made to get Polish industry moving again, for most machines of any value were removed to the Soviet Union and lesser items were looted. The advancing Red Army had taken every available horse, while grain was requisitioned and livestock slaughtered to help feed them. Large landowners disappeared and small farmers were only allowed to keep 100 acres of agricultural or forest land. While the land acquired by the state was distributed to peasants under a co-operative, little could be cultivated without tools or machinery. Starvation, especially in the eastern areas was prevalent and there was even some nostalgia for a German occupation, which had resulted in fewer shortages. Communications were extremely difficult. There was little rolling stock available to civilians though most railway lines were out of action anyway while they were changed to the Soviet broad gauge. Many bridges were destroyed, the roads were in a bad state and to aggravate the chaos, telephone and postal services rarely operated.

At the end of January 1945, the military mission were taken to the newly arrived Soviet commander in Częstochowa, but instead of being received as allies, they were unceremoniously bundled into a cattle truck and sent to Moscow. That other British contact, John Ward, fared better. When the Soviets overran his area, Ward managed to evade capture and joined Stefan Korboński and other underground leaders in Leśna Podkowa. His whereabouts were transmitted to London and were eagerly monitored by SIS and SOE. Arrangements were then made to safely transport Ward home via Moscow. Before he left Poland, he had one last meeting with his AK comrades-in-arms. Stefan Korboński recalled that the C-in-C AK, General Okulicki, decorated Ward with a bar to his Polish Cross of Gallantry, for his extraordinary service during the Rising.[44]

The Soviet grip on Poland was almost complete. AK officers who had not gone into hiding were rounded up in constant NKVD sweeps. The Home Army still aimed to protect the Polish population by armed action against the retreating Germans, but in so doing, risked exposing themselves to the Soviets. A week after the opening of the Soviet Vistula-Oder Operation, it was clear to the AK leadership that their country would soon be completely swamped. Consequently, General Okulicki had no room to manoeuvre and on 19 January 1945, he ordered the dissolution of the Home Army. In his notice in *Biuletyn Informacyjny* he appealed to his soldiers to keep alive the dream of freedom.[45]

The speed of the Soviet advance across Poland was extraordinary, but it was helped by poor German strategy, as the BBC Home Service confirmed:

> The Russian success has been mainly due to their vastly superior forces but they have also been helped by the enemy's mistakes. The Germans moved several Panzer divisions away from Poland in an abortive effort to relieve Budapest, shortly before the great Russian blow fell.[46]

These divisions may have helped the German defence of the Warsaw-Berlin axis, but they could only have staved off the inevitable. Army Group 'A' swiftly collapsed under the shock of the Soviet attack and the Soviet First Byelorussian Front swept onwards towards Poznań, while the First Ukrainian Front raced towards Katowice. Just ahead of them, the SS drove the survivors out of the Auschwitz camps, together with the British POWs from the IG Farben complex. Brian Bishop remembered a terrible journey:

> On 20 January 1945, the Russians bombed our camp. The Germans then started moving out all the Buna prisoners and we followed two days later. We were force marched towards Czechoslovakia to escape the Russian advance. We must have followed the same route as the Jews, because all along the snow covered way (it was nearly 500 miles), lay stripped bodies, left where they fell beside the road. We were pushed on every day until finally our war ended when our guards deserted us.[47]

On the afternoon of 27 January 1945, forward units of the First Ukrainian Front reached the gates of Auschwitz. By the time the 'Ivans' walked into Birkenau, Poland had changed beyond recognition. She had lost 38% of her territory. Furthermore, during the German occupation, nearly all of her pre-war Jewish population of three million had been wiped out together with a further estimated 1.9 million non-Jewish Poles.[48] Resistance in the shape of the Underground State would not be formally dissolved until the following July but its army, the *Armia Krajowa* had already stood down in the face of impossible odds. The Polish people were now defenceless against another tyranny, but this time it was a Soviet one. Poland was once more, alone.

NOTES

1 J. Ward, translated message, 15 October 1944, file ref. 3.9.2.8.9, PUSMT.
2 Major M Pickles (MPP) to Air Ministry, 23 November 1944, and Captain J. Podoski to Major Pickles, 9 October 1944, both HS4/180, NA. See also, Captain J. Podoski to Lieutenant-Colonel H.B. Perkins, 14 October 1944, ref. 71, 3.10.3.1, PUMST.
3 1586 Polish Flight carried out twenty-seven sorties during October, of which four were successful in dropping six tons of supplies. Two aircraft were lost.
4 'SOE: Short History of Air Effort to Poland, 1942–1944', HS4/156, NA. Also 'Summary of Negotiations Taken for Air Supply', 30 November 1944, HS4/157, NA.
5 Lieutenant-Colonel Threlfall to Lieutenant-Colonel Wiggington, 11 November 1944, HS 4/180, NA.
6 Two telegrams from 'Delegate of Cracow District', 14 October 1944, FO 371/39454, NA. The report estimates there were 156,000 prisoners left in Auschwitz at the time.
7 Davies, *Rising*, op. cit., p. 437.
8 David Reynolds, *In Command of History: Churchill Fighting and Writing the Second World War* (Allen Lane, London 2004), pp. 458–63.
9 Captain L. Massey (MPX) to Lieutenant-Colonel Harold Perkins (MP1), 13 December 1944, HS 4/145, NA. Also Fenby, op. cit., pp. 332–9. Also David Dutton, *Anthony Eden: A Life and Reputation* (Hodder Headline, London 1995), p. 209.
10 Lord Ismay, *The Memoirs of General The Lord Ismay* (Heinemann, London 1960), p. 378.
11 Opposition to Mikołajczyk within the Polish Cabinet was ultimately led by the Deputy Premier, Jan Kwapiński; see Captain LM Massey (MPX) to Lieutenant-Colonel Harold Perkins (MP1), 12 December 1944, HS 4/145. Also John Harvey, op. cit., pp. 360–3; David Dilks (Ed.), *The Diaries of Sir Alexander Cadogan OM, 1938–1945* (Cassell, London 1971), pp. 672–3.
12 Lord Selborne to Sir Archibald Sinclair, 30 October 1944, HS4/156, NA.
13 Lieutenant-Colonel Threlfall to AOC Balkan Air Force, 22 October 1944, ref. 75, file 3.10.3.1, PUMST. Also Cynk, op. cit., p. 481.
14 For 'encouraging a rising' and 'submarines', see 'Factors Affecting Flights to Poland', 2 January 1945, HS 4/145, NA. Also, 'General Policy for Kensal', 4 September 1944, HS4/146, NA. For speed of Soviet occupation, see

Report by Major Mike Pickles (MPP) to Lieutenant-Colonel Perkins (MP) of 'Talk with Major Ignatius, M.I.3.c', 28 October 1944, HS4/156, NA.

15 Lieutenant-Colonel Perkins (MP) to Colonel D Keswick (AD/H), 11 October 1944, HS 4/156, NA. Also Brigadier G.A. Hill to Colonel Graur, 7 April 1945, HS 4/142, NA.

16 Peter Kemp, *No Colours or Crest* (Cassell, London 1958), pp. 250–1.

17 Lord Selborne to Sir Archibald Sinclair, 22 November 1944, AIR 19/816, NA.

18 Lord Selborne to Sir Winston Churchill, 24 November 1944, HS4/157, NA.

19 'Allied Prisoners of War' in 'Factors Affecting Flights to Poland', 2 January 1945, HS 4/145, NA.

20 Operation 'Fernham' and 'Flamstead' officially stood down on 27 January 1945. See 'Freston Plans', 11 October 1944, HS 4/156, NA and Jeffrey Bines, *Operation Freston: The British Military Mission to Poland, 1944* (Jeffrey Bines, Saffron Walden 1999), pp. 25–8.

21 The Political ND Party had some links to the extreme right-wing military group, NSZ. Major Mike Pickles (MPP) to Major Boughey (MP1), 'Change of Polish Government', 1 December 1944, HS 4/146, NA.

22 Major Pickles (MPP) to Major Boughey (MP1), 'Change of Polish Government', 1 December 1944, HS 4/146, NA. Also Sir Winston Churchill to Sir Alexander Cadogan, 1 November 1944, AP20/12/508, Lord Avon Papers, UB.

23 'Summary of Negotiations and Measures Taken for Air Supply (SOE)', 28 November 1944, CAB 121/310, NA. Also 'Flights to Poland', 26 November 1944, HS4/145, NA; Threlfall to AOC Balkan Air Force, 26 October 1944, HS 4/146, NA; Lieutenant-Colonel Perkins (MP1) to Major-General Colin Gubbins (CD), 9 January 1945, HS 4/183, NA.

24 WSC to Foreign Secretary, 26 November 1944, AP20/12/553, Lord Avon Papers, UB.

25 Anthony Eden to Prime Minister, 26 November 1944, AP20/11/734, Lord Avon Papers, UB. See also Memorandum undated, HS 4/145, NA, and Prażmowska, op. cit., pp. 191–8.

26 Lord Selborne to Sir Winston Churchill, 14 December 1944, HS4/157, NA.

27 Anthony Eden to Sir Winston Churchill, 4 December 1944, HS4/157, NA.

28 Sir Winston Churchill to Anthony Eden, 14 December 1944, AIR 19/816, NA.

29 WSC to Foreign Secretary, 28 December 1944, AP20/12/712, Lord Avon Papers, UB.

30 Memo, Major Mike Pickles (MPP), 20 December 1944, HS4/146, NA.

31 John Harvey, op. cit., p. 369.

32 Peter Kemp, op. cit., p. 273.

33 'SOE Activities: Summary for Prime Minister Oct–Dec 1944', PREM 3/408/1, NA.

[34] The River Oder formed the post-war boundary between East Germany and Poland. General Rokossovsky's Second Byelorussian Front, took East Prussia and swept over East Pomerania to assist in the final battle for Berlin.

[35] Władysław Szpilman, *The Pianist: The Extraordinary Story of One Man's Survival in Warsaw, 1939–45* (Victor Gollancz, London 1999), pp. 186–7.

[36] Kemp, op. cit., p. 281.

[37] Kemp, op. cit., p. 286.

[38] Report of Interrogation of 542939 Sgt. John Ward, HS4/256, NA.

[39] Memo, Lieutenant-Colonel F.K. Roberts, 9 November 1944, HS4/145, NA.

[40] Sir Frank Roberts to H. Perkins, 8 December 1944, HS4/145, NA.

[41] Ward MI9 Report, 22 March 1944, HS4/256, NA.

[42] Dennis Allen, Foreign Office, 'Report on interrogation of ex-POWs', 17 April 1945, HS4/145, NA.

[43] Ibid.

[44] Korboński, op. cit., p. 362.

[45] For a transcript of his declaration, see Ney-Krwawicz op. cit., pp. 139–41.

[46] Home Service broadcast transcript, 23 January 1945, 7/1/34, Kirke Papers, LHCMA.

[47] Brian Bishop to Author, 10 January 2007. A similar account of life in the British POW camp is held in the Imperial War Museum Sound Archive; see Denis Avey, ref. 22065, IWM.

[48] These are recent and conservative estimates. See 'Poles: Victims of the Nazi Era', United States Holocaust Memorial Museum.

Chapter Ten

Epilogue

During the last tumultuous year of the Home Army's existence, the Polish Government-in-exile made several poor assumptions. They underestimated the power and sheer stamina of the Red Army to come back onto the offensive and occupy large chunks of central and Eastern Europe. They also overestimated the will of Britain to take on the Soviet Union on their behalf. For no amount of Polish losses on behalf of the Allies would ever induce the latter to go to war with the Soviet Union over Poland's freedom or territorial integrity.[1] At the Yalta conference in February 1945, Stalin, Churchill and Roosevelt concluded the border deal or, as Roosevelt delicately put it, 'the Polish headache'.[2] The Soviet Union would keep Poland's eastern territory, including Wilno and Lwów, and Poland would be compensated by the addition of a slice of Germany, including the city of Breslau (Wrocław), to her western boundaries. Any provisional Polish government would have to include democratic leaders and be free of outside Soviet interference. It was all wishful thinking, but it was enough to tempt Mikołajczyk to return and join the provisional government as deputy Prime Minister.

Meanwhile, sixteen leaders from the Polish Underground were lured into a trap, arrested by the NKVD and taken to Moscow for a show trial. In June 1945, all but three of the defendants were found guilty, including General Okulicki ('Bear Cub') ex C-in-C of the AK, who received a ten year sentence. He died (most probably murdered) in prison on Christmas Eve 1946.[3] British diplomatic efforts to help the accused were insipid and some weeks later, with immaculate timing, the British and US governments withdrew their recognition for the London-based Polish Government-in-exile. In late July 1945, following Roosevelt's death Churchill, Stalin and Harry Truman met at Potsdam to iron out details of Germany's borders, including the western Polish boundary. But by this stage, the only internationally recognised provisional government was the Soviet-backed Lublin group. Mikołajczyk persevered with this cabal, but by 1947, it became clear that the democratic elections envisaged at the Yalta conference would never materialise. In the autumn of 1947, Sir Winston Churchill wrote to the new Foreign Secretary, Ernest Bevin, reminding him of the recent fate of Nikola Petkov, the anti-communist leader in Bulgaria and voicing his concern over the threats to Mikołajczyk.[4] These were no idle threats. Tipped off by SIS that he was about to be 'liquidated', Mikołajczyk escaped from Poland and after a brief stay in Britain, decided that the US would offer him a better sanctuary. He was joined by Stefan Korboński, who had also tried to participate in the post-war political map of Poland.

Polish resistance to Soviet domination was not quite over. When the AK was formally dissolved, many members had gone into hiding and formed the 'NIE' (*Niepodległość,* or 'Independence') organisation to keep alive the promise of Polish freedom, despite Soviet domination. But 'NIE's senior commanders, including Major-General August Fieldorf were tempted out of hiding by a bogus amnesty in 1948 and immediately arrested. The Polish communist government under Bolesław Bierut then carried out a number of show trials during the following years, executing many such as Fieldorf, who they claimed had acted against Soviet partisans during the war.[5] Another, more moderate resistance movement, 'WiN' (*Wolność i Niepodległość),* was spawned by the AK and attracted some 60,000 ex-soldiers and activists. It took the Soviet secret police nearly eighteen months to crush most of this organisation. However, their surviving supporters were re-activated by British SIS officers in the late 1940s, only to be finally destroyed in 1952 through infiltration (assisted by KGB moles, including Kim Philby).[6]

Those AK commanders most involved in the fateful decisions of 1944, had already moved on. Lieutenant-General Bór Komorowski, who had spent the last months of the war in Colditz Castle and subsequently Austria, was finally liberated by the US 103rd Infantry Division. After the war he moved to London, where he became active in Polish *émigré* circles and died in 1966. The irascible General Sosnkowski, who was dismissed in 1944, emigrated to Canada, while General Stanisław Tatar settled in Britain for several years after the war, before returning to Poland in 1949. Promises of an amnesty evaporated and the NKVD arrested him. After a show trial he was imprisoned but released in 1956. He died in 1980.

Dr Józef Garliński, veteran of the Home Army struggle and inmate of Auschwitz, made it his mission after the war to chronicle Poland's wartime experience. One of his main achievements in this field was to bring the story of Poland's war to the English-language reader and his output of articles was profligate. After serving in a large number of Polish exile organisations, he died in 2005.[7] Józef Retinger, the intriguer and political 'fixer', continued to be a 'go-between' for international figures after the war. He campaigned for a socialist, united Europe and was a founder member of the Bilderberg Group, a conference of multi-national businessmen, politicians and media controllers, which still meets regularly to promote an understanding between the US and Europe. Retinger died in London in 1960, having given his papers and notes to his secretary, John Pomian, who later recorded his employer's wartime adventures in *Joseph Retinger: Memoirs of an Eminence Grise*.

Colonel Mieczysław Walęga, who with his wife Adela had helped organise AK operations under the very same roof as the Germans, was pursued by the Communist authorities in 1946, and fled to Italy. Adela was also on the run. In 1947, the Polish Secret Police closed in on her as she was leaving her third floor apartment. As she was about to be arrested, a student colleague took her weapon and hid it under his coat. He was arrested and handcuffed to an officer. As he was led away, fearing he would be tortured and thereby compromise Adela, he suddenly jumped down the lift shaft, taking the officer with him. This brave act resulted in his death, but allowed Adela the chance to get away. She later joined her husband and they found sanctuary in London, where, at the time of writing they still live.[8]

Hanna Czarnocka's mother, Halina had been transported from Auschwitz to Bergen-Belsen in January 1945 and survived. At the end of the war, Halina managed to find Hanna and they travelled through a devastated Germany in search of Polish women soldiers of the AK. Although emaciated and physically very weak, Halina was determined to find the women who had been put in the vast 'displaced persons' camps and evacuate them, so they could return to their army units or to take up studies. For her gallant service to Poland, she was awarded the *Wijonny Virtuti Militari* and the *Polonia Restituta*. Later, both Halina and her daughter Hanna settled in England, where they became involved in the Polish Underground Movement Study Trust, Halina eventually becoming Board Chairperson. She died in 1998, but her daughter continues to support the Trust.

Halina Czarnocka had been one of an estimated total of 100,000 inmates still alive when their concentration camps were finally liberated between January and April 1945. When Red Army soldiers reached Auschwitz, they found only 1000 prisoners still living at Auschwitz I, 6000 at Birkenau (Auschwitz II) and 600 at the slave labour camp of Auschwitz III (Monowitz-Buna). Their lives were spared largely because the speed of the Allied advance had overtaken SS plans to annihilate those left, while many SS officers failed to carry out their last orders for fear of retribution by the Allies.[9] It was only after the war that the full enormity of the Holocaust was revealed, but interpretations were varied. The Soviet Union downplayed the suffering of the Jews, preferring to lump all the concentration camp fatalities together as 'victims of Fascism'.[10] In Britain, reports of the liberation of Auschwitz were muted – it was one more horror story in a war of atrocities – but then, British officials had never grasped the enormity of the crime. The British Foreign Office's lame response to contemporary Polish reports on the Holocaust may be explained by a lack of imagination. Additionally, any rational FO official could have been excused for believing that the Nazis would not slaughter a potential slave labour force that could help them win the war. Nor that when faced with a war that was clearly going against them, together with the likely retribution, that the Nazis would engage in an even more furious slaughter of Jews on Polish soil during the summer of 1944. However, it is only now acknowledged that the genocide was inseparable from the German war effort; that the Jews should to be eradicated was as central to Nazi thinking as the creation of *lebensraum* in the east and the associated military operations. Consequently, the logic applied by British officials betrayed a lack of knowledge about both Nazi ideology and its war aims.[11]

If Britain failed to save the Polish resistance during the war, it certainly met its obligations to the Poles after 1945 by offering sanctuary. Before the war there had only been very small communities of Poles living in Britain, mainly in London, Manchester and Scotland. In 1945, as a result of the communist takeover in Poland, the vast majority of the

150,000 Polish service personnel stationed in Britain elected to remain here with their dependents. A Polish Resettlement Corps was established in 1946 – a 'half-way house' military unit, split into an army, navy and air force contingent – which absorbed members of the demobilizing Polish Armed Forces.[12] Their plight was alleviated by the passing, on 22 March 1947, of the Polish Resettlement Act, which provided entitlement to employment and some forty resettlement camps were created in ex-Army bases, airfields or the grounds of large country houses, to house the former soldiers and their dependents. Poles subsequently moved into a large number of communities throughout Britain, and created churches, schools and institutions that remain to this day. While there are now only two major Polish Retirement Homes remaining in Britain, at Penrhos in North Wales and Ilford Park, Stover in Devon, there are many other smaller dedicated Polish support facilities.[13] Since Poland's entry into the European Union (EU) in 2004, increasing numbers of young Poles have arrived in Britain, boosting the economic and cultural identity of Polish communities.

The wartime British Government's attitude towards the Polish resistance may have vacillated but SOE personnel had largely remained dedicated to the cause. Lord Selborne had fought the case for Polish support to the very end. He was constantly reminded by Air Staff of the risk of inordinate casualties in airlifts to Poland, though he knew only too well the cost of personal loss – his son and heir, William, was killed in action in 1942. When the war ended in 1945, Selborne resigned as Minister of Economic Warfare and SOE was closed down the following December.[14] He pursued a number of commercial interests in the post-war years and died in 1971. Another senior SOE figure who had lost a son in the war, Major-General Gubbins, found himself much in demand in a fractured Europe.[15] He became involved again with Retinger in the series of Bilderberg conferences in the 1950s, which aimed to bring together the thinkers and 'big-hitters' in NATO and European affairs. He received a knighthood in 1946 together with a shower of decorations from former occupied countries. Although he was offered a number of directorships and became involved in a textile company, the commercial world never offered him the challenge and excitement of SOE. This 'real Highland toughie' gently glided out of public life, eventually retiring to his beloved Scottish retreat in the Isle of Harris, where he died in 1976.[16]

Some SOE officers felt that their war was not a success. Those who took part in the Freston Operation certainly did not end hostilities on a high note. The team were eventually flown out from Poland to Moscow on 17 February 1945. But the Soviets made sure they hung on to the team sufficiently long enough to outdate any intelligence that the SOE operatives had picked up in Poland. They finally arrived back in London in early April 1945, some six weeks before the end of the war, and in the words of Peter Solly-Flood, the operation 'was in every respect a complete failure.'[17] Yet other SOE officers, such as Lieutenant-Colonel Harold Perkins, were fortunate to complete many of their operations. In May 1945, when Prague rose in revolt against German occupation, Perkins was in place as the British Chargé d'Affaires and on hand to monitor events. When SOE was closed down in December 1945, he, like many SOE operatives moved across to SIS. With the intelligence agency he pursued an eventful post-war career, dealing with operations that included Albania and Palestine. He died in 1965. Lieutenant-Colonel Henry Threlfall, who handled SOE's Brindisi operations and persistently challenged the British Air Ministry over flights to Poland, went on to control elements of the 'Balkan Air Force'. After leaving the army, he joined Siemens, eventually becoming their London Chairman.

The other British soldier who made a significant contribution to the Polish resistance was Sergeant John Ward. Though he never managed to arrange a flight out of Kielce, he kept up his invaluable radio contact with Major Pickles of SOE. On 5 March 1945 he was ordered to report to the Red Army in Warsaw, who were briefed to arrange his transport back to Britain. Leaving Poland, he went via Odessa to Malta and from there, was flown to London to be debriefed by MI9, the branch of the intelligence services that dealt with escaped POWs. Over the successive days, everyone, including SOE, MI3c, MI5 and the Foreign Office, lobbied to interview this extraordinary airman, who by his own initiative had witnessed the rise and fall of the Polish Home Army. On 31 August 1945 he was awarded the Military Cross. He died in 1995, aged 77 years, having never spoken publicly about his wartime activities.[18]

Churchill had, from the very start, committed himself to the sole aim of the defeat of Germany and all other aims were subjugated to this mission. US support inevitably resulted in their dominance over Britain in European affairs, but the really bitter pill that Britain had to swallow involved keeping the Soviet Union as an ally, whatever the consequences for Eastern Europe. No one felt this more deeply than Sir Jack Slessor, who as Deputy C-in-C, MAAF had some very difficult decisions to make regarding relief flights during the Rising, condemning 'the blackest-hearted, coldest-blooded treachery on the part of the Russians'. Unable to contain his anger at Soviet policy, he railed 'I am not a naturally vindictive man; but I hope there may be some special hell reserved for the brutes in the Kremlin.'[19]

Such feelings were not exaggerated. For at the end of the war, the Red Army and NKVD extended its vice-like grip on Polish society. Night-time arrests, especially of intellectuals and professionals, became commonplace. The Church still functioned but priests could not afford to voice opinions. Anyone found outside after curfew without a special permit was executed, as were possessors of radio sets or firearms, and anyone calling a soldier of the communist LWP 'a Berling man' could be summarily shot. Such oppressive measures were not offensive to Red Army commanders reared on Stalin's brutal methods of control. Marshal Konstantin Rokossovsky, who for much of 1944 commanded the critical Red Army thrust through central Poland, ended the war supporting the final assault on Berlin. In June 1945, he was accorded the high honour of commanding the victory parade through Moscow. Then in 1949, upon the accession of Bierut's fully-fledged communist government in Poland, Rokossovsky was 'put in' as Minister of Defence. His period in office was marked by a brutal crackdown on Polish national aspirations. He returned to the Soviet Union in 1955 and subsequently managed, in a profession not known for high survival rates, to retain various military commands until 1962. He died in his bed in 1968 and is buried in the Kremlin Wall.

Another great survivor was General Zygmunt Berling, commander of the 1st Polish Army, fighting under the red banner. His Army fanned out across Poland and by March 1945 had reached its western borders. The Army had suffered heavily since its first engagements in the summer of 1944 – some 20,000 had been killed and over 40,000 seriously wounded. Berling himself was recalled to Moscow but returned to Poland after the war to take up agricultural posts in Bierut's government. He died in 1980.

There can be no doubt that the brief but dramatic US airdrops in September 1944 did boost morale among the Poles. However, it was short lived. The Americans continued to maintain their Poltava base in the Soviet Union through the winter of 1944–45, in the hope that further

'Frantic' missions would be allowed the following spring. But with the collapse of the AK and increasing unease at US bases on Soviet territory, Stalin grounded all remaining US aircraft, effectively ending the experiment.

The Governor-General of Poland, Hans Frank, had boasted at the beginning of 1944 that 'once we have won the war...the Poles and Ukrainians, and whoever else is knocking around, can be turned into mincemeat.' However, the mere whiff of the Red Army approaching Kraków saw him bolting to his home on the Schliersee, in the Bavarian Alps. The Americans arrested him in a nearby village on 1 May 1945. Bizarrely, he turned over his incriminating diary to US forces. His motives remain unclear, though the prison psychologist at the Nuremberg Trials, G.M. Gilbert revealed that Frank's recent conversion to Catholicism had triggered an outpouring of guilt. The ex-Governor of the 'Generalgovernment' of Poland confided to Gilbert:

> The fat one [Göring] is sore because I handed over those diaries – those 40 volumes. He says to me, 'what's the matter with you? Why didn't you burn them?' What does he know about truth and higher values? I remember how I thought it over when the enemy was closing in. They were begging me to burn the volumes before I was captured... When I heard the voice of Christ, something seemed to say to me, 'what, face the enemy with a false face.' You cannot hide the truth from God! No, the truth must come out, once and for all.[20]

It appeared to be an extraordinary transformation from the all-powerful ruler who, barely four years earlier, had noted in his diary that 'the Jews for us represent extraordinarily malignant gluttons'. At the Nuremberg Trials he was found guilty on count 3 of 'War Crimes' and on count 4 of 'Crimes against Humanity.' His only response before execution on 16 October 1946 was 'I deserved it.'[21]

After their crushing of the Warsaw Rising, the SS commanders, Erich von dem Bach and Heinz Reinefarth were both given SS Army Corps Commands in preparation for the German Ardennes Offensive in December 1944. They both survived the last months of the war and in January 1946 von dem Bach testified against his superiors at Nuremberg and consequently escaped prosecution for his war crimes. But he was subsequently convicted of killing German opposition figures in the 1930s and served a number of jail sentences in Germany, dying in Munich

Prison in 1972. Reinefarth meanwhile, escaped any prosecution through lack of evidence and entered German local government. Despite Polish attempts to extradite him, he remained a prominent regional figure in Schleswig-Holstein, until his peaceful death at home in Sylt in 1979.

The more junior SS commanders fared less well. Towards the end of the Warsaw Rising, the remnants of the notorious Kaminski Brigade were withdrawn to the nearby Kampinos Forest, while their commander was ordered to a conference at Łódź. Having stolen large quantities of booty from Warsaw (and not passed it on), Kaminski had incurred Himmler's wrath, and was executed by the Gestapo before he could arrive at his conference. Meanwhile, his brigade was mauled by partisans in the forest and was sent back to Silesia, reporting to a training ground near Stuttgart in November 1944. They were then incorporated, with other RONA survivors, into the newly created General Vlasov's 'Russian Liberation Army' (KONR) – another, more formal attempt to incorporate non-German, anti-Soviet volunteers into German military operations. At the end of the war, under a notorious repatriation agreement, the British handed over large numbers of Vlasov's 'turncoats' to the Soviets, including several thousand Cossack officers, many of whom were undoubtedly murdered by the NKVD.

The other SS brigade commander, Oscar Dirlewanger, whose exploits in Warsaw even the SS found hard to stomach, still found favour with Hitler after the Rising and was awarded the Knight's Cross, Germany's highest award for bravery.[22] After obtaining replacements for his depleted brigade from the criminal and political inmates of various concentration camps, his unit joined the retreat towards Berlin. In February 1945, Dirlewanger was wounded again and disappeared. He resurfaced after the war in Althausen in southern Germany, where he was reportedly murdered in a detention centre.[23]

SS Major Alfred Naujocks, who had famously arranged the bogus Polish attack that preceded the German invasion of Poland, made himself useful at the end of the war. He organised *Aktion Birkenbaum* (Operation Birch Tree), which was a large-scale forging operation giving false papers to escaping Nazis.[24] But it did not work for them all. Many senior SS officers responsible for the crimes at Birkenau and the other Auschwitz camps were apprehended soon after the camps were liberated. Among the Commandants, forty-six-year-old Rudolf Höss was hanged at the scene of his crimes on 16 April 1947, Richard Baer died in detention in

1963, while Arthur Liebehenschel was executed in January 1948. Josef Kramer, another senior SS officer at Birkenau, was promoted to command Bergen–Belsen concentration camp in the later stages of the war, but was finally arrested and executed for war crimes on 13 December 1945. Perhaps one of the worst of the perpetrators of evil at Auschwitz, Dr Josef Mengele, evaded capture in 1945 and disappeared to South America, finally drowning as a free man in Brazil in 1979.

While the SS were justifiably vilified, the German rocket scientists were fêted by the Allies at the end of the war. The German V-2 campaign against Britain had finally ended on 27 March 1945 when the last two rockets fell, one on a block of flats in Stepney, London, killing 134 people and the other in Orpington, Kent. The German rocket units around The Hague withdrew in the face of the Allied advance and eventually surrendered to the US 9th Army on 9 May. Hans Kammler, responsible for so much of the V-2 rocket operations as well as the SS slave labour and concentration camp atrocities, disappeared at the end of the war and despite reports that he had committed suicide, no evidence was ever found. Meanwhile, the main architects of the V-2 program, Von Braun and General Dornberger were prize captives for the Allies. After intensive interrogations, which yielded much important intelligence on rocket science, Dornberger was quietly released by the British in 1947, and emigrated to the US, where he worked on various missile projects. On retirement, he returned to Germany and died in 1980. Von Braun similarly moved to the US and became one of the pioneers of the NASA space projects. He died in 1977.[25]

NOTES

1. Prażmowska, op. cit., p. 195.
2. Quoted in John Charmley, op. cit.
3. Professor Wojciech Rojek, 'The Polish Underground State in the Final Phase of the Second World War', see www.polishresistance-ak.org. Also Ney-Krwawicz, op. cit., pp. 139–42.
4. Ernest Bevin to Sir Winston Churchill, 30 September 1947, AP19/1/20a, Lord Avon Papers, UB.
5. Fieldorf was executed in February 1953. The communist prosecutor at his trail was another Pole, Helena Wolinska, who later settled in Britain. During 2007, attempts were made to deport her to Poland to face charges for her involvement in the show trial.

6 For an analysis of the post-war involvement of SIS in Poland, see Stephen Dorril, op. cit., pp. 256–67.

7 Obituary, *The Times*, 30 December 2005.

8 Adela Wałęga to Author, 2 September 2006. The secret police were part of the 'Ministry of Public Security of Poland (MBP). The Polish state, unlike Germany, has still not opened up its communist-era secret police archives to the public.

9 Laurence Rees, *Auschwitz: The Nazis and the 'Final Solution'* (BBC Books, London 2005), pp. 326–30.

10 Ibid., p. 329.

11 Saul Friedländer explores the theme of Nazi central war aims in *The Years of Extermination: Nazi Germany and the Jews 1939-45* (HarperCollins, London 2007).

12 At the end of the war, there were over 250,000 Polish servicemen and women in western Europe. Some 100,000 returned to an uncertain future in communist Poland, leaving 150,000 in Britain.

13 Alan Brown, *Airmen in Exile: The Allied Air Forces in the Second World War* (Sutton Publishing, Stroud 2000), p. 74.

14 Following Lord Selborne's resignation as Minister for Economic Warfare, Churchill suggested his successor should be 'Foot from MEW'. Winston Churchill to Anthony Eden, 25 November 1945, AP20/12/545, Lord Avon Papers, UB. This reference no doubt refers to Dingle Foot, Parliamentary Under-Secretary at the Ministry of Economic Warfare (MEW).

15 Twenty-two-year Captain Michael Gubbins was killed on 6 February 1944, while serving with the 5th Queen's Own Cameron Highlanders.

16 Leo Marks, *Between Silk and Cyanide* (HarperCollins, London 1998), p. 222. Also Peter Wilkinson, *Gubbins*, op. cit., pp. 238–44.

17 Peter Solly-Flood, 'Pilgrimage to Poland', in *Blackwood's Magazine*, May 1951 (William Blackwood & Son, Edinburgh 1951).

18 MI9 Report, 22 March 1945, HS4/256, NA. Also *The London Gazette*, 31 August 1945.

19 Sir John Slessor, *The Central Blue: Recollections and Reflections* (Cassell, London 1956), p. 612.

20 GM Gilbert, op. cit., p. 52.

21 Ibid., p. 44 and p. 272.

22 Although Guderian, as Chief of the General Staff, tried to stifle this award, several generals from Army Group Centre supported it; see French MacLean, op. cit., p. 17.

23 MacLean, op. cit., pp. 222–6.

24 Michael Elkins, op. cit., pp. 251–2.

25 T.D. Dungan, op. cit., pp. 197–204. Also Frederick Ordway III and Mitchell Sharpe, op. cit., p. 404.

Conclusion

It is very difficult to evaluate the resistance movement in one particular occupied country. Some sources credit the AK with killing approximately 22,000 Germans – a figure similar to those estimated for the Greek and Czech undergrounds.[1] Statistics abound for the Polish Home Army concerning trains and bridges blown, Gestapo and fellow travellers assassinated and German installations destroyed. Yet the debit side of Polish resistance, largely the appalling loss of civilian life during the Rising, looms over every view of its activities. While Britain and its Allies cannot be held responsible for the terrible retribution meted out by the German occupiers to the Polish population, resolute measures by the Allies were distinctly lacking. Furthermore, the British Foreign Office could be criticised for indulging Stalin and promoting a naive view of the Soviet system, even though some elements within the AK leadership felt that a compromise with Stalin and even cooperation with the Red Army was the only solution. However, a totalitarian system offers no compromises.

Poland's sons had sacrificed themselves in large numbers for the Allied cause. Polish soldiers and airmen had died attempting to defend France in the early months of the war, and during the subsequent Battle of Britain. They fell in north Africa, in Italy and in the bitter battles of north-western Europe. They probably made the largest contribution to Allied intelligence of any occupied country and their efforts in forwarding V2 parts and drawings were most valuable. Yet, their hopes of material British and Allied help were doomed.

Geographically, Poland was in an impossible position. Inaccessible to the Allies until Germany was defeated, Britain could not even get close to Poland's western borders, and it was never going to be easy airlifting troops into the country. The Independent Parachute Brigade was certainly squandered at Arnhem, but their injection into the Warsaw Rising would have resulted in almost total annihilation. The Polish Air Force did not have the resources for constant, costly airlifts to Poland and therefore had to wait its turn with all the other lobbies for valuable RAF heavy bombers. During the 339 operational sorties to Poland during 1944, No. 1586 Special Duties Flight managed to drop a total of 238 tons of supplies and 141 agents. The cost was heavy, with 109 Polish airmen killed, 9 missing and 26 taken prisoner. But there is no doubt that the Poles would have flown many more sorties to their homeland, even in impossible conditions, had their flight not been controlled at all times by the RAF.[2]

The Polish wish for independence from British control, especially concerning the secrecy of their cypher codes, can be appreciated, but reserving such independence of action meant that Allied planners were rarely consulted early enough to be able to offer tangible help. This was nowhere more evident than in the run-up to the Warsaw Rising, when Senior British Air Staff and, to an extent, their US counterparts, felt that they had not been properly consulted before Polish action. On 24 July 1944, the Polish Government-in-exile in London passed full responsibility for any rising to the civilian underground government and AK command inside Poland. One week later the Rising erupted. No doubt there was a certain amount of 'pique' involved in the British reaction to General Sosnkowski's demands for instant support. But one week's notice to reallocate Allied aircraft from their main task of bombing the heart out of German industry to bombing Warsaw, Kraków and Łódź and providing relief flights to Poland, was an impossible task.[3] Nonetheless, the Allies knew that a rising was probable, yet did not actively discourage the AK from taking such action. In fact, the Allied Joint Chiefs of Staff had nearly seven months, from the first Red Army crossing into Polish territory in January 1944, to gestate a strategy for dealing with the occupation of Warsaw.[4] One reason for this British inactivity was that the AK fulfilled a useful role in keeping the Germans occupied, pending the opening of a new Western Front in June 1944. But once the

Soviets had taken on that role, the AK became largely superfluous to Allied planners. The fact that the Allies felt they could not afford to goad Stalin by supporting an organisation he wished to crush, further sealed the fate of the Polish underground.

Sue Ryder, who worked so closely with the Poles and who was to do tremendous relief work in the country after the war, recalled that 'the Poles always said, 'it was right to do it', whether they were going to lose or not – it just had to be done.' This logic was never really understood in the British Foreign Office or in elements of the Air Ministry, who continued to exercise stifling bureaucracy as a smokescreen for doing the minimum. Such Polish 'chutzpah' was certainly evident in the motives of the Jewish rising in the Warsaw Ghetto, the previous year. Then, the odds for the Jews had been hopeless, but 'something' had to be done. In the same way, in 1944, Poland felt alone and bereft of allies who could actually achieve anything. After nearly five years of creating an underground state and army, it would have taken extremely tough resolve to watch it being dismantled without a fight. As their candle flickered and a Soviet hand hovered to finally snuff it out, Polish spirit could never allow its flame to die. Even though some Poles were against the Rising, either on the grounds of the expected high casualties or merely because of self-preservation, large numbers of the civilian population chose to remain in the city. They did so, not necessarily because they were trapped. They stayed to maintain morale and support their underground army, and they suffered appalling hardship. That same unity of Polish spirit rose and was crushed by the successive post-war communist leaders, Bierut, Gomółka and Gierek. But in the late 1970s and early 1980s, the population started to take the initiative, buoyed and inspired by the election of a Polish Pope, as well as the creation of a single national trade union, 'Solidarity'. The momentum through the 1980s was unstoppable. The Soviet leader, Mikhail Gorbachev was no longer prepared to support an ailing Soviet Empire and the creaking Polish Government under General Jaruzelski collapsed in 1989. The crowned white eagle finally re-appeared and free elections brought to power a democratic government. Independence was won – this time without the terrible human cost.

The events in Poland during the Second World War, and particularly the climatic year of 1944, continue to torment, as well as intrigue the modern generation. Large numbers of books (largely in the Polish language) are published every year, examining the Warsaw

Rising, the Holocaust and other aspects of the German and Soviet occupation of Polish soil. Polish cinema continues to scrutinize the reaction of its population to this oppression, while modern Polish music can still evoke the anguish and despair of the period.[5] The modern Polish composer, Henryk Górecki drew much of the inspiration for his haunting, but sublime Third Symphony, the 'Symphony of Sorrowful Songs' (*Symfonia Pieśń Żałosnych*) from an event in 1944; an eighteen-year-old Polish girl, Helena Wanda Błazusiakówna, from the composer's home town of Szczawnika, was imprisoned by the Gestapo in their jail in Zakopane. She scratched a prayer, 'No mother, do not weep', onto the wall of her cell.[6] Decades later, the composer came across Helena's words, which seemed to epitomise his people's stoicism when their country was truly 'alone'. It is for this bravery, rather than their suffering, that the Polish people and their resistance deserve to be revered.

---

[1] D.A. Lande, *Resistance: Occupied Europe and its Defiance of Hitler* (MBI, London 2000).

[2] Cynk, op. cit., Appendix 24, p. 652.

[3] SOE Memorandum on 'General Rising by the Polish Secret Army', 29 July 1944, HS 4/156, NA.

[4] Professor Norman Davies, 'Britain and the Warsaw Rising'.

[5] *Ashes and Diamonds* and *Kanal*, both directed by Andrzej Wajda, are notable films in the genre.

[6] Górecki's 'Third Symphony' comprises three movements, each derived from a separate source: Movement no. 1 uses a 15th Century lamentation of the Holy Cross Monastery at Łysa Gora; No. 2 uses Helena's prayer; No. 3 uses a folk song from Upper Silesia, describing a mother's loss of her son in combat.

Appendix

Equivalent Military Ranks

British Army	Wehrmacht	Waffen-SS	Soviet Army
Field Marshal	Generalfeldmarschall	SS–Reichsführer	Marshal
General	Generaloberst	SS–Obergruppenführer	General Armiyi
Lieutenant-General	General der Infanterie	SS–Obergruppenführer	General Polkovnik
Major-General	Generalleutnant	SS–Gruppenführer	General Leytenant
Brigadier	Generalmajor	SS–Brigadeführer	General Major
Colonel	Oberst	SS–Standartenführer	Polkovnik
Lieutenant-Colonel	Oberstleutnant	SS–Obersturmbann-führer	Podpolkovnik
Major	Major	SS–Sturmbannführer	Major
Captain	Hauptmann	SS–Hauptsturmführer	Kapetan
Lieutenant	Oberleutnant	SS–Obersturmführer	Starshiy Leytenant
Second-Lieutenant	Leutnant	SS–Untersturmführer	Mladshiy Leytenant
Sergeant	Feldwebel	SS–Oberscharführer	Serzhant
Corporal	Unteroffizier	SS–Unterscharführer	Mladshiy Serzhant
Private	Grenadier	SS–Mann	Krasnoarmeyets

Glossary of Terms and Abbreviations

Abwehr	German Military Intelligence
AK	*Armia Krajowa* (Polish Home Army)
AMSSO	Air Ministry Special Signals Office
Bureau II	2nd Bureau of Polish General Staff dealing with Intelligence (*Oddział* II)
Capo	Overseer in concentration camp (often a German criminal)
CAS	Chief of the Air Staff
C–in–C	Commander–in–Chief
CCS	Combined Chiefs of Staff
Einsatzgruppen	'Mission Groups' (SS paramilitary extermination squads)
EU/P	SOE Section – Poles abroad
FANY	First Aid Nursing Yeomanry
Gauleiter	Nazi paramilitary rank. Regional Nazi Party leader
Gestapo	*Geheime Staatspolizei* (Secret State Police)
Delegatura	Government of the Polish Secret State (based on Polish soil)
Landser	German soldier, usually of low rank
LWP	*Ludowe Wojsko Polskie* (Polish People's Army – communist Polish Army who fought under the Red Army)
MAAF	Mediterranean Allied Air Forces
MEW	Ministry for Economic Warfare
MI5	Secret Service
MI (R)	Military Intelligence (Research)

MI9	Military Intelligence Section 9 – Escape and Evasion
NATO	North Atlantic Treaty Organisation
NIE	*Niepodległość* ('Independence' movement)
NKVD	*Narodnyi Kommissariat Vnutrennikh Del* – Soviet Security/ intelligence organisation
NSZ	*Narodowe Siły Zbrojne* (Polish National Armed Forces – Fascist resistance organisation
OKH	*Oberkommando des Heeres* (German Army High Command)
OKW	*Oberkommando der Wehrmacht* (Wehrmacht High Command)
OKL	*Oberkommando der Luftwaffe* (German Air Force High Command)
OSS	Office of Strategic Services
PIAT	Projector, Infantry, Anti-Tank (British anti-tank weapon)
PGS	Polish General Staff
POW	Prisoner of War
PWE	Political Warfare Executive
RAAF	Royal Australian Air Force
RCAF	Royal Canadian Air Force
RONA	*Russkaya Osvoboditelnaya Narodnaya Armiya* (Russian Liberation People's Army – Soviet Union ethnic groups fighting for Germany)
SAAF	South African Air Force
SD	*Sicherheitsdienst* (German security police)
SHAEF	Supreme Headquarters Allied Expeditionary Force
SIS	Secret Intelligence Service (MI6)
SOE	Special Operations Executive
SOM	Special Operations Mediterranean
SS	*Schutzstaffel* (literally 'protective shield' – Nazi paramilitary organisation)
Stavka	Soviet Supreme Army Headquarters
Ultra	Code-name for intelligence unit which distributed 'Enigma' deciphered messages
USAAF	United States Army Air Force
V-1	*Vergeltungswaffe* I (flying bomb)
V-2	*Vergeltungswaffe* II (rocket)
Waffen-SS	Armed SS formation

WiN	*Wolność i Niepodległość* ('Freedom and Independence' movement)
WO	Wireless Operator
ZWZ	*Zwiazek Walki Zbrojnej* (Polish Association for Armed Struggle – the forerunner of the AK)

Names

Villages, towns and cities in Eastern Europe are to be seen on maps with various spellings, according to the dominating power at the time. So, the Polish city of Lwów, was previously known as Lemberg (under Austria-Hungary), and latterly as Lvov (Soviet Union). Although the modern Ukrainian city today is styled Lviv, the author has maintained Polish usage throughout the text and maps.

Military Formations

Soviet: The largest formation was the 'Front'. It consisted of 5–9 all arms armies, 1–3 tank armies, 1–2 air armies, 2–5 mechanized corps, 1–2 cavalry corps, together with artillery and support units. In all, a 'Front' could muster over ¾ million men. The Red Army used over ten such vast formations in its 1944 summer offensives.

German: The highest formation was the 'Army Group', which was roughly equivalent to the Soviet 'Front'. In June 1944, Army Group Centre, which faced the Soviet 'Bagration' offensive, comprised five panzer, mechanised or infantry armies. These were further broken down into corps and then divisions. An Army Group could thus contain nearly ½ million men.

Bibliography

UNPUBLISHED SOURCES

National Archives Kew, London (NA)
AIR 8/19/20/23/34/37/40/51 series: Records created or inherited by the Air Ministry, including air drops to Poland; SOE assistance; V weapons; Slessor correspondence; Blizna reports.
CAB 65/79/121 series: Records of the Cabinet Office.
HS 4/6/7/8 series: Records created or inherited by the Special Operations Executive, including Soviet relations; air drops to Poland; Polish GHQ; SOE and the Warsaw Rising; 'Wildhorn' operations; SOE warfare courses; John Ward; V Weapons. The SOE archive is confused and incomplete. Extensive 'weeding' was carried out by inexperienced staff in 1945 and it is believed that a fire in early 1946 destroyed large quantities of material from the Belgian and Polish sections of SOE. It is estimated that the files available today represent only 15% of the original resource.
FO 371 series: Records created or inherited by the Foreign Office, including Eden's relationship with the Poles; air support for AK; Jewish couriers; the 1945 Moscow trial of Polish underground leaders.
K 4, KV2, KV3 series: Records created or inherited by the Security Service (MI5), including German penetration of SOE; Waffen-SS officers; Sikorski crash investigation.
PREM 3 series: Records of the Prime Minister's Office, including Britain's failure to support the Warsaw Rising.

WO 219/229/311 series: Records created or inherited by the War Office, including Operations 'Crossbow' and 'Big Ben'; Polish resistance in 1944.

Liddell Hart Centre for Military Archives, King's College, London. (LHCMA)
The Cold War Television Documentary Archive.
OSS/London: Special Operations Branch and Secret Intelligence Branch War Diaries, GB99 MF 204-211.
Liddell Hart Papers; Hitler's attitude towards Poland, 11/1939/80-83; Newspaper cuttings relating to Soviet capture of Warsaw, 11/1940/69; also Liddell Hart records of interrogations of senior German commanders, LH/15/15/149; also Chester Wilmot's records of interrogations, LH 15/15/150.
General Lord Ismay Papers.
The Trial of German Major War Criminals: Proceedings of the International Military Tribunal Sitting at Nuremburg, Germany, Part 12, 16 April 1946–1 May 1946 (HMSO, London 1947).

Imperial War Museum, Sound Archive, London (IWM)
Oral Testimonies of Dennis Avey: ref 22065 Tauber Biber: ref: 17514 Stephen Dale: ref 14582 Leon Greenman: ref 9274 Kitty Hart-Moxon: ref 16632 Sue Ryder: ref 10057.

University of Birmingham, Special Collections (UB)
Lord Avon (Anthony Eden) Papers.
Neville Chamberlain Papers.

United States Holocaust Memoria l Museum, Washington (USHMM)
Online resource and photographic archive.

Polish Underground Movement Study Trust, Ealing, London. (PUMST)
Polish VI Bureau Papers.
Lieutenant-Colonel 'Mirosław' Stefan Musiałek-Lowicki Papers (relating to Operation 'Wildhorn III').

The Polish Institute and Sikorski Museum, Kensington, London. (PISM)
Papers relating to the Polish Government-in-exile.
Papers relating to the German invasion of Poland, 1939. Papers relating to the Polish II Bureau.

Muzeum Armii Krajowej (Home Army Museum) Kraków (HAM)
Tadeusz Pelczynski, (M. & A.C. Warburton, trans.) *The Polish Home Army and*

the *Warsaw Rising* (published by the museum).
Photographic archive.

Muzeum Powstania Warszawskiego (Warsaw Uprising Museum), Warsaw.
Photographic archive.

Personal Testimonies
Brian Bishop
Walter Davis
Mieczysław Juny
Bolesław Majewski
Bill Steed
Colonel Mieczysław Wałęga
Adela Wałęga
Adam Wykrota
Hanna Zbirohowska-Kościa (née Czarnocka)

PUBLISHED SOURCES

Journals
After the Battle (Battle of Britain International Ltd., London).
The Army Quarterly & Defence Journal (T.D. Bridge, Tavistock).
Blackwood's Magazine (William Blackwood & Son, Edinburgh).
Contemporary European History (Cambridge University Press, Cambridge).
Hansard Parliamentary Debates (HMSO, London).
The *Historical Journal* (Cambridge University Press, Cambridge).
Intelligence and National Security (Frank Cass, London).
Journal of Contemporary History (Sage Publications, London).
The *Journal of Military History* (Society for Military History, Lexington, US).
The *Journal of Slavic Military Studies* (Routledge, London).
Life Magazine (Time-Life Inc., New York).
Military Affairs (Society for Military History, Lexington, US).
Polish Fortnightly Review (Polish Ministry of Information, London).
RUSI Journal (Royal United Services Institute, London).
Time Magazine (Time Inc., New York).

Official Histories
Armia Krajowa w Dokumentach 1939–1945, by Studium Polski Podziemnej.
    (6 Vols). (Studium Polski Podziemnej, London 1970–1977).
British Foreign Policy in the Second World War, by Sir Ernest Llewellyn

Woodward (HMSO, London 1962).

British Intelligence in the Second World War (5 Vols.) edited by F. Hinsley (HMSO, London 1979–1990).

Destiny Can Wait: The Polish Air Force in the Second World War, by the Polish Air Force Association (William Heinnemann, London 1949).

Germany and the Second World War, Volume VI: The Global War: Widening of the Conflict into a World War and the shift of the Initiative 1941–1943, by Horst Boog, Werner Rahn, Richard Stumpf, Bernard Wegner; translated by Ewald Osers, John Brownjohn et al. (The Clarendon Press, Oxford 2001).

Germany and the Second World War, Volume VII: The Strategic Air War in Europe and the War in the West and East Asia 1943–1944/5, by Horst Boog, Herhard Krebs, Detlef Vogel; translated by Derry Cook-Radmore (The Clarendon Press, Oxford 2006).

The Polish Air Force at War: The Official History Vol. 2, 1943–1945, by Jerzy B. Cynk (Schiffer Military History, Atglen, US 1998).

The Royal Air Force 1939–1945, Vol. III: The Fight is Won, by Hilary St George Saunders (HMSO, London 1954).

The Strategic Air Offensive Against Germany, 1939–1945, Volumes I, II, III & IV, by Sir Charles Webster and Noble Frankland (HMSO, London 1961).

Printed Books

Anders, Lt.-General W., *An Army in Exile: The Story of the Second Polish Corps* (Macmillan, London 1949).

_____*Hitler's Defeat in Russia* (Henry Regnery, Chicago US 1953).

Ascherson, Neal, *The Struggles for Poland* (Michael Joseph, London 1987).

Bałuk, Stefan, *Poles on the Frontlines of World War II 1939-1945* (Books International, Warsaw 1995).

Baker, David, *The Rocket: The History and Development of Rocket & Missile Technology* (New Cavendish Books, London 1978).

Barker, Elisabeth, *Churchill and Eden at War* (Macmillan, London 1978).

Bauman, Janina, *Winter in the Morning: A Young Girl's Life in the Warsaw Ghetto and Beyond 1939–1945* (Virago, London 1986).

Beesly, Patrick, *Very Special Intelligence: The Story of the Admiralty's Operational Intelligence Centre 1939-1945* (Hamish Hamilton, London 1977).

Beevor, Anthony, & Luba Vinogtadova (Eds, & trans.), *A Writer at War: Vasily Grossman with the Red Army 1941-1945* (The Harvill Press, London 2005).

Bell, P.M.H., *John Bull and the Bear* (Edward Arnold, London 1990).

Bellamy, Chris, *Absolute War: Soviet Russia in the Second World War* (Macmillan, London 2007).

Bines, Jeffrey, *Operation Freston* (Privately printed, Saffron Waldon 1999).

Binney, Marcus, *Secret War Heroes: Men of the Special Operations Executive* (Hodder & Stoughton, London 2005).

Bonn, Keith E, (Ed.), *Slaughterhouse: The Handbook of the Eastern Front* (Aberjona Press, Bedford US 2005).

Bór-Komorowski, T., *The Secret Army* (Victor Gollancz, London 1950).

Bowman, Martin, *Combat Legend: B-24 Liberator* (Airlife, Shrewsbury 2003).

Breitman, Richard, *Official Secrets: What the Nazis Planned, What the British and Americans Knew* (Allen Lane, London 1999).

Brown, Alan, *Airmen in Exile: The Allied Air Forces in the Second World War* (Sutton Publishing, Stroud 2000).

Cabell, Craig, & Graham Thomas, *Operation Big Ben: The Anti-V2 Spitfire Missions 1944–1945* (Spellmount, Staplehurst 2004).

Charmley, John, *Churchill's Grand Alliance: The Anglo-American Special Relationship 1940–57* (Hodder & Stoughton, London 1995).

Chiari, B., *Alltag hinter der Front. Besetzung Kollaboration und Widerstand in Weissrussland 1941–1944.* Schriften des Bundesarchivs (Droste, Düsseldorf 1998).

Churchill, Winston S., *The Second World War: Volume V. Closing the Ring* (Cassell, London 1952).

Ciechanowski, Jan, (Ed.), *Polsko-Brytyjska współpraca wywiadowcz podczas II wojny światowej, tom II: Wybór Dokumentów / Intelligence Co-operation Between Poland and Great Britain during World War II, Volume II: Documents* (Naczelna Dyrekcja Archiwów Państwowych – Wydział Wydawnictw, Warsaw 2005)

_____ *The Warsaw Uprising of 1944* (Cambridge University Press, Cambridge 1974)

Clark, Alan, *Barbarossa: The Russian-German Conflict 1941–45* (Hutchinson, London 1965).

Collier, Basil, *The Defence of the United Kingdom* (Imperial War Museum, London 1957).

Conversino, Mark, J., *Fighting with the Soviets: The Failure of Operation Frantic 1944–1945* (University Press of Kansas, Lawrence US, 1997).

Cookridge, E.H., *Inside SOE: The Story of Special Operations in Western Europe 1940–45* (Arthur Barker, London 1966).

Cooksley, Peter, *Flying Bomb* (Robert Hale, London 1979).

Cooper, Mathew, *The German Army 1933–1945: Its Political and Military Failure* (Macdonald and Jane's, London 1978).

Crick, Bernard, *George Orwell: A Life* (Secker & Warburg, London 1981).

Curp, David, *A Clean Sweep? The Politics of Ethnic Cleansing in Western Poland 1945–1960* (Rochester University Press, New York 2006).

Davies, Norman, *White Eagle, Red Star: The Polish-Soviet War 1919–20 and 'the* miracle on the Vistula' (Random House, London 2004).

_____*Rising '44: The Battle for Warsaw* (Macmillan, London 2003).

_____*God's Playground: A History of Poland*, 2 Volumes (Clarendon Press, Oxford 2005).

Davies-Scourfield, Gris, *In Presence of My Foes: Travels and Travails of a POW from Calais to Colditz via the Polish Underground* (Pen & Sword, Barnsley, 2004).

Denniston, Robin, *Thirty Secret Years: AG Denniston's Work in Signals Intelligence 1914–1944* (Polperro Heritage Press, Clifton-upon-Teme 2007).

Dilks, David, (Ed.), *The Diaries of Sir Alexander Cadogan OM, 1938–1945* (Cassell, London 1971).

Doolittle, General James, (with Carroll Glines) *I Could Never Be So Lucky Again: An Autobiography* (Bantam Books, 1991).

Drecki, Zbigniew, *Freedom and Justice: Spring from the Ashes of Auschwitz* (Privately printed, Exmouth 2005).

Dungan, T.D., *V-2: A Combat History of the First Ballistic Missile* (Westholme, Yardley US 2005).

Dutton, David, *Anthony Eden: A Life and Reputation* (Hodder Headline, London 1995).

Dziewanowski, M.K., *The Communist Party of Poland: An Outline of History* (Harvard University Press, Cambridge US 1976).

Elkins, Michael, *Forged in Fury* (Piatkus, Loughton 1981).

Engel, David, *Facing a Holocaust: The Polish Government-in-Exile and the Jews, 1943–1945* (University of North Carolina Press, Chapel Hill US).

Erickson, John, *The Road to Berlin* (Weidenfeld & Nicolson, London 1983).

_____*The Soviet Army, 1939–1980: A Guide to Sources in English* (ABC Clio, Santa Barbara US 1982).

Fenby, Jonathan, *Alliance: The Inside Story of How Roosevelt, Stalin and Churchill Won One War and Began Another* (Simon & Schuster, London 2006).

Fest, Joachim, Ewald Osers (trans.), *Speer: The Final Verdict* (Phoenix Press, London 2002).

Foot, M.R.D., *SOE: Special Operations Executive 1940–1946* (Pimlico, London 1999).

_____*Six Faces of Courage: Secret Agents Against Nazi Tyranny* (Leo Cooper, Barnsley 2003).

_____& J.M. Langley, *MI9: Escape and Evasion 1939–1945* (BCA, London 1979).

Friedländer, Saul, *The Years of Extermination: Nazi Germany and the Jews, 1939–1945* (HarperCollins, London 2007).

Fritz, Stephen G., *Frontsoldaten: The German Soldier in World War II* (University Press of Kentucky, Lexington US 1997).

Garliński, Józef, Paul Stevenson (trans.), *Poland, SOE and the Allies* (George Allen and Unwin, London 1969).

_____*Fighting Auschwitz: The Resistance Movement in the Concentration Camp* (Fontana, London 1976).

_____*Hitler's Last Weapons: The Underground War Against the V1 and V2* (Magnum Books, London 1979).

_____*Intercept: The Enigma War* (Magnum Books, London 1981).

Garnet, David, *The Secret History of PWE: The Political Warfare Executive 1939-1945* (St Ermin's Press, London 2002).

Gilbert, G.M., *Nuremberg Diary* (Eyre & Spottiswoode, London 1948).

Gilbert, Martin, *Auschwitz and the Allies* (Michael Joseph, London 1981).

Gladwyn, Lord, *The Memoirs of Lord Gladwyn* (Weidenfeld & Nicolson, London 1972).

Glantz, David, *Colossus Reborn: The Red Army at War 1941–1943* (University Press of Kansas, Kansas US 2005).

_____*When Titans Clashed: How the Red Army Stopped Hitler* (Birlinn, Edinburgh 2000).

Green, William, *Warplanes of the Third Reich* (Macdonald & Co., London 1970).

Gross, J.T., *Revolution from Abroad: The Soviet Conquest of Western Ukraine and Western Belorussia* (Princeton University Press, Princeton US 2002).

Grynberg, Michał, (Ed.), *Worlds to Outlive Us: Eyewitness Accounts from the Warsaw Ghetto* (Granta Books, London 2003).

Hanson, Joanna, *The Civilian Population and the Warsaw Uprising of 1944* (Cambridge University Press, Cambridge 1982).

Hastings, Max, *Armageddon: The Battle for Germany 1944–45* (Macmillan, London 2004).

Harvey, John, (Ed.), *The War Diaries of Oliver Harvey* (Collins, London 1978).

Haupt, Werner, *Army Group Center: The Wehrmacht in Russia 1941–45* (Schiffer Military History, Atgen, PA 1997).

Howard, Sir Michael, *The Mediterranean Strategy in the Second World War* (Greenhill Books, London 1993).

Howarth, Patrick, *Undercover: The Men and Women of the SOE* (Routledge & Kegan Paul, London 1980).

_____*Intelligence Chief Extraordinary: The Life of the Ninth Duke of Portland* (The Bodley Head, London 1986).

Hull, Isabel, *Absolute Destruction: Military Culture and the Practices of War in Imperial Germany* (Cornell University Press, 2006).

Iranek-Osmecki, George (trans.), *The Unseen and Silent: Adventures from the Underground Movement Narrated by Paratroops of the Polish Home Army* (Sheed and Ward, London 1954).

Ismay, General Lord, *The Memoirs of General the Lord Ismay* (Heinemann,

London 1960).

Jeffery, Ron, *Red Runs the Vistula* (Nevron Associates, Peterborough 1989).

Jenkins, Roy, *Gallery of Twentieth Century Portraits and Oxford Papers* (David & Charles, Newton Abbot 1988).

Jones, R.V., *Most Secret War: British Scientific Intelligence 1939–1945* (Hamish Hamilton 1978).

Kacewicz, George, *Great Britain, the Soviet Union and the Polish Government in Exile (1939–1945)* (Martinus Nijhoff, The Hague 1979).

Kemp, Peter, *No Colours or Crest* (Cassell, London 1958).

_____*The Thorns of Memory* (Sinclair-Stevenson, London 1990).

Korboński, Stefan, *Fighting Warsaw: The Story of the Polish Underground State 1939–1945* (Hippocrene Books, New York 2004).

Koschorrek, Günter, *Blood Red Snow: The Memoirs of a German Soldier on the Eastern Front* (Greenhill Books, London 2002).

Lake, Jon, *Halifax Squadrons of World War 2* (Osprey, Oxford 1999).

Lanckorońska, Karolina, *Those Who Trespass Against Us* (Pimlico, London 2005).

Lande, D., *Resistance! Occupied Europe and its Defiance of Hitler* (MBI, London 2000).

Lebert, Stephen, *My Father's Keeper* (Little, Brown and Co., London 2001).

Lewin, Ronald, *Ultra Goes to War: The Secret Story* (Arrow Books, London 1980).

Lomas, Harry, *One Wing High: Halifax Bomber – the Navigator's Story* (Airlife, Shrewsbury 1995).

Lucas, James, *War on the Eastern Front: The German Soldier in Russia 1941–1945* (Greenhill Books, London 1998).

Lukas, Richard C., *Eagles East: The Army Air Forces and the Soviet Union 1941–1945* (Florida State University Press, Tallahasse 1970).

_____*Forgotten Holocaust: The Poles Under German Occupation 1939–1944* (Hippocrene Books, New York 2005).

Lukowski, Jerzy, and Hubert Zawadzki, *A Concise History of Poland* (Cambridge University Press, Cambridge 2006).

Mackenzie, William, *The Secret History of SOE: Special Operations Executive 1940–1945* (St Ermin's Press, London 2002).

MacLean, French, *The Cruel Hunters. SS-Sonderkommando Dirlewanger: Hitler's Most Notorious Anti-Partisan Unit* (Schiffer Military History, Atglen US 1998).

Marks, Leo, *Between Silk and Cyanide* (HarperCollins, London 1998).

Mawdsley, Evan, *Thunder in the East: The Nazi-Soviet War 1941–1945* (Hodder Arnold, London 2005).

Merrick, Kenneth, *Flights of the Forgotten: Special Duties Operations in World*

War Two (Weidenfeld Military, London 1989).

Merridale, Catherine, *Ivan's War* (Faber & Faber, London 2005).

Michaelis, Rolf, *Die Grenadier Division der Waffen-SS: Part 1* (Michaelis, Erlangen 1995).

Mikolajczyk, Stanisław, *The Rape of Poland: Pattern of Soviet Aggression* (Greenwood Press, Westport US 1948).

Miller, Russell, *Behind the Lines: The Oral History of Special Operations in World War II* (Secker & Warburg, London 2002).

Ministry of Foreign Affairs of the USSR (AA Gromyko et al), *Correspondence Between the Chairman of the Council of Ministers of the USSR and the Presidents of the USA and the Prime Ministers of Great Britain During the Great Patriotic War of 1941–1945* (Capricorn Books, New York 1965).

Müller, Rolf-Dieter, & Gerd Ueberschär, *Hitler's War in the East: A Critical Assessment* (Berghahn Books, New York 2002).

Munoz, Antonio, *The Kaminski Brigade: A History, 1941–1945* (Europa Books, New York 2003).

Newman, Bernard, *They Saved London* (Werner Laurie, London 1989).

Ney-Krwawicz, Marek, Krzysztof Bożejewicz (Ed.), Antoni Bohdanowicz (trans.) *The Polish Home Army 1939–1945* (Polish Underground Movement Study Trust, London 2001).

Nicolson, Nigel, (Ed.), Harold Nicolson: *Diaries and Letters 1939–1945* (Collins, London 1967).

Ordway, Frederick, and Mitchell Sharpe, *The Rocket Team* (Heinemann, London 1979).

Overy, Richard, *Russia's War* (Allen Lane, London 1998).

Pawley, Margaret, *In Obedience to Instructions: FANY with the SOE in the Mediterranean* (Leo Cooper, Barnsley 1999).

Peszke, Michael, *The Polish Underground Army, the Western Allies and the Failure of Strategic Unity in World War II* (McFarland & Co., Jefferson, North Carolina, 2004).

Pimlott, Ben, (Ed.), *The Second World War Diary of Hugh Dalton 1940–45* (Jonathan Cape, London 1986).

Prażmowska, Anita, *Britain and Poland 1939–1943: The Betrayed Ally* (Cambridge University Press, Cambridge 1995).

Rapier, Brian, *Halifax at War* (Ian Allen, London 1987).

Raus, Erhard, (Steven Newton, trans.), *Panzer Operations: The Eastern Front Memoir of General Raus, 1941–1945* (Da Capo Press, Cambridge US 2005).

Reese, Willy Peter, Stefan Schmitz (Ed.), Michael Hofmann (trans.) *A Stranger to Myself: The Inhumanity of War. Russia, 1941–1944* (Farrar, Straus and Giroux, New York 2005).

Reitlinger, Gerald, *The SS: Alibi of a Nation 1922–1945* (Heinemann, London 1956).

Rees, Laurence, *Auschwitz: The Nazis and the 'Final Solution'* (BBC Books, London 2005).

Reynolds, David, *In Command of History: Churchill Fighting and Writing the Second World War* (Allen Lane, London 2004).

Roberts, Andrew, *Hitler & Churchill: Secrets of Leadership* (Weidenfeld & Nicolson, London 2003).

Rokossovsky, K., *A Soldier's Duty* (Progress Publishers, Moscow 1970).

Rose, Sonya, O., *Which People's War? National Identity and Citizenship in Wartime Britain* (Oxford University Press, Oxford 2003).

Ross, Graham, (Ed.), *The Foreign Office and the Kremlin: British Documents on Anglo-Soviet Relations 1941–45* (Cambridge University Press, Cambridge 1984).

Rozek, Edward, *Wartime Diplomacy: A Pattern in Poland* (John Wiley & Sons, Boulder US 1958).

Ryder, Sue, *Child of My Love* (The Harvill Press, London 1997).

Rygor Słowikowski, Major-General M.Z., *In the Secret Service: The Lighting of the Torch* (Windrush Press, London 1988).

Sajer, Guy, *The Forgotten Soldier: War on the Russian Front. A True Story* (Cassell, London 1999).

Sanford, George, *Katyn and the Soviet Massacre of 1940: Truth, Justice and Memory* (Routledge, London 2005).

Seaman, Mark, (Ed.), *Special Operations Executive: A New Instrument of War* (Routledge, London 2006).

Seaton, Albert, *The Russo-German War 1941–45* (Arthur Barker, London 1971).

Shirer, William, *Berlin Diary: The Journal of a Foreign Correspondent* (Hamish Hamilton, London 1941)

_____*The Rise and Fall of the Third Reich* (Secker & Warburg, London 1960).

Siemaszko, Z.S., *Działalność Generała Tatara* (London 1999).

Slessor, Sir John, *The Central Blue: Recollections and Reflections* (Cassell, London 1956).

Smith, Myron, (Intro., John Erickson), *The Soviet Army, 1939–1980: A Guide to Sources in English* (ABC Clio, Santa Barbara, Calif., 1982).

Smith, Lyn, *Forgotten Voices of the Holocaust* (Ebury Press, London 2006).

Stafford, David, *Britain and European Resistance 1940–1945* (Macmillan, London 1980).

_____*Secret Agent: The True Story of the Special Operations Executive* (BBC Worldwide, London 2000).

Steinberg, Paul, *Speak You Also* (Allen Lane, London 2001).

Stirling, Tessa, and Daria Nałęcz and Tadeusz Dubicki (Eds.), *Intelligence Co-*

operation between Poland and Great Britain During World War II, Volume 1: The Report of the Anglo-Polish Historical Committee (Valentine Mitchell, London 2005).

Strik-Feldt, Wilfried, (David Footman, trans.), *Against Stalin and Hitler 1941– 1945* (Macmillan, London 1970).

Sweet-Escott, Bickham, *Baker Street Irregular* (Methuen, London 1965).

Świebocki, Henryk (Ed.), *London Has Been Informed: Reports by Auschwitz Escapees* (The Auschwitz-Birkenau State Museum, Oświęcim 2002).

Sword, Keith, (Ed.), *Sikorski: Soldier and Statesman* (Orbis Books, London 1990).

Szpilman, Władyław, (Anthea Bell, trans.), *The Pianist: The Extraordinary Story of One Man's Survival in Warsaw, 1939–45* (Victor Gollancz, London 1999).

Tec, Nechama, *When Light Pierced the Darkness* (Oxford University Press, New York 1986).

Tucholski, J., *Cichociemni* (Instytut Wydawniczy Pax, Warsaw 1984).

Valentine, Ian, *Station 43: Audley End House and SOE's Polish Section* (Sutton, Stroud 2004).

Verrier, Anthony, *Through the Looking Glass: British Foreign Policy in an Age of Illusions* (WW Norton, New York 1983).

Waters, David, *The History of No. 148 Squadron* (privately printed 1998).

Watt, Richard, *Bitter Glory: Poland and its Fate 1918–1939* (Hippocrene Books, New York 1998).

Weal, John, *Bf 109D/E: Aces of the Blitzkrieg* (Osprey, Oxford 1996).

West, Nigel, *Secret War: The Story of SOE, Britain's Wartime Sabotage Organisation* (Hodder & Stoughton, London 1992).

Wiatr, Jerzy, *The Soldier and the Nation: The Role of the Military in Polish Politics 1918–1988* (Westview Press, Boulder US 1988).

Wilkinson, Peter, *Foreign Fields: The Story of an SOE Operative* (IB Taurus, London 1997).

_____ & Joan Astley, *Gubbins and SOE* (Leo Cooper, London 1993).

Williams, David, P, *Nachtjäger: Luftwaffe Night Fighter Units 1943–1945, Volume Two* (Ian Allan Publishing, Hersham 2005).

Williamson, Gordon, *World War II German Police Units* (Osprey, Oxford 2006).

Wilson, Field-Marshal Lord, *Eight Years Overseas 1939–1947* (Hutchinson & Co, London 1949).

Wojewódzki, Michał, *Akcja V-1, V-2* (Instytut Wydawniczy Pax, Warsaw 1970 and revised 1984).

Woltersdorf, Hans, *Gods of War: Memoir of a German Soldier* (Presidio, California 1990).

Wood, E. Thomas, and Stanisław Jankowski, *Karski: How One Man Tried to Stop the Holocaust* (John Wiley & Sons, New York 1994).

Zaloga, Steven, *The Polish Army 1939–45* (Osprey, Oxford 1982).

_____*Operation Bagration* (Osprey, Oxford 1996).

_____*V-2 Ballistic Missile 1942–52* (Osprey, Oxford 2003).

Zamoyski, Adam, *The Polish Way: A Thousand-Year History of the Poles and Their Culture* (Hippocrene Books, New York 1987).

Zawodny, J.K., *Nothing but Honour: the Story of the Warsaw Uprising* (Macmillan, London 1978).

_____*The Forgotten Few: The Polish Air Force in World War II* (Pen and Sword, Barnsley 1995).

Żenczykowski, Tadeusz, *Samotny bój Warszawy* (Spotkania, Paris 1985).

_____*General Grot: U Kresu Walki* (Polonia, London 1983).

Ziemke, Earl, *Stalingrad to Berlin: The German Defeat in the East* (Center of Military History, US Army, Washington US 1968).

Zylberberg, Michael, *A Warsaw Diary 1939–1945* (Vallentine Mitchell, London 1969).

Index

Akins, Lieutenant Francis, 248
Albania, 79, 146, 164, 288
Allerton, Squadron Leader 'Jacko', 237
Allied Chiefs of Staff, 296–7
Anders, Gen. Władysław, 45, 225
Anzio, 176
Appleby, Flight Sergeant John, 104
Arciszewski, Tomasz, removal of Sosnkowski, 94; 'Wildhorn III', 102, 105–6, 108; appointed PM, 270, 272
Arnhem (see also Market Garden'), 247, 251
Atholl, Duchess of, 163
Babington-Smith, Constance, 23
Bach, Erich von dem, hosts Himmler, 115; appointment by Himmler, 209; Dirlewanger, 212; Rising surrender terms, 244–5; AK surrender, 253; fate, 290–1
Baer, Richard, 291
Bagramian, Army General Ivan, 183
Bagration, General Peter, 183
'Bagration', Operation, 172, 183–98
Balkans, 78–9, 81, 88, 146, 175, 256, 265
Banaczyk, Władysław, 266
'Barbarossa', Operation, 42–5, 115, 119, 174, 183, 193
Bari, 78, 154, 189, 215, 267, 273
BBC, 46, 146, 218, 254, 279
Beck, Józef, 29, 34–5
Beck, General Ludwig, 193
Belgium, 40–1, 95
Berezowski, Zygmunt, 90
Beria, Lavrenti, 39, 47
Berlin, 30, 104, 126, 172, 195, 225, 274, 279, 289, 291
Berling, General Zygmunt, background, 45; wartime, 184–5; post-war, 289
Bevin, Ernest, 284
Białystock, 49, 116, 123, 182
Bielany, 275
Bielski, Lieutenant-Colonel Romuld, 93
Bielsko, 132
Bierut, Bolesław, 213, 265, 284, 297
Bilderberg Group, 285, 287
'Birch Tree', Operations, 291
Bishop, Corporal Brian, 128–30, 241, 279
Błazusiakłówna, Helena, 298
Bletchley Park, 121
Blizna, 97–103, 226, 243–4, 267
Bór-Komorowski, General Tadeusz, 70; and Retinger, 93, 105; and Jewish reports, 122; and Rising, 198; AK strength, 204–5; and start of Rising, 207; criticised by SOE, 240; talks with von dem Bach, 245; and civilians, 249; orders surrender, 252; terms of surrender, 253–4; POW opinions of, 255; and Ward, 262; freed from prison, 284–5

Bottomley, Air Marshal Norman, 89, 228
Boughey, Major EPF, 189, 239
Boughey, Lieutenant-Colonel, 255
Boyle, Lieutenant-Colonel Patrick, 176
Brauchitsch, Generaloberst Walter von, 43
Braun, Emil, 74
Braun, Wernher von, 23, 292
Brindisi, 77–81, 88, 104, 155, 157, 175, 207–8, 227, 237
British Army:
Chiefs of Staff, 215, 219–20, 228, 239, 266–7; Eighth Army, 77; Queen's Own Royal West Kent Regt., 163, POWs, 218, 241–2
British Government:
War Cabinet, pre-war pacts, 29–30; talks with Stalin, 31; on invasion of Poland, 32; recognises Polish Govt.-in-Exile, 39; pro-Soviet, 46; at Tehran, 49; on requests to bomb Auschwitz, 136–8; on Poles in UK, 286–7; post-war relations with Soviets, 288–9; Foreign Office, lack of brief on Poland, 67; Jewish deaths reports, 122–5, 133, 136–8; Operation 'Storm', 166; passing intelligence to Soviets, 177; attitude to Rising, 225; Polish cyphers, 270; post-war and Holocaust, 286; Air Ministry, 22, 67, 81, 87–9, 122, 136–8, 145, 147, 216–7, 236, 243, 255, 263, 288, 297; Intelligence Services, MI(R), 34, 145, 151; 'Ultra', 99; receive German decodes, 121; MI9, 157; SIS, and poor contacts, 46; Sikorski death, 47; lack of Polish assets, 86; and Dutch SOE network, 89; V-2 rockets, 95, 97–8; talks with Chmielewski, 108; help from SOE, 145–6; relations with SOE, 146; and Polish II Bureau, 158; abandons contacts, 159; and Rising, 220; cyphers, 276; activates new agents, 284; and Ward 288; Political Warfare Executive (PWE), 166, 194
British Military Mission (1st), 34–5; (2nd), 266–8, 271–2, 278
British Press, reaction to Jewish reports, 139, 173; Soviet power, 178, 240
Breslau, 283
Brooke, General Alan, 149
Brooks, Pilot Officer H, 255
Bruce, Warrant Officer N, 164
Brześć, 183
Bug, River, 67, 72, 100, 182
Bulgaria, 257, 265
Burska, Dr, 197
Byelorussia, 28, 33, 115, 172, 179, 180–3, 190
Bzura, River, 27
Cameron, Flying Officer, 40
Carpathian Mountains, 42, 81, 182, 184, 273
'Case White', Operation, 25–6, 32–3
Cavendish-Bentinck, William, 124–5
Cazalet, Lieutenant-Colonel Victor, 47

Chamberlain, Neville, 21, 30, 32, 40
Chapman, Eddie, 104
Chciuk, Second-Lieutenant Tadeusz, 92, 102, 106, 108, 127
Chelm, 72, 185
Chernyakovsky, Army General Ivan, 183
Cherwell, Lord Frederick, 96, 104
Chmielewski, Jerzy, 102, 106, 108
Cichociemni (silent and unseen), 64–5, 153–5, 162–3, 256
Chiswick, 243
Chruściel, General Antoni, 197–8
Churchill, Winston S, on Teschen, 29; installed as PM, 40–1;death of Sikorski, 48; relation with Sosnkowski, 48; Tehran Conference, 48–9; depicted by Orwell, 49; offers Stalin bomber offensive, 87; meeting with Tatar, 91;V-2 and Stalin, 103; news of Jewish deaths, 121–2, 136; relations with Dalton, 148; and PWE, 166; flagging, 173; and War Cabinet, 173; and Lublin Poles, 213; out of country, 216; Rising, 227; attitude to Soviets, 251–2; bargains over Europe, 265; at Moscow Conference, 265–6; stops SOE schemes, 271; anti-Polish governments, 273
Cieliczko, Roman, 126
Colt-Williams, Captain R G, 152
Concentration Camps:
 Auschwitz system, origins, 116–7; guards, 125; aerial rec., 128, 137; Red Army approach, 241; prisoners escape, 279; war crimes, 291;
 Auschwitz I, 117, 118–9; receives Kocjan, 101; prisoner tally, 119; liberation, 286;
 Auschwitz II (Birkenau), 117–22; arrivals, 119–20; 'Canada', 120; escapes, 126, 264, 279; AK plans, 132–3; Hungarian Jews, 135, 242; summer 1944, 264; liberation, 286;
 Auschwitz III (Monowitz), 117, 128–9, 131, 241–2, 279; 'Capos', 119, 129–30, liberation 286;
 Other camps: Bergen-Belsen, 285, 292; Bełżec, 116, 123, 139; Buchenwald, 96; Chełmno, 116; Dachau, 117; Majdanek, 116, 123, 126, 138–9, 242, 244; Sachsenhausen, 70; Sobibór, 116, 126, 139;Treblinka, 116, 118, 123, 126, 139
Coward, Sergeant-Major Charles, 130–1
Culliford, Flight Lieutenant Stanley, 104–7
Curzon Line, 28, 34, 49, 72, 213, 240–1, 266
Czarnocka, Bohdan, 67–9
Czarnocka, Halina, 35, 36, 67–9, 196, 223, 285–6
Czarnocka, Hanna, 35–6, 67–9, 196, 206, 254, 285–6
Czechoslovakia, 29, 117, 147, 150
Częstochowa, 278
Dalton, Hugh, 21, 49, 145, 148, 252
Danzig, 32, 36, 87, 267
Davies-Scourfield, Gris, 76
Davis, Flight Sergeant Walter, 81, 157, 163–4
Dębica, 103, 226
Debrecen, 189
Denmark, 64, 67, 78, 263
Dirlewanger, SS Standartenführer Oscar, 210–11, 291
Dirschau, 27
Dneiper, River, 43, 172, 182–3
Domański , Jan, 93
Doolittle, General Jimmy, 249
Dornberger, General Walter, 23, 100, 292
Dorotycz-Malewicz, Lieutenant-Colonel Marion, 90, 207
Drohobycz, 189
Duch, General, 41
Dunderdale, Wilfred, 146, 158
Dunkirk, 41
Dvina, River, 192
E715 POW Camp, 128–131, 242, 279
Eaker, General Ira, 215–6
East Prussia, 26–7, 32, 173, 222, 274
Eden, Anthony (later Lord Avon), Curzon Line, 48–9; Soviet help, 78; meets Retinger, 108; meets Karski, 122; receives Jewish Agency, 135–6; orders air rec. over Auschwitz, 137; relations with SOE, 145; with Dalton 148; Katyn, 174; Polish cyphers, 175; approval of Soviets, 176–7; against liaison officers, 239, 271–2; Rising, 216–7; Moscow Conference, 265
Eichmann, Adolf, 138

Eisenhower, General Dwight, 219
'Enigma', 30–1
Estonia, 38, 182, 222
Fiderer, Maria, 257
Fieldorf, Colonel Emil, 74, 254, 284
Filipkowski, Colonel Władysław, 181
First Aid Nursing Yeomanry (FANY), 153–4
Fischer, Dr Ludwig, 196
Foggia, 78, 245
'Fortitude', Operation, 160
Framlingham, 248
Franczak, Pilot Officer Stanisław, 245
'Frantic', Operation, 189, 247–50, 289–90
France, pact with Poland, 30; on invasion of Poland, 32; with Polish GIE; Army operations, 41; Fall of France, 41; deports Jews, 138; Paris re-captured, 221; Resistance Army, 267
Frank, Hans, as Governor General, 37–8; installed in Kraców, 56; retaliations, 73–4; assassination attempt, 155; at Nuremberg, 290
Friedrichshafen, 96, 98
Frulov, Oberst, 210
Gano, Colonel Stanisław, 46
Galbraith, Sergeant-Major Donald, 268
Garby-Czerniawski, Roman, 160
Garliński, Józef, 69, 285
Gdynia, 267
German Aircraft:
 Feisler Storch, 105; Focke-Wulf FW190, 156, 248; JU87 Stuka, 26; Junkers JU88G, 156; Messerschmitt BF109, 26, 66, 156, 221, 248; Messerschmitt BF110G, 156; Nachtjäger, 156
German Armament Works (DAW), 125
German Armed Forces:
 Wehrmacht, early casualties, 36; during Barbarossa, 44; Wehrmacht brutality, 180; discipline, 188, 229; loss of weapons and uniform, 219; casualties in Rising, 236
 Army Groups:
 Army Group 'A', 279; Army Group Centre, 43, 115, 172, 182–5, 208; Army Group North, 26, 43, 192, 222; Army Group North Ukraine, 184, 225; Army Group South, 27, 43
 Armies:
 Third Army, 26; Eighth Army, 27; Ninth Army, 274; Tenth Army, 27; Fourteenth Army, 27; 4th Panzer Army, 184
 Corps:
 II SS Panzer Corps, 184
 Divisions:
 1st Parachute-Panzer Division Hermann Göring, 195,209, 222; 3rd SS Panzer Division Totenkopf, 209, 241; 5th SS Panzer Division Wiking, 209, 241; 19th Panzer Division, 195, 222, 241; Grossdeutschland Division, 190, 222; 17th Infantry Division, 221; 45th Volksgrenadier Division, 221; 73rd Infantry Division, 195, 245; 253rd Infantry Division, 180;'Vengeance' Division, 243
 Regiments:
 111th Azerbaijani Regiment, 209; Cossak Regiments, 209
 Other Units:
 Dirlewanger SS Penal Battalion, 209, 210–12, 226, 247; Einsatzgruppen, 44; SS Helferinen, 121; Kaminski Brigade, 181, 209–12, 226, 291; RONA, 210, 291; Volkssturm (Home Army), 253;
 Luftwaffe, 189, 222, 248; 3/JG 51 Squadron, 248
German Police:
 Gestapo (Geheimistaatspolizei), 37, 56, 59–62, 69–70, 72, 74–6, 93, 101, 134–5, 138, 146–7, 153–4, 192, 194, 226, 268, 291, 295, 298; organisation, 118; successes, 158–9; methods of arrest, 277
 Poznań Police Regt., 209
 SS Security Service (SD), 25, 118
German weapons, 88mm guns, 221; 122mm Artillery Gun, 210; Goliath Mine Tank, 221–2; Nebelwerfer, 187; Panzerfaust 30, 186; Panzershreck, 187; Panther Tank, 190–1, 209, 248; StuG III, 209; SU86 Assault Gun, 210; Tiger Tank, 190–1, 221, 248
Gertz, Wanda, 63

Gierek, Edward, 297
Gilbert, GM, 290
Gleiwitz, 25
Göbbels, Joseph, 47, 100, 127
Golz, SS Standartenführer, 213
Gomółka, Władysław, 297
Gorbachev, Mikhail, 297
Gordziałowski, Otto, 77
Göring, Hermann, 290
Gousev, FT., 225–6
Greece, 42, 146, 255, 265
Gregor, Captain CT, 152
Grossman, Leon, 131
Grossman, Vasily, 138
Groszkowski, Professor Janusz, 100
Gubbins, Lieutenant-Colonel Colin, 151, 177, 270; with
    Military Mission, 34; friend of Retinger, 92; early career,
    147; and Sikorski, 148; appointed Chief of SOE, 148;
    pressure from Sosnkowski, 149; meeting with Tatar, 165;
    SOE in Germany, 194; and Rising, 238–9; post-war, 287
Guderian, General Heinz, 193
Hacha, Emil, 29
Hahn, Dr Ludwig, 208
Haining, Jane, 135
Halder, General Franz, 27, 33, 43
Hankey, Robin, 32
Harpe, Generaloberst Josef, 184
Harriman, Averell, 173, 265
Harriman, Kathleen, 174
Harris, Air Chief Marshal Sir Arthur, 88, 236–7
Harrod, Flight-Lieutenant E, 90
Hart, Sergeant, 40
Hart-Moxon, Kitty, 120–1
Harvey, Oliver, 152, 177–8, 273
Hazell, Major Ronald, 147
Heidelager, (see also Blizna) 97, 108
Hesketh-Pritchard, Major Alfgar, 237
Heydrich, Reinhardt, 25, 74, 115
Himmler, Heinrich, relations with Frank, 37; V-Weapons, 96;
    meets von dem Bach, 115; expands Auschwitz, 117; secu-
    rity apparatus, 118; issues Warsaw decree, 196; and Rising,
    208; appoints von dem Bach, 209; and Dirlewanger, 211;
    orders demolition of gas chambers, 265
Himmler, Operation, 25
Hitler, Adolf, invasion of Poland, 21–3, 30, 32–3, 36, 127; 'Fall
    Weis', 26; strategy and tactics, 27, 43, 183, 191, 222; and
    domination of Europe, 29, 31; lebensraum, 37, 115; and
    Frank, 37; and Stalin, 38, 46; occupation of France and
    Low Countries, 40–1; Operation 'Barbarossa', 42–5;
    secret weapons, 94–6; Auschwitz, 117; Curzon Line, 173;
    July bomb plot, 192–5; and Zeitler, 193; Warsaw and the
    Rising, 208, 265; and Paris, 221; and Dirlewanger, 291
Hołowczyce-Kolonia, 100
Holland, 40–1, 150, 243, 247
Honick, Franciszek, 25
Hopkins, Harry, 241
Höss, Rudolf, appointed Commandant Auschwitz, 116; recall
    to Berlin, 126–7; return to Auschwitz, 135; execution,
    291
Hudson, Lieutenant-Colonel Bill, 238, 268, 273–6
Hungary, 29, 42, 79, 135, 137–8, 146, 245–6, 248, 257, 264–5
'Hydra', Operation, 96–8, 101
IG Farben, 117, 127–9, 131, 242, 279
Ipswich, 243
Iranek-Osmecki, Colonel, 197
Ismay, General Sir Hastings, 32, 266
Italy, allied advance, 71, 77–8; sorties to N. Italy, 79; partisans,
    175; allied pressure, 176; airdrops, 255
Iżycki, Air Vice Marshal Mateusz, 228, 236
Jaruzelski, General Wojciech, 297
Jasieński, Second Lieutenant Stefan, 132–3
Jaźwiński, Major Jan, 89, 155–6
Jebb, Gladwyn, 30
Jedliński, Captain Aleksander, 159
Jeffery, Lance Corporal Ron, 162–3, 195
Jews, population, 28; anti-semitism, 29; attitude to Red Army,

35; Jedwabne deaths, 44; evidence of Auschwitz, 114, 116;
    ghetto system, 114–5, 118; leaders meet Roosevelt, 123;
    Jewish Agency, 135–6; AK section, 132; Polish attitudes,
    133–4, 182; Grynszpan partisans, 179; help from Poles, 179,
    Warsaw Ghetto, 211, 274–5, 297; and Holocaust, 286
Jeziorański, Lieutenant Zdzisław, 105, 127
Jodl, General Alfred, 193
Jones, RV, 96, 99, 103–4, 243
Josten, Oberleutnant Günther, 248
Jula, Operation, 59–60, 75
July bomb plot, 192–4
Juny, Mieczysław, 42
Kaminski, Bronisław, 210, 291
Kammler, General Hans, 242–3, 292
Kampinos Forest, 51, 159, 216, 237–8, 245, 291
Karelian Offensive
Karski, Jan, 92, 122–3, 127
Katowice, 273, 279
Katyn massacre, 39, 45, 47, 174, 185
Keitel, General Wilhelm, 193
Kemp, Major Peter, 238, 274–6
Keswick, Colonel, 165
Kharkov, 47
Kielce, 262, 264, 274, 275
Kietlicz-Rayska, Maria, 211–12
Kiev, 44
Kleczynski, Wing Commander, 47
Kluge, General von, 26
Kochanowka, 97
Kocjan, Antoni, 100–1, 226
Konev, Marshal Ivan, 184, 274
Königsberg, 49, 227–8
Kopański, General, 236
Koppe, General, 74
Koprowski, Flight Lieutenant B, 90
Korboński, Stefan, 71, 214, 218, 278, 284
Koschorrek, Günther, 181, 229
Kossakowski, General Tadeusz, 93
Kostuch, Tomasz, 90
Kraków, 27, 37, 74, 79, 132, 230, 274–5, 296
Kramer, Josef, 135, 264, 292
Krupp, 125, 264
Kückler, General von, 26
Kukiel, General Marion, 182, 270
Kurland peninsula, 192–3
Kursk, 191
Kutno Pocket, Battle of, 33
Kutrzeba, General Franz, 74
Lach, Pilot Officer Tadeusz, 245
Lanckorońska, Countess Karolina, 38
Latiano, 78, 153
Latvia, 38, 222
Lauterbach, Richard, 242
Lawrence, HW, 139, 242
Leliwa, Major Zbigniew, 93
Lerski, Jerzy, 151
Leśna Padkowa, 278
'Lend/Lease' Scheme, 184, 241, 244
Liebehenschel, Arthur, 127, 292
Liddell Hart, Basil, 148
Lithuania, 38, 192, 222; collaboration, 73
List, General von, 27
Łódź, 27, 36, 77, 138, 274, 275, 291, 296
London, 'Enigma' arrives in, 31; Dutch Government in, 40;
    Polish GIE moves to, 42, 46, 48–9, 57–9, 72; SOE HQ,
    78, 152, 165; return of Polish politicians, 90; Tatar in, 91;
    V-Weapons and, 99, 243, 244, 268; RV Jones in, 103–4;
    Retinger in, 108; couriers reach, 123; Auschwitz reports
    arrive, 123; weather and Big Ben, 146; wireless station in,
    159; appreciation to Soviets, 178; Mikołaczyk arrives, 182,
    266; Hugh Dalton entertains in, 252
Łopianowski, Narcyz, 90
Lower Rhine, 247
Lublin, 37, 72–3, 90, 100, 172, 181, 185, 276
Lublin Committee (later Government), 72, 195, 213–4, 226,
    242, 254, 265, 270, 284, 289

Luxembourg, 40, 95
Lwów, 36, 44, 73, 79, 123, 172–3, 181–2, 184, 213, 226, 266, 276, 283
Lwów-Sandomierz Offensive, 172, 184, 195, 226
Maas, River, 247
Maczek, Colonel, 41
Maginot Line, 40
Magnuszew, 195, 221–2, 225
Majewski, Bolesław, 33–4
Makepeace, Flight Sergeant T.J., 164
'Market Garden', Operation (see also Arnhem), 247
Manteuffel, General Hasso von, 190–1
Massey, Captain LM, 152, 243–4
Mediterranean Allied Air Force (MAAF), 78, 176, 215, 245
Mengele, Dr Josef, 292
Miciński, Czesław, 102, 108
Mikołajczyk, Stanisław, appointed to Polish GIE, 39; appointed PM, 48; report from Retinger, 92; removal of Sosnkowski, 94; visits Moscow, 108; relations with Gubbins, 148, on Soviet claims, 173; meets Roosevelt, 182; on Rising, 213; on Curzon Line, 213–4; at Moscow Conference, 265–6; resigns, 270; as ex-Premier, 271; returns to government, 283; death threats and escape, 284
Miłkiewicz, Colonel Leo, 46
Minsk, 172, 183
Mirogorod, 188, 249
Model, Generalfeldmarschall Walter, 183, 185, 208, 222
Molotov, Vyacheslav, 31, 33, 49, 265–6
Monopoli, 78, 93, 153, 218
Monte Cassino, 61
Moravia, 27, 29, 74
Moscow, 43, 115, 193, 267, 278, 288
Murmansk, 42
Musiałek-Łowicki, Lieutenant-Colonel Stefan, 102–7
Narew, River, 225, 255
Narodowa Demokracja Party, 270
Naujocks, Alfred, 25, 291
Nicolson, Harold, 173
'NIE' movement, 284
Niedzialkowski, Mieczysław, 56
Niedzielski, Lieutenant-Colonel, 252
NKVD, 34, 38–9, 181, 244, 262, 276, 277, 283, 285, 289; compared to Gestapo, 72–3
Nordhausen, 96, 98
Norway, 147, 150
Norway Campaign, 40–1
Norwich, 243
Nuremberg Trials, 290
Oder, River, 173, 274
Office of Strategic Services (OSS), 123, 147, 194
Offlag 73, 254
Okulicki, General Leopold, 197, 254, 274, 278–9, 283
Ołtarzewski, Stanisław, 90
O'Malley, Sir Owen, 163, 177
Orwell, George, 49
Osóbka-Morawski, Edward, 254
'Overlord', Operation, 82, 99, 160, 176
Pawiak Prison, 69, 101
Peenemünde, 96–6
Pemberton-Williams, Flying Officer J, 104
Perkins, Lieutenant-Colonel Harold, in Military Mission, 34; stops bridging ops, 87; landing sites, 88–9; removal of Sosnkowski, 94; as SOE Section head, 151; background and character, 151–2; on Soviet strategy, 161–2; interviews Jeffery, 163; with SOE weapons, 165; control of Polish cyphers, 174–5; opinion of Harvey, 178; on Ward, 218; Rising, 230, 238–9; relief air routes, 263; posted to Prague, 267; briefs Freston mission, 268; ceases SOE help, 271; post-war, 288
Petczyński, General Tadeusz, 197
Petkov, Nikola, 284
Philby, Kim, 284
Pickles, Captain Mike, with Military Mission, 34, 102; on 'Wildhorn III', 152; interviews Jeffery, 163; with Tatar, 165; 'Wildhorn IV', 262; anticipates Soviet offensives, 267; criticises PGIE, 270; on Churchill, 272–3

Pietraszewicz, 74
Pilecki, Witold, 126, 131
Piłsudski, Marshal Józef, 27–8
Pińsk, 75, 183
Piryatin, 188
Pitt, Wing Commander W, 80
Piwnik, Jan, 75–6
Ploesti, 78
Poland, pre-war history, 27–32; acquires Teschen, 29; German invasion, 33–4; losses in 1939, 33; 1939 deportations, 35; German administration in, 36–7; Generalgovernment, 37; stripped of assets, 70–1; collaboration, 70–1; POWs of Polish origin, 127; Poles inside Germany, 194; Girl Guides, 196–7; executions, 197; religion, 250, 289, 297; Warsaw civilians, 253; Polish labour in Germany, 269; Poles post-war in UK, 287; Poland's contribution to Allies, 295–6
Polish Armed Forces:
Army:
Polish General Staff (PGS), 46, 255
Corps:
II Corps, 61, 71, 214
Divisions:
1st Grenadier Division, 41; 2nd Rifle Division, 41; 3rd Division, 41
Brigades:
Carpathian Brigade, 42; Pomeranian Cavalry Brigade, 26; 10th Mechanised Cavalry Brigade, 39, 41; Highland Brigade, 39, 41; Independent Polish Parachute Brigade, 165, 219–20, 239, 251, 296
Regiments:
17th Regiment, 60
Air Force, 155, 227–8; Battle of Britain, 41; relocation to Poland, 149
Navy, 39
Polish Government-in-Exile (PGIE), 35, 39; Britain's 1st Ally, 41; established in London, 42; breach with Stalin over Katyn, 47; resistance groups, 56; establishes underground state, 57; and Retinger, 93; response to Auschwitz reports, 133; and PGS, 152; new composition, 252; inertia over Rising, 213, 296; Moscow Conference, 266; pleas from Rising, 214–5; crisis, 269–71; poor assumptions, 283; loses recognition, 284
Bureaux:
II Bureau, 46, 58, 151, 158; VI Bureau, 108, 151, 155, 160, 163, 270
Polish Home Army (AK), origins, 56–8; composition 58–9; lack of arms, 58; sabotage operations, 59; weapons, 61; women, 61–3; publications, 63, 174; assassinations, 69–70; Operation 'Tempest', 72; German retribution, 74; and British POWs, 76; landing strips, 87; units at Wildhorn III, 102–4; wireless stations, 153, 166–7, 174, 214, 227, 276; wireless operators, 159; tying down Germans, 161; contacts with Soviets, 179; treachery, 191–2; and General Staff, 197–8, 207–8; independence from SOE, 150; numbers and arms, 204–5; early success in Rising, 206–7; and Ward, 218; position mid-August, 219; during Rising, 238–9, 253, 274; publications, 251; surrender in Warsaw, 258; arrests by NKVD, 262; enemy killed, 295; role ends, 297
Polish Home Army Units:
Divisions:
5th Infantry Division, 181; 7th Division, 262, 264, 274; 27th Vohlynian Infantry Division, 58, 72, 156, 181
Regiments:
7th (Lublin Lancers) Regiment, 206; 9th Infantry Regiment, 157; 22nd Infantry Regiment, 100
Other Units:
Sosienki Unit, 132; Grey Ranks, 61–2, 196–7Polish Intelligence Services, and 'Enigma', 30–1; established in France, 46; in North Africa, 46; help to British, 81–2; and V-2 rockets, 98; in Hotel Rubens, 158; work in France, 160
Polish partisans, 179–82; 191–2; Bielski Band, 181–2
Polish political parties, Peasant Party, 56; National Democratic Party, 56; Polish Socialist Party, 56; Nationalist Party, 56; Polish Workers' Party, 56

Polish Resettlement Corps, 287
Polish Retirement Homes, 287
Poltava, 188, 243, 249, 289–90
Pomian, Captain Andrzej, 90
Pomian, John, 285
Portal, Air Chief Marshal Sir Charles, relations with SOE, 88, 236; derides SOE, 152; Rising, 215, 273
Pospieszalski, Antoni (Tony Currie), 268
Potsdam Conference, 284
Poznań, 36, 82, 279
Pripet marshes, 72, 181, 183–4
Pruszków, 240
Pustkow, 97–98
Raczkiewicz, Władysław, 21, 39, 48, 252, 270
Radom, 70, 75, 100, 238, 248, 274
Radzievsky, Generalmajor, 195
Rankin, Group Captain, 207
Rataj, Maciej, 56
Reinefarth, SS Gruppenführer Heinz, 209, 211, 213, 290–1
Reinhardt, Generaloberst, Georg-Hans, 222
Retinger, Józef, background, 92; connections with intelligence, 92; 'Wildhorn II', 93; removal of Sosnkowski, 94; poisoning, 94; 'Wildhorn III', 102, 106, 108; first drop, 155; intrigues, 252; post-war, 285
Rhodes, 138
Ribbentrop, Joachim von, 31, 33
Roberts, Frank, 48, 163
Rokossovsky, Marshal Konstantin, during 'Barbarossa', 44; 'Bagration', 183; background, 185; Rising, 225, 230, 241, 249–50; post-war, 289
Romania, 29, 34, 36, 39, 42, 172, 177, 189, 191, 257, 264–5
Roosevelt, President Franklin, 48–9, 123, 182, 227, 241, 266, 283–4
Rowecki, General Stefan, commands AK, 57, 58, 70; death, 208
Royal Air Force (RAF), dropping leaflets, 166; early casualties from Rising, 208
    Commands and formations:
    Bomber Command, 64, 147; 205 Group, 216; 334 Wing, 188
    Squadrons:
    60 Squadron, 98; 85 squadron, 99; 138 Squadron, 63, 66, 79, 263; 148 Squadron, 80, 155, 164, 175, 208, 216–7, 221, 228; 158 squadron, 245; 161 Squadron, 66, 245, 263; 178 Squadron, 216–7, 245, 257; 226 Squadron, 40
    Flights:
    1586 Polish Special Duties Flight, creation, 63, 66, 78–9; early operations, 67; joins 148 Squadron, 80; with 'Base 11', 90; 155, 164, 175, 208, 216–7, 221, 228, 237, 245–6, 256, 263, 266, 296
    Aircraft:
    Catalina, 87, Douglas Dakota, 89–90, 93, 104–7, 263; Fairy Battle, 40; Halifax, 64, 66–7, 79–81, 86–7, 155, 157, 164, 176, 208, 216, 219, 221, 237, 245; Hudson, 88, 90; Lancaster, 227–8; Liberator B24, 66, 79, 208, 216, 219–21, 237, 245, 266; Lysander, 63, 86; Mosquito, 87, 99; Stirling, 263; Whitley, 63
Royal Aircraft Establishment (Farnborough), 101, 267
Royal Australian Air Force (RAAF), 208
Royal Canadian Air Force (RCAF), 250, 252
Rudkowski, Group Captain Roman, 93
Rudkowski, Colonel, 263
Ruhr, 176
Rundstedt, General von Gerd, 27, 37
Ryder, Sue, assessment of Polish Jews, 134; opinion of Gubbins, 150; as FANY, 153; with *cichociemni*, 154–5; Polish signals, 175; Rising, 219; on Churchill, 252; on Poles, 297
Rygiel, Pilot Officer Edmund, 246
Rzeszów, 60, 62, 82, 97, 163, 226, 228, 243
Sajer, Grenadier Guy, 186
San, River, 226
Sanacja Regime, 28–9, 39
Sanders, Colonel TRB, 243, 267
Sandomierz, 27
Sandys, Duncan, 95–6, 243
Sargent, Sir Orme, 177

Sarnaki, 100, 244
Schöngrath, Brigadeführer, 44
Schörner, Generalfeldmarschall, Ferdinand, 222
Schultz, Otto, 74
Selborne, Lord Roundell, 81, 150, 239, 266, 268–9, 271, 273; meets Karski, 122; character, 148; pressure from Sosnkowski, 149; Rising, 215; post-war, 287
SHAEF, 194, 219, 237
Shirer, William, 31
Siberia, 36, 45
Sidlice, 99
Siekierki, 275
Siemens, 125
Sikorski, General Władysław, 21, 39, 47–8, 56–7, 66, 92, 122
Sikorski, Zofia, 47
Silesia, 28, 36–7, 119, 132, 151, 189
Sinclair, Sir Archibald, 136, 149, 218, 266, 273
Skarbeck, Krystyna, 146
Slessor, Air Marshal Sir Jack, 78, 176, 208, 215–6, 229, 263–4, post-war, 289
Slovakia, 27, 29, 117, 162, 264, 267
Słówikowski, Mieczysław, 46
Smith, Sergeant FR, 277
Smuts, Field Marshal Jan, 173–4
Solidarity, 297
Solly-Flood, Major Peter, 268, 288
Sosnkowski, General Kazimierz, 105, 225, 296; flees Poland, 36; appointed to PGIE; appointed C-in-C, 48; pressure on Germans, 149; and Polish Airforce, 155–6; Soviet claims, 173; attacks by Soviets, 178, 182; Rising 213–15; on parachutists, 219; attacks Allies, 236; dismissed, 252; emigrates, 285
South African Air Force (SAAF), 250; 31 Squadron (SAAF), 216–7, 245, 256; 34 Squadron (SAAF), 245–6, 257, 266
Soviet Union, pre-war pacts, 28–32; as German ally, 42; breaks with PGIE, 47; citizens sent to Auschwitz, 117; press, 173; radio broadcasts, 178–9, 195, 214, 226
Soviet Armed Forces,
    Army:
    invasion of Poland, 33–4; 1939 casualties, 33; occupation of Poland, 35; 1941/2 counter-attacks, 45; re-crossing Polish border, 71; at Stalingrad, 88; enters Majdanek, 138–9; arrives at Treblinka, 139; brutality, 180; subsistence, 191; enters Praga, 247; control of Poland, 278
    Red Army,
    Fronts:
    First Baltic Front, 183, 192; Second Baltic Front, 223, 230; Third Baltic Front, 222, 230; First Byelorussian Front, 183, 185, 195, 225, 230, 241, 257, 274, 279; Second Byelorussian Front, 183, 230, 274 ; Third Byelorussian Front, 183, 230; First Ukrainian Front, 182, 184, 240, 230, 274, 279; Second Ukrainian Front, 182, 230; Third Ukrainian Front, 182, 230; Fourth Ukrainian Front, 230
    Armies:
    8th Guards Army, 138, 184, 221; 2nd Tank Army, 185, 195, 222; 5th Army, 44; 47th Army, 185, 209, 245, 274; 60th Army, 276; 61st Army, 274
    Polish People's Army (LWP):
    1st Polish Army, 58, 178, 181, 184–5, 195, 221, 228, 239–40, 247, 252; creation, 45; enlargement, 72–3; infantry and rifle divisions, 221, 222, 275; casualties, 289
    Corps:
    3rd Tank Corps, 195, 209, 8th Guards Tank Corps, 195, 16th Tank Corps, 195, 9th Mechanised Corps, 44
    Soviet Air Force, access to Italy, 78, 188–9, 225; Red air drops, 249
    Soviet weapons, T34 Tank, 185–88, 190; *Katyusha* Rocket Launcher, 187; T85 Tank, 190; KV85 Tank, 190; JS/2 Tank, 190–1
Spanglet, Heinz, 256
Special Operations Executive (SOE), creation, 145–8; air drops, 22; Sikorski's death, 47; early relief flights, 64; and Red Air Force, 78; Italian HQ, 78; Italian organisation, 78; RAF relief routes, 79; problems of flights, 79–80; problems with landing strips, 86–7; Polish Section, 88; relations with RAF, 88; Dutch Section, 89, 151; de-briefing 'Wildhorn

I', 91; 'Force 139', 93, 207, 218; removing Sosnkowski, 94; EU/P Section, 147, 160; withholds drops, 156; money to Poles, 160; 'Station 12', 164–5; 'Station 9', 165; 'Station 6', 165; 'Station 17', 165; 'Station 43', 165; July Bomb Plot, 194; liaison with Red Army, 239; shipyards attacked, 267
Operations:
'Bardsea', 147, 160; 'Dunstable', 269; 'Fernham', 269; 'Flamstead', 269; 'Freston', 268–78, and failure, 288; 'Monika', 147
Speer, Albert, 96
Sporberg, Henry, 151
Stahel, Generaloberst Reiner, 208
Stalin, Josef, talks with Britain, 31; 1939 invasion, 34; Baltic States, 38; reaction to Barbarossa, 44; and Katyn, 45; at Tehran Conference, 48–9; depicted by Orwell, 49; V-2 rockets, 104; Curzon Line, 172–3; future of Europe, 177–9; and Operation Frantic, 189–90; attitude to Rising, 213, 225; US opinion of, 241; reasons for Warsaw delay, 255; bargains over Europe, 265–6; Holocaust, 286; ends 'Frantic', 290
Stauffenberg, Count von, 193
Stavka, 172, 183–4, 257
Stawell, Major-General, 78
Steed, Flight Mechanic W, 80
Steinberg, Paul, 119
Stettin, 227
Storm, Operation, 166
Strang, Sir William, 137
Stromberger, Maria, 121
Struszynski, Marek, 100
Sudetenland, 29
Sweden, 78, 101, 220
Szpilman, Władysław, 274
Szrajer, Flying Officer Kazimierz, 104, 106–7
Szreder, Jan, 95
Tabeau, Jerzy, 126
Taranto, 77, 79
Tarnów, 93, 97, 102, 230
Tatar, General Stanisław, on 'Wildhorn I', 90; attitude to Soviets, 91; background and politics, 92; meeting with SOE, 165–6; and Rising 207; SOE help ceases, 271; and wireless stations 276; fate, 285
Tatra Mountains, 79, 146, 257
Tehran Conference, 48–9, 72, 177, 188, 266
'Tempest', Operation, 72
Tempsford, 66, 78, 80, 87–8, 151, 154, 256, 263
Teschen, 29
Thorpe Abbotts, 248
Threlfall, Lieutenant-Colonel Henry, 78, 93, 104, 155, 165, 218, 220, 267; post-war, 288
Tobruk, 42, 128
Tokarzewski, Karaszewicz, Major-General Michal, 57
'Torch', Operation, 46–7, 88
Träger, 95
Trenchard, Air Chief Marshal Lord, 176
Truman, President Harry, 284
Tuchota Woods, 108
Turzysk, 72
United States Army Air Force (USAAF), 188, 237; 15th Air Force, 215–6; 95th Bombardment Group, 248; 100th Bombardment Group, 248; 390th Bombardment Group, 248; 13th Combat Wing, 248; Aircraft, B-17, 189, 248; Mustang P-51, 189, 248
United States Government, reacts to Auschwitz reports, 123; press and Jewish deaths, 127; press and Majdanek, 139
United States press, 240–1
Ukraine, 28, 33, 43, 49, 67, 72, 189, 265
V-1 Flying Bomb, 95, 98–101, 104, 108, 243
V-2 Rockets, 23, 95–108, 243–4, 267–8, 292, 296
Vasilevsky, Marshal, 183
Victor Emmanuel III, King, 78
Vistula, River, 27, 184–5, 204–5, 208, 220, 222, 225, 228–9, 245, 255, 257, 268, 275
Vistula-Oder, Operation, 247–9

Volhynia, 35, 72, 172, 179
Volksdeutsche, 36, 58, 62, 69, 158, 163
Voss, Brigadeführer Bernhard, 97
Vrba, Rudolf, 135
Vyshinskii, Andrzej, 225
Waal River, 247
Wałęga, Second Lieutenant Mieczysław, 60, 62, 228, 285
Wałęga, Adela, 62–3, 285
Walker, Squadron Leader Tony, 66
Wał Ruda, 105–6
Wannsee Conference, 115
Ward, Sergeant John, aircraft crash, 40; prison escape, 76; arrives in Warsaw, 77; wounded, 77; destruction of Warsaw, 217; Rising, 238; deaths in Rising, 246; post-Rising, 262–3; transmitters, 218; reports, 225–6; wounded again, 250; lays blame for Rising, 255; in Kielce, 274; Soviet occupation, 276–7; with AK commanders, 278; post-war, 288
Warsaw, German invasion, 33, 37, 1939 fall of, 36; relief routes to, 79; V-2 rockets, 100; Ghetto, 123; character of, 195–6; rationale for Rising, 197–8; street fighting in, 223
Districts:
City Centre, 205, 207, 247, 250; Czerniaków, 247; Mokotów, 205, 207, 211, 219, 251–2; Ochota, 205, 212; Old Town, 219, 221–2, 235, 247; Powiśle, 247; Praga, 197–8, 205, 222, 225, 241, 245, 250, 252, 255, 275; Stawki, 219; Wola, 205, 207, 211–12; Żolibórz, 205, 207, 219, 235, 247, 252
Bridges:
Kierbedź, 205, 247; Poniatowski, 205, 214, 247
Roads:
Chłodna Street, 214; Elektoralna Street, 214; Grojecka Street, 214; Jerusalem Alley, 205, 214; Marszałkowska Avenue, 206; Napoleon Square, 221, 235; Pańska Street, 235; Pius Street, 221; Rozbrat Street, 206; Skierniewicka Street, 212; Śliska Street, 235; Sienna Street, 235; Szucha Avenue, 69, 206; Theatre Square, 214; Volska Street, 205; Wawelski Street, 211; Wolska Street, 212, 214; Złota Street, 235
Buildings:
Gdańsk Railway Station, 214; Marie Curie Institute, 211, 226; Polytechnic, 224; St Lazarus's Hospital, 224; The Citadel, 246; YWCA, 223; Żolibórz Viaduct, 214
Watten, 97
Werth, Alexander, 46, 139
Wetzler, Alfred, 135
de Wiart, Major-General Adrian Carton, 34–5
Weizmann, Chiam, 136–7
'Wildhorn I' Operation, 88–92
'Wildhorn II' Operation, 93–4
'Wildhorn III' Operation, 94–108
'Wildhorn IV' Operation, 262–3, 270–1
Wilkinson, Peter, 152–3
Wilmot, Chester, 193
Wilno, 39, 73, 167, 173, 179, 182–3, 276, 283
Wilson, General 'Jumbo', 228
WiN Movement, 284
Witos, Andrzej, 271
Wohiński, Henryk, 132
'Wolf's Lair', 192–3
Wołyn, 182
Wykrota, Adam, 38–9
Yalta Conference, 283
York, Flying Officer Jim, 99
Yugoslavia, 42, 49, 79, 104, 146, 176, 255, 265
Zaremba, Szymon, 70 (as Alun Morgan, 268)
Zawacka, Elzbieta, 64, 165
Zakopane, 298
Zamość, 157
Zahkarov, Army General Georgii, 183
Zhukov, Marshal Georgii, 183, 274
Zeitler, Generaloberst, Kurt, 192–3
Zylberberg, Michael, 134, 158–9
Żytomierz, 72
Żytno, 275